Shooting Stars

Also by Sheridan Morley

Review Copies (Plays and Players 1970–1974)
A Talent to Amuse (The First Biography of Noël Coward)
Oscar Wilde
Sybil Thorndike: A Life in the Theatre
Marlene Dietrich
Gladys Cooper
Gertrude Lawrence
Tales from the Hollywood Raj

Shooting Stars

Plays and Players 1975–1983

Sheridan Morley

Quartet Books

London Melbourne New York

First published by Quartet Books Limited 1983
A member of the Namara Group
27/29 Goodge Street, London W1P 1FD

Copyright © 1975–1983 Punch Publications
The author would like to thank the Editor and proprietors of *Punch* magazine for permission to reproduce the material in this book

Preface copyright © 1983 Sheridan Morley

British Library Cataloguing in Publication Data

Morley, Sheridan
    Shooting stars: plays and players 1975–83.
    1. Theatre—Great Britain—Reviews
    I. Title
    792.9'5   PN2581

    ISBN 0-7043-2388-5

Typeset by MC Typeset, Chatham, Kent
Printed and bound in Great Britain
by Mackays of Chatham Limited, Kent

For Nicholas Matthew and Nicola Young
with love from their godfather

Contents

List of Illustrations	ix
Preface	xi
1975	1
1976	41
1977	73
1978	115
1979	161
1980	205
1981	253
1982	307
1983	347
Index	361

Illustrations

Paul Brooke, Sam Dastor, Peter Gordon, Paul Scofield
and Ronnie Stevens in *The Tempest*   7

Constance Cummings, Michael Hordern, Patricia Quinn and
Tim Woodward in *Stripwell*   33

Maria Aitken and Elizabeth Spriggs in *Blithe Spirit*   62

Lisa Harrow, Alan Howard and Norman Rodway in *Wild Oats*   70

Eleanor Bron, Albert Finney and Leo McKern in *Uncle Vanya*   80

Alec Guinness, Rachel Kempson and John Phillips in *The Old
Country*   102

Jeremy Irons and Simon Ward in *The Rear Column*   121

Michael Gambon, Daniel Massey and Penelope Wilton in
Betrayal   156

Judi Dench, Ben Kingsley, Bob Peck and Roger Rees in
Cymbeline   174

Gemma Craven, David Healy, Diane Langton, Anton Rodgers
and Andrew C. Wadsworth in *Songbook*   192

Judy Buxton, Mike Gwilym, John Shrapnel and Janet
Suzman in *The Greeks*   212

Sheila Hancock and Denis Quilley in *Sweeney Todd*   230

Brenda Bruce, Alfred Lynch and John Salthouse in *The
Shoemaker's Holiday*   272

Simon Callow and Patrick Ryecart in *The Beastly
Beatitudes of Balthazar B*   289

Barry Humphries in *An Evening's Intercourse*   317

Judi Dench, Nigel Havers and Martin Jarvis in *The
Importance of Being Earnest*   335

Selina Cadell, Carole Hayman, Deborah Findlay and Gwen
Taylor in *Top Girls*   350

Preface

With the publication of *Shooting Stars* I am celebrating, though others may well not be, my first twenty years as a drama critic. What follows, however, is not an attempt to give you a complete consumers' guide to the last two decades in the British theatre, partly because much of my earliest theatre writing can be found in another book (*Review Copies*, 1974) and mainly because such a mammoth task is anyway beyond the scope of any single hardback.

I am not, in any case, much of a believer in the theory of the critic as professor of drama: I believe in the critic as traffic reporter, somebody who (in Tynan's immortal phrase) tells you what it was like to be in a certain theatre on a certain night. The alibi I have for presenting this anthology of my *Punch* reviews over the last eight years is a simple one of documentation: the theatre is the most remarkably ephemeral of the arts, and after a show closes you are lucky to pick up a complete cast-list without reference to a press-cutting library.

It has always seemed to me curious that the British film industry (the product of which is anyway perpetually preserved on celluloid) can claim an entire institute dedicated to its history, whereas the British theatre is allowed to drift away overnight as a series of productions are dismantled to make way for the next. This, then, is a record of what has been going on in London and elsewhere in British and (sometimes) New York theatres over the last eight years; it contains no moral, no message, nor even a few hints for aspiring critics. All it has are my memories, assembled in chronological order. I hope they may be of some use to you: they are to me, if only because they explain what I have been doing with the last 1,200 or so nights of my life, apart from sitting in stalls next to Bill Hewison, Art Editor of *Punch*, while he does some stunning theatrical caricatures all too few of which, due to a certain lack of space, are reproduced here.

I will not pretend there are not certain reviews here I would much like, with the wisdom of hindsight, to retouch a little. I have, however, resisted that temptation, although those of you who are not yet readers of the great and good magazine where I first published these might like a brief autobiography of the critic whose views you are about to encounter, if only because another of the many things I have never believed in is the function of the anonymous critic crouching behind a press byline. A critic surely has the duty to make himself known publicly on radio or television or at worst at his local church fête; a reader can then decide either that he looks all right and his views can therefore be trusted, or (equally valid) that he looks appalling and that it would make sense therefore to hasten to all shows of which he disapproves and stay far away from those he likes. A critic can thus be useful whether he is liked or loathed: he is only useless if nobody knows who he really is. For he, please also read she, though since the splendid Hilary Spurling gave up going to the theatre there have in fact been all too few good female drama critics around.

Like Michael Billington, Irving Wardle and an alarming number of distinguished colleagues, friends and near-contemporaries, I got my reviewing start under John Lawrence, a marvellously avuncular Arts Editor of *The Times* in the fifties and early sixties who would let me phone in the occasional despatch from Oxford (under the anonymous byline 'from our special correspondent' which I always liked to think distinguished me from others less 'special' in that same field, until I discovered that we all got the same billing) where I was doubling as an undergraduate at the time. At *The Times*, when I went to work on the staff there a decade later, it was always said of Lawrence that once, left in charge of the Obituaries during a holiday period, he had run by mistake one for the then Duke of Norfolk who had phoned in somewhat indignantly to correct the error. 'But, Your Grace,' asked Lawrence, ever a careful man, 'may I first of all establish precisely from where you are now telephoning?'

He always knew precisely from where I was telephoning, and the further away the better; I rapidly learnt that the chances of getting a review into *The Times* arts page in 1963 (when the going rate was, I recall, £7 for five hundred words) improved in direct proportion to the mileage from London. Lawrence was, like all *Times* executives of his generation, a man who appreciated a bargain and a review from Pitlochry, provided you had managed to hitch-hike there and were not reversing the phone charges, always struck him as better value for £7 than a review from the Ealing Questors. Pursuing this discovery to its logical conclusion, I ended up at the University of Hawaii in Honolulu, from where I was able to file whole-page reports (£30) on the then current state of mid-Pacific theatre.

By the time I got back to London in 1965, I had the beginnings of a family to support and it was clear that an occasional review, for which the going rate had now risen to £8, was not going to be of much use; accordingly I went to work as a newscaster for ITN, but Lawrence let me keep in touch with the theatre and *The Times* by writing weekly profiles of actors or directors or dramatists, a tradition I have happily kept going these last ten years under his successor John Higgins. One morning Lawrence rang up and told me that Noël Coward was staying at the Savoy and had better be interviewed: 'He's getting on a bit and hasn't had a success in a long time, but he's the right sort of chap for our readers and I think you might like him.' That interview began a sequence of four books and innumerable articles for each and every one of which I still have Lawrence to thank.

But the profiles weren't getting me any closer to making my living as a full-time drama critic, something I had meant to do from the age of about ten. I'd come from a family of actors, had indeed made a fleeting stage appearance with my father in Australia at the age of eight (some people don't discover they can't act until they're thirty or forty, and you can see them most evenings on television; I knew before I was ten and so did a lot of Australians). But if I couldn't act, and had no special desire to direct or build scenery (I did a lot of that, too, at the University of Hawaii) the one thing I knew I was good at was talking and writing about plays. Telling people what shows they ought to see, and equally important what shows they ought not to be caught dead at, has always seemed to me the highest possible function of journalism, added to which the whole notion of being paid to go to the theatre was almost too good to be true.

And so for a long time it proved; the only person other than John Lawrence willing to hand over actual money for my views on the London stage circa 1965 was a remarkable lady who, as I recall, came from a family of Devon clergy and operated out of one room somewhere on the Old Vic side of Waterloo Bridge, running a magazine called *Theatre World* for which I and (again) M. Billington and a young LCC town-planning clerk called Clive Barnes would moonlight at about £5 a thousand words.

But by now there were a couple of children and that wasn't going to pay the rent either. I eventually made my way to the *Tatler* where the Editor took the view that handing over actual money as well as free theatre tickets to a critic was far too much of a good thing. It also annoyed him that whereas restaurants and even hotels, assured of a favourable mention in the magazine, were willing to slip in an ad or two, theatre managers were curiously reluctant to follow suit. I spent about a year trying to explain to him that, as (like all monthly glossies then) he went to press about twelve weeks ahead of hitting the bookstalls, few West End managements had the confidence for such forward planning. 'Tell them they'll be getting a good review from us,' he'd say, 'that'll keep them running.' It did, but mainly in some other direction.

To cut what must already be far too long a life-story short, I eventually graduated from the *Tatler* to *Punch* almost a decade ago, and it was only then that I could put 'drama critic' in my passport without feeling the need to add 'part-time'. One of the best things about *Punch* is that in a lifespan of 150 years they seem only to have had about eight drama critics, which suggests a certain reassuring longevity of tenure. My immediate predecessors have included B.A. Young of the *Financial Times*, the playwright Jeremy Kingston and the much-underrated Eric Keown, but there is something undeniably satisfactory about reporting for a magazine which began going to the theatre when Henry Irving was only three. The magazine had of course taken its name from the earliest form of street-theatre locally, and in the first sixty years of its life over 500 plays and sketches by *Punch* writers saw the light of some stage somewhere. The first Editor, Mark Lemon, once toured as Falstaff and President Lincoln was unfortunately assassinated while watching the play of a later Editor, Tom Taylor. He (Taylor that is, not Lincoln) often took part in Victorian benefit nights on stage alongside such other members of the *Punch* table as Shirley Brooks and George du Maurier who of course wrote *Trilby*, thereby allowing Sir Herbert Beerbohm Tree to establish the true definition of overacting.

I have recently been accused, not least by a National Theatre director, of having 'a curious interest in the West End' and to that I plead totally and happily guilty. One of the saddest things to have happened to the general state of dramatic criticism in my working lifetime is that because of an abiding interest in pub theatre (the equivalent, in numerical terms, of constantly reviewing Radio Three) and subsidized theatre, most of my colleagues have turned their backs on both the problems and the admittedly occasional achievements of the commercial theatre in London which is, as a result, in as poor a shape now as I can ever recall it.

But I can't help believing that if the critics generally had put a fraction of the energy, interest and concern into the commercial theatre that they have put into its fringe and state-aided offshoots, then we might by now be beginning to get the kind of rebirth in the West End that has been enjoyed along Broadway these last ten years. A theatre which can only thrive in very small rooms or in very large subsidized culture palaces is not a healthy theatre, and a critical press which made some shaky geographic judgements a decade ago (Glasgow, Manchester, Stratford – OK; Guildford, Farnham, Chichester – not OK) must now look at those judgements again and think hard about the kind of audience the theatre needs for the eighties and where it is going to come from. We need a broad church, not a narrow pulpit.

And if, before embarking on these individual reviews, you would like some overall policy statement from their author I think it would have to be this: a critic is not meant to be an advance ad-man for the theatre, nor an apologist or pleader for special causes, be it the Black One-Armed Lesbian Mothers' Showbiz Co-operative or the Save Shaftesbury Avenue from VAT Campaign. We are, as I was saying when this preface began, traffic reporters, there to tell you about the stage accidents and the places to avoid as well as the best routes to a decent evening out. In that sense, this book may seem somewhat useless, in that it will not tell you anything about where the British theatre is going next. It will however, I hope, tell you something about where it has just come from.

Shooting Stars

1975

Old London Wall

It would be nice to start my life as drama critic of *Punch* in a haze of benevolence by reporting that the Max Wall one-man show (*Aspects of Max Wall*, Garrick Theatre) is the funniest show in town; it would also be nice to report that pigs had wings. The fact remains, however, that survival alone is not enough, even in the theatre, and that a two-hour show based on the single discovery that Mr Wall has lived to tell the tales yet again starts looking more than a little thin well before half-time.

Admittedly the Garrick is not his most likely home, as he himself was (on the first night) at pains to remark; the present show started as a late-night cabaret on the stage of the Greenwich Theatre where I would rather have seen it; in the cold light of the Charing Cross Road one starts wishing he had employed the services of a writer or even a couple of performing seals to fill out the bill.

Yet there is still something deeply endearing about Mr Wall: those Action Man legs, apparently remote-controlled, and that crumpled, despairing face – one which has clearly peered down into too many orchestra pits at too many Monday-morning band calls in the hope of finding somebody there. Now that the Empires have all been lost he is left, an identikit clown basing his act on a kind of weary availability ('I'm happy to be working this lovely theatre . . . as a matter of fact I'm happy to be working'), and the awareness that an audience does not need to be loved or flattered, merely tolerated.

In a deprecatory and seemingly endless act he offers fragments from half-dead routines ('I'm well-known in the field of classical music . . . also in the field behind the gasworks'), which add up to an evening of breathtaking gloom. Yet there he is, a monument to his own survival ('What man has my looks, my physique, my figure? Wish I knew, I'd like them back') and, in his own quietly bitter way, he does make the occasional desultory effort to get his show off the ground before letting it sink back into a sustained monologue about the failings of the world in general and himself in particular. It may well be that Max Wall is the last of the real stand-up comedians; if so, the profession will go out not with a bang but with an angry whisper.

Still in the world of one-man shows, Emlyn Williams is back in London with his evening as *Charles Dickens* (Theatre Royal Haymarket). When he last had this recital in London for a season the stage was used during the daytime for rehearsals of *The Mousetrap*, which gives some idea of how long Mr Williams has been doing it around the world; as a result the evening now oozes a kind of Dickensian fog through which he can be perceived at the familiar red desk (complete with wrist-rest, a natty device which ought nowadays to be used by tele-anchormen) giving us a runthrough of the old set-pieces.

It was originally his achievement (and, since the show insofar as I can remember it has changed remarkably little in a quarter of a century, it remains his achievement) to highlight Dickens as a funnier, bitchier writer than one might otherwise have concluded. Thus we have Mr Podsnap who thought other countries were a mistake, and Mrs Pipchin who was so dark of dress that at night even gas couldn't light her up, and a whole gallery of the lesser-known but more enjoyable characters, each brought to life briskly by Mr Williams who is still evidently having himself a ball with some of the best scripts around. True, he gives us an odd assembly: no Copperfield, no Twist, no Christmas Carol – instead bits and pieces from such lesser-known works as *The Uncommercial Traveller* (a tale worthy of Roald Dahl at his most ghoulish), *The Battle of Life* and *Little Dorrit*, evidently all chosen for their theatricality rather than their familiarity. As an evening it remains more audio than visual, but Mr Williams is still capable of striking a chill even with more well-known material such as the coming of the Revolution in *A Tale of Two Cities*. If, unaccountably, you have not seen him, do so now; if you have, go again – like Dickens himself, Mr Williams gets better every time one goes back to him.

Grandmarlene

Those accustomed to using this page as a consumers' guide to what's currently on in the theatre will have to bear with me for a paragraph or three while I tell you about something you have in all probability just missed. For the last fortnight Marlene Dietrich has been at Wimbledon; not, you understand, because the old lady has fallen on hard times and is reduced to touring England's lesser-known nightspots but rather because Wimbledon happens to have a sizeable theatre which, if you are a superstar resident abroad but intent on packing as many paying customers as possible into a short season, makes it only marginally less attractive than the Palladium, albeit slightly harder to locate on a dark night.

But Dietrich was worth the journey and, since she will undoubtedly be back within the year, hers is not a show which can ever be regarded as closed. There is a chilly magnificence about the lady: alone – save, that is, for William Blezard and a twelve-piece orchestra – she can conjure out of nowhere a kind of theatrical magic which has little to do with age or reality or even humanity but everything to do with stardom. At Wimbledon, after an unusually shaky first half in which she appeared in top hat and tails looking alarmingly like Hetty King, she came into her own with an hour-long anthology of all the classics from 'Lola' through forty years to 'Where Have All the Flowers Gone?'

Her songs are in fact much the same as ever and so is she: Bacharach's arrangements have survived a decade and she herself seems to have survived a century. It is as if we are being sung to, or rather sung at, by the Statue of Liberty: the gestures are still frozen, the voice still sounds as if it is coming from an icebox, and yet still manages to tell you (in Tynan's memorable phrase) that whatever hell you happen to inhabit she has been there before you and survived.

Dietrich and her act are the most remarkable feat of theatrical engineering since the invention of the revolving stage, and age has if anything reinforced her voice to the point where (for 'Lili Marlene') she seems to have within her the strength of entire armies. At the end, as usual, she got a standing ovation and, as usual, it somehow didn't seem quite enough: the first of her kind and almost certainly the last of it, she has to be seen at least once in a lifetime.

In an otherwise thin – not to say barren – week I took the chance of a couple of cast changes to catch up somewhat belatedly with *Kennedy's Children* which can still be found at the King's Head Theatre Club in Islington. To say that it is far and away the best new play I've seen in the past year is not in fact saying enough, particularly as it is in any case not so much a play as a series of five interlocked monologues, spoken by the inhabitants of a bar on New York's Lower East Side – spoken not to each other but to us the audience, since no character will acknowledge the presence or even the sound of any of the others.

Robert Patrick's achievement as a writer is thus all the more notable: having denied himself a plot or any kind of interaction he is left with five characters in search of an answer: each is one of Kennedy's children, linked to the late President not by blood but by the fact that he was the leader with whom they came of age and with whom their hopes died: 'Who needs a leader now? . . . it's not as though we're going anywhere.'

At the risk of oversimplification, the five are the Vietnam GI, the girl who believed in Camelot, the girl who wanted to be the next Marilyn, the off-Broadway actor and the girl who marched; all now find themselves, in mid-afternoon, alone and involved involuntarily in a requiem for the sixties.

If it was right to kill in Vietnam, what's wrong with killing in New York? If Washington was Camelot, what was Dallas? Who can be Marilyn in an age of drag queens? How can off-Broadway survive when it now contains more actors than audiences? How come all the marches through all the sixties only ever achieved the establishment of Jane Fonda? What the hell, since we've already got too many questions here anyway, was all the enthusiasm about, ten years ago?

That, in a nostalgic nutshell, is what *Kennedy's Children* is about; as played at Islington by Shirley Anne Field, Deborah Norton, Richard Oldfield, Don Parker and Pat Starr it becomes an evening of masterly despair in which five people come to the final realization that America in the sixties was not their promised land. The result is a patchwork of disillusion, impeccably directed by Clive Donner in a set by John Scully; as a play it does admittedly owe a considerable debt to Tennessee Williams in general and *Small Craft Warnings* in particular, but as an epitaph for the whole PR industry which

The Tempest Sam Dastor *as Ariel*, Peter Gordon *as Caliban*, Paul Scofield *as Prospero*, Ronnie Stevens *as Trinculo*, Paul Brooke *as Stephano*

adapted Washington and its causes to the needs of Madison Avenue and its campaigns, *Kennedy's Children* is on its own.

Ship to Shaw

This column is going to be very largely about the National Theatre's new production of *Heartbreak House* but before we get to that I would like you to look carefully at the drawing by Hewison which accompanies it. It is, you will notice, of Paul Scofield as Prospero in *The Tempest* (currently to be found at Wyndham's) and it says very nearly all that need be said about that particular performance.

Given that Mr Scofield has the craggiest face in the business, it was clearly only a matter of time before he got around to Prospero and although for most actors the part is merely a foothill on the way up to Lear, Mr Scofield is not most actors and he has chosen to give us his Prospero on the way back from the peak he first scaled with his Stratford Lear all of thirteen years ago.

The showcase here is perhaps a little wan: a production first seen at the Leeds Playhouse last year, one which has all the merits of economy and not much of anything else. But John Harrison, the director of both *Tempest* and Playhouse, has been an associate of Scofield's since the days when both were actors at Birmingham Rep immediately after the war, and he has brought out the best in Scofield himself who drags Prospero's words across the iron grating that is his voice, yet who never seems able to come to terms with the rest of the company or what they are doing around him.

True, Prospero is ringmaster rather than chief clown, and therefore has a right to draw back from all proceedings; Scofield however draws so far back that he appears at times to be in a one-man show while the rest of the cast gather attentively around to watch.

This is a chamber *Tempest*, bleakly conceived and coldly performed, which makes it if nothing else a fascinating contrast to the more lush production offered last year by Peter Hall as his Old Vic inaugural; yet it remains oddly incomplete, a studio performance almost like a final dress-rehearsal and somehow awaiting finishing touches. There is a notable West End début by Nicky Guadagni as Miranda, but elsewhere the casting is at best adequate and the reason for going to Wyndham's must remain solely that of seeing Scofield . . . though that in itself can't be an altogether bad one.

Now, about *Heartbreak House*: the cleansing power of holocausts has always been a shaky dramatic theory in my book, much akin to the idea that earthquakes do wonders for a bad back, and Shaw has not on this occasion done much to help his case by housing it in one of the most unsatisfactory of all his plays (typically, he himself proclaimed it both his favourite and his *Lear*, though it remains on paper a couple of acts of soggy drawing-room comedy foisted onto an admittedly admirable finale).

John Schlesinger's Old Vic production is eminently good, though given a cast headed by Colin Blakely, Eileen Atkins, Anna Massey, Paul Rogers, Graham Crowden and Kate Nelligan it is hard to believe it could have been otherwise. Sadly however, the very excellence of it and them only points up the essential frailty of the play's structure, and the first two acts (well-spoken though they be) have about them an air of claustrophobic interminability.

Blakely's Shotover, halfway from Undershaft to God, dominates where he can, but the focus of these early scenes is so blurred that neither he nor Eileen Atkins' Hesione, dressed like Ottoline Morrell, nor yet Paul Rogers' Boss Mangan, can ever establish enough of themselves to retain our attention. These are cut-out characters, infinitely more fragile than the ideas they are on stage to represent, and on the way from the drawing-room to the holocaust they resemble a team from *Outward* or possibly *Inward Bound,* desperately trying to play a requiem with the wrong instruments.

But all does change, mercifully, with the second interval: the noise of intellectual mills being rather too slowly ground gives way to the noise of a zeppelin and we are left with apocalypse acting of the very best. There is, granted, something a little surprising about a zeppelin dropping bombs over rural England for no explained reason but on this one Shaw was not overly concerned with plot and the device, by the time it arrives, is totally acceptable if only because it gives his characters and the audience something definable to think about.

To drift, Shaw tells us, is the ultimate crime and the zeppelin has come presumably to punish those who are fiddling while the home fires burn, if you'll forgive a mixed metaphor or three. Paradoxically, of course, the ones who are killed by it are the only ones who did actually have some idea of what they were supposed to be doing with their lives, but then that's death for you.

I wish I could be more enthusiastic about *Heartbreak House* as a play: there are indeed one or two *echt* Shavian moments ('Do you believe, Sir, that the laws of God will be suspended in favour of England because you are born in it?') but they are few and hopelessly far between. I also wish that I could join some of my colleagues in believing that this revival, taken together with *John Gabriel Borkman,* marks the end of the National's problems; but any management, given the plays of Ibsen and Shaw and a company of the finest actors in the land, would be hard pressed to fail. The test will come later this year, when they emerge from their current 'safe' period.

Have Show, Will Travel

The one-man show, much like the one-man band, has always been an attractive idea to anyone bent on capturing an audience. For an actor there is still a mystical satisfaction in the solo curtain call, but to be able to go it alone from the very beginning of the evening, and what's more not to have to divide the profits up at the end of it, is a consummation devoutly to be wished, albeit seldom actually achieved.

All the more surprising, therefore, that it was an author rather than an actor who first thought of it: as early as 1853 Charles Dickens was barnstorming the country with 'dramatic readings' of his own work and suitably enough it was Dickens again, though now personified by Emlyn Williams, who provided the basis for the first modern one-man show almost exactly a century later. In the meantime there had of course been others: in Germany in the 1870s an actor called Brandes used to tour entirely alone with a bizarre entertainment known as monodrama, and in America in 1881 Oscar Wilde was to be found touring as a kind of advance-man of D'Oyly Carte's opera company. They were about to present *Patience* to the Americans and felt it might help if Wilde (widely if falsely thought to be the model for Bunthorne) could precede them from town to town declaring nothing but his genius and in the process introducing audiences to 'the aesthete'.

Wilde chose to build this one-man show around the Italian Renaissance and (according to his diary) found himself lecturing one night in Leadville, near Denver, Colorado:

> My audience was mainly composed of miners whose huge sombre hats, red shirts and high boots made me think of the seventeenth-century cavaliers. Indeed they were the first really well-dressed men I had seen since my arrival in the United States . . . I read them passages from the autobiography of Benvenuto Cellini and he proved so popular that they asked as one man 'Why had I not brought him with me?' I explained that Benvenuto had been dead for some years, which elicited the demand: 'Who shot him?'

In this century the one-man show has returned to the clutches of the actors, though not before such distinguished *diseuses* as Ruth Draper, Joyce Grenfell and Beatrice Lillie had all proved between the wars that to keep an audience happy for upwards of two hours a cast of thousands or even two was not strictly necessary. It may not, admittedly, have been quite what theatre architects had in mind, though – all those empty dressing-rooms and scene docks are apt to echo somewhat, and unless carefully organized the first-night cast parties tend to be rather quiet.

But when, at the Lyric Hammersmith in 1951, Emlyn Williams first drew off those white gloves at the lectern and announced that he was Charles Dickens, he can scarcely have realized what he was starting. The success of that solo evening (which Williams had practised at the Ambassadors in between rehearsals for another long-runner, *The Mousetrap*) led him to take it around the world – something that with remarkable resilience he has been doing more or less ever since – and led other actors to start rifling through the library shelves in search of other authors who might stand up to an entire evening's reading. Shakespeare? John Gielgud (*Ages of Man*, 1958); Wilde? Micheàl MacLiammòir (*The Importance of Being Oscar*, 1960); Bernard Shaw? Max Adrian (*An Evening with GBS*, 1966); John Aubrey? Roy Dotrice (*Brief Lives*, 1967). In America Hal Holbrook took care of Mark Twain, and more recently Henry Fonda has been touring with the speeches of the celebrated trial lawyer Clarence Darrow.

Is there, you may now be forgiven for wondering, anybody left? Well, comedians can always do themselves (viz *Aspects of Max Wall*, until recently at the Garrick) and one or two actors have even tried this tack: a relative of mine not too far distant from these pages once took *The Sound of Morley* all around Australia. But if it's classic authors you're after, there are precious few that haven't been tried already: someone might I suppose have a go at An Evening with Samuel Taylor Coleridge but somehow it sounds a little less than promising at the box-office. The Best of Nietzsche? Great Moments from Gorky? Suddenly It's Schopenhauer? I rather doubt it – and them.

The ideal combination is I suppose star plus popular author, hence Williams/Dickens and Gielgud/Shakespeare; how much more courageous, then, of Roy Dotrice (not at the time a fantastically well-known actor), to set up in collaboration with Patrick Garland the evening with John Aubrey which, as *Brief Lives*, lingers in my mind as the best of all the solo shows. Aubrey was a seventeenth-century diarist and compulsive gossip, which made him ideal fodder: in America, however, where audiences had heard neither of him nor of Dotrice nor of Garland in 1967, there was a problem for the publicists – how to sell the show? What they did, after some thought, was to take a series of huge posters and announce on them that Clive Barnes, then newly appointed drama critic of the *New York Times,* had not only seen *Brief Lives* but also liked it. So far, so splendid: except that Mr Dotrice was a little taken aback to be accosted at the stage door one evening by a lady saying, 'Oh, Mr Barnes, I did so enjoy listening to your diaries.'

An Earnest of Good Intent

One of the troubles with the current British theatre (there are in fact a goodly few, but I'll come back to the rest at a later date) is that not enough actors or directors are asking themselves the question why: why are we doing this particular play in this particular year at this particular theatre? 'For the money' is of course a perfectly acceptable answer from those far enough down the cast-list to need it, but from star actors and star directors it simply will not do, any more than will 'because it's there'. What's more, there should be (outside the RSC who presumably need Shakespeare in order to survive) an absolute ban on anyone doing any of the better-known classics until they have at least one good idea about them.

All of which brings me, somewhat circuitously, to Jonathan Miller's new production of *The Importance of Being Earnest* at Greenwich, whither Dr Miller has repaired now that his National shackles are altogether broken off. It was not a production I approached with much glee, having in my time seen *The Importance* done in English, French, American, modern dress, period dress, school, college, field and even on one occasion I seem to remember on ice though that may be nothing more than wishful thinking. Short of doing it under water with a cast entirely selected from the ranks of the Dagenham Girl Pipers there seemed very little that Dr Miller could do to or with the play, which brings us back to the question why?

Happily, Dr Miller has an answer to it: there *are* new things to be done with *The Importance,* and in the current production Miller does them. First, he abandons the idea that Algy and John are a couple of priggish fops waiting only for the next epigram to fall as if by remote control from their lips; instead (in the immaculate performances of David Horovitch and Robert Swann) Miller has them played as members of some pre-Bloomsbury Set, elegant certainly but also thoughtful, affectionate and very funny. And there's better to come: faced with Lady Bracknell and the need to haul her away from the deadly embrace of Dame Edith Evans whose swooping characterization of the role has effectively overshadowed and inhibited virtually all other readings of the part for the last thirty years, Miller has her played by Irene Handl – and, moreover, by Irene Handl not in her lovable cockney mood but instead playing a formidable German Jewess, the inheritor one feels of some huge clothing emporium come to inspect some of the outlying members of her family.

Nothing in the text denies this: there is no reason why (by marriage) Lady Bracknell should not be a German lady inclined to throw up her hands in mild despair rather than stretch them outwards in imperious disdain à la Evans, and through her performance the play is both rediscovered and revitalized. The rest of the cast have clearly also come strongly under Dr Miller's influence to such an extent that some now even walk like him, unconsciously perhaps imitating the long rangy steps of the marshbirds first immortalized by him in *Beyond the Fringe* and now copied in more elegant but no less hilarious surroundings.

As a play *The Importance* remains Wilde's best and – apart from one or two terrible autobiographical portents ('He wished to be buried in Paris . . . that scarcely indicates soundness of mind at the last') it is an evening of total, delirious escapism – a feeling fostered not only by the performances I've already mentioned but also by those of Angela Down and Charlotte Cornwell (as Gwendolen and Cecily) and John Sanderson and Benjamin Whitrow (as Prism and Chasuble).

So hasten to Greenwich – or, if you happen to prefer theatregoing north of the Thames, to the Hampstead Theatre Club where Michael Frayn's *Alphabetical Order* turns out to be a massively comic tribute to the futility of journalism – not that the subject will come as much of a shock to followers of Mr Frayn's novels, which have established him as the only true heir to the Evelyn Waugh of *Scoop*.

Alphabetical Order (admirably staged for Hampstead by the theatre's artistic director Michael Rudman) is set in the reference library of a somewhat rundown provincial paper: as the play begins we find it inhabited by a collection of crumbling desks, filing cabinets and people – among them Billie Whitelaw as the librarian/ den mother, a lady given to providing sustenance both sexual and otherwise for a bunch of reporters who seem urgently in need of the kiss of life.

Chief among them is Dinsdale Landen, offering quite possibly the comic performance of the year as a leader writer incapable of starting a sentence without at least two double negatives and a qualifying clause, the kind of man who comes through doors murmuring 'on the other hand' and, in his own definition, a perambulating heap of blancmange. Into the midst of his cosy, decaying community erupts an assistant librarian (Barbara Ferris, brisk) determined to bring order, sense and logic with her. She succeeds, though not before the paper has closed down, presumably through lack of interest – as Landen says, the trouble with it is that it's produced by the kind of people who read it.

In all, *Alphabetical Order* is a masterly, gossipy play about people living in a verbal junk-room full of useless knowledge, and about the fact that journalists are the last people able to come to terms with reality, possibly because they see too much of it. This may be a small point, but Mr Frayn makes it beautifully.

Thank God for Harry

Although some tidy scholastic minds are doubtless going to be o'erthrown by the fact that Terry Hands has opened his history cycle at Stratford-on-Avon with *Henry V* (only to return to *Henry IV* later in the month) there can be no doubt that this season's first production represents the Royal Shakespeare Company back at the top of their not inconsiderable form.

On a bare stage, surrounded by actors in tracksuits, an eager if somewhat diminutive Welsh Chorus yearns for a muse of fire and one begins to fear the worst as the Archbishops, nattily attired in White City running plimsolls, start to explain Henry's convoluted claim to France. Evidently the RSC are about to show us, yah boo sucks, that cut-price Shakespeare simply doesn't work and that if the Arts Council won't come up with a better cheque this is how we'll be getting our Bard in the future – and in this context, few Shakespearian scenes so amply illustrate the need for costume as the opening of *Henry V*.

But then, praise be, as Henry decides to go into battle, a gun carriage appears and on it are costumes galore – meanwhile a golden tapestry descends from the grid and we are back in the pageantry business with a simple, stunning stage effect owing more than a little to the moment when, in Olivier's film of this very play, the actors leave the Globe Theatre for real settings.

But the crowning achievement of Mr Hands' production is to be seen later: having got his Henry (Alan Howard, in the performance of his career) costumed and armed and to France, he then shows us that here is a play about defeat as well as victory; not only the defeat of the French (ably and almost solely personified by Oliver Ford-Davies who appears to have been cast, in one of the production's true economies, as Mountjoy, the Governor of Harfleur and most of the French court) but also about the near-defeat of the English who so far from being a band of brothers mindlessly triumphing across the countryside are in fact played as a dissident, near-vanquished troop only eventually shoved into the breach once more by the sheer determination of Henry to prove himself a King able to overcome insuperable odds.

When therefore that curious moment comes for the King to be told that he has lost only twenty-five men to the 10,000 dead French, we are in the realm of the supernatural and Howard's realization that God has truly been on his side is admirably chilling.

Beyond Howard, the casting is variable but ultimately more good than bad: Trevor Peacock as a militant Fluellen, Peter Bourke as the Boy and above all Ludmila Mikaël as (at last) a genuinely French Princess are the glories of the evening and apart from a somewhat unconvincing Agincourt done largely on sound effects (O for a muse of fire and a good stereo tape deck) Mr Hands is at his best in the set-piece action sequences, notably the taking of Harfleur. There's a curious and confusing decision at the end to make Emrys James' Chorus double for the Duke of Burgundy, but it does no lasting harm to one's memory of a splendid evening.

Thirty years after Mary Chase's Broadway comedy *Harvey* won a Pulitzer Prize (they were presumably easier to come by in those days) the play is again at the Prince of Wales where London theatre-goers first saw it with Sid Field just after the war. The same director, Anthony Quayle, has now brought *Harvey* back to life, if life it can be called, and his star for 1975 is James Stewart who, not being a man to bestir himself unduly, takes just the three hours to drawl his way through a plot the entire contents of which could neatly and fully be inscribed on a matchbox.

A one-joke play about a man who talks to an invisible rabbit, but believed in all seriousness by some American critics to be a meaningful analysis of the nature of lunacy or maybe just alcoholism, *Harvey* is at best slow and most often stopped. It does however allow a competent supporting cast led by the indomitable Mona Washbourne to group themselves respectfully around their star, and it affords pre-war Hollywood addicts the chance to inspect Mr Stewart at close quarters and ascertain that he is still awake. Just.

A Brittle Light Musical

There's no doubt in my mind that Stephen Sondheim is the most important composer/lyricist to have come out of the American theatre since the war; there is, however, a certain amount of doubt there about whether his latest offering (*A Little Night Music* at the Adelphi) is as consistently splendid as my daily-paper colleagues would have you believe. True, it does offer the best thirty-minute denouement in town: but the two hours it takes Mr Sondheim and his producer Hal Prince to get us there do not exactly fly past and along the way there is time for one or two doubts to set in.

What, precisely, have we here? A presumably conscious decision by the man who has given us in the recent past the best musicals ever written about urban and marital despair (*West Side Story, Company*) to move back into the Vienna Woods or more precisely to turn-of-the-century Sweden. There, thanks to a 1956 Ingmar Bergman film called *Smiles of a Summer Night*, Mr Sondheim has found himself a plot of mind-boggling coyness about an aged Countess Who Has Seen It All, her daughter (an actress) and the latter's attempts to regain an old lover and discard a new one – the entire charade being watched from the sidelines by five largely unexplained ladies and gentlemen who appear to be auditioning for a barber's shop quintet.

Put like that, *A Little Night Music* must sound pretty terrible and in fact it isn't; although it often resembles nothing so much as *Uncle*

Vanya under water, and despite the fact that Mr Sondheim has here allowed his lyrics to get the better of him so that they are too clever and too dominant by half, the evening is pulled through by the sheer efficiency of Hal Prince's production and by the performances of its three stars. As the Countess, Hermione Gingold is, well, Hermione Gingold but never less than a joy to behold. Playing her daughter, Jean Simmons glides imperceptibly through a long first half until, after the interval, there comes the moment for her to sing 'Send in the Clowns' which she does both heartbreakingly and brilliantly: it is at that moment that the show finally takes off and soars into a prolonged finale which comes as something of a release to those of us who were beginning to feel that we have been locked for rather too long in a very small room with all the Strausses.

Joss Ackland as the ageing lover, David Kernan as the younger one and above all Maria Aitken (another Kay Kendall if ever I saw one and until now I never have) each have magical moments but they tend to merge into the suffocating elegance around them so that occasionally Miss Gingold is left with the thankless task of stopping a show which has already halted of its own accord. In short what we have here is a miniature, exquisitely framed but ultimately only rescued from fading into its own background by great Hermione who exhibits from a wheelchair in her late seventies more life than the rest of the show put together.

Talking of the dangers of top-heavy framing, *A Family and a Fortune* (at the Apollo) equally narrowly avoids slow death through drowning in charm, this time thanks to the performances of Margaret Leighton (originally scheduled to play the Gingold part in *Night Music*), Alec Guinness, Rachel Kempson and Nicola Pagett who turn Ivy Compton-Burnett's hymn of hatred to family life into an entertaining if querulous evening. Julian Mitchell's adaptation and Alan Strachan's production are equally waspish, and the result is a distillation of first-class theatrical venom in which the performances add up to rather more than the play, but which should not be overlooked by any of those for whom life has not been quite the same since the BBC stopped repeating 'The Forsyte Saga'.

Twice Knightly

No Man's Land (at the National) 'will not change or grow old or move – it remains forever icy', says Sir Ralph Richardson to Sir John Gielgud at one moment in Harold Pinter's new play, and the line – repeated as the curtain falls – will also serve as a review. For this is Pinter at his most Pinteresque, which is to say suspended in time and space at some unfixed point roughly halfway from Pirandello to Python. From the moment the curtain rises we are made to feel at home, almost indeed at *Home*, for the echoes of David Storey's play in which Sir John and Sir Ralph last shared the London stage are as audible as the echoes of Eliot and Beckett to whom Pinter seems to be paying more direct homage.

But *No Man's Land* could not actually have been written by any other hand: it is a distillation of much of Pinter's earlier work from *The Birthday Party* onwards, an evening with Harold Pinter, in fact. At its opening, an ageing alcoholic man of letters much prone to sudden physical collapse (Sir Ralph) is being visited by a distinctly crumpled poet (Sir John) whom he has encountered on Hampstead Heath where the latter is wont to indulge in a little light voyeurism when not cleaning up the glasses at Jack Straw's Castle.

It later transpires, need I add, that this is no mere chance encounter: the two men are known to each other, inextricably linked by an unseen wife whom one married and the other lived with, and their relationship is as ambiguous as that of the two sinister servants (Michael Feast and Terence Rigby) with whom Sir Ralph shares his house – a house in which the conversation is apt to roam from high comedy ('Lord Lancer? One of the Bengal Lancers, is he?') to lengthy discussions of the impossibility of reaching Bolsover Street by car.

What we have here, then, are four characters in search of several answers ('Tell me about your wife – did she google?'), none of which is forthcoming; along the way, Pinter manages to shape the English language into a spare, ritualistic chant which though never unimpressive remains for me oddly unenthralling. To see Sir John and Sir Ralph together is as ever a sustained joy; to have seen them together in a play rather than a tone poem would have been a still greater one but then that's *No Man's Land* for you: very sparse, very Harold Pinter.

And so to the rest of the week's offerings, the best of which is undoubtedly the Royal Court revival of Joe Orton's *Entertaining Mr Sloane*, first and last seen in London all of ten years ago at which time it caused a considerable furore, exacerbated by the author himself writing indignant letters to the press about 'degradation' and 'theatrical indecency' and signing himself Edna Welthorpe (Mrs).

Seen again in these enlightened times and in Roger Croucher's assured if not over-swift production (with a cast headed by Beryl Reid, Malcolm McDowell and Ronald Fraser) it is hard to remember what all the indignation was about – the late and much missed Mr Orton now seems to resemble nothing more horrific than J. M. Barrie run to seed and his comedy of curious manners, written almost entirely in mid-sixties Colour Supplement jargon, has been overtaken by the infinitely more chilling world of Edward Bond and Howard Brenton.

When it was first produced I seem to remember *Mr Sloane*'s plot (cheerful psychopath with one murder already behind him moves in with middle-aged brother and sister who then do battle for his sexual favours) attracting comparison with Pinter, which in retrospect is much like aligning Coward with Strindberg because they both wrote about marriage.

Jeeves at Her Majesty's is a peculiarly terrible attempt to bring to the musical stage an assortment of the P. G. Wodehouse books, principally *The Code of the Woosters*. The team involved here is a distinguished one (writer Alan Ayckbourn, director Eric Thompson, music Andrew Lloyd Webber) but nothing in their previous experience seems to have saved them from a series of cardinal errors, the first of which is the casting of David Hemmings as Bertie Wooster. Mr Hemmings has an accomplished minor talent for endearing villains (best expressed when he played Mordred in Logan's *Camelot*) but to a part requiring ideally Ian Carmichael and at the very least Richard Briers or Daniel Massey he is woefully ill-suited and resorts all too frequently to the kind of performance which equates charm with twinkling teeth.

Playing Jeeves, Michael Aldridge has an equally impossible task: as a title character his is almost certainly the most underwritten since George and Margaret, and he is moreover denied even one solo song, a denial roughly equivalent to building a film around Esther Williams and then shooting it on dry land.

Faced with the task of making three coherent theatrical hours out of Mr Wodehouse, not known for the lucidity of his plots, Alan Ayckbourn has resorted to a prolonged flashback, irritatingly narrated by Hemmings, in which Bingo Little, Gussie Fink-Nottle, Honoria Glossop and all are shuttled on and off stage in a muddled and often aimless way. The result, give or take a couple of good songs and valiant rescue attempts by John Turner and David Wood, is a disaster of *Titanic* proportions from which Tim Rice (who gave up the lyric-writing at an early stage) and Betty Marsden (whose part was written out of the show on tour) can count themselves lucky to have escaped.

Slow Profile

What José Ferrer's Chichester production of *Cyrano de Bergerac* lacks, apart from a leading actor with enough star quality to carry it off, is a good musical score: seldom if ever have I seen a show so painfully in need of seventy-six trombones and a snappier title (*The Nose Man*, perhaps?) to say nothing of Alfred Drake and a good choreographer. This, in itself, might not be a bad idea: there is no reason why Rostand's buccaneering, musketeering tragi-comic romance should not be staged in terms of a big and brassy Broadway musical so long as the people are there to do it. Through no fault of his own, however, Mr Ferrer (himself a distinguished Cyrano of the past) is faced with a company cobbled together for the summer and plainly at odds with that idea or any other. Thus we have, among the four leading performances, only one that will really do: Barbara Jefford's mature, elegant, tragic Roxane. Among the rest, Christopher Cazenove's Christian is played as a minor Shakespearian princeling, Bill Fraser's Ragueneau is out of Molière, and Keith Michell's Cyrano is a Pollock's Toy Theatre rendering of the role, best symbolized perhaps by his final curtain call which is taken while nervously descending a ladder. Still, it might have been worse – we might have been treated to a glass coach and the kind of waving that Anna Neagle used to do while playing Queen Victoria.

But there is, in all fairness, more wrong with this *Cyrano* than just Mr Michell's inability to project anything more than a cornflake cut-out hero; for although Mr Ferrer has clearly thought a great deal about what the show should look like, he has apparently not thought much about what it should suggest. Thus we have a pantomime, an evening of sound and fury signifying nothing beyond the fact that the director clearly loves a parade and where possible a few acrobats.

To conceive the character of Cyrano as Don Quixote is one thing, and probably fair enough; to play him as the Man of La Mancha is quite another, and leads to a terrible weakening of Rostand's original script, itself in no great shape thanks to the clinking, clanking translation of Christopher Fry.

So what we are left with, across nearly three long hours, is the outward form and trapping of a drama but at its centre only the hollow sound of Mr Michell listening to his own voice. *Cyrano* is, I believe, a masterly play about a great many things including intolerance, platonic male love, and courage; what it is not about is the ranting, raving affectation of Mr Michell's central performance which manages to combine a great deal of activity with very little life.

It is admittedly early in the present Chichester season for generalizations, but the sight of Mr Michell overcasting himself is not a pretty one, especially as he is an actor capable of intelligent minor performances when given the right framework for them. His theatre, which for its architecture and its setting must rank as the most attractive in the country, ought not to have been turned quite so readily into a last resting-place for the kind of cavalier actor-management which went out elsewhere with the demise of Frank Benson and Robert Atkins.

Talking of theatres and their architecture, I have seen the National and, like the future, it may work. Although that towering structure by Waterloo Bridge will not disappoint the long-distance hikers who already inhabit the Festival Hall, and although some of its foyers make London Airport look dwarfish by comparison, it is beyond any doubt the most impressive theatrical structure we are ever likely to see. Holding three separate playhouses (the conventional pros-arch Lyttelton, the workshop Cottesloe and the cylindrical Olivier, this last a gargantuan arena which clearly owes a great deal to Sir Laurence's experience at Chichester in the early sixties) it is apparently designed to be a kind of Theatre City.

Given that the building also houses closed-circuit television, three separate restaurants and innumerable bath- and dressing-rooms it would be possible for a man, even an actor, to live there undetected for several years. The only little local difficulties are going to be in opening up the place and then keeping it open, a feat which will require a regular workforce running into dozens if not hundreds of people.

At present, the interior is admittedly a little bare but that's nothing that several hundred acres of carpet won't cure. Overhead, Denys Lasdun's egg-box ceilings and his determination to build in solid concrete rather than stone suggests a singularly well-constructed atomic shelter, but there are already indications of some nicely quirky decisions like giving the only restaurant with a decent river view over to the actors rather than the paying customers.

More seriously, there is at the moment an ominous hush around the building, as though most of the interior decorators have lost interest or courage, faced with the daunting amount of work that they in particular still have to do. But if our National Theatre, the theatre that David Garrick first tried to build in London almost exactly two centuries ago, is not to sit like some ludicrous white elephant on the South Bank it seems to me that Peter Hall's best bet would be to get his company into those parts of the building (notably the Lyttelton and the offices) which are almost ready for occupation.

Out in the Midday Sun

The plays of Charles Wood (of which the latest, *Jingo*, is in an RSC production by Richard Eyre at the Aldwych until mid-September) have an alarming habit of running to seed almost as quickly as their leading characters. No one who saw *Veterans* or *Fill the Stage with Happy Hours* or such films as *How I Won the War* or *The Charge of the Light Brigade* could doubt that Wood is intermittently one of the funniest dialogue writers around; the difficulty is that his lines and his characters somehow fail to add up to the sum of their parts, so that we are left with a dazzling firework display at which rain has got into some of the boxes.

With *Jingo* we are back in Wood's favourite territory, the loony world of the British army: it is 1941, Singapore is about to fall to the Japanese despite all assurances to the contrary ('the Nippon no petrol have so no march can/Therefore snookered the little yellow man') and Wood's happiest invention is a BBC correspondent, immortally played by John Standing, whose task it is to inspire confidence in the British locals via the twin miracles of wireless and invincible ignorance ('little yellow men cannot see in the dark, therefore we need not fear an attack by night') while his wife (Anna Massey) allies herself to assorted officers and gentlemen and does her best to keep the home fires burning.

Here we are deep in Noël Coward/Celia Johnson country, in a world where there will always be an England, at any rate until about Tuesday, and in which stiff upper lips are so closely linked to stiff upper minds that the resident British colony is totally immobilized by its own confidence. So far, so good; the advantage of crossing R. C. Sherriff with Feydeau is that you get a workable farce at any rate for the first act, and the framework allows both Michael Williams and Peter Jeffrey to do military turns of the kind that the Boulting Brothers used to photograph in the mid-fifties.

The trouble starts round about the interval; by this time the bombs have fallen, Singapore has a naval base full of wet matelots and Mr Wood has run out of ideas: what we get then is Bernard Lee and a Chinese dancing teacher in one rather good albeit disjointed sequence, hotly followed by a collapse as sudden and total as that of Singapore itself. There is a great gaping crater where the second half of the play ought to be, and not even the considerable talents of Standing, Williams, Jeffrey and Miss Massey can disguise the fact that the evening has fallen apart.

Two Septembers ago, a week or two before he was sent by the *Sunday Times* to cover the Arab-Israeli war, and therefore a month or so before he was so suddenly and casually killed, Nick Tomalin appeared in the *Times* office where I then worked and suggested we should lunch. He was carrying two crash helmets – not, he explained, because it was to be a costume lunch but because it would be necessary to reach the restaurant by motorbike, his motorbike. When we arrived and I'd stopped shaking (Nick had a belief shared by Sir Ralph Richardson, but so far as I know none other, that motorcyclists are the children of God, unimperilled by other traffic and answerable only to their own special inscrutable laws of survival) he explained that he was doing a book on the National Theatre and that he thought I might be able to help. It rapidly transpired that I couldn't, not because I wouldn't have liked to but because in six months' research he'd learnt rather more about the internecine workings of that organization than I had in ten years of reviewing its productions and interviewing its directors. The National, he said, was much like the Vatican only funnier and still more Byzantine in its structure, but it had given him immense pleasure to explore.

Although he was sadly never to finish his book, there is now a belated chance for us to share in his bemused pleasure. In what is almost certainly the best-kept secret of the summer (and that too might have given him a degree of wry amusement) the National are doing a season of workshop productions at the ICA, public performances but curiously underpublicized presumably for fear people might actually start going to them instead of the Vic. One of these productions, *Nicholas Tomalin Reporting*, is a three-man reading of his journalism from 1959 to 1973 which I hereby beg Peter Hall to offer to a wider audience since it is far and away the best single entertainment I've come across in London this year. It includes passages from the National book ('laying a foundation stone more than three times is apt to invite sardonic comment') as well as such classics as 'Twenty-four Hours in Piccadilly Circus' and 'The General Goes Zapping Charlie Cong'. It should on no account be missed.

Smiling Through

A play about a derelict pop group reaching the end of the line at a Cambridge May Ball in 1969 may not sound like a barrel of laughs, but in the event David Hare's *Teeth 'n' Smiles* (which inaugurates the new artistic management of the Royal Court) is that and rather more: it's a viciously funny play, certainly the best Mr Hare has yet written – which considering *Knuckle* and *Slag* is already saying a good deal – and it affords far and away the best dramatic entertainment the Court has offered us in a long (indeed too long) time.

The premise of the piece is simple enough: into the privileged, cloistered world of Cambridge University shambles a group led by Maggie, a singer whose ambition it is to reach a San Francisco bar but who is in the meantime pursuing a sustained and exclusive love affair with quarts of Johnnie Walker. Her group also features a bass guitarist on his way to death by drugs, a lead guitar whose passion it is to devise the most boring sentences in the world, and a camel-coated manager who remembers (in a vivid four-minute speech exquisitely delivered by Dave King) being at the Café de Paris the night they dropped the bomb on Snakehips Johnson.

This motley crew is greeted by Snoad, an aged college porter who does at least send out for the group's sandwiches before having them busted, and Anson, a student organizer so bored by the sound of his own voice that he leaves his sentences perpetually unfinished. Together with a songwriter in love with Maggie, and an ageing would-be idol who once backed Eve Boswell, they form Mr Hare's cast-list and what then happens to them is rather less important than what doesn't.

The group slowly get themselves together, play one set, abandon the second and then start removing the college cutlery on the grounds that they might not be paid on account of something in the contract about three complete sets. By then, however, Maggie in one of her rare moments of sobriety has burned down the tent where the festivities are in progress, so by the end of the evening contractual clauses have become more than a little academic, what with the police already there and the group disbanded and Maggie on her way to jail.

That, at any rate, is the plot: but what Mr Hare is really on about here is not the wonderful world of Janis Joplin, nor even the sheer bloody awfulness of being a third-rate minor cult pop group: there are in fact less than half a dozen numbers in the whole show, most sung by Helen Mirren who, playing Maggie, gives what is beyond reasonable doubt the performance of her career. What Mr Hare is on about, through Maggie and those he puts around her, is the generation of twenty-five-year-olds who feel they're on the *Titanic* without much chance of getting it to change course. Maggie is thus not a great tragic figure: she's a girl from Stevenage who thought things might work out better, and now they haven't she's more than ready to try prison as an alternative to the road.

This is not, in short, the kind of instant historical celebration that *John, Paul, George, Ringo . . . and Bert* was; yet there's an auto-destruct process here too ('the louder we play, the sooner we go deaf') which is finally summarized in the song that brings the curtain down. The only difference between 1912 and 1943 and 1969, Mr Hare appears to be saying, is that the bands on the *Titanic* and at the Café de Paris never had agents with the sense to start a little light looting. But in the end none of Hare's characters is waving or drowning either: just trying to make up their minds about the depth and temperature of the water.

India, Whose India?

Tony Harrison's *Phaedra Britannica*, not to be confused with Racine's *Phèdre* to which it owes little more than Shakespeare owed Holinshed, is as fine a piece of theatre as the National has ever offered us, and you'd be advised to hasten along to the Old Vic where it now is with all possible speed.

What Mr Harrison has done here is to uproot Racine's tragedy (itself after all a hybrid from Euripides and Seneca) and transplant it to mid-nineteenth-century India where suddenly – and for the first time in my experience – it all begins to make sense. In a land where the sun explodes, as Maria Casarès once said, Phaedra lies behind closed doors and her passionate love for her stepson, the barbaric horror of his death, the prolonged absence of her husband and even her eventual suicide all acquire a relentless, terrible logic.

Admittedly, once having thought of India, Mr Harrison falls on his feet: the subcontinent can be made to stand for everything untranslatable in the original from '*Venus tout entière à sa proie attachée*' through to the concept of fate itself. India thus becomes the backdrop, the motive, the culprit; she also comes to represent antiquity, guilt, empire, mythology and virtually all the abstract ideas which are needed for an understanding of the play; so when, finally, the monsoon breaks and beats against Tanya Moiseiwitsch's sultry, stifling Governor's Residence there is an almost audible sense of release.

Earlier, within that heavy setting, Racine's duologues about passion and power are given new life, new rhythm and even new purpose by Mr Harrison's couplets which fairly throb through the play, no longer the light rhyming jingles which he used for his earlier National adaptation of Molière's *Misanthrope* but now heavier and more forceful:

My Hell is India, always at high noon,
with no relief of night, and no monsoon,

and under that red sun's remorseless stare
mankind's grossest secrets are laid bare.

True, there are problems here: we are at times only a couplet or two away from the tight-lipped world of Somerset Maugham where anguished upper-class ladies revealed unsuitable passions for local houseboys out in the midday sun; but it is to Mr Harrison's everlasting credit that his verse not only avoids these pitfalls but even manages to convey the supernatural death of Phaedra's stepson ('The brave boy died and left in my embrace/a lump of mangled flesh without a face') without getting an irreverent titter.

Phaedra Britannica thus becomes not only an account of one woman's passion for her husband's son but also a commentary on the British presence in India, a presence which brought colonial settlers into unwelcome contact with forces they neither understood nor were able to control; in this context, Phaedra is no longer Minos' daughter but simply the child of a Judge. Theseus becomes the British Governor, with Hippolytus as his half-caste son now in love not with Arcie but instead with a captive Indian princess called Lilamani. So we are further down the human scale, no longer faced with characters whose connections are godly or at least mythological; this lot belong essentially to branches of the Indian civil service and yet their destiny is no less tragic.

The reason for that lies as much in the casting as in the writing: John Dexter (who like Miss Moiseiwitsch also worked on Harrison's *Misanthrope* which is incidentally still in the National repertoire at the Vic) has again used Diana Rigg, this time with Michael Gough as her husband, David Yelland as her stepson, Alaknanda Samarth as her Ayah-confidante and the impeccable Robert Eddison as Burleigh, all of whom play for everything they are worth which collectively is a very great deal.

Miss Rigg's Phaedra is not, however, the great tragic heroine as specified by the Comédie Française; instead she's an English memsahib, matronly and domesticated, one who can be visualized having trouble with the staff as easily as with her heart and whose ultimate suicide is the action of a woman 'destroyed by lust and Eastern sun'. But the greatest tribute one can pay the creators of this *Phaedra* is that though Mr Harrison may strike the occasional jarring note ('I feel so utterly polluted' really will not do, even in a translation as free as this) together he and Miss Rigg have brought *Phaedra* back from the living death of French classical drama to an accessible theatrical reality – an achievement roughly comparable to that of animating all the statues in the Louvre.

Snarl, Clown, Snarl

Having decided, rightly, that the National should provide a London home for the best of our regional theatre work as well as its own productions, Peter Hall inaugurates that policy with the Nottingham Playhouse Company in *Comedians*, a play by Trevor Griffiths now to be found in repertoire at the Old Vic. The result is an evening of ice and fire (to borrow one of its own lines) which, though fatally flawed in one respect, is in every other well worth your attention.

Mr Griffiths's plot is simple enough: a group of aspiring comedians at night school in Manchester are (in the first act) setting off for the working men's club where they are to audition before a talent scout up from London. The second act consists entirely of their routines, and in the third they gather again before their teacher in his dingy classroom to hear the scout's verdicts.

Like David Storey (*Life Class*) Mr Griffiths has a superb feeling for the atmosphere of a classroom and a painter's talent for sketching detail: unlike Storey however he has a specific axe to grind, and it is that which finally wounds his play. Its beginning is more than promising: having introduced us to the six would-be stars, Griffiths brings on their teacher, himself an ex-professional comic (Jimmy Jewel in superlative form) to establish the ground-rules on which his teaching has been based. Comedy, in Eddie Waters's view, is a roughly equal mixture of technique and compassion, and one somehow visualizes his ideal comic being somewhere mid-way between Dave and Woody Allen.

That view is not however supported by the talent scout, an old enemy of Eddie's who makes it clear even before the audition that what he wants is a generation of Max Bygraves imitators. The second act therefore becomes a conflict between those two schools of thought: trapped in the middle, in a derelict club where the MC is eager to get back to bingo, some perform their monologues as rehearsed by Waters while others adapt to what they think will impress the scout (chillingly played by Ralph Nossek) and the one double-act among them falls apart as one partner heads in each direction.

Then, however, comes Gethin Price: star pupil of Eddie's, albeit not much beloved of him, Price jettisons his script in favour of an ice-cold revolutionary turn advocating death and destruction in the name of social reform. Back in the classroom, Act Three develops naturally enough into a confrontation between Price (Jonathan Pryce) and Waters about the uses and frontiers of comedy. The flaw lies here, though, because what Price has been doing on stage has very little to do with entertainment. So any dispute about what you can and can't achieve in a stand-up monologue becomes almost totally academic, and finally forces itself back into an ancient argument about whether or not there was anything a comedian could do about Auschwitz.

Only if Price, in the club, had done what Lenny Bruce was forever trying could the third act really work: nevertheless on the way to it Mr Griffiths (in his finest play to date) makes some intelligent and chilling points about the 'anything for a laugh' philosophy, and Richard Eyre's production provides three of the best performances currently on offer anywhere in town.

At the other end of Waterloo Bridge, the RSC are reviving Harley Granville Barker's long-lost *The Marrying of Ann Leete* in an elegant Aldwych production by David Jones who, having rehabilitated Gorky as a playwright, is now clearly set to do the same for Barker. But the two writers share more than just Mr Jones and lengthy oblivion: both were concerned with end-of-century change, both chronicled nascent social revolution and both wrote novelish plays in which character mattered more than plot.

In this case the plot concerns Ann's refusal to make a marriage of political convenience and her decision instead to marry a gardener and live with him in a dark hut where contentment appears to be Rousseau and a scrubbed wooden table. But the real interest lies not in Ann herself (who through no fault of Mia Farrow seems at any moment to be about to awake from a deep sleep); instead it lies in the characters Barker has placed around her, ranging from her wholly corrupt father (Paul Rogers), and her smarmy aristocratic suiter (Richard Pasco) through to the simple but honest gardener (Oliver Cotton) helpfully named Abud. Barker's achievement is to get us in one play from restoration comedy to D. H. Lawrence by way of *The Cherry Orchard*: his play is however more impressive in its ambition than its actuality.

Finally, an all-too-brief lament for the death last week of Pamela Brown: I have long cherished a recording she once made of *The Lady's Not for Burning*, and I was lucky enough to see her in several other Gielgud productions of the late fifties. Theatregoers with memories dating back only to the sixties will have little idea of her rare and remarkable talent, one which was lost still more prematurely to the stage where she worked, sadly, so seldom in later years.

Travelling Salesman

'Nobody blame this man. You don't understand: he was a salesman. And for a salesman, there is no rock bottom to life. He don't put a bolt to a nut, he don't tell you the law or give you medicine. He's a man way out there in the blue, riding on a smile and a shoeshine . . . a salesman's got to dream, boy. It comes with the territory.'

Who else but Willy Loman, the perpetually travelling salesman and the figure who outranks even James Tyrone in the gallery of the American theatre's tragic heroes? In the quarter-century since Arthur Miller's play was first staged (in New York with Lee J. Cobb, in London Paul Muni) no single dramatic creation on either side of the Atlantic – not even Osborne's Archie Rice – has ever challenged his tragic glory though in that time there must have been countless Willy Lomans. I have myself only ever seen two: the first, twelve years ago, was in an amateur production presented by the community theatre in Honolulu: in that unlikely setting a man called Norman Wright who was himself a salesman by day (albeit an infinitely more successful and distinguished one) gave a performance which still lives in my memory as one of the greatest I have ever seen at any theatre anywhere in the world, and I like to think it was at any rate partially because he knew, somewhere in the recesses of his memory, what it was like to pack a case of samples in the back of the car and set off into 'the territory'.

The second Willy Loman I saw last week, in an Oxford Playhouse Company production by Anton Rodgers of *Death of a Salesman* which can be found on tour this month in Cambridge, Oxford and Harlow. This time Loman is played by an English actor maybe twenty, thirty years off Willy's age and a whole heritage away from his small-town American background; yet it is no mean tribute either to the performance of Mark Kingston or to the writing of Mr Miller that the play survives intact as a massive theatrical experience even when seen (as by me) in the somewhat chilly surroundings of the Greenwood Theatre, an amiably if anonymously furnished playhouse resembling a sloping aircraft hangar and situated – some might say secreted – behind London Bridge Station. Still, let us not be ungrateful: life, as Willy says, is a casting-off and we should at least celebrate the opening of a theatre on the ground floor of what appears to be a nurses' hostel for Guy's.

Not that a nurse would have been able to do much for Willy: he is dying of failure, a disease which at the time of Miller's writing seems to have been more specifically American than of late. This, then, is *the* American tragedy: Willy, loaded down with suitcases of wares the exact nature of which is never revealed to us, is losing a race to the scrapheap, his struggle for existence merging into a fantasy world in which all his sons are triumphant and all the world loves a laugh. Miller himself once said that in a more benevolent script Willy would have died one Sunday afternoon while polishing the car; but in forcing through a realization that his life has been a hollow, phoney and ultimately senseless charade, Miller also forces through the awareness of something nightmarish at the heart of the American dream. In the course of three hours he gives us a lifetime of Willy, and from its very beginning we are waiting for him to die; when he does, not even his widow can cry. Instead, she notes simply that the last payment has that day been made on the house.

In a cast of twelve there are two or three performances which really will not do for a company of Oxford Playhouse distinction, but Kingston himself, Richard Durden and John Bown (as his sons) emerge with flying colours; Judy Campbell, an actress our theatre shamefully neglects, is equally strong as Willy's long-suffering wife and in the end they are left staring into whatever crater is reserved for burnt-out cases. Suddenly, though, I remembered what made America great: two salesmen, leaving the play's opening performance in New York, were overheard. 'Yeah,' said one to the other, 'I always figured that New England territory was lousy.'

In an otherwise barren theatrical week I have eventually managed to catch up with Agatha Christie's *Murder at the Vicarage* at the Savoy. A cast led by Barbara Mullen as Miss Marple (herself a pale shadow of

Margaret Rutherford in the same role) turn in the kind of 1930s Gothic performances I've not seen since they tore down the Rep in Reading. Nevertheless, lines like 'Disease and glands can play some nasty tricks on a man, Doctor' and 'It's the Colonel – I think he's dead' and 'Grizelda's not one to let her mind dwell on the unpleasant' afford a kind of macabre enjoyment and the whole bizarre entertainment should be preserved in aspic if that's not what has already happened to it. I've seldom seen a more terrible production, but I've also seldom seen a more contented audience leaving a theatre. So much for criticism.

Judgement at Court

Howard Barker's *Stripwell* (at the Royal Court) has the best opening minute of any show in town: a judge, sentencing a man for a flamboyant series of traffic violations, asks if he has anything to say before being sent down. 'Yes,' says the man, 'if you send me to prison I shall escape, and then I shall kill you.' People, as another judge (Brack, in *Hedda Gabler*) once remarked, don't do such things or at any rate they didn't; now they do, and one of Mr Barker's many points here seems to be that we had all better learn to live with and if necessary by violence.

Stripwell is in fact the name of the judge himself, a bizarre figure who tours the assizes in the company of a stripper whom he loves and who dances at nearby clubs while he's up on the bench; though not the habitual fascist loony we have come to expect of judge-figures in plays by any writer younger than William Douglas-Home, Stripwell in Michael Hordern's marvellously rambling performance is not an exactly typical representative of the judiciary either. Whether deciding to leave his wife for the go-go dancer, or shopping his son for smuggling heroin into the country concealed in the private parts of elephants (the heroin, that is, not the son) or simply trying nervously to convince his murderous prisoner that a year inside isn't really a sentence at all, this judge is a crumbling monument of self-doubt.

As a character, in isolation, he is superb: the trouble is that around him Mr Barker has only been able to arrange a series of brief, sketchlike scenes involving the wife (patiently, elegantly played by

Constance Cummings), the son (Tim Woodward) and the dancer (Patricia Quinn) – who decides on balance that she'd rather elope with Stripwell junior. The parts, alas, do not make a whole.

Nevertheless Mr Barker is a witty, literate writer who seems on this evidence to be situated roughly mid-way between David Hare and Christopher Hampton; his point, I think, is that in the end the practical advantages of compromise are no defence against a charge of failing to enact first impulses, but it is a woolly point, confusingly made. Yet Barker uses the English language like a set of carving knives, and his scenes are within themselves a joy to behold, especially those featuring Mr Hordern who, clutching an outmoded sense of 'fairness' around him like an Edwardian shawl, quivers across the stage as if in pursuit of the Alistair Sim award for 1975. Aware that as a judge he has spent his public life 'shifting people from one humiliation to another' he now shifts himself into a series of similar humiliations though the outcome, in the play's

Stripwell   Tim Woodward *as Tim*, Constance Cummings *as Dodie*, Michael Hordern *as Graham*, Patricia Quinn *as Babs*

catastrophic finale, tends to be more wry than tragic. Chris Parr's direction is unobtrusive, and the production as a whole is not helped by a curious decision of the designer (Bob Ringwood) to set the first half against back-projections and the second against three-dimensional reality.

A Little Knight Music

A special kind of awfulness afflicts big musicals in trouble, and *Thomas and the King* has more than its fair share of the affliction: from the moment the curtain rises to discover three buxom ladies with frozen smiles trying to entice King Henry II to bed one is aware that all is not going to be well at Her Majesty's. Mind you, the pedigree is not in itself reassuring: T. S. Eliot's *Murder in the Cathedral* and Anouilh's *Becket* might be thought to have said all that was dramatically necessary on the subject of this particular King and his turbulent priest, and to have said it moreover in the most poetic and elegant of ways. Undeterred by such considerations, Edward Anhalt tries for the hat-trick: having already perpetrated an appalling screenplay for the *Becket* film (one which owed more to the Louis B. Mayer School for Trainee Word Cobblers than to M. Anouilh, and which included such gems of twelfth-century dialogue as 'Will you take her with you or shall I have her sent?') Mr Anhalt has now reconverted his screenplay into the book for a musical of such mind-boggling inadequacy that, even in a year and a theatre which has already visited *Jeeves* upon an undeserving public, it will, I believe, rest assured of a place in the annals of dramatic calamity.

But, such are the eccentricities of West End economics, they might just get away with it; subtitled *A Little Knight Music* or possibly *Dad's Mediaeval Army* it will be remembered for the sets alone, upon which have been lavished at a guess a good £100,000 and all the talents of Tim Goodchild at his most papal. Stained glass windows, leaping priests, movable archways and incense abound: at any moment I myself was hoping for the descent of Anna Neagle on a wire, clutching a wand and murmuring something suitable like 'Arise Saint Thomas – all Canterbury will thank you for this boon.'

Alas, no such luck: instead we are marooned by Mr Anhalt and his collaborators (lyrics James Harbert, music John Williams, production Norman Maen) in the wrong part of *Camelot* country, a never-never land where all the inhabitants look as though they should be on ice skates and where nothing is said which couldn't equally well be sung or inscribed on the back of souvenir ashtrays.

At the centre of this bizarre epic is Richard Johnson, giving the kind of tight-lipped performance of an actor who has mysteriously misplaced his charisma and who in the meantime would like for us to know that he really hadn't meant to be here at all. To this end he stands at the side of the stage, as well he might, while the leaping monks and buxom wenches and hissing bishops prance round him. We are, I suspect, meant to gather that this Thomas Becket is above such worldly problems as choreography and has his mind on Higher Things though just what these things might be is never specified, largely because Mr Anhalt in his infinite wisdom has seen fit to strip the story of all the interest fed into it by Eliot and Anouilh, leaving us with nothing more than a randy King and an uptight Priest eager to assure us that despite all appearances to the contrary they are not in fact in love with each other.

Now, about the actor playing Henry: his name is James Smilie, this is his starring début in London, and it is – taken in isolation – a thoroughly impressive one. Twenty years ago, Mr Smilie would have had little difficulty in becoming Howard Keel or possibly Gordon Macrae: seldom if ever have I seen an actor so patently ready to tell us that there's a bright golden haze on the meadow or else that June is busting out all over. To his credit, he goes through *Thomas and the King* with the kind of energy, enthusiasm and commitment so clearly lacking in his co-star but sadly so totally misplaced in a show which one leaves only hoping that he at least has enjoyed himself.

The rest of the cast includes a lady called Caroline Villiers who in moments of crisis is apt to wander downstage and ask the audience 'Am I Beautiful?' to which the answer is 'Yes, But Is It Enough?' and another lady called Dilys Hamlett who manages to suggest in the one passable number how much better the show would have been if someone had actually considered what it was supposed to be about. Mr Maen's choreography is elsewhere similarly aimless, consisting as it so often does of lining up the cast and having them march around in squares as if involved in some eccentric charity walk. All in all a collector's piece, compulsive viewing only for lovers of gala kitsch and those who want to see what a £100,000 looks like when poured into a structure which resembles not so much Canterbury Cathedral as the model for the visitors' bar at a future Canterbury Hilton.

The Fool and the Playboy

Edward Bond writes some of the best scenes in contemporary British theatre: the fact that they seldom seem to add up to a play, or at least to any one single play, is unfortunate. His last script for the Royal Court, you may remember, was *Bingo*, an apparent life of William Shakespeare which developed rapidly into an attack on sixteenth-century Warwickshire landlords and it may therefore come as no surprise to learn that his new play *The Fool* (also at the Royal Court) is an apparent life of John Clare which develops rapidly into an attack on nineteenth-century East Anglian land-lords. Mr Bond is nothing if not consistent in his views about landlords through the ages; the trouble is that he's less consistent in his views about what constitutes stage biography and as a result we have here parts of at least three separate lives of John Clare.

Let's start with a few facts (we may as well do so here, since the Royal Court has abandoned any idea of programme notes and Mr Bond himself only deigns to give us his central character's surname in the second act): John Clare was the Northamptonshire 'peasant poet' who managed to get his first work published in 1820, when he was twenty-seven, but who spent the last half of a long life as an inmate of the Northamptonshire Lunatic Asylum, apparently unable to remember whom he had married or what had happened to his life. So far, so promising: an epic story containing elements of violence, madness and sex on such an exalted scale that I can only wonder why in the Hollywood forties Cornel Wilde or Tony Curtis wasn't to be found tearing golden locks in the film version. The fact remains, however, that Mr Bond's is the first dramatized biography of Clare and as such it has to be considered a disappointment.

The play opens in 1815 and looks at first as though it's going to be historical: we're entering the Iron Age and sure enough there's a character saying 'We're entering the Iron Age – the horse must go' to set the scene; our first glimpse of Clare (in a superlatively schizoid performance from Tom Courtenay) is as one of what appears to be a band of strolling players – in fact the peasantry, performing a somewhat subdued masque to entertain their lords and masters. But for the rest of the first half, it is the lords and masters who occupy Mr Bond's attention: we learn of their evil capitalist ways, a Parson is stripped of his fine clothing to establish the corrupt wealth of the church, and eventually a friend of Clare's (sternly well played by Nigel Terry) is hanged for attacking the mansions of the rich.

Where, meanwhile, is Clare? On the sidelines, watching, girl-chasing and presumably preparing himself for the poetry ahead. That much we have to guess, because as the curtain rises on Act Two there he is in London being fêted by a rich patron and gently mocked by a joky admiral (Isabel Dean and Bill Fraser, both in fine fettle) while a boxing match is staged in the background presumably – a certain amount of presuming has to be done with Mr Bond's work – to underline the curious values of a society which can encourage boxing and poetry simultaneously. Then, hey presto, we are back in East Anglia and Clare is growing shakier and loonier by the minute. Why? Because his poems aren't selling? Because he has realized the corruption of high society? Because he has married an earth mother (Bridget Turner, hauntingly good) while meaning to marry a gypsy girl he once knew? All these possibilities are suggested, bleakly, by Mr Bond's text but at the end we are left with no more than the image of Clare in the madhouse wondering what happened. Somehow it is not enough, and remarkable acting (not only from those mentioned but also from John Normington as the Parson and Nicholas Selby as the Landlord) cannot blind us to the fact that we have here a disjointed mishmash of an evening in which there are several sparks of light but no steadfast flame.

At the Old Vic, Bill Bryden's National production of *The Playboy of the Western World* makes for the kind of evening the Abbey would be proud of (and in my limited experience all too seldom manages to give its own Dublin audiences nowadays). As Christy Mahon, Stephen Rea finds within himself a wonderful mixture of bemusement and deception so that when he admits (falsely) to killing his own father he seems as amazed as anyone that he should be believed. Margaret Whiting as Widow Quin and Susan Fleetwood as Pegeen Mike offer him strong support, but the real joy of the evening is predictably that band of Irish players (Liam Redmond, J. G. Devlin, Eddie Byrne and P. G. Stephens) who seem to carry between them the whole weight of turn–of–the–century Ireland. Synge's Playboy was perhaps the first of the nearly men, and in reminding us that Christy's success (like that of the Government Inspector) is more a reflection of the derelict community into which he erupts than of his own brilliance, Bryden has done the play considerable service.

Prince Albert

We may live to see more intriguing definitions of *Hamlet* than the Peter Hall/Albert Finney/National epic now at the Old Vic: I do not believe we shall ever see a finer representation of the play as it is written. Across all of four hours, with one twenty-minute break almost three hours in, Shakespeare's text is slowly but surely unrolled to reveal a canvas as vast as any ever conceived by any artist in any medium. This is a massive production, to be judged like all epics not so much by its depth as by its breadth, and on those terms it is truly breathtaking. At the first appearance of Francisco and Barnardo on the battlements a machine is set in motion which then grinds inexorably through to the final command of Fortinbras, and as a feat of theatrical engineering this is far and away the most impressive *Hamlet* I have ever seen.

To some extent it is also a 'Glyndebourne' *Hamlet*: its values are operatic, Wagnerian values and for them to be accepted it is necessary to view the play much as the late Duke of Norfolk used to view coronations – an event, not a drama, but an event no less stirring for being totally predictable, even stately, from the outset. Into this concept of *Hamlet* the play, Hamlet the character fits somewhat unobtrusively: all the cut versions of the text tend to favour him (since it is others whose lines are usually cut) and when, as here, these cuts are restored it becomes not so much *Hamlet* as *Hamlet and Claudius*, a twin-centred play in which it is hard to decide who should ultimately be the focus of our attention, particularly when they are played by two actors (Finney and Denis Quilley) of roughly equal age and vocal strength.

Against John Bury's stark setting – a wall with one large portal at its centre – Peter Hall has arranged a grizzled evening in which it is evident from the first entry of Horatio (a bespectacled, crumbling Philip Locke) that this is no longer to be the play about anguished youth he first gave us with David Warner at Stratford a decade ago.

Instead it is to be a middle-aged evening in which even Laertes and Ophelia (Simon Ward and Susan Fleetwood) seem to be well into their late thirties and Polonius (Roland Culver, the finest I have ever seen) has therefore to seem a hundred.

Style, authority, reliability, all the middle-aged virtues are here in abundance and each of the players I've mentioned (and additionally Angela Lansbury as Gertrude, Robert Eddison as the Player King and J. G. Devlin as the Gravedigger) turns in the kind of star Shakespearian performances I thought to have disappeared with the Stratford of Glen Byam Shaw.

But with all those fireworks going on around him it is perhaps unfair to expect an especially dazzling lone rocket from Finney: in the first half of the evening he seemed indeed (on the first night) to be consciously restraining himself, only to let fly in those moments where Hamlet is anyway at his most theatrical – Ophelia's grave, or the description of the death of Rosencrantz and Guildenstern. His limitations are however only those of the production: lacking a central, guiding thesis and apparently determined not to explore or explain or exploit but merely to exhibit, he and it become a *Hamlet* for all seasons, taking on the complexions of individual scenes and changing as rapidly as they do. For all that, it is a production which has to be seen and will I think never be forgotten.

In an unusually star-studded theatrical week, Graham Greene's *The Return of A. J. Raffles* (RSC/Aldwych) is a literary joke gone wrong; after the success of *Sherlock Holmes*, thought Mr Greene, why not bring back his great contemporary the gentleman cricketer and burglar created by Hornung and supposedly killed during the Boer War? Why not indeed, except that where the *Holmes* script had its own period truth, *Raffles* is a modern parody in which Denholm Elliott's first appearance out of disguise is oddly clumsy and yet sets the keynote for the rest of the evening. The result is a leaden 'entertainment' full of jokes about the queerness of Alfred Douglas but ultimately so lacking in Edwardian confidence that the production is only saved by Paul Rogers' marvellous appearance as the future Edward VII and Michael Bryant's comic German Spy. Other performances are evenly divided between those who go too far and those who don't go far enough, and beyond a curious obsession with the sexual habits of *fin de siècle* celebrities it is hard to see what has drawn either Mr Greene or the RSC to a distinctly lacklustre affair.

Finally, all praise to Ben Travers who at eighty-nine has come up with the best new comedy in town: *The Bed Before Yesterday* (at the Lyric) is a masterly account of a middle-aged gorgon (Joan Plowright) discovering in the nick of time that life is for living. If you're thinking about Christmas entertainment for grown-ups, hasten to the Lyric box-office.

1976

Big Ben

Watching a spotlit Ben Travers raising a glass (of champagne, what else?) from his seat in the stalls to the cast of his fifty-year-old farce *Plunder* at the first night of its revival last week by the National Theatre company at the Old Vic, it was at last evident that our greatest living comic playwright had come into his own. And not before time. Ben Travers is ninety this year and he has been constructing comedies of one kind or another since 1919; yet the British theatre, with its usual remarkable gift for mislaying its own gems, has alternately ignored and taken him for granted.

When *Plunder* first opened in 1928 even *Punch* magazine (which might have been expected to take a special interest in stage humour) totally ignored it, presumably on the grounds that it was just another Aldwych farce, and before we start feeling smug about this latter-day Travers renaissance it might be as well to remember that it has taken the National fully twelve years to get around to him, which seems a little slow even by its standards.

But Michael Blakemore's new production, (coming as it does within a few weeks of Lindsay Anderson's Lyric production of Travers' *The Bed Before Yesterday*), is a sharp reminder of what we have been missing: it is quite simply the funniest evening to be found anywhere in London and for that we have to thank Blakemore himself, Frank Finlay and Dinsdale Landen in roughly equal measure.

Yet it remains Travers' evening: a plot of considerable dexterity takes off slowly, like a classic steeplechase; Dandy Nichols, dressed like a Victorian tea cosy ('You'd have to go a long way to get round me'; 'Yes, I may even have to take a taxi') is claiming to have married above herself and is therefore in dubious possession of a great deal of jewellery. Enter Frank Finlay, all teeth and spats and two-tone hair, determined to burgle the lady with the faltering assistance of Dinsdale Landen, the latter playing the Ralph Lynn part and bearing at times an uncanny resemblance to the only one of the original Aldwych team I ever saw in a Travers farce.

Together, Finlay and Landen form a double-act that is classically perfect, with Finlay, the only actor I know who can almost literally laugh like a drain, leading the inept Landen through a series of misadventures climaxing at their arrival in the dormant Dandy Nichols' bedroom where Landen inadvertently puts himself out with the ether destined for her. It is not, as will already be apparent, that the plot is stunningly original, nor that the jokes are – taken out of context – all that good; what makes *Plunder* such a treasure is the sight of a perfectly tuned theatrical machine grinding into action and then running away with itself along a brilliantly laid track. The overall result is a joyous evening, and if 1976 brings us another such we shall be more than lucky.

Brookery Nook

Like much of the best of Peter Brook's work for the theatre here and abroad over the last decade, *The Ik* (at the Round House) is not so much a play as an event, a bleakly staged documentary but one at which spectators are permitted and, in this case, actually encouraged.

For a week or so before it opened, Brook himself, not normally the most publicly chatty of men, was to be seen and heard ticket-touting on countless radio and television shows so that by the first night some members of the audience seemed to be expecting nothing short of a real-life miracle on ice. What they in fact got was something very different: *The Ik* is neither so theatrically magical as *A Midsummer Night's Dream*, nor so journalistically horrific as *US*; perched somewhere between these two great landmarks of Brook theatre, it is instead a stagey representation of an anthropological truth.

The Ik, such of them as are left, are a North Ugandan tribe living in barren mountainous territory with four inches of rainfall a year; in 1946 the then government of Uganda turned part of their territory into a game reserve, and in the interests of preserving wild life they forbade the Ik to hunt or gather wild fruit. A tribe of hunters was thus supposed to become, overnight, a tribe of farmers and the Ik's inability to do so resulted in their own starvation. In 1964 an anthropologist called Colin Turnbull, who had been at Oxford with Brook, arrived to study those who remained alive, and it is with his arrival (complete with camera, fit-up table and tinned food supplies) that Brook's *Ik* starts.

The tribe itself is represented by five actors from the International Centre for Theatre Research in Paris where this production first opened a year ago, and for ninety uninterrupted minutes at the newly refurbished Round House we watch Turnbull – beautifully played by Andreas Katsulas – as he watches the Ik.

By now they are totally bereft of social responsibilities of any kind: Ardrey's territorial imperative has been reduced to a simple, apparently ludicrous determination to survive no matter how horrific the conditions, how great the degradation, or how brutal the treatment of other tribesmen and women. The Ik expect nothing but grab what they can: a mother burns her son's fingers when he reaches out for food, another refuses to let her father die too close to her, and meanwhile Turnbull's Ik guide (Katsuhiro Oida) filches cigarettes and medicine from the white man. Like Barry Collins' *Judgement*, *The Ik* is about survival at any price and, on a bleak, sand-covered stage surrounded by four unadorned pillars and a few rocks, this bare, minimal drama is staged with a deliberate refusal to shock or move its audience more than is strictly necessary.

The Ik are there, take them or leave them, and most of the world would appear to have left them. Ironically their decimation has been caused by the best of motives: the Ugandan government were simply trying to establish a game reserve, not to destroy a people. That they have almost succeeded in doing both is the intellectual point underlying the Denis Cannan–Colin Higgins adaptation of Turnbull's book; that this can be represented by a handful of actors with tin cans and twigs in a sparse framework where speech rhythms are more important than movement, and where isolated events from the decline and fall of a tribe can be turned into an almost religious experience, is the theatrical point underlying Brook's production. It should not be missed.

Last year's Stratford history cycle has now reached the RSC's London home at the Aldwych, and with a kind of crazy logic it still opens with *Henry V*, presumably on the grounds that it's not only a better play than either part of *Henry IV* but also an infinitely better production. Terry Hands has to his everlasting credit noticed that up to the very gates of Harfleur this King is a loser, reluctantly leading a bedraggled and underprivileged army through the vasty fields of France, instead of being the usual, mindless, boy-scout hero sent off victoriously from Southampton by so many earlier productions.

Visibly flogging himself into action, Alan Howard's nervy, introvert King makes the speeches that are required of him and then finds to his amazement that they actually work – men do go into the breach once more. The production has inevitably lost some of its breadth in the move to the Aldwych, but a smaller set offers instead a greater intensity – one which patently suits Mr Howard. At the end, Emrys James' jolly master-of-ceremonies Chorus still mysteriously becomes the French Duke of Burgundy without so much as a change of accent, but by then we have had a real French Princess and the **best** *Henry V* in years, so who's complaining?

Hampton/Court

Take three characters: two men and a woman, all in their middle thirties, all London-based, all reasonably affluent and all deeply unable to solve the central problem of their lives which for each appears to be an inability to live with, and an equal inability to live without, at least one of the other two. Noël Coward's solution forty-five years ago (*Design for Living*) was to sling all three of them in bed together as the final curtain fell, leaving one to hope for the best. Christopher Hampton's solution (in his new play *Treats* at the Royal Court) is to return at curtain-fall to the original pairing, leaving an odd man out on the grounds that he is the most boring of the threesome and also perhaps the most able to cope elsewhere.

Somehow it doesn't work: Mr Hampton is a master builder of plays, for my money the most able British dramatist to have emerged from the 1960s, and yet it is the sheer overpowering technique of *Treats* which finally destroys any real chance that the play might engage our attention and/or concern. Constructed on a kind of eternal tripod, it rotates the three characters through nine scenes so that each has one scene alone, one with one of the other two and one with them both: there is a kind of perfection here, but it is of the Chinese-box variety and the last box turns out to be very empty indeed. Even Peter Shaffer's *Black Comedy*, another mechanical tour-de-force, had more to say about the people involved in its machinations and their social predicament.

Treats is, across two long hours, about whether Ann (Jane Asher) should carry on living with Patrick (Stephen Moore) who is boring but reliable, or whether she should try to survive on her own, or whether she should go back to Dave (James Bolam) who is a reporter specializing in dictionary jokes. 'Ha!' says Ann at one point; 'Two of those,' replies Dave, 'and you'd be laughing.'

It's that kind of a play: momentarily very funny, occasionally even touching, but totally removed from any touchstones of reality – like a series of conversations in a marooned spaceship. This may, of course, be what Mr Hampton is on about: Ann's flat is symbolically only half-furnished, and when reality does intrude it is only in the form of a street demonstration, distantly heard through a window.

The three of them do, it's true, go to work and come home again but there is an unreality even about that – Dave appears to be a *Times/Guardian* war correspondent able to afford a permanent room at the Ritz, while the office to which Ann and Patrick go each morning apparently intrudes on their existence no more than the street demo. They are record-sleeve people, plastic-coated and vaguely reminiscent of reality, but nine scenes in their company is about six too many. To say that *Treats* has all the makings of a really good half-hour tele-script must sound like an insult, and yet it is – from the interval onwards – an inescapable thought.

The performances, though, are the saving grace of a barren evening: Jane Asher again plays that glazed Hampton lady she created in his *The Philanthropist*, while Stephen Moore offers a variant on that play's central character: a well-meaning but ineffectual bumbler, semi-detached from those around him and in need of reassurance that the police telephone number really is 999. James Bolam is thus left to inject these sketches from unmarried life with something approaching drama, and there are moments when the play seems about to develop through him into an icy tract about repossession and the territorial imperative; curiously, the author of *Savages* has shied away from any such development, and the result is at best a toothless and mildly attractive evening.

At the Mermaid, Mike Stott's *Funny Peculiar* is that rarity of rarities, a really good English farce with the courage of its own central character's sexual obsessions. As superlatively played by Richard Beckinsale, he's a Pennine grocer who progresses from being the author of consoling letters to a local poofter vicar ('if every poofter in the land hanged himself from bell ropes we'd all be deaf') to the realization that the manifold wonders of marital sex have been denied him by an inhibited wife. In search of The Other, he falls in with a couple of experienced wife-swappers, though not before he's come to blows with an irate confectioner in a deluge of flying cream puffs in what is far and away the single funniest scene currently on any stage in London.

Through it all, Beckinsale erupts with suppressed sexual fury, aided and abetted by a wonderfully tasteless loony (Matthew Kelly) and a long-suffering wife (Julie Walters) who only comes to an appreciation of Beckinsale's sexual needs when he's flat on his back in a collection of plaster casts. The belly-laugh is what Mr Stott has brought back to the live theatre, and he has succeeded incidentally in animating and rejuvenating a series of the best seaside-postcard jokes since McGill.

Wiener Schnitzler

I wish I could learn to care for or even about Arthur Schnitzler. I wish I could bring myself to believe, as many do, that he had Meaningful Things to say in his Viennese turn-of-the-century scripts about Life, Love, Sex, Women or even Sachertorte. I wish I could believe that were he alive and working in England now he'd be doing something more significant than cobbling together the occasional script for 'Crossroads'. But I can't.

It is true none the less that as a playwright he's always exerted a unique if incomprehensible hold on drama critics; Robert Muller, among the liveliest *Daily Mail* reviewers of the early sixties, has done some elegant tele-adaptations, while Frank Marcus of the *Sunday Telegraph* is responsible for the translation of *Anatol* currently to be found at the Open Space in a haltingly gracious production by Charles Marowitz.

As played by Derek Godfrey (an admirable and stylish actor here unaccountably giving the kind of arch performance which used to denote greying juvenile leads on their way to the Rex Harrison parts in derelict seaside reps) Anatol himself is the all-purpose Viennese man-about-town who involves himself with six different women (all played by Prunella Scales of whom more in a moment) in six different and self-contained scenes all linked by some decidedly bizarre dance routines in which rather too few ladies do rather too little in costumes that look as though they were originally designed for some weird parody of *Swan Lake*.

The scenes themselves are of unique inconsequentiality, concerned as they are with Anatol in various stages of falling into or out of love with the six aforementioned Scales ladies. These range from a ballet dancer to a circus cyclist, and they are played on a quick-change revue-sketch basis which wins the evening for Miss Scales on points of sheer technique. But in the end only one of the six scenes really works, and that is the one in which Anatol braces himself to break off an affair with a dancer before discovering to his horror that she is intent on doing it first. The other five, intermittently concerned with hypnosis, Christmas shopping, misplaced nostalgia and wedding arrangements, add up to very much less than meets the eye, and a programme note about the 'darker side' of swinging Vienna doesn't help much, since we are then given no more social or historical insight than might be contained in a period commercial for hot chocolate.

All in all it is an ineffably droopy and boring evening, lacking the sexual curiosity of *La Ronde* and loaded with lines like 'men and women are alike, especially women', which look as if they fell off the back of a lorry on their way to the Oscar Wilde Memorial Home for ageing epigrams. The alibi for it all is doubtless 'Six Faces of Eternal Woman' or 'The Battle of the Sexes' but the overall impression is that of being locked in a very small room with all the Strausses while they very slowly construct a musical box made of icing sugar. The Vienna Woods have a lot to answer for.

Meanwhile at the Queen's, Simon Gray's *Otherwise Engaged* enters its eighth month laden with such glittering prizes as the *Evening Standard* and *Plays & Players* awards for Play of the Year, and now starring Michael Gambon who last week replaced Alan Bates above the title. When the play first opened, Barry Took hailed it in my absence from these columns as 'a play to savour' and it does indeed improve the more you throw it around inside your head. But Mr Gambon is more butch than Bates, and the central character's reactions to the intruders (lodger, brother, friend, wife) who disturb a day supposedly devoted to Wagner on the stereo thus appear more defensive than careless.

What we have here is essentially still son of *Butley*, though admittedly he's now a publisher rather than a college tutor. The vitriol of Gray's language ('Australians? All right as dentists – but once you let them into literature they lower the property values. Scribble, scribble, scribble like little gibbons . . .') is a constant joy and it is arguable that he has here collected five of the nastiest people in London for the sole purpose of encircling his hero with them, so that the hapless Wagnerite is left in a perpetual interview-situation asking 'What's it like?' as more and more people burden him with their existence.

'Only Disconnect' is Mr Gray's message, and I begin to find it deeply seductive; to be so far withdrawn from life that you are scarcely visible to the naked eye does have certain advantages, and the final question is whether or not Mr Gray expects us to approve. Bates, in his effortless superiority, was harder to like and easier to fear; Gambon is more visible as a character and infinitely more vulnerable, but I have an uneasy feeling that in the bitter chill of Bates's performance lay the heart of the matter.

The Demolition Man

Watch It Come Down is John Osborne's *Heartbreak House*, and there is something faintly unnerving though hopefully not actually prophetic in that it should have been chosen as the National Theatre's final production at the Old Vic. We, and he, are now precisely twenty years on from Jimmy Porter and *Look Back in Anger*, and the creative fury has been replaced by an acceptance of the holocaust so that the new play ends with a great many bangs and one or two whimpers. It will be a miracle, in short, if we are able to look back in anything.

Set in a trendily converted railway station through which a weekly goods train still thunders, *Watch It Come Down* is concerned, icily and acidly, with Ben and Sally Prosser (Frank Finlay and Jill Bennett) and the commune they have built around themselves as protection for and from each other. There's a dying poof writer of the Florentine school (craggily and quite superlatively played by Michael Gough in what is beyond all likely competition the supporting performance of the year), a living poof housekeeper (Michael Feast), a revolutionary artist (Angela Galbraith) apparently only there to be yelled at periodically, and an all-purpose if weepie comfort (Susan Fleetwood) who finally throws herself under the goods train in a gesture which, one irreverently begins to think, represents the only sensible way out of a weekend in such ghastly company.

But Mr Osborne is not to be mocked, and nor perhaps are his characters: true, they are getting on a bit, less witty than they were in *The Hotel in Amsterdam*, less confident than in *Time Present* and now totally surrounded by hostile outsiders intent on killing first their dog and then them. In the end, *Watch It Come Down* is a play about love and hate but mainly hate: Ben and Sally only come to life when locked in physical combat or when remembering what they achieved without or despite each other. Together they are a disaster area and therefore when the final holocaust comes it is neither unexpected nor very alarming – it is, after all, merely the physical manifestation of the destruction they have already wrought on each other and those around them.

No one chronicles or catalogues hatred more perfectly than Osborne; his speeches at their best (admittedly a condition they achieve less often here than elsewhere in his work) are superlative distillations of venomous indignation, directed now at the British way of country life:

> . . . shotguns in the wood, tea and pearls, rural swank and a tub of money under the chintz four-poster. Fêtes opened by local TV celebrities, restoration funds, old ducks who 'come in and do', village greens, hunting 'manners', indifferent food and pewter candlesticks, over-healthy children home for the hols, greedy Gorgon nannies, undergraduates fumbling behind bushes on floodlit lawns, dancing till dawn with Miss Sarah Crumpet-Nicely of Grasping Hall while Mummy and Daddy look on at all the young people 'having such a good time' against this nasty, brutish issue of English Country Life . . .

So far, so furious; the trouble is that it becomes increasingly difficult to relate the countryside Sally so hates to the country in general, and equally impossible to relate the rest of Osborne's characters to any other kind of people – so that, in the last analysis, a small, nastily incestuous group of failed artists gets its come-uppance beside a symbolically rusting railway branch line. *Watch It Come Down* seethes with distaste, but the demolition man is working on an already collapsed edifice.

At the Arts, E. A. Whitehead's *Old Flames* is an infinitely more chilling account of marital and sexual loathing, this one concerned with four women who invite a man (to whom each of them is linked by birth, marriage or bed) to a dinner party at which he becomes the main course. The concepts of man-eating feminists can seldom have been taken so literally and Mr Whitehead is, at the last, ambiguous about where his own sympathies actually lie; along the way he has however managed to create a disturbing, not to say indigestible, play in which the rich tension of the first act is matched by a post-prandial discussion when the four women – mother, ex-wife, wife, girlfriend – spell out the precise causes of their action in a rap session of ritual fervour. Judy Cornwell, Gary Bond and Anne Dyson, together with Katherine Fahy and Barbara Ewing, make it an unforgettable if uneasy evening.

Grand National

First things first. I have seen the National, and it works. Or rather a third of it does: one of the three proposed stages, the Lyttelton, is this week open for the first time to paying customers along with its bars, cafeterias, cloakrooms and bookshop and while it may not be everything (for that we shall have to wait at least until the winter) it is at least an impressive start. We have, God knows, been waiting long enough: it was in 1848 that a London publisher called Effingham Wilson first thought that a National Theatre for Britain might not be such a bad idea, considering that the French had then already had their Comédie Française for nearly two hundred years without apparent damage to the fibre of the nation, and it was all of seventy-five years ago that Bernard Shaw started campaigning for the same thing, pointing out that whether they liked it or not (and at first they almost certainly wouldn't) the British deserved nothing less.

The fact that now, a hundred and thirty years post-Wilson, we have not only a National Theatre company (in existence since 1963) but also a sparkling concrete-and-carpet home in which they can live and work is a cause for huge celebration and national rejoicing and fireworks in the streets, none of which has actually happened – partly because our economic climate doesn't seem to allow fireworks just at present, and more importantly because Peter Hall has decided to move five already tried-and-tested Old Vic productions (*Hamlet, Happy Days, Watch It Come Down, John Gabriel Borkman* and *Plunder*) into his new South Bank emporium simultaneously, thereby neatly avoiding any one single gala celebration, over-shadowed as that would undoubtedly be by the present – and hopefully shortlived – inability to make public appearances of the man who above all others made the whole thing possible, Laurence Olivier.

But Olivier himself established the Old Vic as the National's temporary home in a similarly unfanfared way, and he too relied on opening productions most of which had been tried and tested elsewhere, in his case at Chichester. What matters now is not the productions but the fact that they are in their own home and that as of this week it will be possible to spend five successive evenings by the Thames in hugely pleasant surroundings seeing the very best that English acting has to offer.

The productions themselves have not much changed since the Vic (though Finney's *Hamlet* is more confident but somehow also more cramped in the Lyttelton and Travers' *Plunder* has blossomed into the funniest show in town) but what we have there now – at a building cost of £16 million and a reputed running cost of another £5 million annually – is the finest company of actors in the land doing their best to show us where the money's gone. It is an impressive sight, and when the Olivier stage opens with Finney's *Tamburlaine* and when Michael Kustow has filled the rambling lobbies with exhibitions and impromptu performances and when the Cottesloe is open for other experiments it will be the most exciting building in the world. And that, of course, is all Bernard Shaw ever wanted in the first place.

Something to Bragg About

George Devine, second only to Tyrone Guthrie in the post–Shavian list of men who have altered the face of the English theatre, was once asked what was the most important thing he'd established at the Royal Court: 'The right,' he said, 'to fail.' It is a right not often extended to authors within the costly and unsubsidized framework of West End musicals and there should therefore be one loud cheer, maybe even one and a half, for the Delfont Organization who have allowed Melvyn Bragg (book), Alan Blaikley and Ken Howard (music and lyrics), Clifford Williams (direction) and Paddy Stone (choreography) to put together at the Prince of Wales an all–English musical about 1917 life in New Orleans which is a massively fascinating disaster.

Called *Mardi Gras*, it is out of Jerome Kern by way of *Ipi Tombi*; it has everything that *Show Boat* had except that it resolutely refuses to float, and at the end of its three hours (by which time water is flooding in through the hold and a number of the cast have actually drowned before our very eyes) one still longs for an explanation.

For, like the *Titanic, Mardi Gras* does not actually deserve to sink; it has evidently been put together with some care by thoughtful men who, though one suspects that they may never have been closer to New Orleans than a cinema showing 'Look at Life' travelogues, have evidently read every book and seen every 'B' movie that could conceivably relate to their theme. The dialogue fairly pulsates with great bad lines: 'I gotta do one last job,' announces the hero, though not before the heroine has noted that the male population of New Orleans 'have bored through me like the Mississippi hitting the Gulf'.

Bragg's book is a literate and loving imaginary look at the last summer of innocence before New Orleans and the rest of America got into the First War, and his plot (local heavy determines to take the town's leading prostitute as his Carnival Queen despite the intervention of lovelorn wandering minstrel) might just have been all right were it not for the second half, in which the book has its spine broken by a series of top-heavily choreographed voodoo spectaculars of the kind which used to be performed by ladies with daggers in their dentures in front of a dropcloth on the ends of piers in the days before they invented the Talk of the Town.

Mardi Gras has in short all the right things in all the wrong places, as if assembled by some mad Frankenstein determined to insert arms into eye-sockets: show-stopping numbers arrive after the show has already stopped, a stunning solo first-half finale by Lon Satton is thrown away because it comes from and goes to nowhere, and even Morgan Sheppard's talkative barman, straight out of *Our Town*, only gets into his stride as the final curtain is falling. The parts are all there, some in good working order, but only the revolving stage ever seems to have been accurately connected.

New Orleans, right? 1917: birth of the blues, Carnival time, the crowning of the Queen of Storyville, say kids, let's do a show. And they have. They've nursed it, they've rehearsed it, and it doesn't work; yet in there somewhere is a great deal of talent (not only Satton and Sheppard but Aubrey Woods and Nicky Henson, though the female casting has admittedly been catastrophic) and also a score which for those of us who intend to buy the record will, I think, improve immeasurably on closer acquaintance. Most important of all, Bragg and Blaikley and Howard have been able to see what the theatre can do for (and against) a script; I long to see their second musical.

The marvellous thing about Barry Humphries (back in the West End at the Apollo with Edna Everage, now ennobled by Gough Whitlam to Dame Edna and otherwise known as *Housewife! Superstar!*) is his quiet good taste. 'Australians–Normal Prices' read signs in the theatre lobby, and 'Paraplegic Toilets Eighth Floor: Please Use Stairs' so that before we even reach our stalls we are back in that bizarre world where, to quote Edna's own theme song, 'It doesn't matter who your Mum or Dad is/As long as you've a lovely bunch of Gladdies.' The trouble is that Edna has now been allowed to dominate the evening with Humphries to the exclusion of much else, with the result that she rabbits on for about half-an-hour longer than is strictly bearable or hilarious. Ian Davidson, credited in the programme with 'executive mise en scène', has singularly failed to fulfil the first task of a director, that of telling his star what and when to cut.

Finally, at the Piccadilly, *Very Good, Eddie* is a small but perfect masterpiece joyously well revived, for the first time in more than half a century, by Bill Gile and a largely unknown English cast. One of the earliest (1915) Jerome Kern musicals, with lyrics by P. G. Wodehouse and others and a book by Guy Bolton, it is far and away the best escapist evening in town. Men in boaters and blazers looking like Bing Crosby's elder brothers sing lovely, lilting, lyrical songs to inane ladies in white organdie, and one is not surprised to learn that this is the show that sent Richard Rodgers into the musical business. Like *Of Thee I Sing* it is one of the great 'lost' shows of our century, and now that Mr Gile has rediscovered it you'd be well advised to share his evident delight at its charms.

Four Hours' Traffic

Let us, for the purposes of argument, assume that Shakespeare was not a fool; let us further assume that when, in *Romeo and Juliet* (this year's initial RSC production at Stratford) he had his Chorus speak of 'two hours' traffic of our stage' he actually meant that the play which followed should last roughly that length of time. If that is so, then a director who wilfully allows his company to ramble on for the best part of four hours, behaving for much of that time as if they were in *Lear* rather than *Romeo*, must have some definable thesis on which to base and justify his production. The difficulty with the present Trevor Nunn–Barry Kyle epic is in deciding precisely what they think the play is about.

The first thing it's about, of course, is a balcony and this year's permanent old-timbered Stratford set by John Napier and Chris Dyer is positively top-heavy with balconies of one kind or another. At the back of a thrust stage now built out into the stalls there are two rows of gallery seats high above the action, where the customers sit in full view of the rest of the audience so that those planning to buy seats there are advised not to nod off and not to mind the sight of a great many necks in rear view since for the most part that's all they'll see from up there. Further balconies exist all around the set, together with a steep stage-left staircase on which the Chorus is discovered sitting in jeans reading a book shortly before leaping to his feet to mislead us about the length of the performance.

From then on in, it's anybody's and everybody's *Romeo*: the two lovers, played by Ian McKellen and Francesca Annis, are not only star-crossed but also visibly into their thirties which makes one wonder during duller moments why they aren't out looking for work or worrying about their children's education. But even allowing for the fact that Veronese teenagers in love were allowed to grow very old indeed, one is still left with an oddly ill-assorted couple either of whom might do well in any one production but not both in the same, if you're still with me. Mr McKellen's Romeo is a leaping, Puckish figure forever on the trot as if determined to prove that whatever else the extra two hours may be they certainly won't be static. Miss Annis' Juliet on the other hand is infinitely still, vastly more mature and seems at moments to be playing his mother.

Then again we have Michael Pennington's Mercutio, a wonderfully queer fellow with, apparently, fond memories of Fellini and Zeffirelli and the lazy, hazy days of an Italian summer, while David Waller's Friar Lawrence and Griffith Jones' Escalus are straight 1950s Old Vic classical. In an altogether different convention (the fifth, before I lost count) is John Woodvine's Capulet, a creature of ice-cold fury who clearly belongs much closer to the heart of the production than his limited allocation of the text allows, despite the fact that his wife (Barbara Shelley) is working in a hands-up-for-the-gasp-of-horror style best remembered from 'B' films of the early 1960s. It is some tribute to Mr Nunn and Mr Kyle that there is seldom a really boring sequence of more than about ten minutes: it is also some complaint that few of the cast appear to belong in the same theatre, let alone the same play.

They do seem, admittedly, to share a general conviction that here is a play about sex and hatred in roughly that order; but beyond that assumption (a welcome one after years in which *Romeo* has been immersed in pretty-pretty boredom) they appear not to have reached much of an alliance, and the four hours' traffic is therefore caught in the kind of jam best witnessed in Rome around lunchtime, where no two cars have any intention of travelling in remotely similar directions. For all that, I'm not suggesting you stay away: Marie Kean's splendidly cackling Irish Nurse and the Act Four discovery of a whole new scene after Juliet's supposed death are well worth a look, even if by the end of the evening one becomes half-convinced that the entire company would have been happier and more united in a revival of *West Side Story*.

Barton Tailoring

Following as it does hard upon the flying heels of Trevor Nunn's manifold *Romeo and Juliet*, John Barton's new RSC *Much Ado About Nothing* (now in the Stratford repertoire) seems a masterpiece of single-minded planning. The play has been lifted bodily into mid-nineteenth century India, much after the fashion of Tony Harrison's recent *Phaedra Britannica* at the National and presumably for much the same reason: just as the sons of Empire were sent into the colonies to 'find themselves' a century ago, so we now send our theatrical classics there in the hope of finding them again.

And it works: the timbered balconies of John Napier's permanent Stratford setting, used last week for the declaration of Juliet's love, now become places to hang awnings and sun-shades out in the midday sun. This is a brandy-and-cigars world where the Governor (Ivan Beavis) is just that and Dogberry (John Woodvine) is a comical native official who seems to have wandered in from television's 'It Ain't Half Hot Mum'. Yet they belie a more serious purpose: in this hot, dusty colonial outpost called Messina where the garrison provides the only real activity as its soldiers play languid games of cricket or gossip about their brother officers' affairs, the on-off love of Beatrice and Benedick becomes suddenly plausible and even touching where all too often in recent revivals it has been churlish and a crashing bore.

Other characters suddenly make sense too: the decision of Claudio (Richard Durden, amiably chinless) to curse Hero at the altar on such slender evidence becomes the mindless reflex action of an officer, gentleman and twit, while Beatrice (Judi Dench) and Hero (Cherie Lunghi) become camp followers until the 'kill Claudio' scene indicates that Beatrice has at last grown up and away from the awful conventions of military life and is about to take Benedick (Donald Sinden) with her.

In these two central roles Judi Dench and Donald Sinden are as individually superb as ever: their difficulty (like that of Ian McKellen and Francesca Annis in *Romeo*) is in forming themselves at the last into a plausible double-act, and their failure in this is to be measured against the huge delight they have separately given us earlier in the evening.

But what Mr Barton has seen in *Much Ado* is a series of codes: not only of the secretive kind (as in Beatrice's early attempts to suggest a kind of love for Benedick, or in the splendid villainy of Ian McDiarmid's dour, academic Don John) but also codes of behaviour – whether in the officers' mess, in Dogberry's ludicrous patrol or finally in the heart of Benedick himself. Throughout, there's a feeling that the parade is about to pass on to some other garrison town leaving behind a group of embittered old maids with a Maughamesque tale to tell; that this never happens, and that by the end everyone's life has been resolved in the usual neat Shakespeare fashion, doesn't ultimately much matter. The joys of the evening are in individual moments: to hear Sinden's colonialist-prig Benedick describing Hero as 'Leonato's *short* daughter' is to understand the disdain that once ruled an Empire, while Miss Dench, alone in my experience of Beatrices, makes it seem eminently likely that a star was dancing on the night of her birth – in the circumstances, that was the very least it could have done.

Dirty Linen and *New-Found-Land* are two new, intricately linked, one-act plays by Tom Stoppard written for and staged at the Almost Free lunchtime theatre in London to celebrate the British naturalization of that theatre's American director Ed Berman. Rising to and far above the occasion, Mr Stoppard has come up with a masterly double-bill in the first half of which a fairly select committee of MPs gather in the tower of Big Ben under the watchful eye of a secretary ('Forty words a minute.' 'Shorthand?' 'No, talking') known as Miss Gotobed; their intention is to concoct a whitewashing report to explain away the fact that 119 of their colleagues have been caught with the same mysterious lady ('never since Dunkirk have so many been in the same boat'.)

The MPs include representatives of the Milk Marketing Board ('an unrivalled record of freedom from suggestions of sex . . . furthermore we are now getting yoghourt to every corner of the globe') and a man with no interests of any kind except his future peerage ('that'll be for Services to the Arts, then') and they are immortally played by a team of the most distinguished light comedians in London led by Peter Bowles, Richard O'Callaghan, Edward de Souza and Benjamin Whitrow.

Into their deliberations intrudes a totally separate play in which two other MPs (equally marvellously played by Richard Goolden and Stephen Moore) debate the rights and wrongs of giving Mr

Berman his British citizenship – a debate interrupted for Goolden to remember Lloyd George and Moore to deliver a ten-minute solo description of a train journey across the States.

Talking of lunchtime joys, the King's Head in Islington has Quentin Crisp in *A Cure for Freedom*, which he himself describes as 'a straight talk from a bent speaker' but which is in fact rather more – a wonderfully rambling monologue on such diverse issues as dust ('it gets no worse after the first four years'), friends ('we'd all like to have them, but if it means listening . . .') and the career of Gilles de Retz who once murdered a hundred and fifty choirboys ('now quantity is not style; still, it's hard not to be impressed'). Other people are, as Mr Crisp notes, usually a mistake; he however is not, and should also be seen as soon as possible.

A Lot of Night Music

If you are only planning to spend one evening in the musical theatre this year I urgently suggest you make it *Side by Side by Sondheim* at the Mermaid. If you are planning to spend two, go twice. Quite apart from the fact that it's far and away the best entertainment I've come across in many months, it affords a panorama of the Broadway musical 1955–75 the like of which you'd be hard pressed to find elsewhere unless of course you happen to have been living in New York throughout those past two decades.

Yet it remains a curiously and ineffably English achievement: *Side by Side by Sondheim* comes out of that Mermaid tradition of composer-tribute evenings which over the past four years has scored two other notable triumphs (*Cole* and *Cowardy Custard*) and it is doubly remarkable, first because Stephen Sondheim (unlike Noël Coward and Cole Porter at the time of their tributes) is neither seventy nor dead but somewhere in his mid-forties, and secondly because his songs unlike theirs are almost all 'book' numbers – songs which one would expect only to work in the context of the shows for which they were written.

That in defiance of both these problems Ned Sherrin (as director and narrator) has put together such an ecstatic evening is largely I believe the result of a partnership he created fully fifteen years ago, at a time when Sondheim had only written three of the ten shows that are used at the Mermaid – a partnership (based on BBC Tele-vision's 'TW3') involving himself, Millicent Martin and David Kernan in which he established them as primarily lyric singers, by which I mean singers who could work fast and almost journalist-ically to reflect real life around them in songs which contrasted starkly with the moon/June escapism of their predecessors. In the years since 'TW3', Kernan (along with Julia McKenzie who makes up the fourth and last member of this superlative Mermaid quartet) has worked in a number of Sondheim shows and as a result the group come together again now as experts in precisely that brand of elegant, acid urban disenchantment which is what Sondheim is all about.

From *West Side Story* through *Gypsy* and *Anyone Can Whistle* to *Company* and *Follies* and even his latest *Pacific Overtures*, Sondheim is explored, annotated and celebrated so that in the closing minutes of the opening performance the Mermaid rang with cheers the volume of which I've seldom heard in that or any other theatre – cheers not only for the great songs and the great shows they came from (many still unseen in London) but the cheers of an English audience waking up to the fact that in Stephen Sondheim we have the greatest lyric poet of contemporary world theatre.

Past Laughter

In a long hot summer, and one which will arguably do more damage to theatre box–offices the length and breadth of the land than was ever achieved by the combined effects of inflation and the bombings, it is not perhaps altogether amazing that London should have fled back to light comedies, and to tried and tested light comedies at that. For their first new production in the Lyttelton auditorium, the National Theatre company have settled on a revival of *Blithe Spirit*, thereby reaffirming an old law (if in doubt, back to Coward) which led them ten years ago to make *Hay Fever* one of the first National productions at the Old Vic.

At the Lyttelton, *Blithe Spirit* (written and first produced in 1941 when jokes about sudden death were not only topical but, more surprisingly, highly acceptable – it ran two thousand nights) is being given a careful and lovingly detailed going–over by a

Blithe Spirit   Elizabeth Spriggs *as Mme Arcati*, Maria Aitken *as Elvira*

company led by such ex-RSC Shakespearians as Elizabeth Spriggs and Richard Johnson under the direction of Harold Pinter. The result, though about fifteen minutes too long on the night I went, is an immensely precise evening in which the gin bottles have clip-tops and the accusations about Elvira's moral untidiness are underlined by the neatness which abounds elsewhere.

Johnson's Condomine is slow, humourless and possessed of a good line in neurotic male defeat, thereby almost perfectly reflecting the character as Coward wrote him though not of course the character as Coward played him. Miss Spriggs, faced with an urgent need to escape the voluminous shadows of Margaret Rutherford, settles for a less lovable Madame Arcati, while the rest of the evening belongs to Maria Aitken whose Elvira is probably the nearest we'll ever come to the memory of Kay Kendall in that role on a brief non-London tour in 1954.

I have, I suspect, raved about Miss Aitken on this page before: quite apart from her timing, which is as near faultless as makes no difference, she is the owner of one of those immensely long necks without which almost no Coward or Rattigan female leads can ever really be adequately played. Her Elvira, back from the dead after a sudden fatal collapse while laughing helplessly at a BBC music programme, is a stunningly attractive rich-bitch ghost, and as Rowena Cooper's Ruth (Condomine's second wife, also destined to haunt him from beyond the grave) is another attractive lady, his final shriek of freedom when both ghosts depart is more than a little difficult to understand. Coward, I suspect, made that final curtain more plausible – but it would be hard to imagine that even his own productions ever treated the play with more affection.

Planetarium theatre, to which the audience is invited largely for star-gazing purposes, continues at the Phoenix with an eight-week season of *The Pleasure of His Company*, an eighteen-year-old Samuel Taylor and Cornelia Otis Skinner comedy originally seen at the Haymarket with Nigel Patrick and Coral Browne, now mysteriously relocated another twenty years back into the past (getting us to 1938) and starring Douglas Fairbanks, Jr, making a return to the West End after forty-two years alongside Wilfrid Hyde White who's returning after a mere five. With them are David Langton (he of 'Upstairs, Downstairs', playing here the part he originally created at the Haymarket) and Dinah Sheridan, so the opportunities for multiple star-gazing are many, especially as the entire cast are inclined to perform as if opening a bazaar, flashing teeth at the customers when the lines fail to sparkle.

That said, let us add that it is good to have Mr Fairbanks back, elegant and insouciant as ever, though I wish he'd chosen a vehicle in slightly better condition: this one has been parked a long time now, there's grass growing through the cracks in the plot, and I'm inclined to remember that even in 1958 it was not considered the best light comedy of its year or even maybe of its month, consisting as it does of echoes of *The Man Who Came to Dinner* and *Present Laughter* all thrown together into a mindless though expensively gift-wrapped saga of a girl forced to choose between her long-lost but charming father and her ever-present but boring suitor. Originally the girl was played by Judith Stott (an actress whose premature retirement has been one of the constant regrets of my theatre-going life) and you cared what happened; but as played, efficiently and coldly, by Belinda Carroll, the girl is no longer of much interest and that alas is also true of the whimsically sub-Douglas-Home comedy around her.

Go, nevertheless: not only to see that Fairbanks is still alive and looking better than all of us, but also and above all to see Wilfrid Hyde White, a consumate light comedian who has thrown away more good lines than anyone else ever collected and whose singing of the first half of 'You're the Cream in My Coffee' is worth crossing England to witness.

Come Dancing

At a very conservative estimate *A Chorus Line* is the greatest thing to have happened to the American musical since *West Side Story* and the greatest thing to have happened at Drury Lane since *My Fair Lady*, all of which means that in fully twenty years there's been nothing to rival it. But there's more to it than that: *A Chorus Line* is *the* American musical because it happens to be about the people who made all the others possible. It's about dancers, not in the schmaltz-ridden sense of 'let's all now remember Gene Kelly', but in the modern sense of workers in an industry, fighting for the survival of themselves and that industry against apparently overwhelming odds.

The show runs two and a quarter uninterrupted hours and the whole of that time is taken up with an audition at which first twenty-seven and then seventeen dancers are being interviewed for eight jobs: in the course of that audition, the director (a fine sinister performance from Eivind Harum) asks them each to tell him about themselves – who they are, where they've come from, why they want to dance, how much they need to work.

The result is electrifying: one by one the dancers step forward, some aggressive, some nervous, some black, some white, some homosexual, some married, some Puerto Rican, and they sing and dance and talk about themselves – their childhood, their mothers, their anxieties, their ambitions. In song after song the same terrible needs emerge ('Oh God I need this job,' 'Give me someone to dance to,' 'I hope I get it,' 'I can do that') and yet all the time there is the knowledge that even if they get into the final eight they are still doomed to tip-tapping anonymity in a line discreetly placed twelve or twenty feet behind the unseen star. None of them is ever going to be Ray Bolger, let alone Fred Astaire, and yet their drive to work, their passion for the trade and their inability to conceive of any other life ('waddya mean Broadway's dying, I just got here') gives them each a unique kind of stardom.

All, perhaps, are stereotypes: there's the girl who escaped from Buffalo ('to commit suicide there would be redundant'), the one who can't sing, the one who can do a hundred-percent split and come up tapping in morse code, and the one who used to live with the director – this last a truly stunning performance from Sandy Roveta. Together, they constitute a line and a show which, marvellous and depressing in turn, is a musical for our time just as surely as *Hair* was a musical for the sixties.

A Chorus Line is about sex and love and hatred and failure and all the things that make the theatre possible: it's also about the technicalities of show business, about how everyone is a star if not to their mothers then at any rate to themselves, and I believe that its book (James Kirkwood and Nicholas Dante) and its score (Marvin Hamlisch and Edward Kleban) will tell you more about the theatre – any theatre – than a whole lifetime spent in drama school.

At the end, all the dancers – the rejects as well as the chosen eight – join in a massive gold-suited number called 'One' which in itself sums up and celebrates a whole generation of Broadway music while it leaves us with two questions – has it been worth it, and will they ever escape from the line? In both instances the answer may well be no: yet along the way Michael Bennett whose show this is (as conceiver, choreographer and director) has distilled the very essence of show business.

In twenty years of almost nightly theatre-going I have never seen a musical which demands so much respect and commands so much enthusiasm, not only for its dazzling professionalism but for the questions it raises about that profession. *A Chorus Line* manages in number after number to capture the best of Broadway, to query it and then to improve upon it. I do not believe the American musical will ever be quite the same again, and if you're not already planning a visit to Drury Lane then you'll have me to answer to: you'll also have a sizeable gap in your theatrical knowledge and you'll have missed one of the great evenings of your life. Any other questions?

Marlow on Thames

The good news, of course, is that the Olivier Theatre is open at last: the largest and most important of the three in the embattled National complex, it provides a central focus for Lasdun's entire South Bank structure and an arena on and around which all things theatrical are possible. The machinery of the Olivier is admittedly not yet functioning, so that Peter Hall's epic *Tamburlaine* could in fact have been mounted at Chichester without much loss of its present effects; but it remains hard if not impossible to think of any other play so perfectly suited to the inauguration of an open stage.

Written in 1587 when Marlow was just twenty-three, *Tamburlaine* is a sprawling four-hour pageant of ritualized violence and death in which there is very little room for characterization, almost no suspense, and about as much subtlety as you'd expect from an Intercity express. And yet the language is magnificent, the scale is awesome and as a central figure Tamburlaine is unrivalled for sheer power in the whole of Shakespeare. Tyrone Guthrie (whose productions in the fifties with Wolfit in London and Quayle in New York are still the touchstones for comparison) called the play 'an orgy of sadism by the light of meteors' and Hall's production seems largely in keeping with that theory.

With Finney in the title role (as for last year's Hall *Hamlet*) both star and director seem content to unroll the play again like some vast tapestry, leaving us to pick from it what threads we will. Philip Locke and Robert Eddison and Michael Gough hover on the sidelines, bringing exquisite diction to a play about bloodshed and slavery and corruption and death and all the other things that made Tamburlaine's life worth living, but the centre of the arena is left to Finney, Denis Quilley (as both his father-and-son rivals) and Susan Fleetwood and Barbara Jefford as their respective wives. The four of them then slug it out, their sound and fury signifying very little but being none the less impressive enough, and as Tamburlaine marches in triumph through Persepolis one starts to long for the colour cameras of Cecil B. deMille. Only Quilley, beating out his brains on the side of a cage, offers any real counter-weight to Finney, but about three and a half hours in there's a finely judged and beautifully played scene with Diana Quick as Olympia and all in all I'd not have missed any of it. But then I've always loved a parade.

Lost Leaders

Lear is the peak: it may not be the greatest of Shakespeare's plays, it certainly isn't the one which works the best, and yet it remains the summit for most Stratford directors, while there can scarcely have been an RSC leading man in the last fifteen years who hasn't at least thought about attempting to scale the character's heights.

Stratford's new King Lear is Donald Sinden, an actor who (despite a deceptively lightweight screen image) has long been a Shakespearian and who brings to the part some superlative moments, whether hurling himself furiously into Regan's front door or entering Goneril's battlements on a cart looking for all the world as though he's about to go into the drinking song from *The Student Prince* but then summoning up fire and fury from a depth that Wolfit himself might have envied.

Yet the production is full of such curious contradictions as this: set in a vaguely Hapsburg area of disintegrating middle Europe in the late nineteenth century, it starts like *The Fall of Eagles* with courtiers in epaulettes and Sinden giving us his Franz Joseph. But once we're into the open air for the mad scenes there's real rain falling and an indeterminate use of costume and setting, while for the end we seem to have arrived at the Crimean War with Cordelia as Florence Nightingale.

This may just be the result of there being no less than three directors (Trevor Nunn, John Barton and Barry Kyle) but it means that the cast have a hard time establishing any real unity of purpose or action. Judi Dench and Barbara Leigh-Hunt do a good evil-sisters double, but Cordelia (Marilyn Taylerson) seems not to belong to their family, while none of them seems to have much of a link to Sinden. Similarly, Michael Williams' Fool (though in its own right a wonderful creation – no longer the young zombie but instead an old music-hall trouper down on his luck) doesn't seem to belong to anyone while Tony Church's elegant Gloucester is straight Old Vic classical.

Whole scenes also operate on this individualistic basis, so that

Richard Durden's final scenes in the camp as Albany work vastly better than I have ever seen them, while supposedly surefire set-pieces like Gloucester on the cliffs near Dover go for very little. All in all an evening of almost constant and alternate surprise, amazement, disappointment and revelation, and at the end of its two hundred and twenty minutes one goes into the night feeling that though the heights have not been successfully scaled on this occasion, a great many interesting paths have been opened up around the rock face.

And from the intermittently sublime to the spasmodically ridiculous Alf Garnett who (in the person of Warren Mitchell) has taken over the Criterion until the end of this week with a one-man show written by Johnny Speight and based in roughly equal measure on the early television shows, a book called *The Thoughts of Chairman Alf* and Mr Mitchell's own ability to revisit music-hall songs of the 1890s. Given the nature of the show, the Criterion is an ideal theatre, designed as it is to resemble nothing so much as a Victorian pub; drinks can be carried through to the auditorium (an innovation all other theatres should copy forthwith) and the atmosphere is ready for a nostalgic singalong some time before we actually get it.

In the meantime Messrs Speight and Mitchell have other plans for us; we are treated first to a complete and utter history of Britain in about thirty minutes flat, with Alf in full racial-bigot flight rambling on about the state of the nation and his own life which, Speight is keen to have us realize, is not what it was.

Alf has lost his wife, his job, and even some of his rancour, leaving us to see only the shell of his former self – still shouting, but now in a curiously hollow voice, like Falstaff after the coronation of Henry V.

Yet in common with Barry Humphries' Edna Everage, Warren Mitchell's Alf retains a good strong line in audience abuse, and whether snarling at the customers ('they sang this rubbish for Gus Elen, you can bloody well sing it with me') or merely hearing his alarmingly Mosleyite views receive even more alarming chortles of delighted recognition from the front stalls, he is in total control of an apparently free-form evening. But in the end it's a curiously derelict entertainment, poised like the Criterion building itself uneasily midway between Victorian nostalgia and present-day Piccadilly tat and still uncertain which of the two ghastly lifestyles it most admires.

Christmas Crackers

Be of good cheer: after an autumn in which it seemed that the London theatre had entirely given up the ghost comes a Christmas week containing an utter and total delight deserving to be with us for several months to come and one well worth a visit over the holidays. The play is *Wild Oats*, a 1791 comedy by John O'Keeffe hitherto unproduced in this century but now rediscovered by the Royal Shakespeare Company and in repertoire at the Aldwych where it rates for my money as the most joyous revival since *London Assurance* all of five years ago.

O'Keeffe was a prolific Irish writer considered by Hazlitt to be the 'English Molière' but possessed of an infinitely livelier sense of dialogue, possibly because much of his life was spent in total blindness and his plays were therefore dictated for the ear rather than written for the eye. Throughout the last century *Wild Oats* was in constant revival by actor-managers such as Wyndham and Phelps and Edward Compton, the latter being the great-grandfather of Alan Howard who is now to be found in the leading role as 'Jack Rover, the bold thunder' himself. It's not hard to see why, in an actors' theatre such as that of the 1850s, *Wild Oats* should have proved so eminently popular; it provides not only one zonking central character (a strolling player much given to quoting Shakespeare in times of stress) but no less than twenty other character parts, all good for a scene or two and all allowed at least one flamboyant, barnstorming moment.

Wild Oats is theatre theatrical: its plot, a shaky one of extreme complexity, has to do with Rover's travels through Hampshire, roaming from theatre to theatre ready to play anything from *Othello* to *Lear* at the drop of an invitation but sidetracked along the way into a whole series of adventures concerning a Quaker heiress, an old sea dog, an evil farmer and sundry other eccentrics.

Few of the clichés of eighteenth-century theatre are left undisturbed, yet O'Keeffe's passion for sham marriages, false identities and speeches starting 'Ever since me bed curtains caught fire', carries us through a raucously funny evening. In the end, *Wild Oats* is about deception and greed and duplicity and corruption and everything that made life worth living in about 1790, but there's a

Wild Oats Norman Rodway *as Sir George Thunder*, Alan Howard *as Rover*, Lisa Harrow *as Lady Amaranth*

manic intensity in O'Keeffe's creation of characters like Farmer Gammon the Hampshire Hog and also in Clifford Williams' swift and sure production, one which ensures that a character having to say 'the dismals are coming upon me' doesn't get the wrong kind of laugh. Like a Ben Travers born 150 years ahead of his time, O'Keeffe has a superlative grasp of mind-boggling irrelevancies and, quite apart from providing the RSC with a surefire moneymaker for weeks to come, *Wild Oats* has two other chief distinctions.

First, it allows a superlative cast (Howard as Rover, Lisa Harrow as his Quaker love, Norman Rodway as the old sea dog, plus Zoe Wanamaker, Patrick Godfrey and Jeremy Irons among many others) to turn in splendidly brisk character sketches. Second, it gives every indication of being the play from which Oscar Wilde lifted the last act of *The Importance of Being Earnest*. I have alas no actual evidence of Oscar's presence in a theatre where *Wild Oats* was playing, despite the fact that I've just spent a year researching his biography; but there was a revival at the Strand Theatre in 1883 and another at the Criterion in 1886, both at times when Oscar was living in London and a regular theatregoer. And if he didn't get his last act from O'Keeffe, the similarity still needs some explaining.

1977

Turning Tables

When Rattigan's *Separate Tables* (Apollo) was first – and indeed last – staged in London in 1954, the general feeling was that here were two thoroughly well-made short plays affording massive stellar opportunities to the only actor and actress (originally Eric Portman and Margaret Leighton, now John Mills and Jill Bennett) allowed to take on new characters after the interval. The rest of the cast, along with the setting (a tastefully and discreetly crumbling seaside hotel in Bournemouth), remain unchanged from play to play, a theatrical device used in no other double-bill I know and one for which the author has been given scant credit.

But then Rattigan must be used to under-estimation by now; his rewards for a lifetime's playwriting have come largely from the bank and Buckingham Palace (where they gave him one of the only two knighthoods awarded to playwrights since the war) rather than from within the theatre itself, where the failure even to include a play of his in the repertoire of the National has been the most regular sin of omission in that company's fourteen-year history.

Maybe the time has at last come for upward valuation of the Rattigan currency: in the thirty years of English theatrical history which separate Coward at his best from Osborne at his, no other writer (not Fry, not Whiting, not Emlyn Williams, perhaps not even Priestley) had Rattigan's grasp of the theatre theatrical, nor did any have his ability to raise laughs and then choke them back within a few short and often curt speeches. His themes (in *Separate Tables* as elsewhere) are loneliness, love, sexual inadequacy and hatred in roughly that order, and he has an unnerving habit of taking stock characters and bringing them startlingly to life, like portrait miniatures suddenly illuminated by a thousand volts of neon.

Separate Tables pre-dates *Look Back in Anger* by about eighteen months, and therefore now looks much like the interior of an arctic submarine released in perfect condition at the end of some marathon ice age. The inmate-residents of the Beauregard Private Hotel are frozen in time, and the director, Michael Blakemore, has wisely decided not to thaw them out but to leave them in the original period, making jokes about Gilbert Harding and Senator McCarthy. Moreover he's put the plays on to a revolving stage, thereby brilliantly if unintentionally evoking an electrified museum showcase.

Peering in through the glass doors, it's possible to see two separate stories, the first of which has never really worked and still doesn't but the second of which is a classic. Play number one (as filmed, if you recall and if you're wise you don't, by Burt Lancaster and Rita Hayworth) has to do with a drunken politician meeting up in the hotel with the glamorous model he once married but subsequently beat up to such an extent that he then went to prison for grievous bodily harm. As performed by Sir John and Miss Bennett, these two vie with each other for implausibility, but are probably played no worse here than they were originally or on screen.

The other guests are imprisoned in the hotel of their own volition: the lonely old schoolmaster (Raymond Huntley), the overbearing matriarch (Margaret Courtenay), the indigent dowager (Ambrosine Phillpotts) and the lovelorn manageress (Zena Walker) have all created their own little cells, often tastefully decorated, and if they are chilly people it is because Rattigan originally hacked them out of glaciers.

But once we have revolved with the set into the second play (the one about the bogus Major and the shy girl who starts to save him from accosting strange ladies in cinemas, as filmed by David Niven and Deborah Kerr) it suddenly becomes clear that no one, not even Coward, was ever as good as Rattigan at recording the intricate trivia and the casual hurtfulness of everyday conversation. This, after all, is Garbo's *Grand Hotel* scaled down to about the right size for West Hampshire, so that the residents are tiny people in trouble rather than Hollywood giants in love: yet behind those clipped, tight monosyllables and the sudden outbursts of anguish there lies a world as enthralling as any ever captured by Maugham in his short stories.

Around Sir John and Miss Bennett, both of whom come as brilliantly to life in the second play as did their predecessors, Mr Blakemore has grouped as good a cross-section of character players as has been seen together since the golden days of Ealing Studios. Moreover he's turned *Separate Tables* into a company production, one which I shall remember as much for the scene between Miss Phillpotts and Miss Courtenay where they read of the Major's indiscretions (which would surely have been of a homosexual nature had the Lord Chamberlain allowed such things in 1954) as for any of the more obvious set-piece duologues between the two central stars.

Vienna Cavalcade

There can't be much doubt that Maximilian Schell's production of *Tales from the Vienna Woods* is the first gold-plated success the National has had since getting established in its new premises last year. The fact that the production comes on stage some minutes before the play and remains there long after the said play has disintegrated, so that what we have here is an absolute triumph of wrapping over contents, need not delay your journey to the Olivier: a marvellous production of a marvellous play would have been nice, but a marvellous production of an occasionally all right play is still a theatrical treat.

The problem does not, I think, have much to do with the Christopher Hampton adaptation, which is fluent and yet wonderfully spare: rather is it, I suspect, that the late Odon von Horvath was fundamentally a writer of scenarios rather than plays. True, this is the first of his to have been given a major English production and we may therefore be doing him an injustice: but something about his plotting (short, self-contained scenes fading into each other or rather revolving into each other, since Schell's use of the everturning Olivier stage is the most brilliant part of a flamboyant evening) suggests a screenwriter born ahead of his time; and if that is true then there is a terrible irony about the circumstances of his bizarre death in June 1938 (killed in the Champs-Élysées by a falling tree in a thunderstorm), since he had just been that afternoon to meet a Hollywood producer.

But back to the play: set in and around Vienna in 1929 it is perched somewhere midway between *Anatol* and *Cabaret* and concerns a group of small-time shopkeepers whose lives, inextricably intertwined in soap–opera fashion, come into focus in a series of tableaux depicting scenes from the pre–war Viennese life as viewed through the wrong end of a telescope. Horvath's people, like Isherwood's later, are losers and like Sally Bowles they've not much idea of the holocaust ahead: their lives revolve around a wastrel (Stephen Rea) and his doomed affair with Marianne (Kate Nelligan) who's also fancied by a neighbouring butcher (Warren Clarke) and ultimately betrayed by Nicholas Selby's suave bystander.

To play this gallery of eccentrics, opportunists, neo–Nazis and old crones Schell has assembled a company (also including Elizabeth Spriggs, Paul Rogers and Ellen Pollock) which must be one of the strongest ever put together for this kind of cavalcade, and my only regret is that they couldn't all have given us *Peer Gynt* instead. Mr Rea, incidentally, is probably going to be the National's first home–grown star; he's noticed, as has Mr Hampton, that Horvath is a lot closer to O'Casey than might otherwise have been guessed and acts accordingly.

Song of the Spokes

Any playwright who chooses to tell the story of twentieth–century Belfast by detailing in vaudeville fashion the marital and other events taking place in one backstreet bicycle repair shop there is bound to lay himself open to charges of whimsy if not of lunatic escapism. The fact that Stewart Parker (whose *Spokesong* has just reached the Vaudeville after successful try–outs at the Dublin Theatre Festival and the King's Head) last month won the London critics' award for the most promising playwright of the year suggests that he's avoided those charges, but *Spokesong* is only saved by its closing sequences from being the *Salad Days* of the 1970s.

This too is a play with music, and the music is by Jimmy Kennedy (he who wrote 'Harbour Lights' and 'Red Sails in the Sunset' and a dozen other popular classics of the forties) so already we are in a lost world: that it's also an Irish world has less to do with the present troubles in Belfast than with the invention there in 1888 of the pneumatic tyre by a local vet, one J. B. Dunlop.

In Dunlop's dream of cycling on air (a transport of delight, as if you hadn't guessed) Mr Parker has seen a metaphor of Ireland and his play is therefore in one sense a dramatized documentary about the evolution of the last development in technology comprehensible to everyone.

But suddenly, and with tremendous effect, we are jolted into present-day reality; cycles have been replaced by cars and cars mean car bombs. Cars are therefore weapons, where the bicycle is a thing of beauty and a joy if not forever then at least until punctured. In the final twenty minutes of *Spokesong*, Mr Parker seems to be telling us that the best hope for the Peace Movement lies in tyres and spokes and crank assemblies.

Along the road he also gives us a selection of brief love-and-hate stories concerning two generations of the Stock family, and these sketches from life are retrieved from the brink of twee charm by wonderfully powerful performances by Annabel Leventon, Niall Buggy and Donald Maciver, interrupted by solo turns of varying success by Robert Bridges.

Spokesong resolutely refuses to take off totally into a world of Emmett fantasy, just as it refuses to take the final leap into political comment: instead it hovers on the verge of commitment until in a final, heroically happy ending the shop is saved from the bombers and bankruptcy alike and a new generation of cycle freaks is if not actually guaranteed then at least heavily hinted. Bittersweet is the cliché for what we have here, but I can't think of a production in recent years (in this case by Robert Gillespie) which has so successfully straddled every possible artistic and philosophic fence without ever toppling off. Add to all that the best title song since 'Hello Dolly!' and it adds up to a long stay at the Vaudeville.

Conjuring in the Dark

Congratulations and celebrations, friends, are the order of the week: on two consecutive nights I have just seen shows either of which would have made my month if not my year. Taken together, they add up to the kind of double which causes me to grin inanely at strangers in bus queues and remember what it was that 150 years ago made me think of becoming a drama critic.

Let's start in Manchester with Leo McKern's *Uncle Vanya*: a great Russian bear of a man, lolloping around the stage propelled by an

Uncle Vanya

Albert Finney *as Astrov*, Eleanor Bron *as Elena*, Leo McKern *as Vanya*

uncertain mixture of hope and despair and forever bouncing off the sharper corners of the other characters until finally they pierce his skin and he is deflated.

The director of this production, Michael Elliott, is also director of the Royal Exchange Theatre which houses it (that remarkable steel and glass bubble suspended from the pillars of the old Cotton Exchange) and the two could have been made for each other: a small, claustrophobic, in-the-round acting arena within a vast outer darkness through which taped thunder rumbles with awesome effect. Moreover Elliott has surrounded McKern with the likes of Albert Finney (as Astrov), Eleanor Bron (as Elena) and Alfred Burke (as Serebryakov) so that we have here one of those Chekhovian first families who by their very presence together on stage start the play on its winning streak.

True, Finney lacks Olivier's seedy grandeur as Astrov, seeming at times more like McKern's tousle-haired younger brother than his eventual rival, but his is a wonderfully chilly performance matched perfectly by the icy aristocratic grandeur of Eleanor Bron. As each of them explores the vacuum into which they have been locked by the others, the life force ebbs away until we are left with Joanna David's final, passionate plea for the possibility of a future. Hasten along even if it means a lengthy journey at current BR prices.

Meanwhile at the Aldwych the RSC have Peter Nichols' *Privates on Parade*, a comedy of Far Eastern army life in the late 1940s which (across three rambling hours) sets out to explain how Britain won the war and lost the peace. To tell his fractionally autobiographical story, Mr Nichols uses all the vaudeville devices of his *Joe Egg* and *Forget-Me-Not-Lane* and adds many more: thus we are given troop-show parodies of Coward and Vera Lynn as well as a highly symbolic sequence in which a British soldier does conjuring tricks in the dark for an audience of bewildered foreigners, to say nothing of songs, jokes, drag acts and all the fun of the Malayan Emergency.

The basis is of course factual: Combined Services Entertainment indeed toured the Far East in 1948, bringing to those dark corners of the world all the joy of the *Fol-de-Rols* and *Jamboree Time*. Nichols was of their number (as were Kenneth Williams, John Schlesinger and Stanley Baxter) but his achievement here and now is to get us away from the farcical level of 'It Ain't Half Hot Mum' and into an area where questions about the British presence overseas, what precisely its troops thought they were fighting to preserve, and how morally they went about that preservation, can all be raised and uneasily answered.

Amid all the queer jokes ('You dare to speak to an Officer like that,' shrieks Denis Quilley, 'and I'll scream the place down') and the camp puns and the twists and turns of a ragged plot, we find that combination of shock and giggles which has always been Nichols' stock in trade. There was no peace in 1945, he tells us, merely a temporary truce and a change of enemy, and the questions he raises about the British are valid above and beyond any single emergency.

Apart from everything else (and there *is* everything else) we have here the first good new English musical in years – performed in suitably nostalgic style by a splendid cast led by Quilley and Nigel Hawthorne in a production which Michael Blakemore has directed as if it were an anarchic Crazy Gang version of *Journey's End*.

Absurd Persons Plural

Alan Ayckbourn is at his best when mocking the afflicted: like all great farce writers (which for this country and this century means just him and Ben Travers) he shares the Groucho Marx view that whereas it is reasonably funny to have an actor dressed up like a little old lady falling downstairs in a wheelchair, to make it utterly hilarious what you'd need would be a real old lady.

Ayckbourn's new *Bedroom Farce* (at the Lyttelton) is a painfully funny play about people in trouble, and is in fact only new to London: Scarborough saw it two years ago, and must have been relieved to discover that their most famous son (and the director of the local theatre) had emerged from the sketchy disappointments of *Absent Friends* and *Confusions* in time to write a classic of the genre, arguably his best play to date and certainly on a par with both *The Norman Conquests* and *How the Other Half Loves*.

What we have here are four couples and three double beds lined up in neat rows across the stage in a long, narrowly partitioned set (by Timothy O'Brien and Tazeena Firth) which might work better were it on slightly different levels, though that is about the limit of my reservations about the entire evening. On our left there's Ernest and Delia (Michael Gough and Joan Hickson), ageing fast, riddled with the damp that a faulty roof is allowing to seep through their furniture, and mildly concerned about their errant son Trevor (Stephen Moore, in the best performance of the evening) and his disastrous marriage to the gangling Susannah (Maria Aitken).

It is Trevor and Susannah who are the odd couple out, that's to say the ones without a bed, not that it stops them occupying (albeit separately) at some stage of the evening each of the other three. The middle bed is owned by Malcolm and Kate (Derek Newark and Susan Littler) who are giving a party to which they've rashly invited not only Trevor and Susannah (whose marital differences cause all other guests to leave it in record time) but also Jan, occupant of the third bedroom and a former girlfriend of Trevor but now married to Nick, an executive who cannot be at the party since he's paralysed in their bed with a slipped disc.

So much for the plot which, like the dialogue, is curiously irrelevant to Mr Ayckbourn's true achievement: sure, there are some funny lines ('What a lovely coat – is there just one of you in it?') but we are not here dealing with tumultuous wit or fantastic storytelling. Instead, this is comedy of character: lines are spoken through gritted teeth, hands extended to be shaken are in fact clenched fists, and his people are forever suffering bad backs, bad marriages or bad breath caused by eating pilchards in bed.

Like Feydeau and Wedekind before him, Mr Ayckbourn is a uniquely funny chronicler of human and marital despair, and it comes therefore as no real shock that the closing moments of *Bedroom Farce* consist of a lady in the dark telling herself that there's nothing to be afraid of. There is of course everything to be afraid of, not least mankind's inhumanity to mankind: 'This old trouble again, is it?' asks Joan Hickson, patting a bedspread and instantly summarizing a thousand sexless marriages. 'How are you?' asks another character of her husband, apparently not noticing that he is even at that moment banging his head against a convenient wall. If there is a message here, it is perhaps that the awfulness of people happily married to each other is marginally less awful than the awfulness of people unhappily married to each other, but even that is a toss-up. As we approach a sort of conclusion, or at least, a temporary truce, Trevor leans nonchalantly against a chest of drawers that Malcolm has spent all night constructing, and the chest instantly collapses into its component parts. But then it would, wouldn't it?

I suspect I have not made *Bedroom Farce* sound as invincibly funny as it really is: the production (by Peter Hall and the author) is a consistent joy and only the thought of where we go from here gives rise to doubt: Mr Ayckbourn has thus far given us tripartite plays set in dining-rooms, living-rooms, kitchens, gardens, and now bed-rooms. I suspect we may soon be off to the bathroom: it's either that or the loft, and considering his characters' constant inability to cope with the wonders of do-it-yourself, I'm not looking forward to the loft.

Super Stevie

At the Vaudeville, *Stevie* is a lyrical and generally enchanting account of the life of Florence Margaret Smith, otherwise known as Stevie Smith the poet of Palmers Green. From her poems, interviews and other semi-autobiographical material Hugh Whitemore has cobbled together a splendid evening which allows Glenda Jackson in the title role and Mona Washbourne as her Lion Aunt to give two of the best performances currently to be found anywhere in London.

Stevie's was by all accounts a curious life ('I'm a friendship girl,' she once said; 'marriage terrifies me') and Whitemore in arranging this gentle lament for a middle-class lady allows her poems to tell the story: her attempted suicide, her refusal to explore her own gifts ('it's like digging up flowers to see how they're getting on') and her hilarious meeting with the Queen are all conveyed briskly and without other comment, but the result (which could so easily have been coy, twee and aimless) is a wonderful display of suburban life. Stevie was, according to the play, a painfully ordinary lady struck by the lightning of her own talent, and the achievement of Whitemore and Miss Jackson is to show us how she managed to live with the lightning.

Rare Jonson

There is a moment during the curtain calls for Peter Hall's new production of *Volpone* (on the Olivier open stage) when you suddenly realize the point of a National Theatre. Purists might suggest that the realization could well have come earlier in the evening or indeed earlier in the National's turbulent history, but for me the moment undoubtedly arrived when Gielgud, having turned in a superlative if all-too-brief Politic Wouldbe, moved gracefully stage left and allowed Paul Scofield his central call as Volpone. Looking from one leading actor to the other, across the assembled ranks of National players, it suddenly became clear that our National

Theatre – or any National Theatre – has to consist of a group of the best actors in the land constantly redefining themselves and their relationships in a succession of roles both major and minor, but remaining ever available even for hardy and turgid perennials like *Volpone* whenever the need arises.

My objection here is not to Jonson's verse, which is admittedly periodically splendid, but to his plotting and characterization which have always seemed to deserve zero-rating. Once you allow that Volpone himself is a crafty fox who will do anything to increase his already considerable wealth, and that those around him differ not in greed or kind but only in degree and intelligence, then what you're left with is a wonderfully ornate portrait gallery in which the frames are mysteriously filled only with unenthralling black-and-white caricatures.

True, Scofield and Hall and their designer John Bury manage to pull the play well away from the over-elaboration in which both Wolfit and Guthrie were wont to smother it, so that what we have here is a super-cool evening through which the two central figures (Scofield and Ben Kingsley as Mosca) glide as though on castors; true too, we have in support not only Gielgud but also Elizabeth Spriggs as the indomitable Lady Wouldbe, Paul Rogers as Castrone and Hugh Paddick as the incredibly ancient Corbaccio, each of whom offers a little revue turn which is more than welcome as the plot grinds its weary way through to the inevitably double-crossed courtroom conclusion. Yet the joys remain incidental here, simply because of the intractability of the central theme. Beware a play in which the subplots are more fun than anything else; beware a play which sets up its central joke (that Volpone will go anywhere, feign anything, sell anyone to increase his own treasure just as his neighbours will do the same to get their hands on it) inside five minutes and then sticks with it; beware above all a play in which the best laugh is the disappearance of Politic Wouldbe inside a tortoise-shell.

The only real surprise of *Volpone* is Mosca's attempted double-cross, and the only surprise about that is that it doesn't happen sooner; none of this, though, can be blamed on Scofield or Hall and if you want to see *Volpone* at its most spacious, elegant and distinguished then see it at the Olivier.

The trouble with *Oh Mr Porter* (at the Mermaid) is alas old King Cole himself: though he did write a lot of good songs, most of them have already been cobbled into previous Porter anthologies so that what we are now faced with are one or two gems ('Miss Otis', 'The Tale of an Oyster') and a fair number of his forgettables. Given the unenviable task of stitching these into a three-hour evening, my colleague Benny Green has come up with an intelligent and highly serviceable plot about ten actors in search of a director to get their show on the road. While they wait for him (or her?) to appear, they work their way through nearly forty numbers all directed and choreographed by Wendy Toye in her most cosily informal 'hey kids let's do the show right here and now' style.

This style has worked well enough for previous Mermaid song-fests, but it depends on massively good casting and superlative lyrics; and now that two *Side by Side by Sondheim* companies in London and New York are employing most of the experts, we are left with a somewhat undercast group in which only Una Stubbs and Kenneth Nelson have the requisite style and charm to carry Cole off. There is also a real problem in that whereas Sondheim and Coward and even Hammerstein have songs recognizably rooted in drama and specific locality, Porter was the Muzak Man whose lesser numbers tell us less than nothing about their singers. Porter's people are a deep-frozen lot, endlessly and inanely in love, and though internal evidence suggests that some of them may occasionally have met a man who knew Gatsby, beyond that they come out of nowhere, say almost nothing, and then go back into nowhere, which is evidently why Mr Green has set the songs within a community of plastic actors.

Yet even in this area Irving Berlin said more about actors in one song from *Annie Get Your Gun* than did Porter in the whole of *Kiss Me Kate*, and by the end of the evening we're missing not only a director but also a composer-lyricist. So, as a musical, no: but as a Porter concert staged for and by addicts so that long-forgotten joys like 'Ladies in Waiting' and 'You don't sing enough/You don't dance enough/You don't drink the great wines of France enough' can be rediscovered, *Oh Mr Porter* has its virtues. Despite an initially rough ride from the daily press, something tells me it is going to keep an awful lot of American tourists very happy this summer.

Maid to Measure

It was in September 1913 that Bernard Shaw found himself in Orleans and began writing from there a series of postcards to that most famous of all his correspondents, Mrs Patrick Campbell:

> I have been all over the Joan of Arc country and shall do a Joan play someday, beginning with the sweeping up of the cinders and orange peel *after* her martyrdom and going on to Joan's arrival in heaven. I shall have God about to damn the English for their share in her betrayal . . . English literature must be saved (by an Irishman as usual) from the disgrace of having nothing to show concerning Joan except the piffling libel in *Henry VI*, which reminds me that one of my scenes will be Voltaire and Shakespeare running down bye streets in heaven to avoid meeting Joan. Would you like to play Joan and come in on horseback in armour and fight innumerable supers?

It didn't of course quite work out like that: when Shaw did finally get around to writing *Saint Joan* a decade later there were no scenes featuring Voltaire and Shakespeare running through heaven, and the Joan was not Mrs Campbell but Sybil Thorndike of whom Agate noted that 'a woman who argues about everything like blazes is bound to be attracted to playing a woman who ends in blazes'. Yet that first London production (a few months after the play had its world première in New York) has set the standards for all which followed, despite the fact that it opened to less than glowing reviews and a good deal of critical doubt about whether a Saint should be played with the rustic accent of a farm girl even if that was what Joan had been in reality. Sybil Thorndike herself thought it a wonderful play and that Shaw should cast himself in all the parts. Maugham however thought that Shaw had put far too many of his own arguments into the play, and a number of other critics objected to what they considered the downgrading of a Saint to the status of a pantomine principal boy.

So much for the birth of a classic: now, almost exactly half a century later, what are we left with? First of all, in the new John Dove production which brings Prospect to the Old Vic at the start of a summer season which will hopefully be the first of many, we have Eileen Atkins in a towering central performance: radiantly sure of her voices, utterly determined to go back to the farm after she has taken Paris, briskly able to cope with the inquisition until the final, awful awareness that death or life imprisonment is her sole remaining choice, this is a Joan as close to the heart of the play and Shaw's intentions as it is possible to imagine.

Around her, all is not quite so well: true, there's a magnificently sinister, cadaverous Inquisitor from Robert Eddison and an interesting Dauphin from Charles Kay, but elsewhere there has been some crippling undercasting from which certain of the non-Joan scenes never get the chance to recover. It is especially unfortunate (and no real fault of the Prospect management) that the touring exigencies of their present situation mean that the upper echelon of their present company (Timony West, Derek Jacobi, John Turner, Alec McCowen) in fact cannot be used in a play which badly needs all of them, and as a result some of Miss Atkins' support was looking distinctly shaky at the preview I witnessed.

Yet this is a production which looks infinitely at home at the Vic: brisk in a kind of no-nonsense Baylis tradition, unconcerned with finer details (Joan's miraculousness is accepted by all save de Baudricourt almost on sight) and cheerfully willing to allow her not only to change the direction of the wind on the Loire as per Shavian instructions but also to cause it to cease blowing altogether for a while, presumably while somebody backstage turns the machine around to fan in the opposite direction. None of that would much have worried Thorndike or Shaw and it probably shouldn't concern us either: thanks to Miss Atkins, it works.

Abigail's Party (at the Hampstead Theatre) is a chillingly well-acted play 'devised' (rather than written, and I'd like to know the difference) by Mike Leigh who also directs. The unseen Abigail is given a teenage thrash and her mother comes next door to join two truly awful couples who for the rest of the evening play out a kind of suburban English version of *Who's Afraid of Virginia Woolf?*, ending in the heart attack of one man while his unloving and unlovely wife lightly sprinkles his face with cigarette ash. Taken all in all, this is probably the best-acted play in town (the five concerned are Alison Steadman, Tim Stern, Janine Duvitski, John Salthouse and Thelma Whiteley) and what they have to say about the social and marital habits of Mr Leigh's chosen slice of life is wholly horrific.

'We're not here to hold conversations,' says the hostess at one point, 'we're here to enjoy ourselves' and in that desperate quest the party proceeds: '*Macbeth*,' says her husband, getting it off the shelf, 'part of our national heritage – not that you can actually read it.' Recipes for pilchard curry are exchanged as lives visibly disintegrate on the carpet, and the recognition laughter of Hampstead audiences is perhaps the most chilling sound of all. Mr Leigh's are undoubtedly what television ads call the 'now' people: snobbish, bitchy, mercilessly wrong about everything from love to the need to ice Beaujolais, and they have been wittily and accurately trapped as if under glass. I don't think I want to meet any of them ever again.

Force of Destiny

In a strong and crowded week, David Edgar's *Destiny* (at the Aldwych) leads by virtue of its sheer scale: thirty years of British home and colonial history, no less, told in an attempt to trace the rebirth of the far political right.

We start in India in 1947: the closing moments of Empire, British army on the retreat, and bringing home not only themselves but a large number of Indian immigrants who are to influence the by-elections of the three ensuing decades. Yet Edgar's play is not political in a solely party sense: it is about the effects of large-scale immigration, bad housing, corrupt management and shaky international ethics on the very mind of England – a mind increasingly open to the tempting arguments of a right-wing Colonel-led party here called Nation Forward.

There is something savagely funny about *Destiny*, just as there was something savagely funny about Brecht's *Arturo Ui* and the two plays have something else in common: both were constructed as overt warnings of the rebirth of fascism, and yet both accept readily the feeble quality of its opposition. We are, notes Mr Edgar, the only nation on earth still inspired by failure rather than success, and all we have achieved is the replacement of the Empire builders by 'sharp young men with coloured shirts and cockney accents reading the *Economist*'. The ones are little better than the others, and as a result Mr Edgar sees an English social river about to burst its banks.

His   right-wing   characters   feel   underwhelmed,   and

understandably, by the arrival on their street corners of Zen macro-
biotic luncheon takeaways, while those to their left are not much
looking forward to the mustering of private armies on the croquet
lawns of our green and pleasant land.

In the end what we have here is a high-class political thriller
which ends with a predictable anti-fascist warning: yet the real
success of *Destiny* is that it explores in magnificently heightened
language the arguments on both sides before finally accepting the
lesser batch of the evils with which Mr Edgar feels us both
threatened and surrounded. Ron Daniels directs a dynamic RSC
cast in which Ian McDiarmid as a dispossessed antique dealer and
Michael Pennington as a Kiplingesque major are superb.

Up the Revolution

Observant readers will have noted that there are occasional weeks
when I feel constrained to take my colleagues to task and this is one
such week. Picking our way tactfully through the Jubilee bunting
and the balloons, it has been possible over the past few days to see
two quite remarkable plays neither of which has been given full
credit by sufficient numbers of my critical brethren.

Let us therefore start (since what could be more exquisitely
timely amid monarchist celebrations?) with a play about the
Russian revolution of 1917: Robert Bolt's *State of Revolution*, at the
Lyttelton, and ironically hit by a backstage workers' strike within
twelve hours of its first performance. Mr Bolt, having already
constructed two massive tapestry dramas covering Tudor England
(*A Man for All Seasons* and *Vivat! Vivat Regina!*) to say nothing of the
Zhivago screenplay for David Lean, has now turned his attention to
the events of 1917–24 in Russia and has come up with certainly the
best-crafted and most ambitiously conceived new play yet seen at
the new National.

For his troubles, however, Mr Bolt has been greeted by a mixed
press and the burden of discontent among those less impressed than
me appears to be that he fails to explain where he stands on the
central issues. Excuse me, Mr Bolt, I wonder if you'd mind answering a few questions for our readers? First of all, in a word, could you
state whether or not the Russian revolution was a Good Thing, with

reasons? Write on one side of the paper only, and having completed that, would you then state whether World War I was fundamentally a better or worse idea than World War II? Now, since time is against us and we still have another thirty years to go, could you outline briefly your opinion of the hydrogen bomb?

The Russian revolution is not, in short, something a playwright can be asked to respond to as though it were an item on an *Encounter* questionnaire about The Playwright In Society, and it is to Mr Bolt's everlasting credit that he has appreciated this. What he has done instead is to animate a historical progression so that by the end of the three-hour evening we feel we have met and even come to know Lenin and his merry men.

We find them first, long before their revolution, on Capri where Lenin (Michael Bryant) and Gorky (Brian Blessed) and Lunacharsky (Stephen Moore, a wonderfully wry narrator) are gathered to plan the upheaval. The play opens in what must be a consciously Chekhovian mood before turning Brechtian as action replaces talk, but all through the evening there is an almost apocalyptic use of language: characters repeat themselves at the end of scenes ('Your day is done, sir.' 'What a pity, Draganov, what a pity.') and generally carry on as if writing themselves into history which of course is precisely what they were doing. Stalin (a bluff, bearlike performance from Terence Rigby), we are told, had the great virtue of not making a hobby of his soul, but Bolt's general conclusion is that such people are formed by events rather than the reverse.

As Lenin proceeds to the construction of the Soviet order, we find ourselves gradually losing sight of the 'ethical clown' Gorky and watching instead the inevitable Stalin takeover: Mr Bolt gives us an old-fashioned and well-made play with a Lenin for all seasons, either too saintly to keep his party together or too incompetent to prevent it falling into Stalin's clutches, depending on how you choose to watch his scenes. Bryant's performance here is masterly, and Christopher Morahan's production falters, like the play, only momentarily: Mr Bolt is still the best historical storyteller in the business.

The other play which seems to me to have suffered unfairly at the hands of critics whose expectations fall far wide of the original intention is *Happy Yellow*, a consistently funny Tina Brown comedy at the Bush about three girls flatsharing in New York. Handled straight, this would have been another portentous *Dusa, Fish, Stas and Vi* and doubtless would then have attracted reviews hailing it as a triumph of social realism. Miss Brown, mercifully, has gone instead after the laughs and there are a very great many, whether from the English girl (Patricia Hodge) who is very into urban poverty and intends taking a taxi to the Bowery, or from the two Americans (Jennifer Watts and Robin Pappas) who are into dog beauty salons and masturbation workshops among other diversions. This is the start of an all-American season at the Bush and if the plays which follow it are even half as enjoyable then we're in for a good summer. In the meantime, if I were a commercial management with a small West End theatre, I'd be thinking very hard indeed about *Happy Yellow* for the tourist trade. Claude Whatham directs.

Slow Death in Dallas

The sight of a great playwright in decline is not a happy one, and there is a case for wondering how much of a service to Tennessee Williams has been done by the admittedly lavish not to say endless production at the Round House of his latest work, *The Red Devil Battery Sign*. This, Mr Williams would have us know, represents him as he is now, more politically and publicly aware than in such earlier (and infinitely better) work as *The Glass Menagerie*, soon to be seen in revival at the Shaw.

For political awareness, we are in Dallas in November 1963 at the time of President Kennedy's assassination there; veiled references to the conspiracy theory surrounding the late President's death are made throughout the evening, and the Bob Ringwood–Kate Owen set offers a stunningly backlit cyclorama of menacing downtown skyscrapers.

But that's about as far as Mr Williams' politics go: true, the Red Devil Battery is an evil big-business conglomerate dedicated to the overthrow of democracy, no less, and possibly involved in Kennedy's death, but as a corporation it has all the definition and detail of the big bad wolf and remains no more than a vaguely unspecified threat.

The Battery apart, we are left with the usual landmarks of old Tennessee: the hotel bar for those dependent upon the kindness of strangers, the penthouse above it where a wealthy lady (not this time a film star in decline but instead the nameless 'woman down-town', linked by marriage to the big bad conglomerate and now being kept a prisoner on shock treatment) and her incurably afflicted and semi-impotent friend can find moments of fulfilment amid the violence.

Already therefore we are hovering dangerously close to the borderlines of Williams self-parody: all we need now is a nameless dwarf called Texas and maybe a tubercular nun once raped by the hero and we're all set for a replay of *Gradually Last Summer*. It is therefore some tribute to Keith Baxter (who co-directs with David Leland and also plays the man, helpfully named not Man but King) and Estelle Kohler (who plays the nameless woman and is required at the final blackout to howl like a wolf) that they at no time provoke even a suppressed giggle, and indeed manage at moments to be undeniably moving despite the considerable awfulness of the dialogue in which they are left slowly to sink.

'Alone is sometimes very lonely' takes some beating, but Mr Williams is up to his own challenge: 'Everything translates to some-thing,' says Miss Kohler, 'when your head is full of tongues' and for a second or two she can actually make you believe that she's said something. But the sound is all: Mr Williams writes as if there was no tomorrow but a very very long today, so that a play whose action could neatly be contained within twenty minutes is allowed to drift on over three hours as we hang around that eternal bloody hotel or King's derelict garden waiting for something to happen.

Gunshots indicate that the President may indeed be dead, and by the end a gang of teenage killers have taken over the stage and Miss Kohler, who may or may not have managed to pass on a package of photostat documents which incriminate the conglomerate in some typically non-specific Williams way. But Williams has apparently no real interest in Dallas, or Kennedy, or American politics in general: he has simply used an arbitrary historical event to provide some phony landscaping for characters who still belong up there on that hot tin roof, and the objection now is to the sheer numbing irrelevance of the proceedings.

Three Mexican guitarists punctuate the action, if such it can be called, Mr Baxter croons a little to pass the time, and in the confusion of guilt and despair and alcohol and uncertainty it is occasionally possible to detect moments of rare Tennessee. But they are few and appallingly far between, and for the rest we seem to be locked into a vast unwieldy play uneasily perched halfway from *Camino Real* to *Flying Down to Rio* but resembling in the end nothing so much as a confused intellectual rerun of *Rich Man, Poor Man*. Skip it.

Chita Rivera, who has been at the Palladium this past fortnight as the brightest and best of all possible Jubilee attractions, is the kind of lady for whom they built Broadway. A survivor of *West Side Story* and *Sweet Charity* and (most recently) *Chicago* she has a steely big-band talent and all the subtlety of a Sherman tank, but that and more was needed for her to rise above (as she undoubtedly did) a first half of mind-bending awfulness even by current Palladium standards.

The problem seems to be that the great cabaret acts of the seventies (Miss Rivera, Shirley MacLaine, Liza Minelli and Joel Grey) have all been built with Las Vegas in mind and thus tend to run about seventy minutes, which is presumably the longest that the locals there are prepared to spend away from the fruit machines. Faced therefore with the need to find something to go before the interval for London audiences who (at top seat prices of upwards of £5) demand a full two hours, yet having apparently already overspent on the second half of the bill, the Palladium is all too apt to dredge up derelict comics, South American showbands and ageing trick cyclists, many of whom cannot have been seen by large audiences since they closed the winter season on the pier at Skegness. My solution would be to forget the first half altogether and fill the spacious Palladium foyers with fruit machines.

Hedda and Hollywood

There are a number of ways of playing Hedda Gabler and (at the Duke of York's) Janet Suzman seems in the first act to be about to try most of them. She comes on as the prowling panther, deeply affected by the portrait of her father and with the gun already in her hand: within minutes we're in near-broad farce, then back again to tragedy, and by the first interval it's hard to know precisely where we are.

True, there are problems here for Miss Suzman: most of the Heddas of the past decade (Jill Bennett, Glenda Jackson, Maggie

Smith) have been either helped or hindered by a single unifying or imprisoning concept of the character: Keith Hack, in his Billingham Forum production (now in the West End for what's billed as 'a special Jubilee season': what price *Richard III* for next year's anniversary of the Coronation?) seems to have decided to let each moment of the play speak for itself, so that in the end we know no more about Hedda than we did when she first appeared.

Is she really having a baby (as the new translation suggests)? If so, is her suicide a final revolt against the imprisonment of motherhood, or an objection to enslavement by Brack, or an admission of guilt over Lovborg's burnt manuscript, or just another bored gesture by a lady who can't think of anything else to do now that her husband has found Mrs Elvsted?

All these possibilities are admittedly built into the text, and Mr Hack is perhaps right to leave his audience to sort the whole mess out: moreover if we are to have a Hedda for all seasons, who better than Miss Suzman who can be inquisitive, vindictive, sarcastic, sardonic and touching all within the space of about ten seconds? Other performances are however more uncertain: two or three are straight Windsor Rep, Jonathan Kent's Lovborg is quirky but ultimately disappointing, and Ian Bannen's Judge Brack is a major problem since he fails to convey any of the sinister charm or power which must be in the man. His final hold over Hedda, the knowledge of whose gun killed Lovborg, must be a real one – here, Brack's threat to Hedda is that at the very worst he may bore her to death.

The triumph of the evening, curiously enough, is John Shrapnel's Tesman: in a performance of infinite subtlety and cunning, he turns what has long been regarded as the least rewarding of the parts into a near-constant focus of attention and interest. In the end, though, we must come back to Hedda and to the fact that Miss Suzman can offer everything except the fundamental single-minded self-destructive egotism of the woman: hers is at the last a soft-centred Hedda, icy in manner but without the steel which is surely in her soul. As a result, we are left with a high Victorian tragi-comedy of manners: Pinero would have been proud of it.

At the Bush, *Are You Now or Have You Ever Been . . . ?* by Eric Bentley is a stunningly good dramatization of the transcripts of the 1946–53 proceedings of the House UnAmerican Activities Committee at the time when they forced a number of leading

Hollywood figures ('neither heroes nor saints nor villains, merely victims') to aid their 'investigations' into a supposed Communist plot to infiltrate Hollywood. In Anton Rodgers' careful, accurate and strong production, much aided by a closed-circuit videotape system, we are in the committee room itself, where the Congressmen now also play their witnesses and where the sheer claustrophobic intensity of those ludicrous depositions is almost too perfectly re-created.

For the first half of the evening (aside from such marvellous irrelevancies as the arrest of the committee chairman Parnell Thomas on tax charges) we are concerned with the crumbling of Larry Parks, Jolson impersonator turned stoolie. Then, after a break for some all too evocative tele-commercials of the period, we have Abe Burrows explaining that as he's just sold the film rights to *Guys and Dolls* for $75,000, a deal now in some jeopardy, 'to have my Americanism questioned is very painful to me'. His alibi is that although conceivably once a Communist he is also a satirist, and Stalin is known for not liking jokes: later we have Lionel Stander demanding they turn off the cameras ('I only appear on television for entertainment or philanthropy and this is neither'), Lillian Hellman making her famous 'St Joan' speech ('I will not cut my conscience to fit this year's fashions') and then the massive closing dignity of Paul Robeson (Thomas Baptiste) making all Luther King's points for him a decade ahead of time. This may not add up, in the strictest sense, to a play: but it is the single most dramatic, most moving and most powerful theatrical evening in town.

His House in Disorder

It is not altogether impossible to see why Granville Barker's *The Madras House* (now in the National repertoire at the Olivier) should have had no major London revival since about 1925. A play running over three hours, in which the principal character has only two scenes, in which there is no readily definable plot, and in which there are a total of twenty-five characters, eight of whom do not appear again after the first scene, does not lend itself readily to the commercial theatre nowadays and it has taken the full revolving-stage resources of the National to open up the museum show-case.

We start the evening up on Denmark Hill in 1910, during what may first appear to be one of the lesser episodes of 'The Forsyte Saga': views of Ruskin's house and the Crystal Palace may be obtained from the verandah, and indoors there's Elspeth March moving like a galleon in full sail across the stage flanked by her six daughters and Paul Rogers as a somewhat defeated paterfamilias. Their family business is to be sold to an American, which is about all we get in the way of a storyline, but Act One seems essentially concerned with the slow stifling of the daughters in an oppressively middle-class home where the height of excitement is the arrival of Lewis Waller's collar, returned in error by a local laundry.

By Act Two we're into another kind of female imprisonment, this time on the shop floor of the family clothing business where Barbara Hicks is to be found dominating a scene of intense embarrassment in which an employee is forced to come to terms with an equally stifling and suspect form of Edwardian morality. By Act Three the debate on freedom and emancipation and femininity has moved to the ornate headquarters of the Madras House, a fashion emporium created by Constantine Madras (Paul Scofield in his *Othello* mood) who has now returned from an eccentric Mohammedan exile to sell up.

But now we've also been joined by Joss Ackland as the American buyer, a man who can discern visions of future glory in canned peaches, and in the ensuing debate it becomes clear that Granville Barker (though fatally less able than Shaw to inject drama into a discussion) had an unexpectedly clear and even comic perception of the polemic that lay ahead as he was writing. His play has never met with much critical favour in the past, largely because it abandons every conceivable rule of stagecraft and ends up as an amorphous mess: but along the way there are some truly marvellous moments, heightened by the classical splendour of one of the strongest acting ensembles ever assembled even by the National.

Scofield, Ackland and Rogers score most of the debating points, but the backbreaking work of the evening is done by Ronald Pickup and Helen Ryan in an extraordinary (and in other hands I'd suspect unplayable) final duologue on the nature and prospects of a modern democracy in which, Barker would have us know, they were already in 1910 paying too high a price for excellence. This, in truth, may not be what the rest of the play has been about, but in a whole new area just before curtain-fall Barker establishes his own claim to social democracy. It is a bizarre evening, perhaps best summed up by the despair of 'Male and female created He them – and left us to do the rest'; still, Gaskill's sharp production makes it the most haunting of museum pieces.

Old Movies (written and directed by Bill Bryden at the National's Cottesloe Theatre) is a play for everyone who has ever queued in the rain outside the National Film Theatre, or wondered why Lucille Le Sueur changed her name to Joan Crawford, or subscribed to the old *Films and Filming*. It is, in short, a movie-addict's play and the fact that it has been shredded by most of my theatrical colleagues is, I believe, a sad reflection not on the play itself but of the ludicrous gulf which separates the National Theatre from the National Film Theatre despite the fact that they both now share the same stretch of Thames riverbank.

True, the play is not perfect: it runs about twenty minutes over-long, and contains at least one character (a suicidal agent) so sketchily drawn as to be unplayable even by the huge and good Trevor Ray. But in its central trio (E. G. Marshall, Fulton Mackay and Kenneth Cranham) and in what they have to say about the past and the present and the future of the film business, *Old Movies* is an intermittently and touchingly splendid play well worth climbing over the reviews to see.

Like Osborne's *Hotel in Amsterdam* (no better a play, incidentally, though one with which this one does have perhaps a little too much in common) *Old Movies* is set in the hotel suite of a Hollywood mogul, in this case seen and played by E. G. Marshall who is himself the walking memory-bank of half a hundred celluloid memories. Marshall, alias Walter F. Bickmore, is in Paris to set up yet another Jesus picture for the scripting of which he has hired Kenneth Cranham, an English playwright ('coupla faggy plays in some theatre I couldn't find and you tell me about integrity?') as well as Fulton Mackay as a Nobel-prizewinning Scots novelist now of course on the bottle; their alliance makes for a very funny evening.

The Prime of Mary O'Malley

For more months than I care to remember, the Royal Court has been in need of a smash hit and at long last this midsummer they've got it from Mary O'Malley, a young Irish writer who is now one of their resident dramatists. Her *Once a Catholic* is essentially the Vatican answer to *The Prime of Miss Jean Brodie*: here we're in a convent school in Harlesden in 1956–7, with Presley on the forbidden list ('I hear good reports of Donald Peers') and girls who go into the toilet together to underline the dirty bits in the Bible being told they may not sit their 'O' levels.

It's a marvellous, irreverent, affectionate and warmly comic play about the confusions and contradictions and general awfulness of being a Catholic schoolgirl, and I'd be more than surprised if it wasn't hugely autobiographical. But the best thing about Miss O'Malley is that she's a genuinely funny woman playwright and, outside of Tina Brown, how many of those do we have around? Her ear for dialogue is if you'll forgive the word immaculate, whether it is Mother Basil telling her class that 'in 1917 a festering abscess broke out on the face of the earth – horrid Communism' or a manic priest wonderfully played by John Rogan informing his girls that for a man to kill his wife may be forgiveable but for him to miss Mass is a mortal sin.

Outside the classroom we're allowed to meet a couple of the girls' boyfriends, one a sexy lad hell-bent on the priesthood. But it is inside the school, watching the extraordinary rituals of silent days and midday Mass spoken in a science laboratory and the sheer ruthlessness of the nuns, that Miss O'Malley's play really shines. This is the *Song of Bernadette* sung out of tune, and it is electrically funny.

As we pursue her girls through the school year via a series of blackout sketches highlighting their lives and eccentric times, Miss O'Malley's theme slowly emerges: to be a Catholic is to be always a Catholic, no matter what moral, mental or spiritual contortion that may entail. The entire class has been christened Mary, forbidden to work at Woolworth's and told that fountain pens may be made infallible by writing the names of Joseph and Mary with them. They've also been told that theirs is the only true God, despite the fact that he went to Nazareth instead of Dublin and turned water into wine rather than Guinness. Who's to be surprised that they grow up blessed but a little loony?

Jane Carr, Britain's oldest living schoolgirl and a *Brodie* veteran, leads a superb cast in which Rogan and Pat Heywood also give the performances of their careers: hasten along.

The Round House in Chalk Farm is always at its best when staging a show which is an event as well as a play, and Howard Brenton's *Epsom Downs* is just that: an episodic, kaleidoscopic account of Derby Day 1977 as seen through the eyes of a cross-section of its participants from jockeys and horses to the Aga Khan and the loonies who are hired to clean up after the race.

There's not much doubt in my mind that Mr Brenton is the sharpest and most assured writer of his generation (*Magnificence, Brassneck, Weapons of Happiness*) but curiously enough what he has to offer here is a straight throwback to those Pinewood slice-of-life films in which a selection of cosily familiar English character-actors ranging from Stanley Holloway up the social ladder to Nigel Patrick would be found intertwining their lives around some major social event such as the sinking of the *Titanic* or the arrival of World War Two or indeed the Derby itself – a film called *Derby Day* released in the early fifties has a lot to answer for in this context.

Thirty years on, what new does Mr Brenton have to offer? He does, it is true, have nude men à la *Equus* to represent the horses, and his scenes from life are somewhat darker than Pinewood would have allowed, but by and large he has settled for the same crowded canvas peopled by half-familiar figures: the weary policeman, the dictatorial trainer, the couple who've put their all on Piggott for the big race, the lapsed evangelist and even the crooked but loveable bookies all turn up here, admirably well played by just nine members of Max Stafford-Clark's versatile Joint Stock company.

And by having every actor play at least half a dozen people up and down the social ladder certain ironies are underlined: the Aga Khan is also the bookie, the evangelist is also a Kermit salesman and the trainer comes to symbolize the course itself with all its treacherous corners. But in the end only the ghost of Emily Davison, who once threw herself under the hooves of the King's horse to dramatize the suffragette cause, has a concise point to make about the Epsom people's festival: 'It's only a picture,' she says, presumably remembering her Frith, 'thin as paint – slash it.' No one does, of course: the race is run, Piggott wins, and another bawdy, funny, brawling day is over.

The Round House, newly turfed, might have been built for this play since the bookies can station themselves in the aisles and kites can be flown from the grid: but at the end of the evening we have learnt no more about human life than can be discovered from a couple of hours in any reasonably crowded pub. I suspect Mr Brenton deep down despises the Derby and everything that is bought, sold and conned in its name: but he hasn't actually said that, and in the end as always it is the sheer sentimental rubbish of the racetrack which starts looking good. A commercial for Epsom '78 could not have been better made or acted, but somehow I don't think that was quite the intention.

From Russia Without Love

We are in a log cabin, in a wood, in an unspecified country that is not England. An expatriate Englishman, his county wife and a couple of curious neighbours are all we see at first, though there's the promise of a distinguished brother-in-law coming for lunch. The talk is elegant, elegiac, discursive: would two men called Johnnie Walker constitute alcoholics synonymous? Could we conceivably be in Scotland? Apparently not, despite an immaculate John Buchan parody delivered by Alec Guinness in the central role of Hilary. Could we be in Rhodesia then? Possibly: the locals certainly seem unfriendly, and the whites seem trapped in their compound. The talk continues to be of England, though of a lost England: the England of Betjeman and Waugh, of *Times* obituaries ('I thought I might write a letter to *The Times* – everyone else has') and of country houses down long drives where men sat having conversations remarkably similar to the ones unfurling on the stage before us: conversations, or rather monologues, about the comparative awfulness of Elgar and Vaughan Williams, and about the fact that zoos are now full of people from the same foreign countries as the animals – gone there presumably in search of a friendly face from back home.

But still, we know not where we are: a Surrey clubhouse mysteriously moved into the Canadian forests? The birds seem not to

The Old Country John Phillips *as Duff*, Rachel Kempson *as Bron*, Alec Guinness *as Hilary*

sing, but there are rabbits to be shot and constant references to exile – Willie Maugham at Cap Ferrat, Max at Rapallo, Hilary in his log cabin in the middle of the wood regretting and remembering. It's his wife who, half an hour into the first act, gives the game away. She (Rachel Kempson in Hampshire vicarage mood) and Hilary are talking about their somewhat recalcitrant neighbours and about the fact that they really have nothing in common: 'Except,' she says, 'that you're all traitors.'

So we're in Russia: Hilary, after the traditional training by Cambridge and the Foreign Office, gave away secrets of state and fourteen years earlier had to disappear overnight from London for fear of arrest by the British. Since then he's been a translator in Moscow ('I sit behind a desk: occasionally people ask my advice and then ignore it: it's much like the Foreign Office') and this is their summer dacha. It may not be Surrey but then is Surrey still?

Into this desolate landscape erupt the brother-in-law, a newly knighted lecturer of considerable distinction and bisexuality (John

Phillips) and his wonderfully bitchy wife (Faith Brook). They have come to bring Hilary home, or to try to persuade him home: the fact that he is to be forcibly swapped for a Russian spy of greater value is kept from him until the very end of the play, in deference to his pride and in the hope that he may decide he wants to go home of his own free will.

But home to Hilary is where the heart isn't: a man with an infinite capacity for melancholy and almost none for love, he lives in a permanently derelict stately home of the mind, the precise geographic location of which is largely irrelevant. That, in essence, is what Alan Bennett's superb new play at the Queen's is all about: *The Old Country* is neither England nor Russia but a country of the mind inhabited by the survivors of a pre-war education which trained them for a non-existent future and flooded them with the memories of an all-too-present past.

Mr Bennett has written no better play since *Forty Years On*, and I have seen no better play in London this year: his ability to contort the clichés by which we live ('We never entirely mean what we say. Do I mean that? Not entirely.') and to provide instant character self-assessments ('I don't bubble over: I've always been at Gas Mark One.') is still unrivalled. But Hilary's dacha is no Wendy House and the Russian woods are no Forest of Arden: we are reminded that men have died for his treachery and that there's a real world beyond the end of the drive, albeit one which Hilary has never been able to enter. His idea of a return home is an appearance on 'Desert Island Discs'; his brother-in-law, fractionally more practical, suggests a bestseller to finance the years after prison.

Yet there are muggers now in Malmesbury, and the North Thames Gas Board is no easier to deal with than the Kremlin: the only world to which Hilary can ever return is one which ceased to exist almost before he was born and it is that which makes him, in the quietly mesmeric presence of Alec Guinness, a truly tragic figure.

The Quick and the Dead

The Ian McKellen *Macbeth* (now in an RSC repertoire at the Warehouse, Covent Garden) is good, though not – as most of my colleagues in the national papers would have you believe – the greatest thing to have hit London since the return of sliced bread. Its director Trevor Nunn has chosen to set a mere dozen or so of his actors in a circle around a bare stage furnished only with upturned orange boxes and a thunder sheet. Within these confines they then play out a straight no frills, no interval tragedy which is to the old red velvet Vic concept of *Macbeth* about as closely allied as is Freddie Laker's Skytrain to a first-class passage on the *QE2*.

Speed is of the essence: the whole show runs barely 135 minutes and at moments you feel you're seeing the *Reader's Digest* version. Yet an immensely sturdy Lady Macbeth from Judi Dench, a wonderfully poetic Duncan from Griffith Jones, a brusque Banquo from John Woodvine and ultimately Mr McKellen's own mannered, quirky, near-epileptic Thane suggest that there is a curious kind of greatness at work here.

Nunn seems to have seen the play as a ritual, a sacred if black magical mass in which those involved are mere acolytes, acting out the will of some malign deity. The result is intense, claustrophobic, sometimes unsatisfactory (the England scenes still seem unplayable and McKellen like Olivier goes from strength to strength in the play's middle reaches but is then deeply unable to cope with the end) yet constantly and uniquely intriguing. As the RSC seem determined to play their greatest recent success only one or two nights a week in a 200-seat theatre, *Macbeth* is inevitably the hottest ticket in town.

Homage to Harlem

I used to think there were only half a dozen truly great Broadway musicals (entries on a postcard please): I now think there are in fact seven. *Bubbling Brown Sugar* is admittedly a late runner, and starts with almost everything stacked against it: first of all it's at the Royalty, a theatre apparently designed to be a combination air raid shelter and all-night Bingo-and-Sauna emporium but mercifully still in legitimate if uncomfortable use. Secondly the show has no plot of any kind, unless you count a random tour of Harlem nightspots 1920–40 as a coherent narrative. Thirdly, although it's almost entirely about black music (most of it vintage, from 'Take the "A" Train' all the way through to 'God Bless the Child') it refuses to look at black culture in any terms other than those of celebration or caricature. 'We may not have had our day,' says one of the all-singing, all-dancing participants, 'but we sure had our nights' and that is the closest we come to an editorial comment of any kind.

Yet the miracle and the utter triumph of *Bubbling Brown Sugar* is that it soars above and beyond these considerations to become the most joyous, the most enjoyable and the most stunningly choreographed show in town. Not since *Chorus Line*, and before that not for the best part of a decade, have I seen a show which can so surely lift the roof of a theatre and the spirits of its inhabitants: *Bubbling Brown Sugar* is the kind of musical you sit through with a permanent grin on your face – and how often has that happened to you lately in a theatre?

Billy Daniels, himself the elder statesman of Harlem and still in wonderfully good voice, leads an immensely strong company in what is quite simply an anthology of all-time Harlem greats: Elaine Delmar, Lon Satton, the director Charles Augins and a sole white man, Bernard Sharpe, all have showstopping numbers but it is in the discovery of Helen Gelzer that the production achieves its final and most unexpected triumph. At the end of two all-too-short hours in which a collection of great singers have sung great songs, she comes out alone to do 'God Bless the Child' and it's fair to say that not since Streisand has there been such a breathtaking debut. *Bubbling Brown Sugar* is at one and the same time a requiem for Harlem and its triumphal procession, and London is more than lucky to have it.

Howard's End

The test of a great Coriolanus is how well he dies: Alan Howard, in Terry Hands' production for the RSC at Stratford, dies as impressively as he has been made to live. Not, granted, as spectacularly as Olivier who in 1959 took one final backward leap off a twenty-foot-high platform on that same stage and then hung about in mid-air while Harry Andrews as Menenius clung on to his upturned foot.

But Mr Howard has little to worry about: his performance across three hours is the single outstanding triumph of this year at Stratford, and when you consider that he is giving it two or three times a week in which he also gives his Henry V and the three parts of his Henry VI then perhaps the time has at last come to recognize that he's finally pulled ahead of all the competition, McKellen's included, and established himself as our leading Shakespearian of the seventies.

The new *Coriolanus* is a tense, spartan affair played out against a black corrugated setting which only heightens the impression that we are here in on some almost magical mystical rite. Howard's is not a flamboyant theatrical leader like Olivier's or Nicol Williamson's: rather he is a warlike Oberon, sent into battle and triumph and eventual self-defeat through force of habit rather than conviction. Dominated by his mother (Maxine Audley in full sail) and totally devoid of the noisy majesty which usually cloaks the man, Howard wafts through the action until the wind gets too strong for him to remain in control.

Up against the nervous, wily, time-serving tribunes of Oliver Ford-Davies and Tim Wylton, this Coriolanus eventually makes his stand as the first of the great fascists. His hatred of the plebeians is inbred and secure where nothing else about him can quite manage such security; Julian Glover's stalwart Aufidius and Graham Crowden's infinitely elegant Menenius (shooting stick at the ready for the lengthier crowd scenes) are both vastly more sure of their identities and considerably more secure in them.

But this is the tragedy of Coriolanus, and when Aufidius has laboriously to work out whether his trouble is pride, a faulty judgement or a defect of nature, we are for once not surprised that he should settle for the third diagnosis. Nature, suggests Mr

Howard, is not to be tampered with and in that conviction he goes to his death – though not before he has been lifted to the Gods on the crossed spears of his supporters, an image which will live with me for very nearly as long as Olivier's dying fall.

Meanwhile the National's Cottesloe Theatre has been continuing what can only be called the Steven Berkoff festival with his *Fall of the House of Usher*, a massively eccentric and compulsively watchable rendition of Edgar Allen Poe in which Mr Berkoff and his wife (the dancer Shelly Lee) and Terry J. McGinity act out the horror story, playing not only all the principal characters but also the house itself in the final stages of its disintegration.

Berkoff is a master of ultimate stage effects, and his Gothic camp theatricality leads him towards an extraordinary mimed, danced, chanted and acted happening in slow motion, one which includes such unforgettable images as that of Madeline walled up in her tomb running her fingernails down the invisible lid with such actuality that you leave the theatre believing you have heard the noise. All in all it's a baroque and bizarre experience, but one which I trust will be back at the National before long.

Another National treasure (though of a vastly different kind) should not be missed: it's an arrangement by Michael Kustow of *The Groucho Letters* immaculately performed by Derek Newark as Groucho and Glyn Grain as his long-suffering stooge. These letters have already been published in book form, and include such gems as the Warner Brothers correspondence when they were objecting to his *A Night in Casablanca* so soon after their own film, *Casablanca*: 'Doubtless,' replied Groucho, 'your great-great-grandfather Ferdinand Balboa Warner discovered the place and copyrighted North Africa, including "Casablanca". But what about "Warner Brothers"? Do you own that too? You probably have the right to use Warner, but what about Brothers? We were professional Brothers long before you were.'

Groucho on television ('little do they know that in a few short weeks I shall have this new medium croaking its death rattle'), Groucho on Lux ('Many's the time people on Hollywood Boulevard say, "There goes Groucho Marx, I marvel at his skin."') and Groucho on Shakespeare ('Do I want to play Hamlet? Play it? I don't even want to see it') are all here, as are Groucho the critic ('What this show needs are more bartenders and fewer actors') and

Groucho the historian ('Sarah Bernhardt was still working at seventy-five when she had hardly a leg to stand on') and the overall collection is one of the funniest late-night shows in town.

Relative Values

Filumena (at the Lyric) has almost everything going for it. First of all it reunites the Eduardo de Filippo–Joan Plowright–Franco Zeffirelli team who gave the National Theatre one of their greatest successes with *Saturday, Sunday, Monday* (also adapted from the Italian by Keith Waterhouse and Willis Hall). Secondly, it's another bitter-sweet Neapolitan family saga, this one admittedly less boisterous and less complex and also less hilarious than the last. Thirdly, it brings into the West End an air of assurance, comic style and sheer professionalism which leaves the average Shaftesbury Avenue comedy whether ancient or modern looking like a try-out for 'The Generation Game'.

The play in fact dates from 1949, and it belongs to that group of de Filippo plays which inspired and sustained not only an entire theatre company in Naples but also countless Mastroianni–Loren movies of the middle and late 1950s. This is the one about the middle-aged lady of uneasy virtue who tricks her wealthy lover of twenty-five years into marriage by feigning death. The curtain first rises at precisely the moment when he (Colin Blakely) has discovered her deception and she (Joan Plowright) has leapt out of bed to celebrate the long-overdue solemnizing of their relationship.

Two servants (wonderfully lugubriously played by Patricia Hayes and Larry Noble) watch in stony silence as their employers lay about each other in a slanging match so powerful that it seems the play has nowhere to go from there but downhill.

Not so. Blakely gets the marriage annulled, Plowright then tells him that one of her three illegitimate sons is in fact his, but refuses to specify which: thus by the middle of Act Two we're into another marathon row and by the beginning of Act Three Blakely has again been brought to the altar, though not before a desperate and very funny cross-questioning sequence in which he tries vainly to establish which of the three likely lads might be his, a mystery he is never allowed to solve for fear of favouritism.

Stated as baldly as that, the play must sound more like Strindberg than an Italian comedy of appalling manners: but in fact *Filumena* is, thanks to the performance of Miss Plowright in the title role, a glowing and heartwarming and generally glorious evening shot through with de Filippo's passionate belief in the importance of the family and its survival, at whatever the cost, through hell and high water.

Zeffirelli has directed in an almost operatic convention within an oppressively heavy set by Raimonda Gaetani, and though his production takes its time (three hours on the first night) it gradually becomes clear that what he is aiming for is not so much a play as a ceremony. At its conclusion, within seconds of the final curtain, there is a moment when the now safely married Filumena discovers that for the first time in her awkward life she is able to cry real tears. If I had to pick a single moment from any performance currently visible in London to preserve for posterity as an example of what acting is all about, I think it would be that one.

More Sinned Against than Sinden

Shut Your Eyes and Think of England is one of those farces on which theatrical fortunes can be based: what you hear, echoing around the Apollo Theatre, is not mirth so much as money. Written by Anthony Marriott (he of *No Sex Please – We're British*, now if you can believe it possible the longest running comedy in British theatre history – where's your Oscar Wilde the noo?) and John Chapman (a veteran cobbler of ancient Brian Rix jokes), this is some considerable way from being a great play and carries a plot which might generously be described as inadequate.

But, in the credit–card, multilingual, executive–class, airport world that now supplies Shaftesbury Avenue with much of its audience, *Shut Your Eyes* is clearly a goldmine. It is a play to which you could safely and simultaneously take fifteen deaf Japanese businessmen and your mother and a man who might be about to run off with your daughter in equal expectation of a happy or at any rate peaceful evening.

There are of course always going to be the ungrateful few among us who will complain about computerized jokes, caricatured characters and the impossibility of a storyline which has a junior accountant cheerfully taking over an entire corporation while his boss lies apparently dying of sexual over-exertion in a neighbouring bedroom. There may even be one or two of us who think that once we've heard one joke about Arabs turning St Paul's into a mosque we've heard them all, though we are in the event proved wrong as Mr Marriott and Mr Chapman mercilessly proceed to demonstrate that it is possible to think up two entire hours' worth of shaky Sheikh jokes.

But even for us, the unfaithful few, there is the miraculous Donald Sinden: Mr Sinden, you may recall, has already given us his Lear and his Benedick this year, and after this masterly comic turn at the Apollo he may for all I know be planning to do *Peter Pan* on ice atop the GPO tower. For the moment however he's installed in the West End giving yet another of the performances of his career, turning a thankless and underwritten role as the downtrodden worm-will-turn accountant into a massive comic creation, capable of demolishing a telephone merely by looking at it. Sinden's Arthur Pullen is a walking disaster area, and when he finally engineers his sexual and financial triumph over the sharks around him it is a moment of genuine theatrical delight which has a great deal more to do with acting than writing.

Around Sinden are assembled the likes of Frank Thornton, Jan Holden, Peter Bland and the inimitable Ken Wynne (about the only actor who might just manage to inherit the leading role when Sinden eventually departs and still keep it funny) but they are lumbered with a series of gags rather than people and thus cannot be blamed for firing their characters off at the audience rather than playing them.

It is unfortunate for Messrs Marriott and Chapman that their play should have opened in the very week that W. H. Allen publish five classic farces by Ben Travers, since they have managed to break every one of the three cardinal rules of the art pioneered by Big Ben: their characers are unbelievable, their jokes often unrelated to storyline and their denouement implausible. They have however been saved by Mr Sinden and I trust they are giving him a very large percentage of their undoubted profits.

Thanks for What Memory?

Aware as you doubtless are of my intensely youthful not to say lovely appearance, it will come as something of a shock to discover that this week I celebrate my fifteenth anniversary as a professional drama critic. There are of course those who would question the celebration, let alone the professionalism, but this is a forgiving time of year and I therefore wish my enemies nothing but peace and joy and two tickets to the first underwater *King Lear*.

It was not of course on this page that I started: my first critical job was on a monthly magazine renowned for its photographs of immensely chinless young men called Nigel who were usually seen sharing a joke or a horse with Fiona at a hunt ball in Warwickshire. Only a few months before my debut the magazine had in fact been closed down by Lord Thomson as uneconomic (there being in his view an impending slump in the hunt-ball business) but an enterprising publisher in Nottingham had worked out that if he could get a dozen photographs on to every page, and if each photo could contain at least six people accurately captioned from left to right (or in many cases far right), that would give him a guaranteed buying readership per page of seventy-two plus friends, relatives, neighbours, private detectives, etc.

The magazine was thus revived, the formula worked, and after a while he agreed to spare one or two pages for actual words: one of those pages was, he decided, to be about the theatre and accordingly I set off to my first professional assignments as a reviewer with a high heart and an amazing ball-point pen of which the tip lit up in the dark until I used up its batteries and discovered they could be replaced by personal callers only at a shop in North Korea.

After a month or two I noticed that something else had gone wrong, too: I wasn't getting paid. Accordingly I took myself to see the editor. 'Paid?' he echoed, with a faintly bemused smile: 'paid? You want to go to the theatre every night, have a ticket not only for yourself but also a spare one to take wives and/or friends, see a show and then get paid as well?' That, I told him, was the arrangement to which Bernard Shaw had come with the editor of the *Saturday Review* and though I would not of course be expecting the late Mr Shaw's rates right away, a little something on which to live when I wasn't actually sitting in the darkness might be nice. He agreed, albeit grudgingly, and I stayed with the *Tatler* for another five years.

So what, you will doubtless wish to know, are the many theatrical changes that I have seen in my time? It's hard to know where to start: ten years ago this week the Royal Shakespeare Company's *Macbeth* was at the Aldwych whereas now of course it is at the Warehouse, a good five minutes' walk away. Engelbert Humperdinck was at the Palladium instead of Tommy Steele. Donald Sinden was in a farce by John Chapman called *Not Now Darling* whereas now of course he's in a farce by John Chapman called *Shut Your Eyes and Think of England*. The National Theatre was doing *Volpone* with Colin Blakely whereas now of course they are doing *Volpone* with Paul Scofield. And *The Mousetrap* was celebrating its fifteenth anniversary instead of its twenty-fifth: only by keeping closely in touch with the many tumultuous changes that overtake our theatre in each decade can the drama critic hope to remain useful.

And how, you will doubtless also wish to know, has the experience of seeing roughly four shows a week fifty weeks a year for ten years (or, according to my trusty Hanimex pocket calculator, two thousand shows averaging, say, two hours each, that's four thousand hours of my life, or, dividing by twelve, the exact equivalent of 333 entire days) changed me?

Am I still that stagestruck, bright-eyed young man who set off to the theatre every night with a spring in his step and an expectant smile on his lips? No. On the other hand, he was called Max Beerbohm and died in 1956. What then have I, let alone the British Theatre, achieved in fifteen years – which is, you will recall, roughly twice the length of time needed by the Tsars to build the Winter Palace in Leningrad?

First of all, I have seen my name immortalized on posters outside theatres: 'the best revival of *Candida* in Leatherhead since the war' was one of mine, as was 'lots of laughs' and 'very exciting', though I cannot alas lay claim to the immortal 'it will run and run', widely attributed by showbiz scholars to Mr Fergus Cashin.

Nor have I yet achieved the classic one-liner, perhaps because plays have always seemed to me too complicated: the man who reviewed Christopher Isherwood's classic *I Am a Camera* in the three unforgettable words 'Me No Leica' was conceivably a great wit but not a good critic. Nor have I ever come across a single line of dialogue which begged an immediate audience response, unlike Bosley Crowther of the *New York Times* who was lucky enough to be at the press preview of Hedy Lamarr's film *White Cargo*. 'Me Tondelayo,' she said as she first appeared on the screen, 'me stay.' 'Me Bosley Crowther,' came a voice from the stalls, 'me go.'

Those were the days, and I seem somehow to have missed them: great insults in theatrical journalism are now few and far between, which is why we still recall Kenneth Tynan on Anna Neagle ('her Nell was not the broadest of Gwynns, and there was a heated division of opinion in the lobbies during the interval. A small conservative majority took the view that it might be as well to remain in the theatre: there was always the chance that Miss Neagle might come bowling on as Boadicea with a knife between teeth') just as we still recall Noel Coward on *Camelot* ('like *Parsifal* without the jokes') and on the Guinness–Signoret *Macbeth* ('Aimez-Vous Glamis?'). Critics have grown milder and alas more responsible than in the great days of the late fifties when Levin and Muller were the tabloid butchers of Shaftesbury Avenue and when Tynan could cause a queue to form halfway down the King's Road with a single good *Observer* notice for a play at the Royal Court. It is also the actors who have gone quiet. Twenty, even ten years ago the occasional giant still bestrode our stages: Olivier, Redgrave, Thorndike, Edith Evans all played as if it was their duty to light up the sky around their theatres. They were like human firework displays, and certainly on occasions the rain had got into a few of their rockets: but they left you in no doubt that they were theatrical, and it is, I think, to be mildly regretted that with the advent of a directors' theatre has come a scaling down of performances and a general fear of rising above 'the group' for any solo shows of force.

And finally, since we seem to be in nostalgic vein and since his death a fortnight ago was reported while I was abroad, a word about Terence Rattigan. The only playwright apart from Noel Coward to have been knighted since the war, he was our last surviving link with the master craftsmen of the British theatre. Starting in the middle 1930s with *French Without Tears* he wrote a succession of comedies and dramas (four once ran simultaneously at neighbouring theatres along Shaftesbury Avenue) which established him as the heir apparent not only to Coward but to Maugham and Pinero and Galsworthy as well. His fate was however to be the last son of a dying monarchy, and from heir apparent he was shunted by the Court revolution of the fifties into the role of exiled

Duke long before he was ready to go.

Nevertheless, plays like *The Deep Blue Sea* and *The Winslow Boy* and *The Browning Version* will, I believe, one day be recognized for the masterpieces they are; in the meantime, the fact that the National has in its fifteen-year history as a company never once done a Rattigan play is nothing short of a National disgrace. Now, Sir Peter Hall, is still not too late.

1978

Stage '78

January: Following the immense success of his *Ipi Tombi* (now entering its third year) Ray Cooney announces a season of all-African Rodgers & Hammerstein revivals. The first three are to be *Ipi Oklahoma!*, *Ipi Carousel* and *The King and Ipi*. Anna Neagle announces she will not be starring in a musical life of the Queen Mother. *The Mousetrap* celebrates its twenty-five-years-and-three-months anniversary.

February: New financial crisis hits National Theatre: plans to turn the Olivier foyer into a bingo hall and take-out hamburger centre are rejected by the Arts Council. Peter Hall threatens not to resign. Rock Hudson announces he will not be starring in the first-ever musical *Macbeth*, provisionally entitled *The Horror Rocky Show*.

March: Danny La Rue announces he will not be starring in a musical life of the Queen Mother. The Royal Shakespeare Company, in the expectation of another bumper season, puts in for temporary control of nineteen London and regional theatres plus a further seven in Scotland and four in the Seychelles. Eddie Kulukundis threatens to return to shipping.

April: John Curry to star in *King Lear* on ice at Wembley for the summer: believed to be a world record. *The Mousetrap* celebrates its twenty-five-and-a-half-years anniversary. Cicely Courtneidge announces she almost certainly will not be starring in a musical life of the Queen Mother. Peter Hall announces plans to charge £5 a head for skateboarding along the National's terraces. Sir Bernard Miles says there will be no *Treasure Island* at the Mermaid next Christmas due to the retirement of his parrot. Five plays by Alan Ayckbourn open at adjacent theatres along Shaftesbury Avenue. Jessie Matthews says she is seriously considering making a stage comeback in a musical life of the Queen Mother.

May: Cliff Richard opens at the Palladium in *Billy!*, a musical life of the great evangelist, Billy Graham. Milton Shulman says he has seen the light. Meanwhile, plans to flood the Lyttelton Theatre and stage the first ever underwater season of plays by the late Sir Terence Rattigan are rejected by the National Theatre Board as 'irresponsible and wet'. Four more plays by Alan Ayckbourn open in the West End.

June: Strike by Watney's lorry drivers seriously threatens the future of several pub theatres. Arts Council say they disapprove of a scheme to stage *A Midsummer Night's Dream* on the escalators at Green Park station (Victoria Line). London Underground Players thought to be responsible but not very.

July: Bernard Levin rejects offer to become chief drama critic of *Pravda*. Gracie Fields says she has no knowledge of a musical life of the Queen Mother. Trevor Nunn, following the triumph of his *Comedy of Errors* (a musical loosely based on Shakespeare) is now said to be at work on a dramatization of *The Boys from Syracuse* (Shakespeare loosely based on a musical). Robert Bolt's *State of Revolution* invited to play Moscow and Leningrad: cast said to be examining airline tickets with some care.

August: Penelope Keith says she is 'surprised' by suggestions that she should play the Queen Mother in a musical biography. Stanley Baxter is now believed to be considering the offer. Prospect announce that in order to ensure their continuing survival at the Old Vic in difficult economic times, theatregoers will have to pay not only to get in but also to get out. Charges will be on a sliding scale, with those who leave at or before the first interval paying most.

September: West End Theatre Managers decide that in response to the changing nature of West End audiences and in view of increased box-office charges, interval drinks and ice creams will henceforth only be priced in Japanese yen. Theatregoers wishing to pay in English currency should give at least two days' written notice and a bankers' reference. Lionel Bart says that he has written first ever comedy musical about North Sea oil. Irish National Theatre announces a season of plays by Reg Prentice.

October: Brian Rix says he is 'seriously considering' title role in a new farcical musical about the Queen Mother. Ray Cooney opens five new theatres along Ealing Broadway. Arts Council say that GLC bye-laws forbid ten-pin bowling down aisles of any National Theatre auditorium. RSC say they are willing to take over the National as a temporary London home until the completion of their

Barbican scheme, now scheduled for 1994. Vanessa Redgrave turns down *Maggie!*, a drama about the formative years of Margaret Thatcher.

November: William Douglas-Home knighted at last. Celebration season of his plays at the Theatre Royal Haymarket is attended by Aiec Douglas-Home, Henry Douglas-Home and Charles Douglas-Home, all of whom also have books on sale in the lobby. Glenda Jackson turns down *Maggie!*, also a musical about the Queen Mother. Emlyn Williams said to be considering solo show about the life and writings of Sir Keith Joseph.

December: The Muppets to star in ice spectacular about the Brontë Sisters at Wembley. Queen Mother declines to make her stage debut in solo musical about her early life; also declines to play Gracie Fields in eighty-first birthday tribute for Lew Grade. *The Mousetrap* celebrates its twenty-six-years-and-two-months anniversary by moving to the National Theatre where it is played simultaneously on all three stages. Peter Brook buys Zambian rights in *Bubbling Brown Sugar*. Angela Rippon to play Anna Neagle in stage musical entitled *Anna!*

Seeing Stars

Peter Hall's new *Cherry Orchard* (at the National) is as remarkable for what it avoids as for what it achieves. To a play traditionally the intellectual province of its director he has brought no guiding thesis, no theory, no historical or social or political comment. He has simply allowed Michael Frayn's super-cool translation to speak for itself and cast it, as they used to say at MGM, with more stars than are in the heavens. Thus for starters we have Albert Finney (Lopakhin), Ralph Richardson (Firs), Dorothy Tutin (Ranyevskaya), Robert Stephens (Gayev), Judi Bowker (Anya), Susan Fleetwood (Varya), Ben Kingsley (Trofimov) and Nicky Henson (Yepikhodov), all rattling around John Bury's sets of which the interiors look as though they belong to a vastly expanded doll's house and the exteriors to one of those children's picture books about Russian landscapes.

Frayn's translation is also a model of non-commitment; thus we have, more or less as Chekhov ordained, a Lopakhin who is no

ignorant peasant, a Trofimov who is not the voice of the revolutionary future, and a Charlotta who is not a comic turn. Where in
the recent Riverside production by Peter Gill (neither better nor
worse than this one, merely as different as chalk from cheese) we
had anguished people in search of their comic salvations, here we
have overgrown children in some eternal nursery watched over by a
group of more or less benign guardians.

The children are of course led by Tutin's Ranyevskaya (and if I
dwell on performances here it is because they are what the evening is
about – never has the Olivier stage so closely resembled a portrait
gallery): seventeen years on from her Varya (at the Aldwych) this is
a muted, gently haunting lady unlike the grande dame we have
come to expect in the role. Her cry 'Without the cherry orchard I
can't make sense of my life' works as it has never worked before,
simply because we are offered here a very confused woman,
genuinely unable to understand that if you spend money it can no
longer be found at the bottom of a purse the next morning.

Opposite her, Robert Stephens (in a hugely welcome return to
the National) turns in an equally childlike Gayev, adrift in a world
where even the furniture seems no longer quite as friendly as once it
was, and of the other children at the heart of the play only Judi
Bowker's Anya, the youngest of them, makes you believe that she
has a chance in hell of survival once the orchard has been sold. Susan
Fleetwood's Varya, played old enough to be Tutin's elder sister
rather than her adopted daughter, has the ritual moment of collapse
after Lopakhin's non-proposal, but inside she has been collapsed for
so long that it seems almost irrelevant.

Of the guardians, Ralph Richardson's Firs is a masterly creation
worthy of the Moscow Art at its Stanislavsky best: a crumbling,
doddering retainer with a soul of ice and steel. Albert Finney, in Leo
McKern mood, makes of Lopakhin an acceptable face for capitalism
and Nicky Henson's Yepikhodov is a wonderfully comic turn, all
the more to be admired because of the courage needed to go over the
top in a production where everyone else has got their heads down.

True, it's not all perfection: Frayn's translation has one or two
shudders ('silly Billy' has unfortunate Yarwood connotations, and
'chippity choppity' is less than ideal for Firs) and there is a faint
danger in Acts I and IV that we're about to cross the perilous
threshold into Dodie Smith country where a twee gentry are
bemoaning their losses. Danger circumvented, we're left to reflect
that this production, like the 1963 Chichester *Vanya*, will grow in

the mind: already it's grown sufficiently to fill the vasty spaces of the Olivier.

Gray Matter

We're in the Congo in June 1887: Stanley (of Livingstone fame) has gone to rescue Emin Pasha from the clutches of the Mahdi, leaving behind a rear column to guard his supplies and bring up eventual reinforcements. Major Barttelot (Barry Foster) leads this column, assisted by the faithful Jameson (Jeremy Irons) and soon joined by three adventurers from home – a doctor there for the money (Donald Gee) and two officers and gentlemen (Simon Ward and

The Rear Column   Jeremy Irons *as Jameson*, Simon Ward *as Ward*

Clive Francis) there to see what the Congo has to offer. Five men, surrounded by death and disease and hostile natives, thrown together in a store room by the Arruimi River, and they are what across nearly three hours Simon Gray explores in his *The Rear Column* at the Globe.

For the playwright of modern, urban, semi–detached and other-wise engaged London to turn his attention back a hundred years to a historical incident famous for the subsequent row it provoked in *The Times* requires some explaining. Possibly Mr Gray had long wanted to write his own *Journey's End*, or at least his own *Conduct Unbecoming*, and that is more or less what he's done.

In the first two acts of Harold Pinter's taut production we hover perilously close to the border of Hollywood stiff-upper-lip stereo-types: there's the mad Major, the coward, the joker, the sensitive soul and the doc all locked together in a tropical nightmare. No one actually says 'It's hell out there' or 'The natives are restless' or 'God, Carruthers, I can't take much more of this heat' but, and this is the acid test, we'd not be altogether surprised if they did.

Gradually and predictably the façades crumble: cannibalism, child flogging and morphine addiction overtake the group until Stanley returns (a fact which the cast list should have hidden from us) to find his hopes of fame shot to hell by the collapse of his rear.

Mr Gray has achieved the tension of all enclosed groups, from *Twelve Angry Men* to *Above Us the Waves*, and he half-explains the changeover from civilization to cannibalism in the least suspect of the cast. So far as it goes, we have a well-made military drama in which men go to pieces like men. Hovering over them is the unseen (until the last moment) presence of Stanley, whose officers, like Stoppard's Rosencrantz and Guildenstern, obey him from con-fusion rather than loyalty.

And so to Hampstead, where James Saunders' *Bodies* is *Private Lives* seen from the other end of the analyst's couch: two couples (Dinsdale Landen/Gwen Watford and David Burke/Anne Stallybrass) meet again nine years after they have swapped partners and then reverted to their original mates. In the meantime the latter couple has been through a particularly severe therapy, which has relieved them of neuroses but also of nearly all other human feelings. Thus they are sitting targets for Dinsdale Landen, gleefully determined to play a variation of Albee's 'Get the Guests' when they come to dinner. Recollections of pain and delight, we are told, must not be cut out because they are the life force itself: gut a person, and you gut all there is to live for. This may not be a new argument (*Equus* was also built around it) but Saunders expresses it forcefully and elegantly and funnily, reminding us along the way of the filial debts he's owed by Gray and Hampton.

And finally Arnold Wesker's *Love Letters on Blue Paper* at the National's Cottesloe Theatre: an extended tele-play written in a kind of lyrical blank prose, it concerns a dying trade unionist immortally well-played by Michael Gough who can communicate with his wife (a stoical Elizabeth Spriggs) only by a series of letters which grow more passionate at the daily approach of death. As a long-playing record it might be marvellous: as a play it has some stunningly good moments but no central energy, so that the language is all and ultimately it is not enough.

Life Class

I've said it before in these pages and I'll say it again until somebody somewhere takes some action: it is immoral and idiotic and wrong to stage a play as new when it has in fact been seen some years previously on television. Not that I've any objection to television work being seen later on the stage: many of the best broadcast dramas deserve a longer life and to be seen by people who happened to be otherwise engaged on the night of transmission. But to stage a play like Brian Clark's otherwise admirable *Whose Life Is It Anyway?* (now at the Mermaid) and give no indication to paying customers that they may in fact be shelling out two or three pounds to see a play they already know – and don't tell me that happens with *Hamlet* because I already am aware of that – is to discourage theatregoers at a time when there's already enough concern about their diminishing native numbers.

A line on the posters reading 'originally televised in 1972' is not likely to act as a deterrent to those who missed it or want another look; the absence of such a line looks like a case for the Trades Descriptions people.

That said, it needs to be added that the Mermaid have, and deservedly, got themselves a big success – one likely to outlast the year. Clark's play is essentially a debate about the ability of a paralysed man on a life-support machine to have that machine turned off when in his right mind he considers his life to be no longer feasible. In writing it as a black comedy reminiscent of Nichols' *Joe Egg*, Clark has been able to highlight the arguments on both sides and to arrive at a remarkable, joky, bitter, clever play about the rights of man over machines. Tom Conti's is a stunningly good central performance, powerfully supported by Jane Asher as a sympathetic doctor, Richard Leech as a less sympathetic one and Sebastian Shaw as the judge who has to make the final decision. If you missed it on television, catch up with it now.

Meanwhile at the Savoy for a limited eight-week season is a revival of Tony Shaffer's *Sleuth* containing the best performance I've yet seen in that thriller's central role: Patrick Cargill may be a less distinguished actor than either Anthony Quayle (who created the part on stage) or Laurence Olivier (who played it on film) but he comes infinitely closer to conveying the eerie bisexuality of Andrew Wyke on which the last scenes hinge. Seeing the play again is in fact an utter and total joy: *Sleuth* is one of those rare thrillers which, like *Rope* and *Witness for the Prosecution* and *Dial M for Murder* and that's about it, work even when you already know the ending.

Partly of course it's the language: Mr Shaffer writes with a kind of Edwardian elegance which manages at one and the same time to celebrate and mock its own genre: a detective story, being 'the last refuge of snobbish, outdated and ignoble minds', has a sort of awful fascination and (in an enthralling programme note which is in itself worth the price of a Savoy stall) the author maps out for us the perilous borderline he is treading.

Any lover of Sayers, Christie or Cluedo has got to admit that the body in the library no longer casts quite the same spell, and moreover that the whole 'But Inspector How Could You Have Known?' species is extinct not only because of the arrival of television reality but also because of the suicidal snobbery of its participants. Comic maids, plodding policemen and faithful near-sighted butlers are hard to come by these days, and in making Wyke a smug, class-conscious cobbler of smug, class-conscious thrillers Shaffer has been able to examine his entire craft while practising it.

That achievement apart, he's also got himself a marvellous plot I intend not to divulge in case there are any of you who've been orbiting space since 1970. Suffice it to say that Cargill is archly triumphant, Tony Anholt a convincing partner and Hugh Goldie's production redolent of the days when detectives were titled and every cabinet minister had a thriller by his bedside. *Sleuth* is essentially about the games people play to hide their own truths, and it remains an immensely enjoyable evening in the theatre.

Ten years ago this month, researching a biography of Noël Coward, I noticed that in all the reviews dealing with his boyhood as a child actor in the London of 1910 he was bracketed as 'up and coming' with another child actor known as Alfred Willmore. All newspaper references to Willmore ceased in 1917 however, and after a long and (I thought) careful search for him as an eyewitness to Coward's early years I came to the conclusion that he must have come to a sudden death in the First War. A month or two later, to my huge delight, I was sent to Dublin by the BBC to interview Micheàl MacLiammòir, whose death at seventy-eight was reported last week. 'How did you start your career?' I asked. 'As a child actor in London,' he replied, 'called Alfred Willmore.'

For a child to start out as Alfred Willmore doing charity matinees at the Crystal Palace and end up as the leading Irish actor of the twentieth century is a considerable feat and one that I reckon could have been accomplished by nobody but Micheàl: he will be much missed.

Forsyth Saga

In a degeneration game, all the players are losers: proof is to be found at Her Majesty's from where *The Travelling Music Show* should be asked to move on as soon as decency and financial arrangements allow. That will not alas be for some time yet: thanks to the dubious miracle of television, Bruce Forsyth is a very big star indeed, and his name over the title here was able to guarantee £100,000 or so in the box-office before the curtain went up which, if the first night was anything to go by, should never have happened anyway. The performance bore all the traces of a singularly under-rehearsed Variety Club gala benefit night, one of those occasions on which charity and goodwill are supposed to make up for the absence of plot or planning. Here, however, paying customers without hot food are being offered a show of such appalling inadequacy that to have Mr Forsyth in his curtain speech telling us we weren't a very good audience was like being accused of lying by Richard Milhous Nixon.

Mr Forsyth is alas where the trouble begins and ends: financially he may be the saving of this sorry show but artistically he capsizes it merely by his curiously unlikeable on-stage presence. There is, contrary to all present evidence, in fact quite a lot to be said for a Bricusse–Newley 'songbook' anthology; there is also a lot to be said for involving Burt Shevelove as director, since he's a man with a good Broadway pedigree and *A Funny Thing Happened on the Way to the Forum* to his credit. There is however nothing of any kind to be said for involving Mr Forsyth, who is so deeply unsuited to the material at hand that mid-way through a long evening I began to long for Vera Lynn.

Bricusse and Newley write three kinds of songs: heartbreak songs ('What Kind of Fool Am I?', 'Who Can I Turn To?'), triumph songs ('If I Ruled the World', 'Gonna Build a Mountain', 'Nothing Can Stop Me Now') and London Pride songs ('Candy Man', 'London is London', etc) and nearly all of them are worth hearing again in the right conditions. Only Lionel Bart has done as much to keep theatrical music alive in this country since the war, and the present farrago of Bricusse-à-brac should not blind us to the fact that, whatever *The Travelling Music Show* may look like, we are not in fact dealing with rubbish.

Lacking however the confidence to do a *Side by Side* or even a *Cole* kind of anthology, Shevelove and his fellow conspirators have come up with a uniquely catastrophic framework in which Forsyth, pandering to all the worst 'laugh clown laugh' elements in Newley's repertoire, plays one Fred Limelight, a vaudeville trouper understandably down on his luck and forced to present at mysteriously short notice a musical for which one of the cast goes missing, the only surprise here being that the rest of the cast haven't gone too. As they haven't, we are offered nearly three hours of increasingly desperate revue turns by Mr Forsyth, who drags from the ragbag of his talent assorted impressions, tap-dance routines and jokes all of which would have looked shameful on the pier at Southsea in its worst days.

The Travelling Music Show is considerably more tatty than the one it's satirizing, and infinitely more disgraceful since there is the money here to do something better, or at any rate more coherent: to see Mr Forsyth fractionally disguised as a park-bench tramp singing Newley standards is to realize that unsuitability can go no further.

Aware presumably in the course of a long tour that *The Travelling Music Show* was in some kind of artistic trouble, which is much like saying that the boats in Pearl Harbor had a navigational problem, Mr Forsyth steams to the rescue, firing on all guns and sinking everything within a fifty-mile radius including himself.

The sadness lies in the waste: a chance to hear numbers from *Roar of the Greasepaint* (Newley–Bricusse's best score and still hugely underrated) is thrown away in the desperation of Forsyth's bid for solo success, and the result is a gimmicky, pleading, pathetic apology for a theatrical evening which appears to have been put together on the backs of old envelopes then reused to paper over cracks in a doomed edifice. Bricusse and Newley deserve a lot better than an orgy of Forsythiana, and the sight of Bruce himself releasing underwound clockwork butterflies from beneath his jacket serves as a horrendous epitaph for the chances of the British stage musical.

By way of joyful contrast, *Lark Rise* (at the Cottesloe) is an enchanting 'promenade performance' which, borrowing a trick of two from *Orlando Furioso* and *1789*, allows its audience to wander around and through the midst of a group of actors playing out scenes from Flora Thompson's countryside classic *Lark Rise to Candleford*.

We're in an Oxfordshire village, at harvest time, towards the end of the last century: the postman, the fishmonger, the publican, the gossip and the gentry are gathered around the pub and the church arguing and storytelling and dancing and harvesting and living out lives of idyllic pastoral calm interrupted by occasional reminders of war and social injustice.

The result could all too easily become a period 'Archers', or the stage equivalent of one of those plastic villages built by Americans to remind tourists of their heritage. Instead, thanks to the immensely tactful direction of Bill Bryden and Sebastian Graham-Jones, *Lark Rise* is a lyrical and marvellously uplifting account of Victorian life and times.

Table Talk

There are those who will tell you, and with some justice, that Alan Ayckbourn belongs with Noël Coward and Ben Travers to that trio of English comic dramatists who, unrivalled in their chosen field, have kept British theatre audiences falling about the aisles for the best part of the twentieth century, so neatly timed, moreover, that Travers looked after the twenties, Coward coped with the thirties and forties and Ayckbourn has been mirthmaker to the sixties and seventies. In the fifties we don't seem to have laughed a lot.

There are also those who will tell you, again with some justice, that Ayckbourn belongs in fact to an infinitely darker and more committed school of writing, and that his purpose has been nothing more nor less than the terminal demolition of our most cherished middle-class securities. It is the former collection of his admirers who are going to be happiest with *Ten Times Table* at the Globe.

As that title might suggest, the star here is a conference table around which are grouped ten (well, actually nine plus a last moment walk-on) people intent on planning a summer street-pageant for their now over-urbanized community. The first four scenes cover planning meetings held between November and the fateful June, and the final one deals with the dread pageant itself, heard rather than seen, while a manic old lady rehearses 'Soldiers of the Queen' on the piano and the other committee members form themselves into the two opposing armed divisions to which they have been driven by the events of the previous meetings.

We have of course the usual Ayckbourn gallery of cross-sectionalized social types: there's the bossy county lady (Julia McKenzie, splendidly managing to breathe new life into what can only be called the Penelope Keith part), her henpecked husband (Paul Eddington in the harassed role usually reserved for Richard Briers) and the social rebel with an eye for the girls (usually called Norman as in *Conquests* but here passing himself off as Eric). There are, though, a few newcomers, including the marvellously mad and deaf old biddie (Matyelok Gibbs in the best creation since Margaret Rutherford) and a girl who can only speak in whispers (Diane Bull).

They form into two groups: the middle-class elite led by Miss McKenzie versus Eric and his students, who are determined on a workers' rally rather than a pageant. Not that it much matters: Ayckbourn's jokes are here of the most basic tight-trousered variety, and the master playwright of social unease seems to be going for the belly laughs rather than the groans of recognized truth.

Directing his own work solo for the first time in London, Ayckbourn has urged his company into a brilliant technical display of matter over mind, so that in the speed of the quarrels and the ultimate technical débâcle we manage to lose sight of the fact that this is really a play about remarkably little.

Like Travers, Ayckbourn now has his own stock company of actors and characters, and whether he groups them round a conference table or in the living-room really doesn't much matter. The result is a very funny evening: mindless, but very funny.

A conversation piece of an altogether different and infinitely more disturbing kind is to be found at the Royal Court, where Nigel Williams' *Class Enemy* has transferred, and justifiably, from the Theatre Upstairs to the main stage for the remainder of this month. A member of the BBC2 cultural mafia, but hitherto unknown to me as a playwright, Mr Williams writes with a raw and brutally funny gusto about six schoolboys, the scum of the blackboard earth, awaiting the arrival of their new teacher in a singularly derelict South London comprehensive.

Only the class is 5K and the teacher never comes: the last one got hit over the head with a hammer while trying to explain about Antony and Cleopatra, and this time the school seems to have decided that 5K may be left to their own nasty devices. Accordingly, each of the boys teaches a five-minute lesson to the others; for one it's sex, for another it's the making of bread puddings, for a third the growing of flowers in a window-box.

But as its title suggests, the real concern of *Class Enemy* is hatred. Barricaded behind their desks the six stereotype boys (the black, the swot, the schizo, etc.) reflect the unacceptable face of *Once a Catholic* (interestingly the only other real Court winner in the last two years, and also to do with the perils of education). Lessons aren't education, says one of the boys, 'I'm education – we're all education' and Mr Williams' point, at the end of a horrendously violent, savagely written and generally very powerful play, seems to be that any society which can tolerate a class like 5K fully deserves the hooligans it breeds.

But after an hour or two spent reflecting and detailing the

mindless hatred of boys whose minds have been allowed to rot away (the girls have presumably long since fled the class) Mr Williams pulls a subtle switch. No longer the fearful aggressors, the pupils are suddenly seen as survivors clinging together in a sort of educational lifeboat waiting for a pilot who never bothers to show up. All in all it's an immensely impressive London stage début.

Hare's Breadth

Time plays are among the hardest to achieve, as will be evidenced by anyone who has sat through the intermittently splendid, sprawling, nine-hour soap-operatic epic that is Shakespeare's *Henry VI* at Stratford last summer or at the Aldwych last week. This week, two more modern attempts at social and political history, both to be welcomed unreservedly.

David Hare's *Plenty* (at the Lyttelton)˙is one of the most ambitious new plays the National has yet attempted: set across two decades, from 1943 to 1962, it's a mordantly funny, savage and cynical play about the betrayal of whatever complex ideals may once have been symbolized by an English girl in the French Resistance. We start in a Knightsbridge house whose possessor has been stripped of everything including his clothes: to explain how he and we got there, we then flash back to a wartime French field where the girl (Kate Nelligan, in the most stunningly good central performance even she has yet given us) is watching a squabble over parachuted supplies between different Resistance fighters. But there, anything is possible: away from loveless England, where even passion comes at you down a blocked nose, there's a chance that the future can be made to work, that the fight may not be futile. In the scenes which follow, that futility is measured, examined and angrily recounted.

From petty ambassadorial betrayals to the infinitely greater treachery of Suez, Mr Hare charts a nation in decline: writing like some latterday Rattigan crossed with Charles Addams, he produces as playwright and director a black comedy so stylish, so acidly funny and so broad in its measure that we end up with an epic of disillusion and articulate rage.

In defining the gradual disintegration and reformation of one lady's spirit, Hare's message is that power rots but money rots faster: his world is one where it has taken 6,000 civil servants to dismantle an Empire built by 600, and where an ex-Embassy staffer (Stephen Moore at his most hesitantly urbane) can look back in nostalgia because 'say what you like about the Foreign Office, at least they were hypocrites; in the City they don't even try that'. Mr Hare's message, sent back from the outer reaches of disillusion, is that finally the only dignity lies in being alone, since together we've managed to ruin even twenty years of peace.

A national failure of guts and of truth is what Mr Hare is on about here, and he writes with a coherent and committed though well-controlled rage which makes him, on the evidence of *Plenty* and his other work for the stage, the most powerful young writer around. He also of course has the regular help of the incomparable Miss Nelligan and (on this occasion) also of Julie Covington playing the eventual inheritor of what little there is left. Together they've delivered the National an impressive package. If you listen very carefully, you can even hear it tick.

Meanwhile, at the Shaw where they're starting a major revival of the complete Wesker trilogy, there's the chance of another look at *Chicken Soup with Barley* which I'm still inclined to think of as the best of all the blessed Arnold's plays. Set across twenty years (from October 1936 to December 1956) in the home of one East End Jewish family, it's an account of how three wars (the Spanish Civil War, World War II and the Cold War climaxing in the 1956 invasion of Hungary) affect the Communist faith of one household.

We start with them defying Mosley and his blackshirts in Cable Street ('I'll clean this and bring it back to you,' shouts Monty, grabbing Sarah's best poker to fend off Sir Oswald) and as Mosley is turned back at Gardner's Corner there's a feeling of real triumph and exultation: we appear to be in for an upbeat 'Fiddler on the Carpet' where the pogroms are unsuccessful and benevolent Socialism can conquer all.

But Mr Wesker is a better and more thoughtful playwright than that: in the midst of this first-act joy the father of the family is already nicking cash from his wife's handbags, and by the second postwar act he's already an out-of-work loser taking his revenge on the world by retreating from it. Already it's all gone wrong, already: the dreams of 1936 are looking tarnished even in the first flush of the Labour government, and the family is starting to slip away, not only from Communism and even from Socialism but also from each other. Nothing seems to matter any more: this happy breed of men has become a nation of nervous, acquisitive, self-seeking shopkeepers and we're into an altogether different scene, one which appears to be the East London answer to Eduardo de Filippo's Naples in *Filumena* or *Saturday, Sunday, Monday*. Now only the family triumphs: gossiping, bickering, loving, hating but always in the most closely guarded domestic terms. By Act Three and the final disillusion of Hungary, only Sarah, the mother, is left to plead a broader cause than sitting-room survival, and in a great and powerful final speech she turns on her son, the last of the Socialist deserters, and gives him the choice: despair and die or live and care. The two go together: 'if you don't care, you'll die'. Mr Wesker's play is as simple, as romantic, and as great as that final speech, and I doubt that we shall ever see it better played than by Barbara Young and Martin Friend in Anthony Cornish's careful and lovingly detailed production.

Orphan Annie

'Oh for a spoonful of acid,' said the legendary Mrs Patrick Campbell coming out of the first performance of *Peter Pan*, 'to take away the taste of all that sugar.' *Annie* (at the Victoria Palace) could do with a little more acid too, but being at its London premiere last week was like witnessing the ceremonial opening of a goldmine. Never in the whole history of Broadway can a musical have left so little to chance: this one has winsome orphans, a dog that does everything but sing, and a plot of relentless lovability. For good measure it also borrows the 'Shall We Dance?' routine from *The King and I* and the result is nothing more nor less than the American *Oliver!*: a marzipan-coated, gold-plated smash hit that doesn't so much tug at the heartstrings as tie them in little knots.

The plot, such as it is, concerns the meeting of America's cartoon-strip heroine Little Orphan Annie with her father-figure millionaire Oliver Warbucks during the early Roosevelt years. The rich little poor girl is played by the Broadway original Andrea McArdle, now looking old and confident enough to adopt her own missing parents should she ever find them. Her friendship with Warbucks (Stratford Johns) is thus only saved from being thoroughly sinister by Mr Johns himself, who turns in a musical performance of massive dignity, unlike Sheila Hancock who has elected to play the orphanage manageress as the wicked witch of the West End.

Faced with cut-out cartoon characters, the rest of the cast follow her eccentric lead; but in among all the schmaltz *Annie* does in fact contain one of the dozen all-time great Broadway scores, and for that alone it is well worth a visit: children under twelve and Japanese tourists especially welcome.

Of all Pinter's plays, *The Homecoming* (now in its first major London revival at the Garrick) is probably the most readily accessible: an Ortonesque comedy about a grotesque North London family who send their newly acquired relative to try her luck as a prostitute on the streets of Soho, it affords four out of six marvellous parts and is perhaps the only Pinter in which these parts are considerably greater than the whole.

Menace and ambiguity, which any second-year drama student will tell you are the playwright's especial stock-in-trade, hardly exist in *The Homecoming* at all: instead we have a logically plotted piece about the territorial imperative, dominated by the magnificent creation of Lenny, a character Pinter himself once played and who's to wonder since it's about his best ever. Lenny is a vintage semi-literate thug ('Apart from the known and the unknown, what else is there?') and a marvellously anarchic theatrical creation who, were he in television, would already have his own series and possibly a chat show as well. Whether arranging for his sister-in-law to go on the streets or merely paying tribute to his father ('I respect him not only as a father but also as a first-class butcher') Lenny is one of the great characters of the modern British theatre and Michael Kitchen plays him for all he's worth which is a great deal: Timothy West playing his grizzled butch thug of a father, Charles Kay as the queer uncle and Roger Lloyd Pack as the boxer brother manage not to get outpointed, and it is left to Gemma Jones and Oliver Cotton to play the less rewarding couple.

On the National's Olivier stage, Christopher Morahan's four-hour *Brand* is simultaneously impressive and very dead, like a lying in state: it will doubtless please those who believe the National to be a place for ritual and dutiful celebration, like Radio Three, but it comes as a sharp reminder that the play itself should never be taken off the page. A sprawling poem with an immensely effective last line, it totally lacks the action of *Peer Gynt* or the concise impact of *Master Builder* or *Enemy of the People*. The only way it can work is if (as in a production I saw by the Brandes Theatre in Riga on a Russian journey last December) the central actor is so mesmeric that the behaviour of those around him becomes comprehensible in the way that an old Billy Graham crowd was comprehensible. Michael Bryant is many things as an actor, including excellent, but mesmeric he's not and nor is he helped by having in the company (as the Mayor) the one current National actor who could just possibly make the play work – Robert Stephens.

Brand needs to be compulsive rather than coldly efficient, and that goes for the production here as well as the central performance: the rising and falling ice blocks of Ralph Koltai's stunning set are the most moving things around, and they alas are not enough to get us through 225 minutes. A better *Brand* was achieved with infinitely less time, money or resources by a Trevor Nunn student production I was lucky enough to see in Edinburgh some fifteen years ago.

Albert's Opera

Brave is the company which tackles *Macbeth* so soon after Trevor Nunn's RSC production (in which, you'll recall, twelve actors led by Ian McKellen working with upended soapboxes and not much else turned Shakespeare's tragedy into a two-hour Satanic thriller with overtones of a black mass) and at first I feared the worst for Albert Finney, opening at the National just three days after McKellen had finally closed.

The Finney–Peter Hall production, on the Olivier's open stage, gets off to a bad start with bearded witches and a lot of soldiers wearing saucepans for helmets (other leading players like Daniel Massey as Macduff and Nicky Henson as Malcolm get to wear kettles instead) and a feeling that we are about to be plunged straight back into Irving's Lyceum or at any rate a Donald Wolfit tour. Yet nothing he's played at the National, not Hamlet nor Tamburlaine, has ever technically suited Finney so well as Macbeth: physically he is the Thane and we have only to wait for him to come into his own.

True, it's a long wait: the first hour of this 140 minute, no interval production seems to have the red velvet shadow of Michael Benthall hanging heavy upon it. As at the Old Vic in its worst mid-1950s, the play is not so much explored or interpreted as entered into the record: there's no feeling that either Hall or Finney or their designer John Bury has actually thought about why they are doing this play here and now. Like Everest, *Macbeth* is there, and has presumably to be climbed by a major subsidized company every decade or so. As a result the play is left looking like a great uncharted cliff-face.

'Stands Scotland where it did?' 'Alas, poor country, almost afraid to know itself': no, not Jimmy Hill and the World Cup squad but Macduff and Ross in Act IV, by which time it's clear that Sir Peter is intent on turning the whole thing into a full-scale Glyndebourne evening. Thus we've already had a chanting Hecate, no fewer than six witches and the play's ritual obeisance to Elizabeth I's ancestors, sequences almost always cut by directors who wish to get on with the plot.

What Sir Peter wants to get on with is the ceremony, and by Act V we're well into *Götterdämmerung*: it's here though that Finney can at last get going. After the deadly feeling of a duty being done, we at last move into an area of fire and passion as Birnam Wood starts its move to Dunsinane and Finney gets the bit between his teeth. Until then the company seem long before Lady Macbeth (Dorothy Tutin at her most birdlike) to have been sleepwalking, alternating sonorous monotones with wide-eyed manic stares. But by 'tomorrow and tomorrow and tomorrow' Finney has decided to go for the full Robert Newton, and I by that time would also have welcomed the parrot and the wooden leg. It's an act which makes one long to see Finney as Richard III, but not one which justifies the rest of a curiously aimless evening: John Russell Brown shares the directing credit with Hall and must therefore also share the blame for what's gone astray, and principally for reinstating some age-old cuts. If a scene has been deleted from playing versions for the best part of a century in a not over-long script, there's usually a valid reason and the reason the Hecate scenes have always been cut is, alas, that they're terrible.

Party Piece

Every Good Boy Deserves Favour (at the Mermaid) is a party piece played at concert pitch. Six actors and a thirty-piece orchestra (it was originally conceived for the LSO) are gathered together on three acting areas and a concert platform to perform a words-and-music work jointly written by André Previn (music) and Tom Stoppard (words).

Stoppard's short scenes, divided by long sections of Previn's music, are concerned with two inmates of a Soviet mental asylum. One is there because he thinks he owns an orchestra, the other because he has dared to write to *Pravda* pointing out that some of his friends seem to have been locked up for reasons not wholly or indeed fractionally concerned with criminality or insanity. Both men are attended by a doctor who happens to play in a real orchestra, and the only three others we meet are the dissident's son, his strict party-line teacher and a comic-opera General who arrives at the last possible moment to release both inmates, not because of a change of Soviet heart but because of a confusion over their respective identities. Rosencrantz and Guildenstern are alive and well and living behind bars.

What we have here, then, is a collection of vintage Stoppard sketches interlinked by an orchestra: the cellos are rubbish, the Jew's Harp has applied for a visa and if you had to find a word for the cellist herself that word would be plucky. So much for the jokes.

Ian McDiarmid, as the genuine orchestra-hearing loony, lacks the manic intensity of John Wood who created the role for its only other performance last summer at the Festival Hall, but he seems to have been hearing the music ringing in his ears for several decades longer; similarly John Woodvine as the dissident lacks the absolute power of Ian McKellen while managing to look more deeply incarcerated. Frank Windsor, as the doctor, is a distinct improvement on the original casting.

All credit to Stoppard for having the courage, signally lacking in his contemporaries, politically to deal with present-day Soviet barbarities and theatrically to write a play for thirty musicians. Such doubts as there are about the validity of the piece arise from the constraints of the form. Within seventy minutes, half given over to

Previn's score, it's too much to hope for a genuine resolution or a serious look at the subject. Instead, we get a series of tumultuous semantic leaps, a sketchy kind of reality and as eccentric a theatrical event as even Stoppard has ever devised.

Onto an infinitely moral Shavian premise he has grafted a series of music-hall jokes ('He has an identity problems, but I forget his name') and some intensely good, bitter writing ('Tell them Yes if they ask whether you agree you were mad, No if they ask whether you intend to persist in your slanders, and Sorry if they ask how you feel or if you didn't catch the question') but in the end the danger here is that a trendy mixed-media event has replaced what might have become a fine and serious full-length play. What we have instead is a play for concertgoers and a concert for playgoers.

Meanwhile the best thing that ever happened at the Shaw Theatre, Anthony Cornish's revival of the Wesker trilogy, is drawing to its close this month with *I'm Talking About Jerusalem*, the final and perhaps least impressive of the cycle. We're away from the East End now and away too from Beatie Bryant's *Roots* though still in Norfolk. Dave, the idealist from the Spanish Civil War, has decided to flee the city and set up as a country craftsman: it's 1946 already ('Out go the slums – in comes the Welfare State') but Dave and Ada are escaping back into the William Morris past rather than coming to terms with the new urban order. Leaving Communism behind them they've turned back to the countryside, where progress means waiting for Calor gas and where even the wells are biblical. The city, we're told, makes strangers of husbands and wives: for Dave and Ada there's to be togetherness working on the Colonel's estate.

Except that Dave, remembering old factory practice, filches a couple of unwanted rolls of lino and is sacked for this offence against the country code: his old RAF mate mocks him for not going into real business, his apprentice deserts him for better money elsewhere, and nobody wants to buy his expensive handmade armchairs. Something has gone very wrong with the William Morris scheme of things, and by the end of the play it's 1959, the Tories are on their way back to power and Dave and Ada are off, defeated, back to the city.

A couple of moving men are there at the beginning and the end, like a Greek chorus underscoring Wesker's lyrical tragedy, and there are two caricature aunts for comic relief, but in the end this is the most bitter of all the plays and the only one which allows of the impracticality and indeed the impossibility of the Socialist dream. For that reason it has seldom been well played: lacking the ice and fire of *Chicken Soup* or the Beatie of *Roots, Jerusalem* may well be the weakest link in the chain, yet it has here been given its due and then some by a superlative cast led by Jonathan Blake, Adrienne Posta and of course Frank Baker as the ubiquitous Ronnie Kahn. All I'd like now would be to see the Shaw following RSC practice and staging the complete trilogy one Saturday from morn till night.

Viva Eva

A musical which opens to the best publicity build-up since *My Fair Lady* and has £800,000 in the box-office before the first night needs critics the way it needs a musician's strike. What matters, though, about *Evita* (at the Prince Edward which is the Casino by any other name) is not that it's perfect, which it isn't, but that for the first time in eighteen years (*Oliver!* was the last) we've actually got a home-grown British musical which could be sent across the Atlantic with pride rather than embarrassment.

True, 'homegrown' only relates to the music and lyrics and design and casting: the director and choreographer are both Broadway men, and to them (Harold Prince and Larry Fuller) has fallen the task of converting the Tim Rice–Andrew Lloyd Webber bestselling LPs into a stage show. This they've done by cutting some of the numbers (notably 'The Lady's Got Potential' which was politically the strongest of the songs), reducing the narrator Che (David Essex) from a young Guevara who happened to be a pesticide salesman in Perónist Argentina to an infinitely more anonymous anchorman, and putting in some marvellous choreographic jokes about the inefficiency of the army.

The result is a tumultuously good first half, followed by trouble: we go in brilliantly, with an open-air screening of the kind of appalling B feature Eva herself once starred in being interrupted by the news that Santa Evita is alas dead. From there to the funeral, and so back to the beginning of her life: picked up first by a seedy nightclub singer (whose 'Night of a Thousand Stars', the 'big number' apart from 'Don't Cry for Me, Argentina', can now be seen as the parody it was always intended to be) and then by Perón himself (whose rise to power is told simply and superbly in a game of musical chairs) Eva goes from showbiz to political strength, until by the end of the first half she is appearing as the full Lana Turner, every Argentinian's dream of what a leader should look like.

Elaine Paige, tiny and very powerful in the title role, and Joss Ackland as her thug husband (the only two featured characters apart from Che in the whole musical) both manage Rice's cynical lyrics superbly: 'Showbusiness has kept us alive/Since 17 October 1945' and 'They need to adore me/So Christian Dior me' are lines Porter himself would have envied, and by the interval it seems nothing can go wrong.

Yet by then it's all over: Eva has come to power, and we're left with nothing but the rainbow tour of Europe and her lingering death. Denied the joky funeral we've already seen up front, we have only Che to bring the blackout with the information that her body then disappeared for seventeen years. It's not enough: until that moment we've only been given the haziest and most simplistic account of Perón (no mention of the Nazis) and if we're to add bodysnatching to his many crimes then we need to know more.

Despite brilliant use of newsreel footage, this second half is a distinct anti-climax, and it is here that the lack of any political base for the show is most crippling. The objection to Eva as superstar is that she was a nasty, corrupt Fascist lady who deserves the star build-up about as much as Lucrezia Borgia. Yet Rice's lyrics suggest he's well aware of this: *Evita* on record is anti-Perón but on stage, with the inevitable glow from the footlights, it becomes if anything pro-Perón.

Not even this, though, can alter the fact that the show is not only a distinct improvement on the same team's *Joseph* and *Superstar* but also the best thing by far to have happened to the British musical theatre in the seventies.

Frying Tonight

Few playwrights this century have been so highly praised and roundly condemned (often simultaneously) as Christopher Fry: at the height of his 1940s fame, when there had been five major productions of his plays and translations in as many years cast with

the likes of Olivier, Gielgud, Scofield and Burton, *The Times* took
the view that he was a lyric poet who had 'blazed into the greyness
of the postwar British theatre with all the colours of the rainbow'.
Tynan was less impressed: 'Mr Fry,' he wrote in 1952, 'is like an
energetic swimming instructor giving lessons in an empty pool.'

Now, for the first time in London in all of thirty years, there's a
chance to inspect the play that's generally been reckoned to be Fry's
masterpiece: *The Lady's Not for Burning* is at the Old Vic in a loving
if faintly ossified production by George Baker, a longtime Fry
advocate which is no easy thing to be in the present climate of
theatrical opinion. His production has already met with the rage of
one or two critics who, echoing Tynan (and indeed Agate who once
said that Fry was the kind of man who'd write a play called *Turn
Right for the Crematorium*), cannot bear to find a British stage being
used for a purpose which is not strictly naturalistic. The French have
no such objections (not by chance has Fry been an Anouilh
translator) but in this country a general press loathing of the poetic
finished off John Whiting and might have done much the same for
Fry had he not proved resilient enough to go off to Rome and write
Ben-Hur for Charlton Heston.

The trouble is, of course, that Tynan's followers have a little right
on their side: any playwright who can describe tears as 'wandering
dews' must have a faith in Equity membership and British audiences
which is not borne out by recent experience, and the arch self-
mockery of much of *The Lady* suggests nothing so much as Oscar
Wilde rewritten on a cold morning by Dylan Thomas.

And yet there is a case to be made for Fry, and a very good one, on
the evidence of this play alone: the story of the 'witch', Jennet
Jourdemayne, who wants to live and the soldier, Thomas Mendip,
who wants to die could be one of the great stage romances of all
time. In fact, it has always suffered from distinctly neutral casting
(Pamela Brown and John Gielgud in 1949, Eileen Atkins and Derek
Jacobi now) so that the passion which should erupt through the
poetry has, I suspect, never been seen in its full sexuality. Yet the
comedy is still here: Michael Denison playing the Mayor like Lady
Bracknell with a nasty cold, John Savident still doing his Peter Bull
imitation as Tapercoom (and why not, since the part was created by
Mr Bull?) and Robert Eddison giving one of the best performances,
even of his career, as the Chaplain ('My friends tell me I exist, and
by a process of faith I have come to believe them').

Fry is beyond all doubt the major dramatist of a poetic movement in the theatre which began with the bang of Eliot's *Murder in the Cathedral* and ended with a whimper in Enid Bagnold's *Chalk Garden*: his language is sometimes heightened prose, sometimes high camp, but it is never thin or boring or familiar and the central argument about the life force and the redeemability of man ought to drive the play forward to its surprisingly optimistic conclusion. The point of *The Lady* is that 'something condones the world, incorrigibly' and Fry has chosen to make that point in an arch and fey and intermittently enchanting script which depends crucially on wonderful performances. The fact that the Prospect company is still something less than wonderful, that Eileen Atkins has seen her Jennet as a minor-key rerun of her St Joan instead of the great blazing romantic star turn we need, and that the younger quartet of lovers and nephews has been horrendously undercast, doesn't help this evening at the Vic.

For all that, I'd not be inclined to miss it: more than just a period piece, more than just a 'verse drama' with all the awful condescension of that phrase, *The Lady's Not for Burning* is at one and the same time an example of Fry's lyrical brilliance and an explanation of why it led him and the British theatre down a blind alley. In the end, amazingly enough, words do not make a play.

The Theatre at New End in Hampstead now has an all-star female cast (Susannah York, Julia Foster and Stephanie Beacham) in Simone Benmussa's stage adaptation of the George Moore story, *The Singular Life of Albert Nobbs*. Already highly acclaimed in Paris, and now played to perfection in the claustrophobic intimacy of the New End, this is the one about the waiter at Morrison's Hotel in Dublin in the middle of the last century who was in fact a woman in male disguise, not for any sinister sexual purpose but simply because it was the men who got the work in those days and she badly needed the work.

At one and the same time a fable, a short story, a one-act play and a fantasy, *Albert Nobbs* is an eccentric and poetic gem much in the style of an Oscar Wilde prose poem: Albert is discovered by yet another woman in male attire, falls in love with a chambermaid but dies alone as he/she has always lived, neither man nor woman but a 'perhapser'. Because it stops short of an overtly political or sociological message, *Albert Nobbs* is all the more damning in what it has to say about Victorian chauvinism: if there's a better evening to be found around the London fringe, I've yet to hear of it.

Minor Master

There are a great many very good Noël Coward comedies in need of a revival: *Look After Lulu* is neither very good nor wholly Noël Coward nor in need of a revival but that, such is the luck of the draw, is the one currently on show at Chichester so we'd better have a look at it.

Written in 1958, when the Coward fortunes were at an unusually low ebb, *Lulu* is a farce based none too lovingly on a Feydeau original called *Occupe-toi d'Amélie*. The idea of Feydeau in a Coward adaptation is already an uneasy one: rather as if Ben Travers' *Rookery Nook* had been rendered into French by Sacha Guitry. The clash of styles is all too apparent: where Feydeau dealt in lightning action, Coward paused for the jokes. Thus we have a highly active semi-circular plot involving Lulu and her many lovers, interrupted by long stretches of dialogue which would work better in almost any other context.

The adaptation was originally nailed together as a cross-Channel vehicle for Vivien Leigh, and staged at the Royal Court since they too had reached a low ebb by 1959 and were looking for a solid commercial money-maker. John Osborne, walking into the stalls during an early rehearsal and seeing Coward, Vivien Leigh and Anthony Quayle on stage, thought he was hallucinating or had been mysteriously transported to the Theatre Royal Haymarket. On its first London outing the play did neither Miss Leigh nor the Court nor Feydeau nor Coward much good: on Broadway it had already been turned down by Shirley MacLaine and Carol Channing and was eventually done, though without much success, by Tammy Grimes. It was, after more than fifty plays, Coward's first adaptation and he was only to repeat the experiment once more in a long and varied career.

Why then have we now got *Lulu* back? Largely I suspect because of Chichester's current passion for female-star vehicles: here we have an opportunity for Geraldine McEwan and Fenella Fielding to go as far over the top as even they could possibly wish. Miss McEwan, in the title role, twitters and flutters her way through a complex bedtime story involving trouserless Russian princes while Miss Fielding contents herself with one of those *grand dame* offerings which used to be the province of the young Martita Hunt. Neither is however here able to do more than caricature an already contorted piece, since Coward himself (with a fatal lack of faith in the original) has contrived an archly camp evening.

The result is a comic opera desperately lacking a score, in which only Clive Francis (replacing Malcolm McDowell) is able to give a genuinely funny performance that is also true to Feydeau. The mock marriage in Act Three, which turns out to be all too real, also works wonderfully well and it is just possible that Miss McEwan and Miss Fielding (along with Kenneth Haigh as the Prince and Nigel Stock doubling as a couple of heavies) will be a lot funnier when they cease trying quite so hard to be. For the moment however we have Feydeau adapted by Coward and, in Patrick Garland's boisterous production, then filtered through Brian Rix. The only hope for Amélie/Lulu now is to see if she'd work any better on ice or set to music, though it's only fair to report that the Chichester audience on the first night fairly fell about. Then again, it was Goodwood Week.

There is a theory, widely held by my critical colleagues, that Revue in this country is only fractionally less dead than Canute: when therefore, as has just happened at the Hampstead Theatre, a good new revue raises its head above the footlights it is rapidly battered to death by them lest the theory should be proven false.

Revue is in fact alive and well and living in *Beyond a Joke*, a three-character Oxford graduate show conceived as a vehicle for Rowan Atkinson who's an eccentric comedian pitched somewhere halfway from Dustin Hoffman to Jonathan Miller. True, not all the jokes are hilarious or brilliant, and though the title is presumably an intentional echo of *Beyond the Fringe* some of the sketches go back a great deal further: indeed if I had to find a mother-ship for this particular UFO I'd suggest *Pieces of Eight*, a 1959 Kenneth Williams–Fenella Fielding classic which included a remarkably similar French restaurant number.

Yet were I the owner of a small West End theatre such as the Fortune or the Duchess I'd invite *Beyond a Joke* in for a year or two: like *Drop of a Hat* and the original *Fringe* it neatly taps the English love of faint amateurism in the theatre while remaining just pro-fessional enough to get by. No one has told Mr Atkinson that all his monologues go five minutes over; nor are his two Oxford col-leagues (Elspeth Walker and Peter Wilson) much more than all right. Moreover Michael Rudman, the director, has gone for an unusually slow pace. But in the end the jokes are enough: the concept of a Barclays Bank Christmas musical, or better yet a child called Wycherley-Williams-Wocket being asked to discuss the contention that Cleopatra had the soul of a rolltop desk and then, by an increasingly irate schoolmaster, if he has a good lawyer, taken together with a savagely good Carpenters parody add up to a highly entertaining evening which deserves a longer life than a summer month in NW3.

Look Back

When next they ask you what's so great about John Osborne, take them to *Inadmissible Evidence*: when they ask you what's wrong with him, take them to it again. The play is now back at the Royal Court with its original star, Nicol Williamson, in the first major revival it's had since opening there precisely fourteen years ago this month and if you see nothing else in the London theatre in 1978, see this.

Osborne himself once said that *Inadmissible Evidence* was the point at which he lost the critics and found his own form, and as if to prove the point he has littered the Court programme with hostile reviews. Not altogether fairly: few critics in 1964 failed to recognize that there was a curious kind of greatness here, both in Williamson's performance and in the play itself. True, it could still be brought in at less than three solid hours; true, it's a one-character play which seven other actors have to try and make you believe is about them too; true, it is a desperately parochial piece when set alongside *Death of a Salesman* with which it begs comparison if only because Bill Maitland is, as Bryden was the first to realize, 'Willy Loman in striped English serge'.

But what makes *Inadmissible Evidence* so powerful and so unforgettable is simply Maitland himself: a solicitor who is fast losing his grip on life ('I'm not equal to any of it; I can't escape it, and I can't begin again') he is Jimmy Porter run to seed, Archie Rice without any footlights. Fourteen years ago Nicol Williamson seemed to me precisely the right age for the role: he still does, which means that Maitland is somewhere between twenty-six and forty, though with a failed marriage and a teenage daughter behind him the logic is presumably closer to forty. All that matters about Maitland is that he's failed: the entire play, from a nightmare opening trial to the final rapidly darkening wasteland, is about a man whose fingers are being prised open from their grip on life. Taxis won't stop for him, janitors won't talk to him, telephones ring and there's no one there or else don't ring and there is someone there, clients all look alike (because they're played by the same actors in the same clothes) and all he knows for certain is that everyone, wife, mistresses, daughter, secretary, partner, wants to leave him.

But to leave him with what? Nothing more nor less than a kind of patriotic rage: culture has become a Sunday supplement joke, London is peopled by Female Guardian Menstrual Lib, youth is not only swinging but callous to a point of murderous indifference, and there are people who drive fifty miles into the countryside to watch the long-distance lorries rattling past. Maitland is cracking up, and with him goes his and Osborne's nation.

It may be a familiar shout by now (first heard from Jimmy Porter in *Look Back in Anger*) but Maitland shouts it best: held together by his three-piece suit and not much else, turning a single vowel into a yelp of pain, desperately peering through the darkness to see if anyone is still out there listening or loving or even hating him, just so long as they're still there, telephoning them to make sure that he's still there, constantly convinced that he's ceased to exist, Williamson's Maitland is one of the great epic performances of the postwar British theatre and fourteen years have done nothing to diminish his stature in the role.

Around him Osborne (here his own director) has gathered a respectable if none too inspiring Court cast led by Clive Swift as the all-too-orthodox partner and Marjorie Yates as a succession of clients. But to see *Inadmissible Evidence* again is in fact a mixed blessing: on the one hand it's the best example of Osborne's talent for exploding the structure of a play with the sheer vehemence of its tirades, but on the other hand the explosion can be followed by nothing but another interrupted soliloquy. *Inadmissible Evidence* is *Butley* multiplied by a thousand, but that still doesn't make it a great play: what makes it finally less than *The Entertainer*, perhaps even less than *Luther*, is that by the time he got to it Osborne had lost interest in plots. For all that, it's a great one-man recital.

On the National's Lyttelton stage there's a stylish revival of *The Philanderer*, a very early (1893) and seldom seen Shaw comedy which the director Christopher Morahan has sensibly cast from the

National's *Plunder* company, thereby preserving the superb
Dinsdale Landen–Polly Adams–John Standing team intact and
inadvertently reminding us that the play is a good deal closer to
early Travers than later Shaw in any case. The philanderer of the
title is Leonard Charteris (Landen) whose eccentric romantic
attachments to two women (Polly Adams and Penelope Wilton)
form the peg on which Shaw has chosen to hang a whole series of
random attacks on Ibsenism, the New Woman, drama critics,
doctors and the divorce laws. The beginnings of *Candida* are here,
and those of *The Doctor's Dilemma*, and though this is a relatively
minor frolic it allows of some very high comedy playing indeed,
notably from Landen who is a constant joy, nowhere more so than
when, having clambered up a library ladder at the end of a chase,
he's faced with the awful realization that there's nowhere to go but
down again. It's that kind of evening, played with an elegant
confidence which suggests that the National may at last, if only on
its Lyttelton stage, be finding some sort of a house style: Basil
Henson's archetypal army man and Frederick Treves as the
Telegraph's legendary Clement Scott suggest it's also finding some
respectable character actors.

Out for the Count

There are so many things wrong with *Dracula* (at the Shaftesbury)
that it would perhaps be charitable to start with what's right,
namely the eerie Gothic stage settings of Edward Gorey. Faced with
having to design a somewhat creaky revival of the old 1920s chiller
about men going into bat, Gorey has come up with a trio of truly
stunning sets (living-room, bedroom, vault) in which everything
from bedheads to curtain pelmets are bat-shaped. Situated somewhere halfway from Mabel Lucie Attwell to Charles Addams,
Gorey has disproved once and for all the notion that a bat is a bat is a
bat: somewhere on stage he manages friendly bats, hostile bats,
young bats, old bats, bats in love, and when you can no longer bear
the performances being given in front of them, which is to say
roughly ten minutes into Act One, I'd be inclined to settle back and
feast your eyes if you'll forgive the phrase.

This of course is what audiences on Broadway have been doing this past year; indeed when I first saw the show there one hot July afternoon there was a moment at the very end when the cast left the stage and the audience rose, rightly, to cheer the scenery. But on Broadway Dennis Rosa's production also had the advantage of Frank Langella, a magnificently starry actor who has seen in Dracula the unacceptable face of Ivor Novello and decided to play the part accordingly, as if in some baroque Ruritanian musical that's suddenly turned nasty.

For this country, the management have unaccountably (sorry) cast Terence Stamp, an actor with almost no stage presence of any kind but a quiet line in chat that might just get by for, say, a television production of *Alfie*. As a result, on the first night at any rate, a kind of desperation set in all around him: the rest of the cast, attempting to fill the space where Dracula should have been and all too clearly wasn't, went up and over the top as if about to do the transformation scene in a Palladium pantomime. There is anyway a severe problem here which is that Hamilton Deane, who first adapted Stoker's novel half a century ago, fancied himself not as the dead Count but as the avenging Professor Van Helsing which is therefore much the best part: at the rival *Passion of Dracula* (Queen's) where George Chakiris plays Dracula and Roy Dotrice the Professor, the battle is roughly evenly matched since Chakiris has a useful, toothy, foreign quality. At the Shaftesbury, there is so obviously no contest of any kind that Derek Godfrey might as well stay home and phone it through.

All of which is to say the least a pity: there was once a big and confident Broadway hit here and to see it reduced to a thoroughly uncertain parody-pastiche (from being originally an impressive period piece) through a major but to me incomprehensible error of casting is to be aware of the massive waste of those stunning Gorey sets. Perhaps if they could be moved to the Queen's, all might not be lost.

At the Young Vic Peter Brook's *Ubu* is a massively eccentric knockabout farce based on the two Alfred Jarry plays *Ubu Roi* and *Ubu Enchaîné*. Working with a company of ten and virtually no scenery, Brook has created a sort of pantomime for academics in which Jarry's notions about freedom and captivity are turned into an evening of marvellous moments. To see a march-past at which just one soldier has to double up as both cavalry and infantry, or a Czar of all the Russias emerge from a basement dugout looking and sounding like Chico Marx, is to be reminded that Brook's powers of invention work for comedy as well as they can for weightier texts: what we have here is essentially a stage cartoon (one which has been travelling the world since it first opened in Paris a year ago) which ends up looking like *Macbeth* by way of *Hellzapoppin*.

And talking of eccentric vaudeville turns, last week saw the long-awaited London début (at the Palladium) of Bette Midler, an American superstar about whom anything I have to write will have to be read with caution since it was I who, a fellow student of hers at the University of Honolulu fifteen years ago, suggested she might like to think of some other sort of career. Her current world tour is reputed to be worth at least half a million dollars, which gives you some idea of the scale of my mistake, but I still think I may perhaps be forgiven for it.

For she is not a star like any other star you've ever seen. Where MacLaine and Streisand and Minelli are packaged to within an inch of their vocal chords, Midler lets it all hang out: her first preview at the Palladium ran well over three hours, in which time she'd done everything from imitations of Franz Kafka to a bizarre wheelchair number for which she appeared strapped to a palm tree. The result was an evening of tacky camp schmaltz, yet a predominantly middle-aged and apparently married audience cheered her to the rafters. I'm still not entirely sure what they were cheering, but I think it probably has to do with courage and vulnerability and above all the sheer unexpected nature of most of what she does on stage. She is, as they say, one of a kind and despite my early doubts about her professional chances, something now tells me she's going to be around long after more conventional and predictable stars have vanished from the scenes.

The Glenda and Alan Show

The new Peter Brook *Antony and Cleopatra* (RSC at Stratford) is neither very Brook nor very *Antony* and therein lie a good many of its troubles. Perhaps unfairly, sometimes wrongly, we have come to expect a very great deal of Mr Brook: the guru of postwar world theatre, his theories about acting spaces and holy theatricality are taken very seriously indeed by a number of actors, critics and other directors so it is more than a little surprising to find here an *Antony* which could well have been done, and maybe should have been, by almost any other producer currently attached to the RSC.

Brook's last three RSC Shakespeares – the *Dream*, the Scofield *Lear* and *The Tempest* – were productions of such identifiable and unforgettable magic that to find him now doing an *Antony* with apparently no fundamental attitude of any kind to the play or its chief participants seems more than a little strange. True, this is not the easiest of plays: always denied its place in the big four (*Hamlet, Lear, Macbeth, Othello*) *Antony* has two entire last acts and a broken-backed structure which has always clouded the fact that this is also intermittently the most poetic, the most lyrical, the most touching and the most believable of all the great tragedies.

Antony and Cleopatra have to carry not only their present but also their past around with them: they have to be plausibly the most powerful people on earth, and they have also to be in decline. We seldom see them. Only four previous revivals at Stratford this century, presumably because of the difficulties of finding a sufficiently and equally starry couple: the play usually suffers from either a good Antony and a poor Cleopatra, or the reverse, or (as in the last McCowen–Tutin production at the Vic) a fundamental incompatibility.

Here we are at least spared these hang-ups: from their first entrance, Alan Howard and Glenda Jackson are a visibly crumpled and sexy couple who have evidently spent much of their time together in bed. So far, so domestic: Brook's staging uses a few glass panels and almost nothing else to indicate the luxury of Egypt or the austerity of Rome, and it is in this elegant kind of summer house that we first get to know the world's greatest lovers. Egyptian decadence seems to consist of a few cushions, and there is no attempt to suggest that either Antony or Cleopatra have ever been in charge of more than a few under-furnished rooms in a palace.

Alan Howard, beyond question the greatest Shakespearian of his generation, is no general: he suggests not so much power in collapse as insecurity in the usual ascendant. Similarly Glenda Jackson is a curiously modern sphinx, whether scratching at the floor of her monument or the chest of her lover, and there is a constant mockery in her voice which undercuts whatever passion may also be there.

But there are along the way some incidental triumphs: to play 'Fulvia is dead' as a laugh line is a stroke of sheer callous brilliance and Miss Jackson, throwing herself around in a series of nifty *Vogue* kaftans, plays much of Act One as if it were the Egyptian *Private Lives* which in a way of course it is. But later, as the shackles of the tragedy tighten around her and her Antony, it is clear that a terrible price is about to be paid for her early flippancy. If all we have here are a couple of middle-aged lovers trying to sort themselves out, then are they really worth armies and a war? If Antony is no real threat to Rome, let alone Cleopatra, if he appears frequently incapable of leading himself out of a doorway let alone half the world's troops, then what is Octavius worried about?

In Enobarbus we have a leader: Patrick Stewart's magnificently grizzled, poetic soldier seems in this production not only to remind Antony of what he is supposed to be but also of what he never was. In a taut, ungimmicky production marked by a general arrogance he alone stands and eventually falls for issues of honour and nobility and power, issues which the play is meant to be about. Even Jonathan Pryce's fine, mesmeric Octavius is a petty conspirator by comparison and it is only very minor figures who are allowed to indicate virtues.

In his eagerness to cut through the banners, to get away from pomp and circumstances, Brook has also got away from greatness and if this is not a play about greatness then it is no more than a *Romeo* for the middle-aged. Devoid of any subtext, shorn of all subtlety, this production declines slowly into an endlessly non-commital final act. By now there are splashes of blood on the panels (Brook's only concession to the outside world, unless you count a naval battle indicated by dimming lights) and a very faint awareness that something might be about to happen. In an atmosphere of spartan gloom, enlivened only by the clown who brings the asps and does a music-hall turn while he's about it, Cleopatra gets ready to die. The bright day is done, and we are for the dark: but we have in fact been in the dark all along, despite the glare of Nick Chelton's lighting. At no point has Brook bothered to get us away from gymnasium pranks. It is therefore left to Mr Howard and Miss Jackson to pull us through a four-hour evening, which they do with a considerable fund of comic and dramatic expertise. None of it, though, has much to do with greatness.

Hello Solly

In a year which has given us both *Evita* and *Annie* it would, I suppose, have been too much to hope for the hat trick: yet *Bar Mitzvah Boy* arrived at Her Majesty's with the best musical pedigree in years (music by the man who wrote *Gypsy* and *Funny Girl*, lyrics by the man who wrote them for *Billy*, script from an award-winning TV original and production by the man who wrote and directed *Annie*) and one could therefore be forgiven for expecting something more than the pleasantly melodic little show which will doubtless survive 1979 and then disappear from the British theatre without leaving a single memorable song behind it. In that respect, *Bar Mitzvah Boy* is much like *Billy*: inflated from a slender original to fill a wide stage, it suffers from some very visible stretch-marks and the fact that, thanks to three BBC television repeats, we now all know the story of the thirteen-year-old boy running away from his bar mitzvah and ultimately returning to accept his family on its own horrendous level. Father (Harry Towb in the performance of his career) is a cabdriver in a sustained state of shock at the cost of the celebrations; mother (Joyce Blair) thinks of the great day as 'not so much a religious ceremony, more a hairdressing contest' and it is left to the sister (Leonie Cosman) to bring the boy if not back to the synagogue, then at least back to the chicken livers.

Jule Styne's score is, as ever, only as good as his lyricist and in this case Don Black's lyrics are bland beyond belief; Jack Rosenthal has had the sense to keep his basic tele-script very much intact, but it is therefore up to Martin Charnin (as director) and his superb choreographer Peter Gennaro to breathe life into an evening which can all too easily develop into 'Fiddler on the North Circular'. This they do by taking the dancing into the very heart of the action, so that every bit-player is a star here for at least ten seconds. Yet there's still a fundamental conflict between the central storyline, which is in the Mary O'Malley tradition and could have been called 'Once a Jew', and the old Jule Styne–Broadway tradition which would demand Ethel Merman as the mother. Barry Angel as the boy is capable of a great deal, but falls short of carrying a £300,000 show on his slim shoulders: in the attempt to spread the load, both focus and a centrifugal force have had to be sacrificed. Still, there's a lot left, and

if you can't get in to *Evita* or *Annie* then this, as they say in the
American Express ads, will do nicely.

Molly (at the Comedy) is another television original transplanted
to the stage, though in this case the management (unlike that of *Bar
Mitzvah Boy*) lack the grace or the honesty to say so. Based on
'Death of a Teddy Bear', this is Simon Gray's reworking of the Alma
Rattenbury murder of the 1930s and therefore provides an intriguing though minor and low-keyed companion piece to Rattigan's
last play on the same theme, *Cause Célèbre*. Where Rattigan was
concerned with what the case had to say about English legal and
social conventions of the period, Gray is concerned purely with its
central characters. Thus we have Billie Whitelaw as the gin-soaked
Moll, married to a deaf Canadian boor and escaping into an
eerie childlike world reminiscent of Giles Cooper's *Happy Family*.
T.P. McKenna as the husband, Anthony Allen as the killer chauffeur
and above all Barbara Atkinson as the housekeeper in love with
Molly do what they can with a slender script, but it is Miss
Whitelaw's evening and the better she gets the worse the play is
made to seem. By its end the only real mystery is why she's not
setting off to storm Broadway in *Private Lives* instead of settling for
a lovelorn life near Guildford.

At the Garrick, Ira Levin's *Deathtrap* is quite simply the best
thriller since *Sleuth*: a once-famous Broadway playwright, now
down on his luck, receives through the post a brilliant whodunnit
by a former pupil. The playwright must then dispose as best he can
of the student and take over the new play as his own, and within that
theatrical framework Mr Levin has achieved some genuinely heart-
thumping moments. Denis Quilley in the lead, under Michael
Blakemore's deft direction, has decided to let the play speak (and
sometimes scream) for itself rather than turn it into the massively
eccentric star vehicle which John Wood made of the same script on
Broadway, and the result is that current West End rarity, a rattling
good yarn.

Night Extra

Two plays this week about the practices and malpractices of British journalism: one by Tom Stoppard, the other by Michael Frayn. Stoppard's will perhaps come as the greater surprise, if only because it's not another of his literary wordplays, and nor (despite a couple of very good jokes) is it another of his comedies. Instead, *Night and Day* (at the Phoenix) is a serious and alarmingly topical consideration of the current state of the fourth estate which just happens to have reached London within a fortnight of the likely closure of Times Newspapers. But what we have here is not another printer-bashing piece: instead it's an armed debate set in Kambawe, a fairly fictitious African country where there's a rebellion against a dictator.

Night and Day is essentially about two journalists: on the right hand there's Wagner ('I go to fires. I don't file prose, I file facts.') the archetypally hard-bitten Australian reporter who regards journalism as a trade rather than a calling and who believes that the bosses can only be beaten by union solidarity around the typewriters. On the other hand there's Milne, an idealist who's already been blacked by his union and who now, through his own enterprise and individuality, has scooped Wagner on an interview with the rebel leader. The argument (an old but valid one) is about the industrialization of newspapers and the extent to which union rules are valid in a profession originally built on non-union lines: it ends in yet another strike and, on the battlefield, an exceptionally bloody and futile death in which context it is hard not to think back to Nick Tomalin. But along the way, Stoppard's curious achievement has been to dramatize what might so easily have become another *New Statesman* leader, and to set a play entirely about Fleet Street entirely in Africa.

He has also managed to turn an intractable, emotive (to those involved) and often intensely boring (to those not involved) subject, that of press democracy, into an often moving and powerful evening, a task for which he has been much helped by John Thaw and Peter Machin as the journalists and Diana Rigg and David Langton as the settlers in whose home they fight out their war.

With Michael Frayn's *Clouds* (at the Duke of York's) we return to easier and more familiar territory, not only because the play was first seen at Hampstead fully two years ago but also because (as readers of Frayn's novel *Towards the End of Morning* may be glad to note) it marks a return to that most favourite of his themes, the journalist on a freeloading travel jaunt, known to the trade as 'a jolly'. In this case the jolly country is Cuba; there, in the office of the Minister for Overseas Affairs, two writers come face to face, each convinced that the other is the Minister. One in fact is a lady novelist ('I write books.' 'What sort of books?' 'Oblong books.'), the other a neurotic Fleet Street hack, and they have, as they subsequently discover to their mutual horror, been sent by rival Sunday colour supplements to do Cuba pieces.

The rest of the play, set on a bare stage with just six chairs and a table, is about their journey through Cuba accompanied by an over-eager American academic, a manically cheerful chauffeur and a wonderfully listless guide. But it is on the two journalists (Tom Courtenay and Felicity Kendal) that our attention is focused as they fall slowly into and out of love while touring the requisite collective farms, sewage works and new towns on their route. Alternately waspish and bitchily bemused, they are a splendid double act; Courtenay in particular having developed a good post-Ayckbourn line in nervous intensity.

And finally to the Cottesloe, where *The World Turned Upside Down* is another epic production from the folks who brought you *Lark Rise* and *The Passion*. This time we're in Cromwell's 1650 England: the old world is 'burning up like the parchment in the fire', King Charles has gone to his scaffold (a nobly poetic performance from Gawn Grainger) and the country is overrun by a variety of specialist groups ranging from soldiers to preachers by way of out and out nutters, psychics, politicians and not a few revivalists. Order has been fragmented and the production (by Bill Bryden and Sebastian Graham-Jones) is based on the *Lark Rise* principle.

Here as there, the problem is that the cast has to create instant characters for short sequences, much after the fashion of guest stars in Hollywood war films of the 1950s: thus an actor has to come on and be Cromwell or Charles I or the Mad Cavalier without any real background or development, and inevitably some actors are very good at that and some are terrible. The Cottesloe company has temporarily lost both Michael Gough and Mary Miller, who are much missed, and though *The World Turned Upside Down* has the same dramatist in Keith Dewhurst it desperately lacks the unity of one village at one moment in history which was the making of *Lark Rise*. We are left with a bitty, scrappy, sketchy affair, full of very good moments and others at which it appears the whole thing has been devised as a tourist pageant by American Express. An historical and sociological mishmash, it lacks only a soldier saying 'A revolution, Oliver? Here in Britain? But what will become of the King?' to qualify for the vintage movie award of the year.

Dearth in Venice

Readers in search of theatrical treats this Christmas have just about the best selection I can recall this decade: three major musicals (*Annie, Evita, Bar Mitzvah Boy*), a new Tom Stoppard (*Night and Day*) and a new Pinter, though *Betrayal* (at the National's Lyttelton Theatre) is admittedly something of a mixed blessing. It can't be easy to be Harold Pinter, and still less easy to be Harold Pinter working at the National: the expectations are vast, and it would perhaps have been sensible to slip this play (like the Stoppard) into the West End rather than leave it in those vast South Bank sub-sidized halls where it looks about as much at home as would *Private Lives* at Stratford-on-Avon.

For what Mr Pinter has chosen to give us here, and good luck to him, is the straightest of romances: a total cast (excluding waiters and publicans) of three form themselves into a classic triangle – wife, husband, lover – and the play is a stark and bleak account of their relationship. True, there's one essential twist which is that we start at the very end of the affair and then work our way gently back to the beginning by way of a Venetian holiday, but beyond that reversal of the hour-glass anyone expecting any of the ambiguity or menace of the earlier Pinters is in for a sharp disappointment.

Yet Pinter's reputation has never rested solely on his pauses; he has for years been the director of the glossier plays of Simon Gray and it's a fair guess that his writing of *Betrayal* more or less coincided with the time he was directing Coward's *Blithe Spirit* for the National. What more natural, then, than that he too should have decided on a boulevard piece with which to confound his many thesis-writers?

The trouble is that it's not, as boulevard pieces go, a very strong one; it starts wonderfully, with the adulterous Jerry (Michael Gambon) and Emma (Penelope Wilton) meeting in a pub some two years after their affair has come to a halt, but once this requisite information has been fed into the scene and it becomes clear that we're to get precious little more in the way of amazement or even surprise, the evening grinds along with all the predictability of the

Betrayal
Daniel Massey *as Robert*, Penelope Wilton *as Emma*, Michael Gambon *as Jerry*

revolving stage on which it is set. True, we also get to meet Emma's husband Robert (on stage as in real life, Daniel Massey) and the three of them then give performances which must be among the best ever seen at the National. By about the middle of the second scene, what they are doing is not so much *Private Lives* as *Design for Living*: three people, locked together by their love for each other (not only do the two men fancy Emma, they have, it seems, in the past also fancied each other) and unable to live either apart or together for the age–old reason that three's a crowd.

Appearance is all: 'I ask about your husband,' says Jerry at one point to Emma 'you ask about my wife. You know the form,' and the form is really what *Betrayal* is about. Jerry is an author's agent: Robert is a publisher. Both have children, both belong to the high-society publishing world which now seems to have taken the place of the Embassy nightclub for purposes of gentle social satire. With one bound we're back into *Pumpkin Eater* territory (another project with which Pinter was involved, for he wrote the screenplay) and what we've got here are nine scenes from married life all immaculately staged by Peter Hall but all ultimately as empty as a dead bottle of Cinzano.

Stage by Stage

1978 has been a year of great musicals, good one-man shows, and faint but distinct signs of a return to some sort of life in the West End. Let's start with the musicals: *Evita* is the first West End big-band show in fully a decade which could be sent to Broadway with pride rather than deep embarrassment, and *Annie* has confirmed that Broadway is still the musical Mecca we should be turning towards. True, there have been some homegrown disasters, including no less than three Leslie Bricusse catastrophes (*The Travelling Music Show*, *King & Clowns* and *Beyond the Rainbow*) but both *Oliver!* and *Elvis* are holding up well and in any lesser year Jack Rosenthal's *Bar Mitzvah Boy* would look positively sparkling. In a boom year, it looks just about all right.

Among the one-man shows, I'd be inclined to remember Dave Allen's sell–out solo at the Vaudeville, Gordon Chater's stunning Australian transvestite in *The Elocution of Benjamin Franklin* (not to be confused with Barry Humphries' stunning Australian transvestite at the Piccadilly, where Dame Edna incidentally deserves a special award for the wittiest neon sign of the year – 'Nice Australian model, turn left'), James Earl Jones as Paul Robeson, and Quentin Crisp's eccentrically splendid monologue at the King's Head. But the two best solos of the year have undoubtedly been Alec McCowen's rendering of St Mark's Gospel, not a reading nor a recitation but a performance of rare and true brilliance to be compared only to Gielgud's *Ages of Man*, and Nicol Williamson's revival of Bill Maitland, the greatest of all Osborne's stage characters, in *Inadmissible Evidence*. There are of course those who would have you believe that *Inadmissible Evidence* is a play rather than a one-man show, but I am not among them.

In the subsidized theatre, the Royal Court continues to lurch along in search of a policy (both *Once a Catholic* and *Prayers for My Daughter* were strokes of luck rather than sustained judgement) but the National has at last managed to narrow the RSC's long-sustained artistic lead to the point where the two companies go into 1979 more or less level. Typically and predictably, given the flair for bizarre timing that has long been a feature of Sir Peter Hall's South Bank administration, the moment in about mid-autumn when the whole operation at last seemed to come together, with hits on all three stages, coincided with news of yet another artistic reshuffle. Still, it would be churlish not to note a totally superb *Double Dealer* on the Olivier stage, the return of Robert Stephens back at the very top of his considerable classical form, and, at the Cottesloe, the village wonder that was *Lark Rise*. True, there was also that disastrously operatic Finney *Macbeth*, and indeed a *Cherry Orchard* considerably outpointed by a Peter Gill production at Riverside; but to set against those there was also the triumph of Kate Nelligan in David Hare's *Plenty*, a distinguished Shaw rediscovery (*The Philanderer*), and a sensible revival of *Plunder* by our greatest living comic dramatist Ben Travers who, if the Honours system in this country bore any relation to reality, would already be Sir Ben.

Over at the Royal Shakespeare Company, this has been the year of the Peter Brook *Antony and Cleopatra* (a somewhat austere couple in Alan Howard and Glenda Jackson) and not a lot else, unless you count Mr Howard's continuing triumph as *Coriolanus*, a production which actually started in 1977. At the Aldwych the RSC too were considerably outpointed in their *Changeling* by an infinitely more thoughtful Peter Gill production at Riverside, so this might be the moment for a special award to Mr Gill himself. Operating in the disused BBC television studios down by the river in Hammersmith he has, in the uneasy economic climate of 1978, yet to come up with a loser.

Disappointments of the year have included two Simon Gray flops (*The Rear Column*, which deserved to succeed, and *Molly* which should have been left in television where it belonged) and the continuing inability of the West End to sustain anything heavier than Ayckbourn comedies (*Ten Times Table, Bedroom Farce*), Haymarket revivals (*Waters of the Moon, The Millionairess*) and 'dramas' like *Whose Life Is It Anyway?* which is Somerset Maugham's *The Sacred Flame* by any other name, a fact which appears to have gone curiously unnoticed.

But the closing weeks of 1978 did bring a new Tom Stoppard to the West End: his *Night and Day* is undoubtedly the best new play of the year and not, gentle reader, just because it deals with journalists. Like Michael Frayn in an infinitely lighter piece (*Clouds*) Mr Stoppard has seen in journalism a mirror for countless social and political images and it is to the Phoenix that I would urge you for proof that the West End is still alive and kicking. Just.

Prospects for 1979: doubtful for Prospect itself, which after some valiant work at the Vic is still being cold-shouldered by the Arts Council, who should be thoroughly ashamed of themselves and doubtless are not. A 'major' Pinter to make up for the somewhat lightweight *Betrayal*. The arrival from Broadway of *Dancin'* and the new *Sherlock Holmes* which comes complete with its own on-stage thunderstorm.

Special 78 award: to Ray Cooney, for buying a Broadway theatre. Always an impresario keen to stick his head in the lion's mouth, he now owns the den.

1979

Minstrel Mistake

First Pearl Harbor, and now this. The Success Motivation Institute of Japan are presenting, at the Cambridge Theatre, a musical called *Troubadour* of such stunning, nay breathtaking, awfulness that medallions should be struck and ties woven with special symbols, perhaps a crossed crusader, so that in twenty or thirty years' time we few, we unhappy few, we band of brothers, we who actually sat through *Troubadour*, can gather together at annual reunion dinners and lick our wounds.

What we have here, such as it is and that is not a lot, appears to be a musical about the Crusades: set in 1190, give or take a decade, it concerns one Ermengarde, Viscountess of Narbon no less, who is given to declaring her love for her native province in such musical couplets as 'Narbon I have loved you beyond myself/Everything else I've put on the shelf.' There are forty other thespians on the stage, twenty-seven musicians in the pit and, at least until the first interval, almost as many in the stalls; those that did stay through the interval sat with their mouths open, in a kind of stunned and disbelieving silence, wearing that shell-shocked expression I last encountered in the audience shown by Mel Brooks to be sitting through his 'Springtime for Hitler' routine in the *Producers* film.

But until you've seen twenty dancers gyrate through a number called, if my programme notes are to be believed, 'Onward to Jerusalem' or heard Ermengarde utter that other immortal couplet 'Today in Narbon there is only Jubilation/For our nephew has lived up to our Expectation' you really haven't lived. The entire project, written by Michael Lombardi and Ray Holder, directed by James Fortune and produced by Mr Lombardi ('we name the guilty men') makes *Beyond the Rainbow* (now in its third amazing month at the Adelphi) look almost adequate; *Troubadour* is much like building the *Titanic* out of matchsticks – a doomed and costly project, rumoured to have set its makers back almost £400,000. Even if you manage not to pause and wonder how many of the Vietnam boat people could have been housed and clothed and fed for the rest of their lives on that kind of cash, it is still worth wondering how a musical apparently set in the lobby of the Mediaeval Hilton and containing such other utterances as 'You must be celestially favoured/Given a job for which you have laboured' could have reached the stage of a professional theatre in what is supposed to be the theatrical capital of the world.

Camelot, said Noel Coward once, was like *Parsifal* without the jokes; *Troubadour* is like *Camelot* without the plot. True there's a battle sequence, taking place we are told within the third Crusade, just in case we might have idiotically thought it was the second Crusade, during which one poor benighted or possibly beknighted extra, told to stand stage centre and say something, was heard the night I was there to declare 'these Crusades are spreading like wildfire'. I also quite liked the three consecutive lines which ran 'I wonder as the years go by/Has my life been one big lie/Is this the way I shall die?', the latter a question a number of drama critics must have been asking themselves by the end of the first half. John Watts and Kim Braden lead a large company, all of whom deserve special merit awards for carrying on to the bitter end of an evening of baroque rubbish. If this is where the Success Motivation Institute of Japan is at, something tells me I shall not be enrolling there this year.

Meanwhile at the Aldwych, the Royal Shakespeare Company's New Year romp is *Saratoga*, an 1870 American comedy by Bronson Howard now being seen for the first time in London. As a 'rediscovery', it rates a good long way below such other RSC gems as *London Assurance*, *Sherlock Holmes* and *Wild Oats*: this is a mindless and larky little piece subtitled *Pistols for Seven* and concerning one Robert Sackett who, the castlist tells us, 'loved not wisely but four well'. Always beware joky castlists: they indicate, rightly in this case, that the author is better with a pen than with a plot. Howard in fact went on to found the American Dramatists Club, and is rightly credited with being one of the first men to make the American drama both respectable and interesting: *Saratoga* however shows him as a kind of minor Feydeau, forever trying to get characters in and out of a series of doorways.

Nor is Ronald Eyre's somewhat humourless production helped by the central casting of Dennis Waterman, who fatally lacks a lightness of touch until, too late in the evening, he is able to display an altogether different talent and go into a brilliant soft-shoe shuffle with a group of negro waiters who act as the production's chorus and its only real attraction.

Turned into a Jule Styne musical called *Saratoga!* this might just have worked: done straight, it emerges as the North American *Charley's Aunt* and a very pale shadow of innumerable European light comedies of the period. But a strong RSC cast (James Laurenson, Polly James, Jeffery Dench, Maxine Audley and the altogether superb Keith Hodiak as the leader of the singing waiters) do what they can to breathe life into a period piece which is historically but never dramatically interesting: it's the kind of show which ought to be staged and then examined by students in the drama department of a mid-western American campus. Thrown into the Aldwych, where the shadows and the memories are longer, it looks more than a little shaky if you go along expecting another unknown classic. If all you want is the occasional laugh, it might still be all right.

Half Marx

A Day in Hollywood, A Night in the Ukraine (on the stage of the New End Theatre in Hampstead) is an eccentric sort of movie addicts' treat. The first half (the *Day*) consists of an hour-long revue cobbled together by Dick Vosburgh from his apparently inexhaustible fund of vintage Hollywood rubbish. Thus we have songs, impressions, jokes about the moguls ('The trouble with *The Good Earth*,' said Louis B. Mayer, 'is that Chinese movies don't stay with you: an hour later you want to see another.') and a general hotchpotch which none the less deserves your attention if only for the sake of a song, hitherto unknown to me, entitled 'She's the Girlfriend of the Whirling Dervish but She's Giving Him the Runaround'.

This is real Denis Norden–Philip Jenkinson country: patchy, intermittently very funny, waspish ('When Zukor laughed, dust used to fall from his mouth'), required watching for people hooked on late-night television movies, and as a show considerably helped by some stunning Bette Davis and Katharine Hepburn impressions from the redoubtable Paddie O'Neil. Whether recalling Dorothy

Parker writing a Nelson Eddy musical ('Let me out of here, I'm as sane as you are') or merely noting that Hollywood was the place where mind-readers starved to death and where nothing was ever so wrong that six good writers couldn't fix it, this half of the evening forms the kind of entertainment which would run about thirty years in some off-Broadway piano bar.

Then, however, we get to the second half, which is both more ambitious and less successful: *A Night in the Ukraine* is, wait for it, Dick Vosburgh's adaptation of Chekhov's *The Bear* as it would have been performed by the Marx Brothers. Except of course that it wasn't. So what we have here is Sheila Steafel (as the wonderfully silent Harpo), John Bay (as Groucho) and Frank Lazarus (as Chico) camping their way through a shaky pastiche. By some eccentric accident of birth-timing, Mr Vosburgh never actually got to write for Groucho: his script here suggests, however, that he has spent about thirty years watching continuous screenings of *A Night at the Opera* and as a result he comes up with some very plausible dialogue (Chico: 'You live here?' Groucho: 'No, I came from Moscow.' Chico: 'Have a rough trip?' Groucho: 'No thanks, I just had one.'). But we are still dealing here with impressionists, and only Miss Steafel, she of the rubber face and the manic stare, really gets away with it, allowing her Harpo to go further and further over the top until finally she/he becomes the star turn of an evening which is otherwise somewhat secondhand.

For all that, I'd not be inclined to miss it: the Vosburgh show was the best thing about a lorrystruck and trainless London last week and, given the right small-scale theatre, I think it might achieve a West End life of its own for all those whose idea of heaven is being hit over the head with bound volumes of *Picturegoer*. Ian Davidson's production of a camp evening is deft and swift and loving, and that faint creaking you hear is the sound of Chekhov and Groucho turning, gently, in their respective graves.

On the main stage of the Royal Court, David Edgar's *Mary Barnes* is a remarkable documentary play based on a book by the lady of that name and subtitled *Accounts of a Journey through Madness*. When we first meet her on stage (she was also sitting in the audience at the first night, an eerie case of double vision) Mary Barnes is an apparently normal if tight-lipped staff nurse. A dotty outburst soon reveals that she's nothing of the sort: in an advanced state of what looks like schizophrenia (though the play is devoted to querying such easy identification tags) Miss Barnes has come to a South London psychiatric commune staffed by people who want to get patients away from drug-based hospital 'cures'. 'Curing,' says one of them later in the play, 'is something you do to bacon, not to people,' and Mr Edgar is concerned here with the alternative possibilities.

In this closed community (which in real life was R. D. Laing's Philadelphia Association) Edgar examines not only Mary Barnes, a central and crucial and stunning performance by Patti Love, but also the varying and various motives of those around her. An all-too-predictably stuffy family (mother and brother) are contrasted with the 'family' Mary has acquired through her illness, and though it may be thought that she was unusually lucky to have found no less than four psychiatrists ready and free to devote themselves to her case, Edgar's point is that they too, like Mary, are in fact trying to escape a real world where insanity has for too long been regarded as a clinical rather than a human problem.

This community (like that of the tent-builders in Storey's *The Contractor* or of the footballers in his *Changing Room*) rapidly acquires its own momentum and its own characters: there's the drop-out, the eccentric, the orthodox and the rebel, each of them coming into some sort of contact with Mary and either staying or going as a result of that contact, until at the last it is Mary who has become the central upholder of the community that was originally gathered to save her. The mission accomplished, there is no easy ending: but along the way there's a lot of hope and a lot of humour as well as one or two very nasty visual and verbal shocks. By any standards, 1979 has started with a major play and Peter Farago's production draws not only on Miss Love but also on superb support from Simon Callow and Katherine Kitovitz.

Court Jesters

The Royal Court has returned to one of its earlier and better traditions: alongside the pioneering of new writers, George Devine was always ready to look at a neglected classic (long before the present revival of interest in *The Changeling*, it was his 1961 rediscovery that made the names of Robert Shaw and Mary Ure) and now Stuart Burge in the wisest decision of his two-year management has come up with *The London Cuckolds*.

Written in 1681 'by Edward Ravenscroft, Gent' the play had its last known performance on stage at Covent Garden in 1782. Since then, despite some fervent Radio Three championing by Raymond Raikes, it has been totally ignored by the British theatre and it would be good to know how successive playreaders at the RSC and the National have managed to blind themselves to a minor but undoubted classic. For not only is *The London Cuckolds* the funniest revival in town, it also rates as the most interesting and worthwhile rediscovery since *Wild Oats*.

We have here two aldermen of the City (Alan Dobie and Roger Kemp) and one lawyer (Barry Stanton) all obsessed with the honour of their wives – an honour which is swiftly and well lost to a succession of lovers in a plot of infinite complexity. The result is a period *Bedroom Farce*, but one built like a steam engine so that, once fuelled, it gathers momentum and runs away with itself. Along the way, there are some marvellous set pieces: Loveday (Brian Protheroe) in love with one of the wives and knowing her to have a lover and a ready-cooked dinner hidden away in a cupboard, convinces her husband that by witchcraft he can summon up a meal. He thus gets fed, the lover gets to escape, and the wife has eventually to show Loveday her gratitude in bed. In these games husbands are not the only losers: one hopeful lover (Kenneth Cranham) gets himself wedged into a grating while chamber pots are emptied over him. Asked to relate what has happened to him later he merely murmurs, 'Fire, rape, confusion and misfortune,' as though they were daily occurrences, which of course is what they are in Ravenscroft's randily eccentric world.

Stephanie Beacham is rampant as one of the wives, Deborah Norton and Nina Thomas complete that unholy trinity, and there are superlative supporting turns from Christopher Hancock, as a misunderstood valet inclined to raise false alarms, and Michael Elphick as the drinker Townly ('a gentleman of the times, careless of women, but fortunate'). Ravenscroft writes with an acid elegance ('Forgive my excess of wonder – your growth and the smallpox have altered you quite') and his plot is one that even Feydeau or Travers might have marvelled at. This production would do considerable credit to a major subsidized theatre on a huge budget with a permanent company: for it to have come from the Court, where there are none of these advantages, is an added miracle. Hasten along.

At the Round House there's a chance to catch up with Ronald Harwood's splendid adaptation of *The Ordeal of Gilbert Pinfold*, a theatrical evening chiefly notable for Michael Hordern's grouchily superb portrayal of Evelyn Waugh. True, the production by Michael Elliott is less than perfect: for the opening scene, for instance, clearly modelled on Waugh's infamous BBC tele-interview with John Freeman, it is pretty unforgivable to have the actor playing the interviewer do an impersonation of Alan Whicker, and a shaky one at that. Once we get on to the ship, however, the Round House's new permanent stage comes into its own, and there is a genuinely frightening claustrophobia about Pinfold's cabin, scene of his mental collapse and, as he says with his usual understatement, 'hardly the Connaught'.

Though the novel must have appeared at first intractable, the play Harwood has fashioned from it is far and away his best, since it tells us both about the book and about Waugh. The original Manchester Royal Exchange cast give patchy support, but this is Hordern's evening and he makes the very best of it all.

If, as we smugly tell ourselves, we are the theatrical capital of the world, then how do we explain a fiasco like *Forty Love* which arrived at the Comedy last week and departed four days later, in my view not a moment too soon? Though it doesn't hold the record for the world's shortest run (there was a memorable 1930s revue which closed at its first interval), the mystery about *Forty Love* is how it ever got into the West End at all. The original star, Bernard Cribbins, having been taken to hospital (though not apparently as a result of having read the script) his part was taken over by the author Leslie Randall who acts fractionally worse than he writes. A lumbering, mindless and aimless attempt to do an English Neil Simon farce, this might just have worked for about fifteen minutes on a bad ITV Monday night. Stretched across two interminable hours it was an absolute disgrace to the theatre and to the management involved (Paul Elliott – we name the guilty party). It also raises the question of whether we need some kind of minimum acceptability test before a show gets into the West End: the major subsidized companies have their own fail-safe system of artistic direction, but for as long as central London theatres are as easy to rent as flats, there remains the danger of a catastrophe like this. It didn't just lose £30,000: it lost the goodwill of every theatregoer unfortunate enough to see it.

Dark Victory

The shadows are darkening on the Ayckbourn lawns. His latest London play, *Joking Apart* (at the Globe) may not be as knockabout-hilarious as *Bedroom Farce*, nor as cunningly contrived as the *Norman Conquests* but for all that it's a haunting and intermittently very funny account of the awfulness of perfection. Richard and Anthea are the perfect couple: rich, successful, glamorous, instinctively lucky, charming, naturally elegant, infinitely kind, eternally considerate. Blessed with clever and lovely children, they live in a large house to which they invite, over the play's twelve-year time span, a group of friends who are slowly but surely (and in one case quite literally) driven mad by the lucky couple's everlasting goodness.

The play is, as Ayckbourn himself concedes, one of his 'winter' works, a category into which he also places the infinitely less successful *Just Between Ourselves* and the patchy *Ten Times Table*; written in a Scarborough December 'whilst the North Sea storms hurtled round the house and slates cascaded from the roof', and during which the author suddenly came to realize that his son was already eighteen, *Joking Apart* is therefore not the most carefree of plays. Perhaps for that reason, it has had a distinctly grudging reception from many of my colleagues who appear to want nothing more from Mr Ayckbourn than everlasting rewrites of the *Norman Conquests*.

The clown who wants to play Hamlet is admittedly not a new figure in our theatre, and many comic dramatists (Neil Simon to name but six) have come badly unstuck when turning to something more serious: but Ayckbourn here goes from strength to strength. True, his central characters, though admirably played by Christopher Cazenove and Alison Steadman, suffer from a certain invisibility: but then the play is not really about them at all. It is about their devastating effect on the others: on Sven for instance, the Finnish business partner (immortally played by Robert Austin) who is finally given a heart attack by his attempt to beat Richard at just one thing, tennis, even though Richard is at the time predictably playing him with the wrong hand. And on the loony local vicar (Julian Fellowes, hovering perilously close to parody but staying just the right side of that fence) who falls hopelessly in love with

Anthea. And on his wife, who by the end of the evening is a basket case.

It is their final realization of their own total defeat that is the most chilling part of this evening: when Sven, spokesman for the unsuccessful, finally confronts the golden couple's equally golden daughter and tells her that she has been born 'not with a silver spoon in your mouth, but with a whole canteen' it is an admission of the eventual unfairness of life. In earlier Ayckbourns, the escape routes are left open, even if they only lead (as in *Bedroom Farce*) to the joys of eating pilchards out of a tin in bed. Here, they are all sealed off: the golden couple get progressively more bronzed, the others simply fall apart mentally, physically, spiritually, even vocally.

This may well not prove to be the most commercial of the Ayckbourns, but in the final reckoning I think it will live a lot longer than most: the mechanics are less obtrusive than elsewhere, the characters more thoughtfully drawn, the jokes more integrated. The production is also all his own work.

Sherlock and Fats

'People, my dear Watson, tend to remember a one-legged man travelling through the streets of London with a pygmy': who else but Sherlock Holmes, back in the West End in the most scenically lavish and spectacular show since Beerbohm Tree set fire to Her Majesty's in an attempt to lend credence to his Nero. *The Crucifer of Blood* (at the Theatre Royal, Haymarket) comes in fact from Broadway, where it was presumably inspired by the success of such other revisitations from the past as the Dracula shows: here a young American author-director, Paul Giovanni, has had the brilliant wheeze of transferring not a single Conan Doyle story to the stage but a kind of amalgam of them. His play is fundamentally *The Sign of Four*, to which he's added other extracts from Conan Doyle's writing in the *Strand Magazine* stories.

Purists will doubtless object: but as a child's guide to Holmes and Watson, incorporating the best of their adventures and eccentric personal relationship, the evening is an out and out triumph. It opens on the battlements of the Red Fort at Agra in 1857; the British are under siege, a dastardly Wazir is hiding up in the hills and the

black devils are everywhere. Suddenly, the Wazir's jewels are pur-
loined: mysterious deaths occur ('This curse business – is there
anything to it?') and hey presto we're back at 221b Baker Street
thirty years later. There Holmes (a pipe-smoking, cocaine-taking
performance from Keith Michell) and Watson (not the old
Hollywood buffoon but a young romantic played by Dennis Lill,
he who was 'Lillie's Edward VII for ITV) are confronted by a
distraught Susan Hampshire. Her father has gone spare on receipt of
a blood-soaked piece of parchment, there's a madman in a wheelchair out at Maidenhead, the treasure has disappeared and there's
this pygmy up a tree blowing poisoned darts. And still we haven't
even reached the interval.

Along the way we also get a complete thunderstorm for which
the lightning strikes from the back of the dress circle across the
audience and forward on to the stage, ships passing each other on the
foggy Thames, a scene in an opium den and a denouement for
which Miss Hampshire changes out of her hitherto virginal white
dress into a flaming red velvet number, thereby indicating that
something dashed rum is still afoot. Oh yes, and just as you think it
has all finally been solved, a man runs in bearing tidings of this giant
rat he's seen in Sumatra.

But what makes Giovanni's production such a splendid evening
out is not only that you can see where your ticket money has gone;
it's also that he's held the whole show together easily on the right
side of parody (not a feat always achieved by the recent Dracula
producers) and that he's elicited some superlative performances, not
only from Dennis Lill but also from Edward Petherbridge and John
Quentin as the two Indian army officers who start it all. An Easter
holiday must for children of all ages.

Feeling distinctly outnumbered by its enthusiasts, I have been
trying to like *Ain't Misbehavin'* (now at Her Majesty's) ever since I
first saw it on Broadway last year. I still hate it. The show seems to
have been put together by Murray Horwitz and Richard Maltby Jr
purely as an excuse for the singing of thirty of the songs of Fats
Waller. That's not to say thirty songs by Fats Waller: some he
merely made famous as singer and/or pianist, some he wrote the
music for, virtually never does he seem to have been a lyricist. The
songs are admittedly done with vivacity and a certain raucous
charm by five singers (on and off stools) and one pianist, together
with a backing group of six jazzmen, but nowhere in this long

evening is there any attempt to explain who Waller was, where he came from, what he believed in or why he should matter enough for us to spend two hours in the company of songs he once sang.

Unlike some of my more austere colleagues I happen to love the songbook format: shows like *Cowardy Custard, Cole* and *Side by Side by Sondheim* taught me more about Coward, Porter and Sondheim than I would ever have gathered from any one individual musical or biography, and I believe that at the end of those concert evenings audiences went out into the night with a genuine knowledge of the making of a songwriter.

Not here; if anything, I knew less about Fats Waller at the end of *Ain't Misbehavin'* than I knew at its outset, and nowhere along the way was there any attempt to set him in any kind of social or musical or personal or national or even historical context. So what are we left with? A show which works infinitely better on its own original-cast recording, a show which is no more dramatic or theatrical than a Radio Two concert, a show which in short doesn't need to be seen at all.

Enthusiasts tell me this doesn't matter a jot: that *Ain't Misbehavin'* is not meant to be about Waller but about the effect he had on people and the atmosphere he created around his music: the trouble is that never having seen the gentleman, who died in 1943 at the age of thirty-nine, I have no way of knowing whether Maltby's production has anything at all to do with Waller or not.

Will Power

Cymbeline (RSC, Stratford-on-Avon) is the impossible one. Three and a half hours of long-lost sons, men hiding in chests, mistaken identity, murder, visionary Gods descending from the heavens, war, romance, drugs and a final happy ending in which so many loose ends have to be tied that the last scene plays all of forty minutes. It is consequently not often revived, and the last two Stratford productions have taken easier ways out: in 1974 some heavy cuts were made, and in 1962 it was built around a star turn from Vanessa Redgrave.

For the new production (the last on Stratford's main stage by David Jones before he starts this autumn to build his American

Cymbeline Bob Peck *as Cloten*, Ben Kingsley *as Iachimo*, Roger Rees *as Posthumus*, Judi Dench *as Imogen*

Shakespeare Company in Brooklyn) there are no such simple solutions. Instead of the usual woad-painted fairy tale, or indeed any real attempt to make a confusing narrative simple, Mr Jones has chosen to tell the play just like it is, conflicting styles and all.

The result is *Reader's Digest* Shakespeare: highlights from *Romeo and Juliet, Othello, Lear, Timon, Twelfth Night* and *As You Like It* all cobbled together into an epic folly which, typically, contains some of the very best of all Shakespearian verse. *Cymbeline* is the script Tennyson asked to have buried with him in the coffin, not to be forgotten but presumably to be remembered. It's the one that contains 'Fear no more the heat of the sun' and 'Boldness be my friend' but it's also the one in which a character desperately trying to unravel the denouement is forced to begin a speech 'O Gods, I forgot one thing'. It is in short a patchy affair, written by the Bard when, like his Prospero, he was nearing the end of his creative powers and eager to start messing around with them for their own sake.

The new production opens with Griffith Jones, elder statesman now of the RSC, on a bare white stage being told a story: within seconds we are deep into comedy, tragedy, intrigue, poison, passion, a father cruel and a stepdame false. Not only is the present plot complex beyond all belief, but to have a hope of following it we have first to grasp a still more complicated sequence of events which took place years ago. Bernard Shaw thought it all 'vulgar, foolish, offensive, indecent and exasperating beyond all tolerance' which of course *Cymbeline* is; it's also funny, touching, magical and unlike anything else Shakespeare ever wrote, no matter how often scholars try to link it to *Pericles*.

Whole acts here revolve around moles being conveniently discovered on left breasts; whole battles are fought apparently in downtown Milford Haven. This is perhaps our only truly local epic, Britain's answer to *Ben-Hur*.

Nature is perceived in a state of imbalance: court life is wild; the wild woods are tame; the universe is visibly cracking up; and the golden lads and lasses must, as chimney sweepers, come to dust. I think maybe *Cymbeline* needs to be a musical.

But the RSC are never better than when faced with this impossible kind of challenge, and they go after it hell for leather. Judi Dench as Imogen, Bob Peck as the idiot Cloten, Roger Rees as Posthumus (asked to begin and end the action, but left off stage for fully two hours in between) and Ben Kingsley as a wonderful evil Iachimo have all grasped one essential – the only way *Cymbeline* can work is if each scene is played true to itself. Coherence and continuity are no more relevant here than they would be to a conjuror who having produced a rabbit from a hat then proceeds to saw his wife in half. What matters is the achieving of single effects in their own time and for their own purpose, and that Jones' production does brilliantly.

Talking of the rehabilitation of impossible plays, Manchester's Royal Exchange company have brought to the London Round House, but for a month only, Michael Elliott's stunning production of T. S. Eliot's *The Family Reunion*. This, you'll recall, is the one about Harry versus the Eumenides: Harry (Edward Fox) is the patrician son who returns to his ancestral home convinced he has pushed his wife into the sea, only then to discover even darker family secrets and to encounter the Fates themselves who (for the

Round House) surround him and the stage like two-tier ghosts in long white sheets. At its worst, the play is out of Dodie Smith by way of Enid Bagnold. Tynan, no great lover of Eliot, said it was about 'the cerebral acne in the monastery garden' and many of his readers thought that a quotation from the play which it very nearly is: we are told in the course of the dialogue of 'chilly pretences in the silent bedroom' and of 'clocks stopping in the dark' and of 'casual waste in an orderly universe' and of 'seasons of stifled sorrow' and of the maze in the garden being too reminiscent of the maze in the brain. It's a play of guilt and expiation in which people are forever finding themselves on the other side of despair: yet by an act of almost superhuman willpower Mr Elliott has convinced an incredibly strong cast (Fox, Pauline Jameson as the mother, Avril Elgar as the eerie aunt, Joanna David as the cousin, William Fox and Jeffry Wickham as the bluff uncles) to believe in the play and therefore to make us do the same. Again the Round House has proved a perfect home for the best of Manchester's theatre.

Still Afraid

James Saunders' *Bodies* (now at the Ambassadors, but first reviewed here last March when it opened at Hampstead) improves on further acquaintance; it is the closest the British theatre has yet come to performing the game of 'Get the Guests' which Albee invented for his *Who's Afraid of Virginia Woolf?* two decades and a continent away. The guests in this case are David and Helen (David Burke and Angela Down) who nine years ago had extramarital affairs with their hosts Mervyn and Anne (Dinsdale Landen and Gwen Watford). That is to say, in case you were visualizing something sexually more eccentric, that Anne had the affair with David and Helen with Mervyn. But since those halcyon wife-swapping days of yore something very strange has happened to David and Helen: they have been living in America, and while there have undergone a violent if unspecified form of therapy which has relieved them of all their neuroses but also of nearly all other human feelings. Now they are back, semi-lobotomized and thus sitting targets for Mervyn who in Dinsdale Landen's epic, raging, hilarious and massively powerful performance sets out to prove in the course of their uneasily shared evening that even the worst sort of feelings are better than no feelings at all.

True, this is not virgin theatrical territory: Peter Shaffer's *Equus*, you may recall, was built around precisely the same thesis. But Saunders writes with a forceful kind of elegance, rounding his dialogue and his thoughts like a master craftsman and thus making his infinitely careful play stand head and shoulders above a currently vacuous West End. *Bodies* needs to be seen for Landen alone: seldom can so fundamentally light a comedian have been given a role which allows him to rage like Lear and camp like Butley within the space of a few long speeches. The pity of it is that he is not given any worthy opponents: though Gwen Watford as his wife is given a superb opening monologue, her character is then shoved back on the shelf marked 'bitchy wife' and left there undeveloped, while David and Helen are by the very nature of their American affliction unable to challenge Mervyn save with platitudes.

True, the play is about something more: it's about one of Mervyn's pupils, an unseen lad who has driven a motorcycle very fast into a brick wall and whose flickering life thus becomes a sort of focus for Mervyn's arguments. *Bodies* is never less than compelling: what stops it being a great play as well as a great vehicle is that it never really gets off the Scrabble board. David Burke and Angela Down are excellent at looking mentally vacuum-cleaned by their therapy, and around them Landen prowls like some manic evangelist for the imperfect society. It's an award-deserving performance in a stylish play.

Writing this page from New York about four years ago I suggested that the musical *Chicago* (now at the Cambridge in Peter James' production from the Sheffield Crucible) was Broadway's last trumpet-call, the show with a little bit of everything from every other Broadway and Hollywood hit you could think of and then some. I still think the clue to the whole enterprise lies in a lyric from the big 'Razzle Dazzle' number which goes 'Long as you keep 'em way off balance/How can they spot you got no talents?' and that *Chicago* is sleight of hand, a massive circus trick which happens so fast and so noisily that you forget to notice there isn't anybody up there on the high wire at all.

But the triumph of the English production is that for the first time in my experience it is actually a great deal better than the Broadway original: where that looked simply tacky and derivative, Peter

James and his Sheffield company have managed to instil a Brechtian sense of purpose which gives the lie to the old theory that nobody can do American musicals as well as Americans.

The writers of *Chicago*, John Kander and Fred Ebb, are at their best in single moments or numbers which don't have a lot to do with each other. There is certainly a good basic idea here, to show that Chicago in the twenties got the gangsters it deserved and that if you treat Capone or Pretty Boy Floyd as media stars then you may as well set their murders in a showbiz circus. The result is a sort of vaudeville about Death Row, highlighted by some good lines ('We broke up because of artistic differences: he saw himself as alive, I saw him as dead') and some big-band numbers in the convention of *Mame* and *Dolly* and all the other staircase shows.

But there are only so many times you can stop a show that has never really started, and *Chicago* suffers terribly from divided loyalties: are we in fact witnessing a musical about Chicago itself, or about all those Cagney–Bogart 'Roaring Twenties' films, or about the Busby Berkeley dance routines that coincided with them, or about the old Broadway habit of covering everything, even murder, in stardust? The writers seem never really to have decided that, and the show suffers from their indecision. For all that, I'd not have missed Ben Cross doing 'Razzle Dazzle', Don Fellows doing 'Mister Cellophane', Hope Jackman doing 'When You're Good to Mama' or Antonia Ellis and Jenny Logan doing 'Nowadays'. All in all, a show in which the parts are a lot better than the whole and the numbers fail to add up, great though many of them are individually.

Maugham Rendered

When, soon after the death of Somerset Maugham, a faintly scandalous account of his homosexual life was published with considerable profit by Beverley Nichols, somebody asked Noël Coward for a reaction. 'I think it is lovely for dear Beverley,' replied the Master, 'to have discovered all that gold down in Somerset.'

Since then Somerset gold has been somewhat scarce, but it is good to report that in their continuing hour of industrial trouble the National Theatre company have managed to dig up a little more of the precious substance: their current Lyttelton stage production of Maugham's *For Services Rendered* (directed by Michael Rudman), while something rather less than the revival of a great play, is for all that one of the most fascinating evenings the 1979 theatre has yet given us.

Though this was not (despite some misleading current publicity) by any means Maugham's last play, it is true that during the writing of it he had announced his imminent retirement from the theatre. The year was 1932, and Maugham had made a number of discoveries, not least that he much preferred being a novelist, where the money was a great deal better and the interference of others a great deal less evident.

Unlike his earlier successes (*The Letter, The Sacred Flame* and others mostly premiered by my grandmother Gladys Cooper during her management of the Playhouse Theatre in the late 1920s) *For Services Rendered* is a defiantly uncommercial piece: 'I expected nothing of it,' Maugham wrote later, 'and during rehearsals I amused myself by devising the way in which it could have been written to achieve popularity . . . the characters had only to be sentimentalized a little and everything might have ended happily. But that would not have been the play I wished to write.'

It is a pity that in a batch of more irrelevant quotations from Maugham running through the programme the National has chosen to ignore that one altogether, for it tells us a good deal about Maugham's frame of mind at the time. The play he wished to write was as defiantly anti-British as Coward's *Cavalcade* (written two years earlier) was defiantly pro-British. Maugham's message to the nation was that the whole bloody thing had gone wrong, that the First War had been fought largely in vain and that there was another awaiting just around the corner. Not surprisingly, that was not a message the theatre-going audience of 1932 wished to hear and the play, though it made a star of Flora Robson and established both Ralph Richardson and Cedric Hardwicke, survived a mere seventy-eight performances on its first outing.

It is set at the home of a wealthy solicitor in a mythical Kentish country town called (not I think irrelevantly, since the theme is ultimately one of lack of decision or purpose) Rambleston. He (Leslie Sands) has a wife (Jean Anderson) and three daughters (Barbara Ferris, Elizabeth Romilly and Alison Fiske); there's also the usual Maughamesque doctor-narrator (Robin Bailey), a drunken son-in-law (Ian Hogg), a blind son (Harold Innocent), a bankrupt war hero (John Quayle) and a lecherous nouveau-riche neighbour (Peter Jeffrey) and his bossy wife (Phyllida Law). That, give or take a maid, is the entire company and at first it looks as if we might be in for an English countryside rerun of *The Three Sisters*, all longing for the big city and an escape from the claustrophobia of home.

But it soon becomes clear that Maugham has a darker purpose: the blind son, the drunk and the bankrupt are all walking wounded from the First War. Now, fourteen years after Armistice, society is being asked to cope with them and society in the shape of the solicitor is refusing. There is apparently a time limit on those kind of debts and time is up: the 1930s are not a time for casualties, however honourable, and what we instead get is the unacceptable face of all those Dodie Smith–Douglas-Home comedies about upper-crust family life: *For Services Rendered* is, in short, *Dear Octopus* turned rancid. It's a cynical, bitter, prophetic, intriguing, unwieldy stage machine in which the decline of post-World War I England is mirrored through the affairs of one quasi-typical family.

By the end of the play we have one daughter gone mad (though her final loony singing of 'God Save the King' is oddly muted here), one gone off to evil ways in the big city, mother about to die but father wonderfully unaware of the wreckage littered around his own hearth: 'Well,' he says jovially in a final speech so heavily ironic as to be almost unmanageable, 'I must say it's very nice to have a cup of tea by one's own fireside . . . this old England of ours isn't done yet, and I for one believe in it and all it stands for.'

Seen in the week of a General Election, in a theatre surrounded by picket lines, *For Services Rendered* seemed a curious historical leftover, but Maugham's point in 1932 was that England, his England, was in fact already done for – only the residents appeared not to have noticed. *The Times*, which in 1932 was still appearing with some regularity, thought that Maugham had 'severely underrated the healing powers of time'; we at *Punch* thought the play 'tragic, memorable, full of the intolerable constrictions of human bondage and deeply moving for all its angry bitterness'. I'm inclined to think that we, rather than *The Times*, got it about right.

Bent Double

As the curtain rises on *Bent*, Martin Sherman's chilling new play at the Royal Court, it is clear that we are in a flat owned or at least inhabited by a homosexual nightclub dancer and his friend Max: the time and place are left unspecified, and for the first few minutes it looks as though we are in for a queer rerun of *The Odd Couple*.

But then it becomes all too clear: the year is 1934, the place Berlin, and it's the morning after Hitler's notorious homosexual purge in the Night of the Long Knives. Immediately therefore, Max and his friend are on the run, and much of the rest of the first act is taken up with the unacceptable face of *Cabaret* – nightclub scenes from Berlin life intercut with indications that to be homosexual in that time and that country is only fractionally easier than being Jewish.

For a while, this remains a comedy, albeit a very black one: the scene on a park bench between Max (Ian McKellen) and his uncle (Richard Gale) who, though also homosexual, refuses to come out of the closet but cannot resist looking over the 'fluff' is a little comic masterpiece, and Sherman's throwaway references to Berlin ('I know pain is very chic here right now, but I still don't like it') are, I suspect, closer to the truth of that time than many of Isherwood's.

Thus, by the end of Act One, we have two innocent queens bickering, bitching and finally bludgeoning their way through German society. All the way to Dachau.

By Act Two we are no longer in some uncensored version of *Some Like It Hot*: we are in a concentration camp where to be homosexual is now actually worse than to be Jewish: Max, forced to beat his friend to death by the guards, is now a determined survivor in a camp built to defeat survival. It is 1936 ('We'll miss the Olympics') and in a deadly second act a curious love story develops between McKellen as Max and Tom Bell as the taciturn Horst.

In the end, *Bent* is a play about straightening up and admitting what you are even in the most hostile surroundings imaginable: there is no way the play can be recommended as a cheerful evening out for all the family, but I doubt that there are two finer performances in London at the moment than those of McKellen and Bell in Robert Chetwyn's production. I also doubt that there has ever been a better play about homosexuality; it is *The Boys in the Band* rewritten in blood.

Minority Verdicts

Right, friends, this is it: it's me or them. For some weeks past I have been coming to the slow but sure conclusion that my critical colleagues along Fleet Street have begun to lose their marbles, and the last few days have proved the clincher. Not only have they collectively savaged a very funny new David Mercer nostalgia piece at Hampstead, they've also treated Simon Gray's eccentric plunge into the somewhat stagnant *Waters of the Moon* as though it was a major new play instead of a pallid rerun of some earlier and better work by Maugham and N. C. Hunter.

Let's start with the Mercer: called *Then and Now* (Hampstead Theatre) it's an account of the past and present tensions of two people immaculately well played at twenty and fifty by Mike Gwilym and Morag Hood. He is the cynical son of a dead miner ('Will Socialism invent a pit that won't kill miners?'), she an aristocratic filly whose mother considered it was middle-class to think about the future. They meet in Yorkshire in 1945; by V.E. Night they're in bed together at Claridge's, and by the time we leave them thirty-four years later he is a much-married surgeon and she a nymphomaniac archaeologist.

What Mercer is on about here, and not for the first time, is the collapse of postwar Socialist ideals: but what makes *Then and Now* so hugely enjoyable is that he's decided to go for the laughs as well as the despair. Thus we get a series of sketches from postwar British life which add up to a stylish comedy about the havoc of time. In the end, nothing matters half so much as nothing: the surgeon doesn't care about his patients ('They're not bodies to me – just an endless series of threats to my reputation') and the archaeologist doesn't care about her ruins, not even those she herself makes of the people around her. Togetherness is a bad joke ('I've been taking a look at our marriage.' 'Oh, does it show?') and Mercer, like Pinter in the not dissimilar *Betrayal* and Hare in *Plenty*, has constructed each of his scenes like a short story, complete in itself but still adding to a greater whole. Robin Lefevre's production (like his recent Hampstead *Bodies*) should be sure of a longer West End life later.

I wish I could care half as much for Simon Gray's *Close of Play* (Lyttelton); given the full National treatment (production by

Harold Pinter, cast headed by Michael Redgrave, John Standing, Anna Massey, Michael Gambon, Zena Walker and Lynn Farleigh) this turns out to be one of those skeleton-in-the-closet unhappy family pieces that used to turn up at the Haymarket thirty years ago with titles like *A Hundred in the Shade* or *A Day by the Sea*, vehicles primarily constructed to give ageing *grandes dames* a good scene each and Felix Aylmer a telling role as the Judge. Clearly Gray and Pinter would like us to think they've got something more here: to that end there are some tricky changes, a momentary lurch into Christopher Fry, and a hesitancy in explaining to us whether Sir Michael Redgrave (silent in an armchair all evening) is actually alive, dead or merely dying.

In a hugely welcome return to the stage (and in what can only be called the Lewis Casson part) Sir Michael is cast as an old Professor each member of whose family feels obliged to come on stage alone for a 'big scene' and reveal dark and terrible secrets. One son is a BBC alcoholic, another a faithless doctor, a third dead because that was what he most wanted to be; the second wife is a gibbering bore immortally well played by Annie Leon, and of the daughters one is a compulsive mother who wishes her children dead, another a guilt-ridden novelist and the third just rotting away. Mr Gray's message would seem to be that first there is Life and then there is Death and there's precious little anyone can do about either except · maybe try not to hate each other.

As portraits of terrible filial gatherings go, Giles Cooper did it better in *Happy Family*; as for anything more significant, it does Mr Gray's play no service to stage it on the same boards and in the same repertoire as Maugham's *For Services Rendered*. True, Gray is an acidly funny writer ('Sodomy, buggery, public schools are much more fun that state schools. Nothing furtive or passionate in state schools. Nothing to prepare you for life.') and Redgrave's basilisk stare is wonderfully sustained, to a point of such blank distaste that you begin to wonder if he is viewing his family or the play itself. Following this and Gielgud in *Half-Life*, I can't imagine why the National don't now go the whole hog and revive *The Holly and the Ivy* with *Dear Octopus* for matinees.

War Games

Michael Herr is a thirty-nine-year-old American freelance journalist who went to Vietnam to cover the war for *Esquire* ('*Esquire*? What are you here for? To tell them what we're wearing?') and ten years later turned his notes from the battlefield into a book called *Dispatches*. Sections of that book have been used by Coppola for his *Apocalypse Now*: both film and book find some sort of a starting point in Conrad's *Heart of Darkness*. Now Bill Bryden and his permanent company on the National's Cottesloe stage have put together what is effectively a magic-lantern slide show of the book. Fragments of dialogue, sketches for a scenario too horrible to contemplate, hospital and trench and war-zone scenes, have all been nailed into some sort of shape, and the result (which I saw at a preview) is the unacceptable face of *M.A.S.H.*

Chaos is what we have here, but if every war gets the play it deserves then *Dispatches* is right for the shambles that was Vietnam; none of your *Journey's End* poetry here, just a collage of limbs and limbo. In so far as it can be held together, it is by Jack Shepherd as the man from *Esquire* who went to cover a war and found instead that it had covered him. In a performance remarkable even by his standards, Shepherd drifts through a waking nightmare, stumbling up against such familiar figures as General Westmorland and Sean Flynn, the actor's son who seems to have thought the whole affair was just another movie through which he could journey on a motorbike, an easy rider on a road all too obviously mined.

Other characters are inevitably stereotyped: the black, the cockney, the druggy, the lady reporter all form part of an ever-changing background in which death and madness are the only constants. The triumph of Bryden's production doesn't have much to do with characterization or dialogue from the book, but it has a great deal to do with capturing for the stage the mood of Americans in Nam, a mood perhaps best known to English readers not from Herr at all but from the late Nick Tomalin's classic 'The General Goes Zapping Charlie Cong'. In the end *Dispatches* is a catastrophic tapestry of confusion and irresponsibility; in theatre terms it's also one of the best things the National has yet done.

Mickey's Mouse

There was an audible groan around the West End last week at the news that the Palladium's triumphant return to *The King and I* (of which more in a paragraph or three) is to be followed by London revivals this autumn of *My Fair Lady, Hello Dolly!* and *Oklahoma!* Presumably the thinking on Broadway is that if we can send them Bruce Forsyth, they are justified in sending us just about anything.

Yet, sadly, the general critical hostility to musicals in this country is such that not only do we fail to recognize great old musicals when we get given them, we also fail to recognize great new ones. For every Rodgers and Hammerstein retread that hits town there are predictable queries about the whereabouts of the great musicals of today. Typically, when one did actually open here in the very same week as *The King and I*, few critics bothered to celebrate the fact.

But *Flowers for Algernon* (at the Queen's) is a great little musical and it is at least fairly new; true, the novel by Daniel Keyes on which it is based has been around America for a decade or more, and has already been used for a film called *Charly* which won Cliff Robertson an Oscar in 1968. But Charles Strouse (who did the music for *Bye Bye Birdie* and *Applause* and *Annie* among many other Broadway blockbusters) and David Rogers have done such a superb conversion job, and Michael Crawford is so marvellously cast and used in Peter Coe's production (one which originated in Canada) that *Algernon* is one of the very best things about the West End this summer.

It's not, at first sight, an obvious subject for a musical: the central figure is a mentally retarded baker's boy who risks a new kind of brain surgery, becomes a genius, and then finds himself regressing to his original state and in danger of losing even the memory of what it was like to be brilliant. All along, this progress is forecast by that of a mouse called Algernon who has undergone the same kind of surgery; together, man and mouse struggle their way through a huge steel maze which becomes the focus of Lawrence Schafer's dazzling set. In the end, of course, the two of them, Charlie and Algernon, do a number together which becomes an object lesson in the art of the musical – not since Gene Kelly danced with a cartoon mouse in a Hollywood movie thirty years ago has there been anything like it, and this mouse is real.

Crawford himself has never been better: abandoning the more obvious lunacies of 'Some Mothers Do 'Ave 'Em' he charts Charlie's mental progress and regress with infinite care, from the first day at the clinic ('Dear Progress Report, I report no progress') through to the final and terrible realization that for every step forward he's about to take two back. In the end, *Algernon* is an infinitely touching and immaculately crafted special plea for the taking of mental-health risks, and for those of my colleagues who raised smug doubts about the borderlines of showbiz good taste I have but one question: how come those same doubts were not raised by those same critics at the time of Peter Nichols' *Day in the Death of Joe Egg*? Is it just possible that there is still one law for the straight play and another for the musical?

And so to the Palladium for an evening with Yul Brynner. *The King and I* was of course the show which thirty years ago made him a star, though only after Rodgers and Hammerstein had tried and failed to get Alfred Drake, their original *Oklahoma!* lead, for the role. They also briefly considered Rex Harrison who'd played the part in a non-musical film version of *Anna and the King of Siam*, which raises another intriguing thought. What we have here is the age-old story of the Victorian governess who goes out to educate the children of the King of Siam and stays to educate him too: a strong-willed woman overpowering a still stronger-willed man. Does that not suggest to you not only the plot of *The Sound of Music* (which R&H did a decade later) but also the plot of *My Fair Lady*? *Pygmalion* would of course always have existed; but would it have become a musical had it not been for the success of *The King and I*?

And another thing: most of my colleagues would have you believe that *The King and I* is just another relic, a kind of leftover 'Tale from the Siamese 'Woods'. Not in fact. For its time (1951), it was as brave and experimental and revolutionary a show as *Flowers for Algernon*. No previous musical had allowed its central character to die lengthily and on stage; no previous musical had allowed its hero and heroine to go through an entire three-hour score without a love scene or even a kiss. Only twelve shows ever ran longer on Broadway, and it could be argued that this one has been running somewhere ever since that first performance; the career of the show is a mirror of Brynner's rise to stardom. When it first opened Gertrude Lawrence was alone above the title and he some way beneath it; a decade later, for the film, he was above the title but co-starred with Deborah Kerr. For London, a decade later still, he's alone above the title with Virginia McKenna, who has a great deal more of the show and the score to carry, now well beneath it. Such is progress, but Brynner remains good value for money. He turns in an infinitely royal performance, appearing at times to be not so much the star of the show as some immensely distinguished foreign dignitary paying it a State visit.

Grand Hotel

'My God,' muttered a distinguished West End impresario sitting in front of me at the first night of the National Theatre's new production of *Undiscovered Country*, as yet another extra came on stage wearing a dress that would not have disgraced Anna Neagle in her prime, 'I couldn't afford to put a star into clothes like that, let alone somebody who's only going to speak a line and a half.' And sure enough, after a long winter of economic and industrial discontent, Peter Wood's staging of the Schnitzler marriage-go-round on the open Olivier boards does look like a gesture of pre-revolutionary aristocratic defiance, an immense show of monetary strength involving thirty characters in search of two authors.

For what we have here is Schnitzler adapted by Tom Stoppard and played by a hugely starry cast headed by Dorothy Tutin, John Wood (back from a year on Broadway), Michael Bryant, Anna Carteret and Joyce Redman, all parading through some vastly elegant garden and hotel lobby settings by William Dudley. But why? What has convinced one of the strongest production teams in town that this is the play on which to spend their energies? There is of course the old Everest argument, 'because it's there'; but so too are other and better Schnitzler plays, notably the *Anatol* sequence. True, *Undiscovered Country*, though premiered simultaneously in nine European cities in October 1911, has never before been seen over here, so what we also have is a Grand National First. And, if you accept the reference-library theory of a National Theatre, which argues that certain writers need to be 'made available' there, then Schnitzler is worth a shelf or two.

Then again, it's possible that in Schnitzler's long, languid tracts of semicircular dialogue Stoppard has found some kind of challenge, though lines like 'He wouldn't have been seen dead with a suicide note' suggest that this may be a somewhat free translation. Or it's even possible that their success with *Tales from the Vienna Woods* a year or two back has given the National management a taste for building immense productions on shaky foundations, so that in the end the staging is all. But none of that can disguise the fact that what we have here resembles nothing so much as bits of *Ivanov* and *Hotel Paradiso* cobbled together on a bad afternoon by Noël Coward.

At the play's centre is Hofreiter (John Wood), a successful industrialist whose friends have a habit of dying in vaguely mysterious circumstances; he and his wife (Dorothy Tutin) seem to be involved in an everlasting kind of mixed doubles and *Undiscovered Country*, if it's about anything, must be about the games people played in a generation which had time to kill and people to kill too. Sexual games, social games, financial games, word games: all are played with a lazy kind of elegance by people who seem to wish they had either something better to do or less time to do it in. By the third of five acts we've left the Hofreiters' garden and travelled to a Dolomite hotel lobby for an hour or so of undiluted Vicki Baum. Characters, some already familiar, some totally new, drift in and out, use the fully functioning lift, give us a line or two into their personalities and then drift off again, presumably to board the Ship of Fools.

Never mind the plot, feel the aimlessness: even the roses have stopped bothering to grow, and by the time (two and a half hours into a three-hour evening) that Schnitzler decides to pull it all together and give us a duel and some sort of resolution, there is a terrible danger that we are well past caring. The performances are, as we have every right to expect in such a showcase evening, superb: not only Tutin and Wood (the latter finally stung into a fight to the death with a youth whose crime is not just the seduction of Tutin but more importantly being a youth) but Bryant as the hotelier, Redman as the actress-mother and John Harding as a local Viennese twit of the year are all collectively and severally superb. But it still isn't enough.

Word Plays

'If it goes on beyond half-past ten,' says one critic to another in Tom Stoppard's 1968 *Real Inspector Hound*, 'it's self-indulgent'; his *Dogg's Hamlet*, newly arrived at the Collegiate Theatre near Euston, barely makes it from eight to eight-forty but must be regarded as the most self-indulgent thing he's ever done. It forms the curtain-raiser to an infinitely better piece called *Cahoot's Macbeth* and though there has been a half-hearted attempt to make you think there's only one play here (principally by shifting one character from the first play through to the second) I'd remind you that *Dogg's Hamlet* has in fact been around in one form or another for the past five years. Performed once on the pavement outside the National Theatre, it seemed just about adequate if you happened to be passing at the time and in no particular hurry; done now before paying customers it seems pretty unforgivable, though hedged around with so many good causes (the returning of the Collegiate to mainstream theatres and the launching of Ed Berman's BARC, an Anglo-American repertory company who have broken through the usual Equity barriers and plan to perform the show across both nations) that it's hard to separate the criticism from the charity.

All that said, *Dogg's Hamlet* remains a one-joke show, the joke being that you can do *Hamlet* in ninety seconds instead of four hours; had this been done in perhaps *Beyond the Fringe* or one of the old Max Adrian–Joyce Grenfell revues, it would have remained a very funny minute and a half; padded up to thirty minutes and then some, overloaded with Wittgenstein jokes about linguistics and full of men named Able, Baker, Charlie who have but that one claim to our attention, it comes to resemble a Senior Common Room end of term romp that has somehow been allowed to drift on way past its dubious prime.

But then we get an interval, for which relief much thanks, and following it comes *Cahoot's Macbeth* for which Stoppard has clambered off the Scrabble board and come up with an infinitely stronger and surer one-acter, though one strongly reminiscent of the aforementioned *Real Inspector Hound*. What we have here is a truncated *Macbeth* performed (as it was by Pavel Kahout in Czechoslovakia a few years back) in a private living-room by a group of actors whom the State has denied access to a more public stage. Into this chamber tragedy erupts the Inspector, immortally played in the one really good performance of the evening by Peter Woodthorpe: 'If you'd any pride in your home,' he tells the lady of the house, 'you wouldn't take Standing Room Only in your sitting-room lying down,' and from there on we're into a half-hour of vintage Stoppard in which social, political and linguistic jokes are cobbled together into an alternately depressing and uplifting account of the survival of Shakespeare in a police state.

Macbeth is of course a 'dangerous' play: 'Words,' remarks the Inspector in the key speech of the play, 'can be your friends or enemies. It depends on who's throwing the book,' and Kahout himself (playing Banquo) is in some danger – 'You're a great favourite down at the nick – we're thinking of making you Writer in Residence.' But *Cahoot's Macbeth* is actually about something – it's about freedom, and it's about the power of language, and it's about Pirandellian concepts of theatrical reality. It's also very funny: 'May I remind you,' inquires the Inspector plaintively as the confusion on stage grows apace, so that the Third Murderer has mysteriously become a removals man from Leamington Spa, 'that we're supposed to be in a period of normalization?' The only pity is that neither Stoppard nor his director Ed Berman seem to have been capable of finding a halfway adequate piece to precede it. I'd have even settled for a rerun of *Hound* rather than *Dogg*.

At the Queen's, C. P. Taylor's *And a Nightingale Sang* is one of those musical nostalgia shows that once seemed the exclusive pro-vince of Peter Nichols. The setting is World War Two Newcastle, the cast are all members of one vociferous family (or their lovers) and despite the title we're a long way from Berkeley Square.

But if you can imagine Coward's *This Happy Breed* somehow merged with *Close the Coalhouse Door* and *Forget-Me-Not Lane*, then you'll have some idea of what's afoot here, confusing though that must be to the busloads of Japanese tourists even now wending their way down Shaftesbury Avenue. Mr Taylor doesn't seem to have a lot he wants to say, except that girls with limps can be taught to dance if they're truly in love, and that the family that preys together stays together.

True, there are some rich and ripe performances: Patricia Routledge as the manic Catholic mother, Arthur Blake as the dotty old grandfather, Gemma Jones as the narrator daughter, Roger

Avon as the piano–playing father, forever halfway into the Vintage Hits of Vivian Ellis, and Ray Brooks and Christian Rodska as the two no–good soldier boyfriends, all look as they they should be part of some long–running tele–soap opera: 'Yet Another Family At War', perhaps.

If you know a lot about the suburbs of Newcastle there are doubtless some good local jokes, and if forty years later the most you want of a wartime play is sentiment and schmaltz, then hurry along; but try to forget that Nichols, Alan Bennett, indeed Coward himself all managed to cover this territory more crisply and more thoughtfully. What we end up with is an old box of 1940s chocolates from which somebody has carefully removed all the hard centres.

Song by Song by?

It was just ten years ago that a one–off charity midnight matinee in honour of Noël Coward's seventieth birthday led to the concept of *Cowardy Custard* and a whole series of (usually Mermaid) musicals built around the songbook of a single composer: *Cole* and *Side by Side by Sondheim* were followed by a more recent Yorkshire Television series called 'Song by Song' and the format is now well enough known to have produced its first–ever parody. *Songbook* (at the Globe) is an entire evening of the songs of Moony Shapiro, who never existed.

His inventors are Monty Norman and Julian More who back in the 1950s did the English version of *Irma la Douce* as well as *Expresso Bongo*, and in choosing to build an entire musical around the life of a mythical Liverpool–American composer who very nearly also manages to be Jewish they have come up with a format which neatly sidesteps the old English inability to come up with a decent musical plot, while also allowing them to ransack the entire twentieth–century history of popular songwriting for their parodies.

The result is probably the best all–British musical in a decade (*Evita*, you'll recall, has an American director and choreographer) and though that's not saying a lot, it's saying enough for *Songbook*. Its start is brilliant: Moony (played chubbily by David Healy and narrated elegantly by Anton Rodgers) is, we are told, the only

Irish-born songwriter ever to have met Hitler. Having fought his way all the way to the top of the songwriting racket, he then fought his way all the way down to the bottom again, and although the lights went out all over Broadway the night he died, the cause was a power cut. But when he first arrives in New York, a penniless orphan off the Irish boat, there they all are: 'Say Moony, I'd like you to meet the kids – George and his little brother Ira, Jerome, Oscar, Richard . . .'

So far, so splendid: the first half of *Songbook* is a brilliant and merciless parody of every songwriter's autobiography, and it allows a superbly versatile cast of five (Rodgers and Healy plus Gemma Craven, Diane Langton and Andrew Wadsworth) to do everything from Busby Berkeley numbers to marvellous Dietrich and Trenet mockeries. By the interval Moony has got his first divorce (citing the Barrymores – John, Lionel and Ethel) and returned to London in time to write a horrendous Cicely Courtneidge wartime musical; if Jonathan Lynn's production had ended there, my love for it would be unqualified.

Songbook David Healy, Anton Rodgers, Diane Langton, Andrew C. Wadsworth, Gemma Craven

The trouble is the second half. By now we're into the 1950s; Moony is trying to catch the *Oklahoma!* bandwagon with *Happy Hickory*, and the show soon has to move into Beatle and Disco parodies which are only retrieved from disaster by the sustained brilliance of Mr Rodgers. The problem seems to be twofold: the fifties and sixties are nowhere near as parodiable yet as the twenties and thirties, and the authors are suddenly determined to give *Songbook* a real plot by marrying Moony off to an amalgam of all the Mitfords. Somewhere around here the rot sets in, and the confusion is summed up by a number called 'Nostalgia' which dies away with the composers unable to decide if they're meant to be celebrating it or attacking it.

Since the death of Alfred Lunt and the retirement of Lynn Fontanne, there's not much doubt that Hume Cronyn and Jessica Tandy are the most distinguished double-act in the American theatre; like the Lunts they're a middle-range couple, more Clements than Casson perhaps, and while he gives the impression of having gone straight from Banquo to Duncan without ever scaling Macbeth, they both manage in a rare and remarkable way to complete each other's performances, so you feel that you are watching one actor rather than two.

It is therefore thoroughly shaming and embarrassing to every commercial management in the West End that Mike Nichols' Broadway Pulitzer-prizewinning production of *The Gin Game*, of which Hume Cronyn and Jessica Tandy are the stars and entire cast, is being presented here not by a British management but by an American one made up of the Shuberts and the cast and director themselves. True, D. L. Coburn's study of two welfare veterans suffering from an advanced case of old age in a somewhat seedy retirement home is something less than acid or Chekhovian; yet it does make a marvellous vehicle for two cantankerous character studies in Geriatric Lib, a vehicle that will doubtless be hijacked by countless other ageing theatrical couples in the future.

Coburn is sharp enough to spare us a sentimentally happy ending, and his play is about hatred rather than love; his old man is a compulsive card player (hence the title) forever losing, angrily, to his old lady who is forever lucky at cards and has been disastrously unlucky in everything else. Both are divorced, loathed by their families, and compulsive rebels, eternally bickering if only to prove that they're still alive. Yet we are never really allowed to know enough about them to form independent judgements: Coburn seems to sense that in the end the unacceptable faces of Darby and Joan are going to crack into some sort of a smile and that the wrinkled pumpkinheads are going to appear lovable in spite of themselves. The result is a mannered, precious, highly theatrical evening.

Charms and the Man

John Dexter's return to the National Theatre after several years at the Metropolitan Opera in New York has produced a deeply operatic, fairly charming but also top-heavy *As You Like It* at the Olivier. Gone is the brisk spartan clarity of his earlier National work and instead we are treated to an endless kind of harvest festival, one which may have a lot to do with the pastoral spirit of Arden but threatens to swamp a lightish comedy.

This *As You Like It* weighs in at three hours and comes complete with orchestra and chorus; at times we appear to be in a yeast commercial, at others witnessing a masque about Fertility and Mother Nature.

Deep in the forest something is stirring, but not a lot; Michael Bryant does a good melancholy Jacques, converting 'All the World's a Stage' into an audience participation show, but neither Simon Callow as Orlando nor Sara Kestelman as Rosalind are able to cut their way through the undergrowth for long enough to convince us that this is anything more than a wayward pastoral.

Before reviewing *The Man Who Came to Dinner* (at Chichester) I have a goodly number of personal interests to declare. I was born on its original London first night thirty-eight years ago and acquired the Christian name of its title character, Sheridan Whiteside, a role my father happened to be playing at the time. Because Whiteside is modelled, albeit none too lovingly, on Alexander Woollcott I also acquired him for a godfather, though we never actually met; one morning when I was about three he went into a New York grocery, ordered a large tin of biscuits to be airlifted to his English godson, went on to CBS to do his weekly radio show, collapsed in the studio and died a few hours later.

All that was a long time ago, but the production which opened last week at Chichester is, surprisingly, only the second major British revival of the play in my lifetime and I therefore approached it with some trepidation. In fact, the play has worn a good deal better than I have; true, some of its references are not so much dated as historic, and its characters (among whom are to be found parodies of Coward, Gertrude Lawrence and – at least in theory – Harpo Marx) are all now as dead as Woollcott himself. Yet so brilliantly did Kaufman and Hart, who have never here been given the classic comic status that is their due, build their play that it remains, alongside *The Front Page*, the funniest American comedy of the first half of this century.

It is, granted, deeply unfair to Woollcott himself who was a complex, unhappy, homosexual and immensely powerful American literary and dramatic huckster of the 1930s. The power he wielded over books and plays and films, through a syndicated column and a network radio show, made him a kind of amalgam of Connolly and Tynan at the height of their fame; the play treats him at best as a querulous Gilbert Harding.

Yet by engineering around this caricature of Woollcott a hugely complex farce involving a cast of forty, all of whose lives are totally disrupted by the fall that causes Whiteside to billet himself for the winter on a small-town Ohio family, Kaufman and Hart have managed a masterpiece of comic invention. *The Man Who Came to Dinner* is a three-hour romp involving four penguins, a Cole Porter parody of a Coward song, six choirboys, an Egyptian mummy-case and a denouement in which an axe murderess is unmasked

All credit therefore to the Peter Dews management at Chichester for coming up with a revival which the National should have been on to a decade ago, and all credit to Charles Gray who makes of Sheridan Whiteside an immensely strong and believable yet oddly touching grouch around whom the rest of the action can revolve. Jill Bennett as his lovelorn secretary and Barry Justice in the Noël Coward role are also immensely good, having discovered the old Feydeau principle that farce is funnier the more truthfully you play it.

The problems, in Patrick Lau's agile production, are to do with the rest of the casting; inevitably in a scratch summer-stock company such as Chichester's you are not going to get thirty-seven good supporting players, and only Rosamund Greenwood as the mysterious Harriet gets it absolutely right. The rest of the family upon whom Whiteside forces himself, his eccentric friends and his plans for a better life forfeit all claims to our sympathy or interest by a matching set of appalling performances, and the contest is thus somewhat one-sided. Only by caring a little about the Stanleys can we get the true measure of Whiteside's awfulness.

Moreover Ken Wynne's eccentric decision to play the Banjo character as Jimmy Durante rather than Harpo Marx makes nonsense of some first-act references to his brothers Wacko and Sloppo, and a number of lesser members of the cast clearly think they are working in some kind of Equity charity pantomime rather than a classic farce. Nor is this truly a play for the open stage, though it would be lovely if they could do a little recasting, lop ten minutes off the running time, and find themelves a proscenium-arch London home for the winter. With the RSC about to revive *Once in a Lifetime* next month, it looks as though at long, long last Kaufman and Hart may be going to get the attention they deserve.

Tricky Dick

With the Royal Shakespeare Company economically embattled but still in full London and Stratford swing, who needs Shakespeare at the National? Christopher Morahan's new *Richard III* (suitably enough on the open Olivier stage, since it is still Olivier's performance on stage and screen which dominates and even conditions most thoughts about the play) raises the question simply because it is the third Shakespearian disaster the NT has had there in less than two years. One or two might be forgiveable; three, in the Lady Bracknell's phrase, begins to look like carelessness.

There is so much wrong with this *Richard* that we had better start with what's right; clearly the NT is right to have given John Wood his hunch, specifically because he made his name in the role as an Oxford undergraduate a quarter-century ago. Equally the opening seconds, in which Richard's long misshapen shadow stretches across the back of the stage before his first appearance, are chilling and brilliant. From there on, though, it's all downhill. Wood and Morahan have somehow conceived Richard as an Iago in perpetual search of Othello; the villainy is there, and the long, knowing, leering asides to the audience, but there is absolutely no indication of a framework within which this Richard could possibly be made to work. Desperately lacking character actors of any real distinction, hopelessly lacking any kind of continuing Shakespearian tradition which would make them aware of the verse, the NT forces stumble through a ritual pageant which all too soon degenerates into 'Carry On Up the Throne Room'.

Of course Wood is right to search for the comedy in the role, since there is a great deal there; of course he is right to avoid all Olivier's old effects, scarcely even reacting when the awful child York refers to his hunchback; and of course he is right to curl up at the last on his own battlements, the *enfant terrible* returned at last to the womb. In these split seconds, most of which have as much to do with David Hersey's lighting as with Morahan's production or Ralph Koltai's stone-grey set, it is possible to see how this Richard might have been made to work. But they are scant compensation for the rest of a mocking, mannered, campy, eyebrowed evening in which the single most dramatic device is to have streams of blood trickling down the guttering of the set until the stage itself becomes a peninsula.

John Normington and Jeremy Kemp are woefully under-strength as Clarence and Buckingham, and it is left to the three royal widows (Anna Carteret, Mary Wimbush and Yvonne Bryceland) to give the evening what guts it has; the rest of the company appear to have drifted in from a conference of civil servants, and the result is at best comic opera. Wood never for a moment chills the blood, and lacking any worthy on-stage opponents (though there are several in the text) he is increasingly forced to conduct a one-man band very loudly. We are left with the worst of the old-fashioned star system: a one-performance show, lacking any real motive or sustained approach. Like Everest, *Richard III* is there and needs occasionally to be climbed; but not, surely, in so ramshackle a way as this.

Meanwhile the RSC at the Aldwych are continuing to mine Maxim Gorky, and have now reached *Children of the Sun*, the play he wrote in 1905 while in prison for his part in the January workers' march. Considering that, it is a surprisingly joky, reflective play in which the inevitable revolution is foreseen for entirely non-political reasons. The 'children' of the title are a household of wealthy amateurs: Pavel (Norman Rodway) is a scientist who cannot be bothered with a little local outbreak of cholera. His sister Lisa (Sinead Cusack) is a dotty poet half in love with a suicidal Ukrainian vet (Alan Howard); then there's a wealthy widow (Natasha Parry) who loves Pavel, and a visiting artist (John Shrapnel) who loves Pavel's wife, thereby completing a kind of eternal rectangle.

What Gorky gives us here is the turn–of–the–century Russian answer to Bloomsbury; romantic intellectuals without a single practical skill between them, so totally immersed in their own semi–incestuous relationships that they are unable to recognize even a cholera outbreak as a sign that all may not be absolutely all right in the outside world. Even when Pavel is beaten up in his own garden by a marauding band of peasants, it fails to occur to him that the times may just possibly be a–changing. That, at some length, is the play's central proposition and its running gag.

If you can imagine *Uncle Vanya* rewritten by Feydeau, you'll have some idea of what's afoot; a ruling class whose brains have been allowed to rot, yet who remain totally convinced of their artistic brilliance, thrown into sharp contrast with a new and changing world beyond the gates. It is not clear from Terry Hands' brisk and agile production that Gorky intended his play to be wholly satirical, or hostile to its central figures; many are written with a lyrical kind of regret, and they are played with considerable wistful charm, notably by Howard and Miss Cusack as the local small–town Ophelia.

Three hours may be a little long for this collection of character-studies; yet so sure-footed is the RSC's Gorky house style, so confident are they of each other's mannerisms, so fundamentally familiar are they with each other and their setting, that the result is as good as *Richard* is bad. The children of the sun, Gorky seems to be saying, were so confident of their place in it that they failed to see an eclipse even when it was upon them; what makes the play remark-able is that it was written at the time, not with the wisdom of hindsight.

Full Marx

In the early hours of the morning of 16 December 1969, an anarchist railway worker called Giuseppi Pinelli was scraped off the pavement outside Italian police headquarters in Milan. The late Mr Pinelli, said police regretfully, had during interrogation 'shouted "Anarchy is Dead" and then pushed past policemen and leapt through a fourth-floor window which was open because the room was very stuffy'. Milan police, who were at the time investigating some bombings at railway stations and the Agricultural Bank, soon found themselves having to answer one or two questions themselves. Questions about just how 'stuffy' a Milan police station would be in the middle of a December night, and about how a suspect managed to 'push past' no less than seven policemen in a room no more than twelve foot by eight. One or two local papers even began to suggest that Mr Pinelli's departure from the police interrogation room and this life had received considerable assistance or, to cut a long story short, a shove.

Improbable as it may seem, the real-life (or rather real-death) Pinelli story now forms the basis of one of the funniest shows London has seen in a very long time: to the old Half Moon Theatre in Aldgate, the touring Belt and Braces company (one of those potentially threatened by Arts Council cutbacks to which we'll return in a paragraph or three) have brought Dario Fo's *Accidental Death of an Anarchist* and if you can possibly imagine the Marx Brothers running a documentary inquiry into the death of Blair Peach then you'll have some idea of what is afoot here.

Mr Fo, a distinguished Italian comic, has rightly reckoned that farce is a lot more bearable in the theatre than polemic, and that in the end it can make the same political points. His play, as adapted and directed for Belt and Braces by Gavin Richards, is a savage and satirical attack on police brutality and corruption, made triumphant by the central performance of Alfred Molina as a kind of latter-day government inspector, a maniac buffoon who sets himself up as a police investigator only then to uncover some distinctly dodgy goings-on. How is it, he inquires at one moment, that if Mr Pinelli made this sudden and unexpected dash for the window shortly after midnight, a police ambulance had been ordered fully ten minutes beforehand? Ah, say the police, recognizing a tricky question when they hear one, 'we often order ambulances on the off-chance'. Whether doing half-hearted Tommy Cooper imitations or merely lumbering around the stage like a comic Orson Welles, Mr Molina is a consistent and utter joy and the best knockabout farceur to have arrived in our midst in a very long time.

True, the strength of the evening is dissipated by its closing minutes in which the company, having linked the events in Milan to events not a million miles from Southall (in itself a dicy comparison), then send one of their number forward to make a somewhat pathetic plea for public money, arguing that if such money is not forthcoming then our theatre will be reduced to Brian Rix and *Oh Calcutta!* As *Oh Calcutta!* is now closing, and there hasn't been a Brian Rix farce in the West End or indeed anywhere for the best part of a decade, it would be good to know when Belt and Braces last took stock of the situation in general theatrical terms. True, the threatened Arts Council cutbacks (by no means yet confirmed) are appalling; but it ill behoves a company having achieved such an anarchically good box-office hit to turn round and demand public money for it. Belt and Braces does after all indicate some form of self-support.

At the Royalty, *For Colored Girls Who Have Considered Suicide When the Rainbow is Enuf* is one of those inexplicable Broadway hits which should have been drowned somewhere in mid-Atlantic on the way over. Admittedly, a programme note in which the author Ntozake Shange describes her work as 'a Choreopoem' and goes on to talk about 'acceptance of the ethnicity of my thighs and backside' does not lead one to expect a jolly evening out, and sure enough her collection of turgidly choreographed little poems is an appalling leftover from the days when to be black and female gave you the right to bore people rigid.

    For Colored Girls, etc. (beware long boring titles; they usually indicate long boring shows) is the musical of the Me generation, an el cheapo production (cast of seven, music on tape) which suggests that *Chorus Line* got it all wrong. To succeed nowadays you don't have to worry about pleasing directors or managers or even audiences; you merely have to please yourself. The result is a zonking great self-indulgent soporific bore which I do not think will be long for this London life.

Face the Music

Amadeus: loved by God? Lover of God? Whatever the interpretation, it is clearly central not only to Wolfgang Mozart's name but also to the play about him and his would-have-been assassin by Peter Shaffer, now on the National's Olivier stage in an operatic production by Peter Hall.

    Two-man conflicts are of course close to the heart of Shaffer's best writing: Pizarro and Altahuallpa in *Royal Hunt of the Sun*, the psychiatrist and the boy blinder of horses in *Equus*, and now Salieri and Mozart. The latter needs, as they say, no introduction; about the former it just needs to be recalled that he was the Viennese Kapellmeister who took in later life to claiming that he had poisoned Mozart because the child prodigy ('all smugness and seduction') had inexplicably been given by God the gift of musical genius, one to which Salieri fancied he had the greater claim.

Shaffer's play starts, like *Brief Lives*, with a dotty old man gossiping about the past in an unwelcome present ('Opera used to be about the raising of the Gods – now it's all Rossini and the escapades of hairdressers'). But then, abruptly, Paul Scofield, in a magnificently starry and never offstage theatrical performance, throws off thirty years and we are back in the court of Josef II, marvellously inanely played by John Normington.

Enter Mozart (Simon Callow), a blaspheming, sexy and bowel-obsessed lad capable of making music so divine that Salieri is reduced to quivering envy; that, give or take an attempted seduction of Mrs Mozart (Felicity Kendal in good joky form), is the first half. And splendid. The second half is however inclined to fall away sharply, partly because we've already learnt all we need to know and mainly because in pushing his story from a natural two to an over-extended three hours Shaffer makes us aware that the demands of the gargantuan Olivier stage have led to a kind of terrible swelling – this is actually a smaller, tighter, brisker and shorter play than it is made to seem by the use of extras peering at it and us through the scenery.

The result is a repetitive and overblown second act built around a single joke about the constancy of mediocrity; but *Amadeus* is still well worth your attention for the Scofield–Callow double act and for the reminder that Shaffer remains the most eloquent and elegant of playwrights.

Give My Regards from Broadway

A once powerful nation, now having trouble getting its own people out of a Teheran embassy captivity, is apparently in no mood for courageous experiment either in the Arts or anywhere else. The big news along Broadway this Thanksgiving week is that, wait for it, next August Richard Burton will be returning to the New York State not in the *King Lear* he has so long been promising but instead in a revival of *Camelot*, the 1960s musical once beloved of President Kennedy. The first President Kennedy, that is: doubtless they will now be trying for an endorsement from Teddy, even if his own endorsement for the White House is still looking a little shaky.

In times of crisis, Broadway has always been good at examining its own navel. The current hits here include a Neil Simon musical about songwriters, a thriller about a thriller writer, and a romantic comedy about two romantic comedy playwrights who spend eleven years deciding whether or not to fall in love. But by far the biggest hit on Broadway, at a significant and symbolic five feet three inches, is Mickey Rooney.

Mr Rooney, who sings worse than he dances and dances worse than he acts, is currently starring here in a show called *Sugar Babies* alongside Ann Miller, who was the 1940s' Hollywood answer to Jessie Matthews. Their show, billed as a tribute to the good old days of vaudeville and burlesque, is giving useful employment to twelve dancers and some of the oldest jokes in the business, as well as to several variety stars who look like they last worked the World's Fair of 1939. If you can imagine a pre-war American seaside special, you will have some idea of what is at present passing here for great entertainment.

The other big star on Broadway at present, also not much higher than the average kneecap, is a lady billed as 'the Divine Miss Midler'. She's here in concert and also in a film called *The Rose* for which the queues grow longer by the hour. As Bette Midler is the only star I ever went to university with, unless you count Michael York, I find it difficult to assess her critically except to note that what she is doing in *The Rose*, one of the great bad movies of all time, is playing the doomed singing junkie Janis Joplin in a tearful account of her life which makes all three versions of *A Star is Born* look like masterpieces of quiet good taste and restraint. Regardless of the fact that Miss Joplin died alone in a motel room, Miss Midler dies on screen at a rock concert before just the 500,000 screaming fans. Alan Bates, playing her manager, looks understandably appalled throughout, while Miss Midler remains the only singer I know who can make her shoulders sweat during a big number. There's an awful lot of sweat in *The Rose*.

Back on stage, Broadway's revivalist season does, however, contain a totally magical *Peter Pan*, turned into a musical by Jule Styne, who also wrote *Funny Girl* and *Gypsy*. While for far too many years we in Britain have allowed Barrie's masterpiece to degenerate into a series of increasingly tacky and tatty Christmas revivals featuring ever more unsuitable leading players, Americans here have taken the old play, revitalized it, and come up with a Christmas show worth the Atlantic air fare to witness. For the sake of all our children at home, we should start campaigning now for this musical to reach London for Christmas 1980, complete with its laserbeam Tinker Bell, its miraculously camp Captain Hook from Christopher Hewitt and its totally enchanting star, a lady called Sandy Duncan.

The Broadway *Evita*, though again directed by Hal Prince, turns out to be a pale shadow of its London original and politically even more confused, perhaps because along the Great White Way a star has always to look holier than the Pope and Eva thus emerges as a cross between Anna Neagle and Mary Baker Eddy. The three central players all have trouble living up to the first or indeed the second London cast.

The only straight non-musical hit of the season thus far is a play called *Romantic Comedy* by Bernard Slade, who is the Canadian Neil Simon and may be remembered in London for his *Same Time Next Year*. What we have here is an eccentric reworking of *Present Laughter* which frequently acknowledges its debt to Coward without ever quite managing to live up to its masterly source. By a rare but eccentric stroke of casting genius, the star of *Psycho* and the star of *Rosemary's Baby* are here locked together in a sort of drawing-room comedy. But neither Anthony Perkins nor Mia Farrow, in her Broadway début, seem to know a lot about the timing of this kind of stylish caper and the result is that Perkins looks like Leslie Phillips imitating Coward and Farrow looks like a winsome Oxfam refugee mysteriously set down in an elegant Manhattan apartment. Mr Slade is, I think, trying to tell us that light comedy is dead and that there will never be any more *Philadelphia Stories*. The trouble is that his play indicates all too clearly in its writing and its playing just why the death has taken place.

Ticket prices hovering around and sometimes above twenty dollars for a front stall mean that Broadway is actually taking more money this year than almost ever before, but behind the neon smiles there is an uneasy awareness that in a normally lush pre-Christmas period, theatres are only averaging seventy-five per cent capacity. The big moneymakers are still the big musicals, and in this context the most reassuring is Sondheim's *Sweeney Todd*, which last week took $230,000 at the box-office, surely something of a record for a show which resolutely refuses to play the old Broadway nostalgia game and instead sends its audiences out into the night humming the joys of baking human meat pies.

One of the more attractive aspects of Broadway is, incidentally, its habit of publishing every Thursday its box-office takings for the previous week. The sooner the West End does the same, the sooner it will attract investors currently nervous of the kind of accountancy going on there.

The bad news here is that they are about to tear down three of Broadway's most historic theatres to make way for yet another hideous convention hotel housing hideous conventions. The good news is that they have at last discovered the totally effective diet. It is called the President Carter diet, and those following it only eat when he does something right.

1980

Oxford Blues

Doug Lucie's *Heroes* (at Hampstead's New End Theatre) is a double-bill linked much after the fashion of Rattigan's *Separate Tables* by precisely the same cast in exactly the same setting. Here however we find ourselves not in an out-of-season Bournemouth hotel but in the living-room of an Oxford house inhabited by undergraduates of (for the first play) 1969 and (for the second play) 1979. It does not therefore require an immense leap of the imagination to assume that Mr Lucie is through his plays trying to tell us something about the way that students, or at any rate Oxford students, have changed over the past decade.

His first play opens somewhere around the middle of the age of Aquarius: the students here are a couple of spaced-out druggies, a rich bitch, a radical loser and the budding feminist organizer of the student commune in which they are all living. It takes an outsider, a likely lad on the make, to show us the self-delusions of the other five but the overall mood here remains curiously optimistic; knives may be flashed, the pot may turn to heroin and so may the heroine, but all is surely going to be all right in a world where so many are so caring about, well, just about caring.

Ten years on, all that has changed. The commune has become a safe middle-class abode whose students are obsessed with the need to vote Conservative and get a good degree. The age of Aquarius has become the age of ICI student grants, there has been a congealing of kindness and the only refuge now appears to be the convent or the gas oven. The actors who played the hippies have become respectively an oarsman and a society hostess, and the outsider is now a Cowley car-worker, come to remind us that a different world lies only four miles beyond the university gates. Self-sufficiency is the name of the new game, and the weakest are going to the wall so fast they can barely be counted.

The trouble is, of course, that it's all too neat; Mr Lucie has assembled a roomful of interesting 'types', transformed them a decade later into an altogether different roomful, and left it at that. He could as well have made them all outpatients at an Edinburgh infirmary or occupants of the Leatherhead station waiting-room as Oxford undergraduates, for although it is true that the university has changed in ten years, and quite possibly moved in the conservative direction he suggests, such generalizations cannot be sustained through a set of intriguing but disconnected character sketches. *Heroes* tells us no more about Oxford life than 'Fawlty Towers' tells us of the state of the Torquay hotel business. For all that, it's an enjoyable double, and one which might well manage to sustain a West End life in a small theatre, so strong are the cast of seven under Penny Chern's direction.

Unknown Soldiers

Since they found Joe Orton in a pool of his own blood fifteen years ago, black comedy has been in something of a decline; whether out of a faint realization that nobody did it better than Orton, or simply because black comedy is traditionally not a box-office winner, there have been precious few managements willing to risk it, for which reason all credit to the Oxford Playhouse Company whose production of Howard Barker's *The Love of a Good Man* paid a flying visit to the reopened Royal Court last week.

What we had here was an evening of gala bad taste and several very good, one might well say appallingly good, jokes; if you can imagine *Journey's End* rewritten by necrophiliacs you'll have some, though admittedly not much, idea of what was afoot or rather underfoot. Set on the fields of Passchendale in 1920, Mr Barker's play opens with the arrival of the Prince of Wales muttering vaguely about erecting a flashing neon sign which in coloured lights would spell out the single word 'Sorry' high above the acres of war dead. It rapidly transpires that not only His Royal Highness but also a profiteering funeral director from Peckham (immortally well played by Ian McDiarmid) are standing on a million dead Englishmen, a good many of whom now have to be removed from the earth ('fertilizing on this scale is unprecedented') and placed in neat rectangular boxes under neat white crosses in neat green plots kindly supplied free of charge by a grateful brave little Belgium.

So far, so macabre; enter now an aristocratic Englishwoman looking not a million miles removed from, say, Vita Sackville-West, who has decided that corners of foreign fields are all very well but she'd like her son back home underneath the apple tree in the orchard.

Finding him, or rather several connected bits of him, proves surprisingly not to be difficult since by this time Mr Barker has lost some interest in the intricacies of his plot; instead, he's into a jet black farce about the rotting of the English both above and below ground. His one likeable character, the caretaker sent out by the English to catalogue corpses (Edward Jewsbury in craggily good form) is by now loony, and the rest of them are involved in a murderously bitchy and caustically funny survey of English attitudes to war and death.

Writing in a kind of heightened prose which sounds like John Whiting by way of Edna St Vincent Millay, Barker veers from the knockabout comedy of McDiarmid and his lugubrious undertaking partner (Anthony Pedley) to the more serious commentary on a corruption of the flesh living as well as dead. He has a sharp eye for the greater lunacies of our national heritage ('If you love someone,' HRH tells the dowager, 'you want to give them everything you have. I happen to have Cornwall.') And though he hasn't yet quite got this play right – a final seance hopelessly fails to turn any tables – there are indications that Mr Barker is still at work on it and that one day it may turn out to be as entertaining as *Mr Sloane*.

Georgia on my Mind

Any week which brings a new comedy by Michael Frayn and even in these troubled times, a complete Soviet theatre company from Georgia, to say nothing of a kind of one-man promenade concert devoted to Sir Thomas Beecham and (venturing northwards) a stunning revival of *Oklahoma!* has to indicate that maybe the British theatre is not yet as terminal a case as many at last Tuesday's Drama Awards presentation were inclined to believe.

Guests first: at the Round House the Rustaveli *Richard III* is quite simply a Georgian epic. Clearly this theatre company relates to Moscow in much the same way that the Abbey Theatre, Dublin relates to London, which is to say hardly at all. Political objections (such as the opening night's mini–demonstration) are therefore largely irrelevant: Georgia appears to be a law unto itself, and nowhere is this better expressed that in Robert Sturua's vast, sprawling pageant of a production. Its star, Ramaz Chkhikvadze, appears to be the local Donald Wolfit: his is a matinee–idol Richard, only very faintly misshapen and inclined to head straight for the nearest spotlight and stay there while the rest of the company form respectful circles around his bravura turn. But Sturua has had some vastly good ideas, not least the use of Queen Margaret as prompter and stage manager, the permanent shadowing of Richard by an unusually sinister Richmond, and the final struggle between these two men literally draped in a torn map of Britain. It's a performance that Barnum, Bailey and Cecil B. deMille might have considered unrestrained, but joky and electrifying and illuminating by turn and coming complete with a superlative score by Gia Kancheli; there's been nothing quite like it in our (or I suspect any other) theatre in my lifetime, and we owe the Georgians a considerable debt of fascination and gratitude.

Back on home ground, Michael Frayn's *Liberty Hall* (at Greenwich) starts from a wonderfully funny premise and proceeds to go gently downhill. We are at a writers' rest home in Balmoral Castle; it is 1937, and the revolution of twenty years earlier came not in Russia but here in Britain; survivors of that revolution include such 'acceptable' writers as Enid Blyton, Godfrey Winn, Warwick Deeping and Hugh Walpole, all now about to be exhibited to a visiting journalist from the wicked capitalist press of Moscow. Unfortunately, however, Walpole drops dead after a bit of a squabble with Winn, and has therefore to be replaced by the dour Scots janitor. From here on in, a thoughtful comedy rapidly turns into a corpse-disposal farce, and in this league Frayn is not quite the intellectual answer to Ben Travers. Along the way however we do get two masterly performances (from Rikki Fulton as the janitor and George Cole as his defeated superior) and some very joky moments until the last scene is finally strangled by its own contortions. Whoever it was said there are no second acts in American lives might have added that there aren't many in Michael Frayn's plays either.

Pieces of Atrium

Of the ten plays that make up the current cycle of *The Greeks* (Royal Shakespeare Company at the Aldwych) seven are by Euripides, one is Homer as adapted by John Barton, one is by Aeschylus and the tenth is an amalgam of Sophocles, Euripides and Aeschylus. Already therefore it should be apparent that what we have here is a kind of instant guide to classical drama, one cobbled together by Mr Barton himself and his translator Kenneth Cavander to provide a nine-hour theatrical epic. Such epics are not of course unknown to the RSC or to Barton: in 1964 they did *The Wars of the Roses*.

But there all such comparisons must end: where in the *Roses* we had a sustained narrative, here we have ten totally separate plays ranging in style and tone from magnificent sacrificial tragedy (*Iphigenia in Aulis*) to campy comedy of the old Giraudoux 'classics can be fun' school (*Helen*). Wisely the RSC chose to show the entire cycle to the critics on a single marathon day, and that is far and away the best arrangement for general audiences too. Seen across three separate evenings, the problems of the weaker plays would become all too apparent: seen together, they cease to have such individual failings and become part of one great rolling event.

And the event is all: for the actors, for Barton himself (and finally at the end of the first day for the audience too) the applause was to denote that we had all got through it together. There was something both moving and fascinating about starting out a day at ten in the morning watching a group of giggling Greek girls gathering at Aulis to watch the great ships depart for Troy and ending it at eleven at night with these same women, ravaged by seventeen years of sacrifice and war and bereavement and murder and rape and madness, being told by one of the Gods who have destroyed their lives that, all in all, the best idea is compromise.

On John Napier's bare, dust-bowl set, a company of forty work their way through the saga in the simplest possible terms: Barton and Cavander have gone for a prose style of stark simplicity to match both the setting and the acting. *The Greeks* is not a day of metaphor or of subtlety. Instead, everything is up front, laid out before you from Astyanax to Zeus like some appalling tapestry of blood and revenge. For Agamemnon, having butchered his own child, to tell his grieving wife as he sets off for Troy that he 'may be some time' is admittedly a little anti-climactic, but it is in keeping with a pageant which by its very nature has to lurch from idle gossip about the Gods to the equivalent of *Hamlet* Act V within a matter of minutes.

What we have here, then, is the cartoon-strip history of the classical world, one which can incorporate characters as diverse as the dizzy blonde Thetis (Annie Lambert) apologizing to her son

The Greeks   John Shrapnel *as Agamemnon*, Janet Suzman *as Clytemnestra*, Mike Gwilym *as Achilles*, Judy Buxton *as Iphigenia*

Achilles for having been so forgetful about his heel, and the massively tragic Clytemnestra (Janet Suzman) who having killed Agamemnon (John Shrapnel) for what he did to their daughter is then in turn butchered by her own children Orestes and Electra who have (in one of the rare production mistakes of the epic) been allowed to grow up into modern-dress urban guerrillas.

Such occasional errors of judgement arise from the same source as much of what is best about Barton's production: an utter determination never to bore or confuse or forget its audience. Gone forever are rows of chorus ladies chanting in white sheets; gone too are the unwieldy and stagey translations of the past. It is something of a surprise, even so, to discover about eight hours into the epic that Helen was never living in Troy at all, and that Iphigenia never got herself sacrificed either: the whole of the Trojan Wars has been some terrible black joke perpetrated by the Gods. But people have lived and died through them, some have even survived them, and that too is what *The Greeks* is all about. Like forty ancient mariners, the RSC company fix you with glittering eyes and proceed to tell you their terrible tales. But, thanks to Suzman and Shrapnel, to Billie Whitelaw, to Mike Gwilym and Lynn Dearth, and to a whole host of supporting players including Judy Buxton, Eliza Ward, Tony Church and Oliver Ford Davies (and to Nick Bicât's score), the parade passes by in fine fettle. True, its final sequence runs downhill so fast that even the cast seem breathless, but if you take my advice and see *The Greeks* at one sitting that will only appear as the inevitable anti-climax to the war itself.

Tour de Force

At the Bush, which has long been London's most distinguished pub-theatre, Tom Kempinski's new *Duet for One* is an acidly funny and very moving two-character play about a world-famous violin-ist condemned by multiple sclerosis to a wheelchair, and about the psychiatrist determined to prevent her suicide. The violinist is played by Mr Kempinski's wife, Frances de la Tour, and her psychiatrist by David de Keyser, and if we get two better performances or a better new play than this in the rest of 1980 then I shall be more than a little surprised.

At this point you may have to forgive a certain note of I-told-you-so smugness; last year, asked along with more than a dozen other national critics to name a 'most promising playwright' I was alone in choosing Mr Kempinski (on the basis of his earlier *Flashpoint*) and never in my life have I seen a promise so rapidly realized.

Duet for One is a major play, at times alarmingly biographical and maybe even autobiographical, about analysis and the life force itself. Though, or perhaps because, occasionally given to pious platitudes ('The Tree of Life has more than one apple') de Keyser's Harley Street psychiatrist is wonderfully convincing, never more so than when sitting in perfect stillness watching his patient gradually tearing herself apart and then starting on the long and slow process of reconstruction.

But it is Miss de la Tour's evening and she makes of it a feast of fine acting; the final moments of the final scene are perhaps inclined to cop out, but that is a very small price to pay for what, in Roger Smith's tense and taut production, has been an immensely strong and timely reaffirmation of the power of thoughtful drama. *Duet for One* deserves to be played for months if not years, and in the West End at that.

Greenwich Mean Time

Arguably the greatest comedy written in the English language since *The Importance of Being Earnest* (which preceded it by thirty-five years), *Private Lives* is a technical exercise of immense difficulty for two superlative light comedians plus a couple of stooges. It contains the second most famous balcony scene in the whole of dramatic literature, but precious few actual jokes ('Women should be struck regularly, like gongs' is more of an aphorism and anyway now considered somewhat unfeminist) and almost no action of any kind. A couple of divorcees on second honeymoons meet accidentally at a hotel in the South of France, decide they prefer being married to each other rather than their new partners, and run away together to Paris. And that, across three entire acts, is more or less that.

When Noël Coward first sent the play to Gertrude Lawrence, for whom he'd written it as a kind of apology for not casting her in his *Bitter-Sweet* on account of her voice not being good enough for its score, her wired reply was 'Nothing that can't be fixed.' 'The only thing to be fixed,' replied Noël, 'will be your performance,' and from there they started rehearsals, watched over by Robert Montgomery and G. B. Stern in the villa Gertie had appropriately rented on Cap Ferrat.

It was the summer of 1930, and when they first opened in London (opening also the Phoenix Theatre) one critic wrote that it was like watching 'buckets of filth being thrown around the stage'. But Aimee Semple McPherson (also at the first night, sitting next to Lawrence of Arabia) approved, and Lawrence added that he had closely examined the script and failed to find in it 'a single redundant syllable'.

Noël and Gertie only played it for twelve weeks in London and another twelve on Broadway, Coward's boredom threshold in performance being somewhat low; he never played Elyot again, she only played Amanda again once, for a week in 1940 at a summer theatre on Cape Cod. So the whole Noël and Gertie legend rests on twenty-four weeks and a scratchy gramophone record on which the great love scene is reduced to about three and a half minutes, mainly about the flatness of Norfolk and the potency of cheap music. But since their time, scarcely a month has passed without *Private Lives* being staged somewhere in the world and usually fairly badly. The last major London revival was a decade ago, with Robert Stephens looking uneasy and his then wife Maggie Smith unaccountably doing impressions of Margaret Rutherford.

Now, however, praise be, the Greenwich Theatre have come up with a winner, thanks largely to their casting of a lady called Maria Aitken who, since the premature retirement of Kay Hammond and equally premature death of Kay Kendall, is the nearest our stage has ever come to that leggy aristocratic jokiness which was Gertrude Lawrence's peculiarly evanescent stock-in-trade. Miss Aitken makes a perfectly ravishing Amanda and the miracle is that Michael Jayston, cast against type as Elyot, manages to keep up with her, largely by reminding us of the underlying seriousness and sadness of a play about two people who find it impossible to live apart and equally impossible to live together.

The director at (and of) Greenwich, Alan Strachan, was involved in both the great Mermaid Theatre nostalgia songfests, *Cowardy Custard* and *Cole*, and this new production exudes a kind of 1930s confidence. True, it is a little anachronistic to have Elyot at the piano do a rendering of 'These Foolish Things' which was actually written some months after the play, but beyond that the period accuracy is well-nigh faultless and Ian Collier in the old Laurence Olivier role makes a splendidly blustering stooge as does Jenny Quayle playing the unfortunate Sybil (so christened to allow Elyot to utter his immortal 'Don't quibble, Sybil'). It will be sad if this production does not find a central London home for the summer, not least because of Miss Aitken's rare ability to stand around like an elegant alcoholic lamp-post.

Mirror Images

The historical costume drama is back, forsooth. Ever since the days of *Marie Antoinette*, and I mean the Norma Shearer MGM movie of 1936 rather than the unfortunate lady herself, there has been a sneaking feeling that what we really needed were more plays like *Richard of Bordeaux* and *The Duke in Darkness* which took real-life historical events, preferably to do with royalty and death in that order, and cloaked them in sentimental drama. Now for the first time in years, we have a new example of the genre in the West End, suitably enough at the Theatre Royal Haymarket which itself looks like the sort of place mobs would have stormed in search of a decent evening's entertainment.

What *Reflections* by John Peacock really lacks is Tyrone Power, or at the very least Cornel Wilde, standing at the door shouting, 'The coach is without, Madame, and time will not stay,' or words to that ludicrous effect. We have already got Donald Pleasance, shaved to look like Yul Brynner's grandfather, doing impressions of George Arliss as the evil Englishman who has captured Madame du Barry in her own gracious château and is now about to hand her over to the guillotine. We also have Dorothy Tutin as the anguished Madame, and so would you too look anguished if you have to stand around in three hundredweight of costumes listening to lines like, 'With the du Barry, love was an art,' or worse still having to say, 'My ambitions are only of the heart,' without giggling.

By setting the whole eccentric affair in a cut-down version of the Versailles hall of mirrors (hence the *Reflections* of the title) Mr Peacock may well think he is telling us something meaningful about the way we see ourselves or each other; he has also, in the story of the Englishman who became a professional helper of other people's revolutions and ended up half in love with the du Barry, got himself a minor historical footnote which might just about have done for a 1953 Monday afternoon drama on Radio Four. But set across two short yet interminable hours at the Haymarket, where lines like 'The Republic Will Happen' are sent winging up towards the chandeliers and where for some reason the peasants have taken to scrawling graffiti in English on the walls of the set, the whole baroque mishmash looks like an unholy alliance of Clemence Dane and Gordon Daviot on a bad day. Brave performances come not only from Miss Tutin and Mr Pleasance but also from Jeffrey Kissoon as an understandably bemused Indian servant and Gordon Gostelow doddering through as the ancient retainer. What they all think they are doing in a vehicle that even Greer Garson might have had second thoughts about remains a mystery, but I bet they do good business at the midweek matinees.

At the Queen's, thanks almost solely to its star Jane Asher who rediscovered the play and set about finding it a production, there is an intriguing and admirable opportunity to reconsider Rodney Ackland's *Before the Party*, first (and last) seen in London in October 1949 with Constance Cummings playing the widow back from Africa with the terrible secret of her husband's mysterious death. But what is so good about *Before the Party* is not in fact the way that it transfers a rather hackneyed Somerset Maugham melodrama of death and drink from page to stage; what is so good is that the play rises above its original source to become a savagely funny attack on the hypocrisy of England in the late 1940s.

In a splendidly thoughtful and minutely detailed production by Tom Conti (his first for the English stage) we are shown the Skinner family life; father (Michael Gough) is an ambitious solicitor hoping to become a Conservative candidate for the next by-election; mother (Phyllis Calvert) is a semi-abstracted cloth-head worried only about cook's imminent departure from the kitchen, for what is a little murder in the family compared to that impending disaster?

Apart from Jane Asher the family have two other daughters, one a bitterly sex-starved spinster, the other an already deeply cynical twelve-year-old through whose eyes Mr Ackland lets us witness the greater lunacies of postwar middle-class life. The play, unlike the story, is shot through with a deep hatred for what England has become in the immediately postwar years; a nation, if Mr Ackland is to be believed, of selfish hypocritical snobs desperately trying to prop up a crumbling social order.

The result is a richly comic period piece which makes one realize just how good a playwright we have so long neglected in Mr Ackland; while preserving a certain sense of the old Maugham morality, he has added to it layer after layer of other observations about a nation in decay and decline; 'All that sleeping on top of each other in air-raid shelters has changed our social habits,' says mother, but in the end the play is about a family for whom the decencies have never been quite as strong as perhaps they should have been. *Before the Party* is in many ways the play that Coward tried often to write after the war and never quite managed; it's a comedy of expediency, about the fundamental corruption of apparently decent people; it's also a murder play and a comedy of class warfare and to have got all of that into a seven-character drama based on a short story is no mean achievement. The previous collaboration of Tom Conti and Jane Asher was (in *Whose Life Is It Anyway?*) a play about the right of a man to choose his own death; this, equally fascinatingly, is about the right of a woman to choose her own life, and Mr Ackland's final triumph is to have created a play which Maugham himself, in the days when he was writing *The Sacred Flame* and *The Letter*, would have been proud to have his name on. It may not be another *Crime and Punishment*, but it's the best revival in town.

Aussie Acting

Sydney

I am not, I fear, very Australian. My brother, ten years younger, thinner, sexier and resident here this past decade with a mahogany tan to prove it, reckons this is because I lack the secret of youth. I on the other hand incline to the view that Australia is actually too old for me rather than I for it, and take consolation from the fact that seventy-five per cent of local Sydney schoolchildren, asked what they would most like to be in life, said retired. There is not, so far as I can make out, a lot going on here. True, there is my father, giving what I would tell you, were I not his son, is the most marvellously touching and bittersweet portrayal of the reluctantly homebound spy eking out the last days of a Russian exile in Alan Bennett's *The Old Country*, a production in which Wallas Eaton (he who was once our very own Wealthy Wal in 'Take It from Here') is also infinitely more joky and moving than the original London casting of the role. But beyond that, what? Well, in the thirty-one years since I was last here, when the going rate for a child actor (which I occasionally was) ran to two shillings per matinee, they have of course built the

Sydney Opera House, a flamboyantly if irrelevantly winged structure which rises out of the harbour like a baroque National Car Park, and under those wings there is now a new theatre where Frank Thring, irreverently known locally as the Thring from Outer Space, is playing the Michael Redgrave role in Simon Gray's *Close of Play*. This too seems to have improved on its journey to the other side of the world: both plays were in London treated by actors and directors alike with a kind of desiccated respect, and there isn't too much time for that sort of thing down here, where the dramatic priorities appear to be getting on with the jokes and trying to make sure that the customers understand the plot, or at least enough of it to get down the final curtain. I do not wish to suggest that Australians are not natural theatregoers, merely that they look curiously relieved once on their way back to their cars.

This must be the only nation in the world where seven is a winning score on 'Mastermind' and where tele-commercials exhort us to Think Australia. I keep thinking of the twenty-four-hour plane journey out here, which resembled nothing so much as a Darby and Joan airborne outing that all the Darbys had somehow missed: they even played Bobby Howes on the headphones. 'What do you think of Australia?' a brave journalist once asked my father, who as it happens has always loved it; 'What does it matter what I think of it?' replied Robert, 'You're the one who has to live here.' But they do seem to like to know what we think, and what I think is that the best thing about Sydney is the Nimrod. Situated in what appears to be a disused air-raid shelter near a shop calling itself the Depilatory Capital of New South Wales, this is a theatre complex which has already given the world *The Elocution of Benjamin Franklin* and much of the best of David Williamson, including his *The Club* which is still to be found at the Old Vic. But the surprising thing about *Traitors* is first that it's not in fact yet another Williamson, and second that it's the work of a young Brisbane writer with only one other play to his name. This one is set in Leningrad and Moscow in 1927 and tells simply, if often brutally and bloodily, the story of the collapse of the Russian Revolution.

Ten years on from the dreams and ideals of 1917, communism has disintegrated into a savage internal struggle between Stalin's thugs and the last of the Trotsky idealists and around that theme of disillusion and death Stephen Sewell has woven an admittedly overlong three-hour drama of immense raw vitality. The message of the play is that communism, like capitalism, was built out of the blood of the workers, and though this may place Sewell politically some way to the right of Barker, Brenton and Hare his writing has many of their strengths. Nimrod has recently been through considerable internal troubles of its own, but this production by their new artistic director Neil Armfield promises well for the future and needs to be seen soon in London: Michele Fawdon and Barry Otto lead a grittily good cast.

Over on the other side of town, just near where a shop is selling packets of wine dust (not a ready mix, you understand, but for sprinkling over your bottles to make them look as though they've been in a cellar and not the local supermarket) Mollie Sugden from 'Are You Being Served?' is to be found in a ramshackle farce, soon to be followed by John Inman in one even more ramshackle. Once you've got a hit tele-series out here, the thing to do is apparently make a dash for the theatre and clean up before the customers forget or move on to another series. English actors appearing here ought to be made to sign a declaration that the show they are playing is one they would be willing to have the West End see them in.

But the Australian theatre is even more perilous than most: my brother, who is a producer here (a job not unlike running a car-wash concession in the desert) found himself the other night talking to a fellow theatregoer in the interval after the first act of Derek Jacobi's visiting *Hamlet*. 'Bloody long,' said the Sydney man; 'Yes,' agreed my brother, 'the first act of *Hamlet* has been that long for about 400 years.' 'Then you'd think,' said the Sydney man, 'that by now they'd have done something about it.'

Rained Off

'It's a crazy business,' said the producer of last month's *Umbrellas of Cherbourg*, announcing its closure after nine performances to a loss of £140,000; 'we were slaughtered by the critics.' Quite apart from the medical impossibility of slaughtering what was a corpse long before it hit the stage, the craziness of the business may have a certain amount to do with the belief that it is possible to find a waterlogged French film from the 1960s, take away its sole remarkable asset (Catherine Deneuve) and cobble the leftovers together as a stage musical. Whoever could possibly imagine that an old film could be turned into a hit musical? The producers of On the Twentieth Century, perhaps. They are alive and well and living at Her Majesty's Theatre just a few hundred yards away from where the Umbrellas have so recently been taken down. As the man says, it's a crazy business.

Meanwhile, one of the best musicals I have seen in a long time still seems to be in search of a central London home, though my fervent hope is that by the time you read this it may have found one. Ned Sherrin, master compiler of the songbook show, and his co-director David Yakir have recently assembled the words and music of Jerry Leiber and Mike Stoller into an altogether joyous celebration called Only in America. Leiber and Stoller are probably best known over here as the writers of such Elvis hits as 'Jailhouse Rock' and 'Hound Dog', but by digging up another fifty of their numbers in the best Sherrin Song by Song style, the compilation manages to establish its two music men as one of the most remarkable teams in the modern history of popular songwriting.

Leiber and Stoller did not just write songs; they wrote records. Their backlist is an entire chronicle of Tin Pan Alley, from Peggy Lee's Brechtian 'Is That All There Is?' (given here in a shamefully truncated form at the final blackout) all the way back through 'Jackson' and 'Kansas City' to such relics of the 1950s as 'Lucky Lips'. They were, perhaps still are, the twin wizards of the juke box; their songs are the defiantly unromantic laments of the used-car lot and the drive-in movie. Songs of the Bronx, maybe, or Pittsburgh, Pennsylvania, or Southside Boston, or the no-name towns on the train tracks between Washington and New York. These are not the race-conscious songs of the Deep South, nor yet the sunshine-and-orange-juice songs of California; they are the songs of inner-city decay, songs for people on the corner of 12th Street and Vine with zips all over the sleeves of their black leather jackets.

The fact that every singer from Piaf to Debbie Reynolds found a song of Leiber and Stoller's worth recording is a tribute to their versatility or maybe just to their sheer survival; yet this is the first time that these hamburger-stand numbers have been anthologized and put back into their correct settings, so that, for example, 'Hound Dog' becomes the shout of a big black Mama (immortally well played by Bertice Reading) to her no-good lying husband who is already halfway back to 'Jackson'. Even if this show remains unable to find a West End theatre, I trust someone will have the sense to record it, thereby giving us the best original-cast album in years.

You only have a couple of weeks left now in which to catch Ralph Richardson as the dying politician in David Storey's *Early Days* (on the National's Cottesloe stage) and it is not to be missed. Though lacking both the depth and the length of the earlier Storey–Richardson *Home* (this one runs a mere ninety minutes including interval) it is a marvellously resonant dramatic tone poem about old age and loneliness and the recollection of one single unnerving childhood incident. Mr Storey's point is that life does not go on for good, it goes on for bad; this other point is that the journey actually narrows the mind, as does most travel. Against Jocelyn Herbert's Chekhovian garden setting, the little drama played out here shares many of the obsessions of Alan Bennett's *Old Country* and Simon Gray's *Close of Play*. Sir Ralph makes it all infinitely poetic, and though the play is more than a little sketchy (other characters eminently well played by Rosemary Martin and Gerald Flood get barely a look in) his performance is one to cherish and remember long after the precise details of its surroundings have slipped away.

Rough Knight

Playwrights from Chekhov all the way through to Clifford Odets have succumbed to the temptation to write the one about the old actor nearing the end of his days in states ranging from nostalgia through alcoholism to penury. Reflections in a dressing-room mirror have always had this understandable Pirandellian fascination; if what the actor does for a living is by definition unreal, how real can the rest of his life hope to be?

Now, at the Queen's Theatre, we are asked to consider a specific case history. In his programme note the dramatist Ronald Harwood is eager, some might say rather too eager, to have us understand that though his new play *The Dresser* is partially about Sir Donald Wolfit (for whom Harwood spent five postwar years working as dresser) it is not wholly or solely about him. Nor, Mr Harwood hastens to add, should we assume that 'Her Ladyship' in the play bears any relationship to Lady Wolfit.

Yet a great deal of this play cuts closer than such absolute comfort in the programme might indicate; the fact that Harwood had collected here a vast range of backstage jokes (most concerning *King Lear*) and cobbled them together into a kind of Garrick Club benefit night does not detract from his searing insights into Wolfit and the nature of the actor-manager in decline.

In that sense, *The Dresser* is a tragedy, a long day's journey into would-be knight at the end of which we are left with a mixture of relief and sadness that the days of tacky Shakespearian provincial touring have long gone. The title character is immortally well-played by Tom Courtenay as a waspish, intermittently savage homosexual manservant all too well aware that his task is not just to dress this Lear but also to play his offstage Fool. The old actor, a no less impressive or important performance from Freddie Jones, is therefore the other half of this odd-couple relationship. Back from the brink of a nervous breakdown and heading rapidly for on- and offstage death, 'Sir' (as he is known throughout the play) is admittedly a collage job. There are bits of Martin Harvey in there, and not a little of Bransby Williams and Robert Atkins as well.

The running joke is that we are in the midst of a 1943 air-raid; the Luftwaffe are thus providing the sound effects for this *King Lear*, and Herr Hitler has left Sir with a company comprised solely of 'old men, cripples and nancy boys' with which to carry the immortal words of the Bard out into the number three touring dates around England. It is not, however, made clear how much (if any) better Sir's company would have been in peacetime, and although Harwood may have had (as he says) the intention of re-creating the 'magnificent tradition' of such old tours, he has allowed his impressions of company characters to degenerate into novelettish glimpses of lovelorn spinster stage-managers or angry young rebels.

Actors will recognize a lot of truth in the two central characters, both of whom theatregoers of thirty and up could easily have encountered as late as 1960; but with the exception of Lockwood West (marvellous as the old 'play as cast' company man hauled in to give his Fool due to the unexplained but all too obvious police detention of Mr Davenport-Scott) the rest of the characters are mere caricatures sent on, like those in Sir's company, to 'keep your teeth in and serve the playwright'.

In the end *The Dresser* is a very schizoid play, hugely entertaining but reflecting only Harwood's own inability to decide whether his love or his hatred for the last generation of the great over-actors should emerge strongest. Suitably enough, therefore, the performance is all: Courtenay and Jones are a stunningly good double-act, so good that it is already impossible to imagine that any of the many actors doubtless already longing to get their hands on this play will ever be better. The idea of a *Lear* being acted both on-stage and off is also stunningly effective; it is in the trappings, in the play's willingness to incorporate a whole treasure trove of green-room wit and wisdom, that some of the power of *The Dresser* is lost. Harwood seems to have been torn between saying something historically very interesting about the way our theatre has changed, and creating a lovable old wreck married not to 'Her Ladyship' (to whom he has declined marriage on the grounds that the prerequisite divorce from a first wife might injure his fading chances of a knighthood) but to his equally wrecked dresser. For all that, *The Dresser* remains the most quintessentially theatrical play we have had since Osborne's *Entertainer* fully twenty years ago.

From out of a bottom drawer, Harold Pinter has dug his 1958 *The Hothouse* and his own production of it, the first ever, can now be seen at the Hampstead Theatre where it emerges as a black, Ortonish little comedy about life and sudden death in a sinister state mental home. These were the pre-*Caretaker* days, when Pinter was still writing revue sketches for Kenneth Williams, and the highlight of the present proceedings is a scene where the loony commandant of the clinic hurls glasses of whisky over an ever replenishing assistant. For the rest, it's an elliptic early attempt at a power play, almost a parody of what we now call Pinteresque. Kafka is somewhere in there too, but the overall impression is that of a game of Scrabble from which someone has removed the board. Edward de Souza is briefly superb as the man from the Ministry, and Derek Newark carries most of the rest.

Class Struggle

At a time when the West End theatre is starved of economic shows, where indeed the Mayfair Theatre is actually closing because of a shortage of same, it is a gesture of eccentricity bordering on the loony for the Royal Shakespeare Company to stage Willy Russell's *Educating Rita* at their Warehouse in Covent Garden. For what we have here is an eminently commercial two–character comedy, better indeed than most comedies currently on offer in the West End, which has nothing at all to do with the RSC and still less to do with the experimental nature of the Warehouse. Moreover there is a Pavlovian critical reflex whereby a play opening at, say, the Fortune or the Ambassadors is treated totally differently from a show opening at the Warehouse, and had Mr Russell gone to either of the former homes I suspect reaction to his play would have been a great deal warmer.

True, *Educating Rita* owes a lot to *Butley* and a great deal more to *Pygmalion*; it concerns a jaded university lecturer (Mark Kingston) into whose study one morning swans an Open University pupil wanting nothing more nor less than a total literary education. He who has hitherto had to suppress a deep desire to throw pupils through windows suddenly finds himself with the perfect recipient for his words of wisdom; she (quirkily and twitchily and marvellously played by Julie Walters from the Victoria Wood telemusicals), progresses from a state of unholy ignorance to one of such utter intellectual and social confidence that she finally has no need at all of her teacher.

What we have here therefore is both a comedy and a tragedy; Mr Russell (he of *John, Paul, George, Ringo . . . and Bert*) has some good jokes, and though he has borrowed his two main characters from earlier and better plays he gets a lot of good fun and even some moments of real drama by throwing them together and watching them operate on each other. Mike Ockrent's production is swift and fluid, and in Rita's getting of wisdom there is something both hilarious and very touching. Her tutor, naturally enough, prefers her ignorant even if this does mean she approaches E. M. Forster with a 13-amp plug on account of his 'Only Connect'; she, on the other hand, cannot wait to put her little learning into action and the end result is an inevitable reversal of roles once we have been through the confrontation immortalized by first Shaw and then Lerner–Loewe as 'I can do bloody well without you'. True, Mr Russell has yet to find his play an effective end, but for all that *Educating Rita* is a lot of fun.

At the Criterion, *Tom Foolery* is essentially *Side by Side by Lehrer*, a two–hour choreographed concert of the American campus satirist's songs from the late 1950s pleasantly hosted by Robin Ray and performed, sometimes rather over-exuberantly, by Jonathan

Adams, Martin Connor and Tricia George under the direction of Gillian Lynne. Tom Lehrer himself gave up writing and performing his own material in about the year that Kissinger got the Nobel Peace Prize, reckoning that satire could go no further. His songs therefore belong to a lost world of undergraduate revue, but that is not to say they have lost their point. His immortal 'Vicar of Bray' number about Wernher von Braun is as true as ever it was, and the 'Old Dope Peddler' turns up in a marvellously sinister and almost whispered rendition by Mr Ray which suggests that more of the numbers might benefit from a quieter and less produced approach. One or two numbers, notably a venereal disease hymn entitled 'I Got It from Agnes', may well come as new, and though it is chilling to find thirty-year-olds in the audience who have never actually heard of Lehrer I suspect there are enough of us forty-year-olds around to fill the Criterion with nostalgia for quite a while – especially now that the tourist season is at last upon us.

On the National's open Olivier stage (and looking about as misplaced there as *Educating Rita* looks at the Warehouse) Alan Ayckbourn's *Sisterly Feelings* is another of his multiple-choice comedies. But whereas *The Norman Conquests* offered you three altogether different plays (albeit with the same characters) if you went back on three different evenings, *Sisterly Feelings* only offers you a choice of middle scenes. Acts One and Four remain constant, and Acts Two and Three are determined by an actress flipping a coin at the end of Act One and then making a partnership choice at the end of Act Two. This power to decide what happens next must be a lot of fun for the actress up there on stage (in fact Penelope Wilton, joined at the National by such other old Ayckbourn hands as Stephen Moore and Michael Gambon) but is rather less fun for us in the audience since we're allowed no hand in the decision. The trick is therefore a lot more impressive in theory than when you have to sit there watching it performed, and in order to stretch a thinnish twelve-character comedy over four possible evenings Ayckbourn is forced to build up a stage machinery that is both creaky and top-heavy because it has to accommodate so many potential alternatives. There are some strong performances here, notably from Andrew Cruickshank as the old paterfamilias, and from Anna Carteret and Miss Wilton as the two sisters of the title, plus a splendid turn from Michael Bryant as a paranoid copper; but what this fragile little jest is doing sprawled out evening after evening across the Olivier stage is something only Sir Peter Hall could explain. It may well be that what has gone wrong in the current West End is as much a loss of purpose as the imposition of VAT or the drop in tourism; but that situation is not helped by both the RSC and the National now taking over plays whose rightful and only logical place is Shaftesbury Avenue.

Young Nick

There are a number of stunningly theatrical moments in the Royal Shakespeare Company's epic new nine-hour dramatization of *Nicholas Nickleby* at the Aldwych, but none better than the final one: after all the loose ends have been interminably tied into one of Dickens' most sentimentally happy endings, the recently married young Nicholas strides down to the footlights and scoops up into his arms one of the destitute lads who have newly been freed by him from the dread Dotheboys Hall. This is not, as some of my critical colleagues would have you believe, merely the gesture of a man about to adopt some poor and unwanted orphan. There is a look of such inner rage on the face of Roger Rees (as Nicholas), and the child is held out to the audience with such defiance, that it is clear he is being offered up as a symbol of poverty and illness and corruption, and as a reminder that when all is said and done, even at such length as here, there are no happy endings.

At which point we'd better go back to the beginning. This *Nickleby* project has been around the RSC for more than two years now: it first emerged partly out of a suggestion by Peter McEnery that Dickens was about due for stage treatment other than those of Lionel Bart and Emlyn Williams, and partly out of an accidental discovery that Dickensian dramatizations are a regular feature of subsidized-company repertoires in the USSR. So if there, why not on home territory?

One reason is of course the sheer scale of the venture: *Nicholas Nickleby*, as dramatized by its cast and stitched together by David Edgar, requires a cast of fifty and nine hours to say nothing of a score (by Stephen Oliver) which would not have disgraced a David O. Selznick movie, and a set (by John Napier and Dermot Mayes) which has entailed the virtual rebuilding of the Aldwych proscenium.

If the question is do we actually need a stage *Nickleby*, the answer must, I believe, be yes; if the question is do we need one at quite this length, the answer gets a bit more uncertain. Since the 1940s movies of David Lean (and *Nickleby* must have been the only one that starred neither Alec Guinness nor John Mills) Dickens has been musicalized out of all existence; *Nickleby* itself has twice been plundered, once for a tele-musical called *Smike!* and on another occasion by the Sherrin–Brahms team who limited themselves as I recall to two major sequences, Dotheboys Hall and the Crummles touring players. Both these sequences are of course in the first third of the book, and there's no denying that by the break in the present production, roughly four hours in, there's a distinct feeling that we've had not just the best of it but virtually all there is worth remembering about the story. We've by then had Mr Squeers (marvellously leeringly played by Ben Kingsley) and we've had the old actor-manager Crummles (equally definitively intoned by Graham Crowden) leading us up to a brilliantly camp first-half finale in which the RSC disguised as the Crummles company solemnly perform the happy–ending version of *Romeo and Juliet*.

If you plan to take in only one part of *Nickleby*, therefore, it has got to be part one; part two, though much more densely packed with characters and sub-plots, is something of an anti-climax unless you believe, as the directors Trevor Nunn and John Caird clearly do, that the event is all and that you have to experience it wholesale, preferably in one day-long sitting. It is an understandable belief, particularly if you happen to be running a company of fifty eager character actors only about half a dozen of whom have had enough to do in part one; but it is here that the sheer intractability of much of the material begins to defeat everyone. Dickens was himself of course no stranger to theatre; not only did he effectively create on American recital tours the notion of the one-man show, he also himself witnessed pirated stage versions of the school scenes from *Nickleby* which were being staged even before he'd completed the rest of the part-work novel. Had he wanted to make *Nickleby* a play rather than a novel he could very well have done so; what stopped him, by all accounts, was a realization that themes of poverty and injustice can only effectively be staged in the very narrowest frames of references. Once you take the whole of London as your canvas, and a hundred and fifty of its citizens as your characters, realistically the stage cannot be expected to cope.

Still, anyone who has recently witnessed *The Greeks* or the closing minutes of *Once in a Lifetime* will tell you that the RSC is currently in a Cecil B. deMille frame of mind, and it has led here to a patchwork tapestry offering (at best) performances like that of Edward Petherbridge as the gently decaying Newman Noggs and (at worst) sequences which appear to have been staged exclusively for an RSC Christmas staff treat. There is a lot of self-indulgent pantomime performing going on here, but there is also a lot that is as powerful and valuable as the performance of John Woodvine playing the evil Ralph Nickleby. His suicide, and the quieter yet infinitely sadder departure of Crummles and his diminished troupe for America, are pictures which will linger like those of Boz. With maybe ninety minutes shaved off its overall running time and some minor performances toned down, *Nickleby* as a whole might be equally triumphant; as it is, we are left to reflect that outside of Russia the RSC must be the only theatrical company capable of such a massive endeavour as this.

On His Todd

Writing this page from New York a year or so ago I put it to you that *Sweeney Todd* was the most important musical of the 1970s. Seeing the show a second time, in Hal Prince's new production at Drury Lane, I am prepared to revise that judgement. It is also the most exciting and innovative attempt to drag the stage musical into the second half of the twentieth century since *West Side Story*, which was also of course a part-Sondheim show.

It will doubtless be argued, indeed is already being argued, that *Sweeney* has lost money on Broadway and can never be regarded as a great or classic show because it breaks all the old laws of the musical theatre. I cannot vouch for its commercial life (though I would remind you that *West Side Story* ran into precisely these objections in 1956 and took a very long time to get its money back at home and abroad) but I can tell you that *Sweeney* matters precisely because and not in spite of its refusal to be yet another cosy Victorian singalong ballad show.

There are no chirruping lines of cockney orphans chanting Lionel

Sweeney Todd Denis Quilley *as Sweeney Todd*, Sheila Hancock *as Mrs Lovett*

Bart pit-a-pat rhymes, no cuddly Annie-type heroines, no affir-
mation that when you leave the theatre you will feel falsely cheerful;
the greatness of *Sweeney Todd* can be measured in terms of the
distance it soars above both *Oliver!* and *Annie*, both easier journeys
along the same period route. Where they were in the business of
happy endings, *Sweeney* is a jet black, vitriolic and viciously brilliant
show played at and on the razor's edge.

In that I have recently published a book about Sondheim and am
an occasional narrator of *Side by Side*, it could be argued that I am
perhaps more committed to him than the ideally if impossibly
neutral critic ought to be; but *Sweeney* is not, as he would I suspect
be the first to admit, a Sondheim show in the sense that, say,
Company was a Sondheim show because if you stripped it of its
diamond-hard lyrics you had nothing left. *Sweeney* by contrast is
the equal achievement of three men.

First, Christopher Bond the playwright who took the old *grand
guignol* legend of the murderous barber and his neighbour who
turned their victims into lunch and gave it a shape and a purpose.
Pre-Bond, Sweeney had always been played as a loony villain; by

constructing a plot about a wrongful arrest, an Australian exile and an abducted daughter Bond has turned the show into a Victorian revenge drama. We now know, as never before, why Sweeney is a killer and who in particular he is setting out to kill.

Second, Stephen Sondheim, who with Hugh Wheeler took Bond's play and gave it a musical shape so that the show is now in fact eighty per cent sung. That means no sudden lurches from dialogue to big number, no lines of chorus dancers aimlessly approaching the footlights, no deathless pause before the star does his second-half solo. Instead, a total and semi-operatic construction comparable to *Peter Grimes* or *Threepenny Opera* in both its ambition and its achievement.

Third and most important, since this is one long and massive production number, the director Hal Prince who with his designer Eugene Lee has turned the Theatre Royal Drury Lane into a micro-cosm of London at the very centre of the Industrial Revolution, thereby giving us not just a murder mystery but a running commentary on the dehumanizing effects of poverty and progress and injustice.

Early preview reports from Drury Lane last week (including that of the editor of this magazine, over whose raised and spirited objections to the show this review is now being written) were not good, and I began to fear that the usual sea change had overcome *Sweeney*, and yet again a show once great on Broadway had become somehow muted and less successful on its journey across the Atlantic.

Not so. If anything, *Sweeney* is in fact stronger in London because of the presence in the title role of Denis Quilley who brings to the demon barber a classical-theatre strength and authority which was inevitably missing from the range of the American actor Len Cariou. This in turn makes the partnership of Sweeney and Mrs Lovett more equal, and though Sheila Hancock is as yet no match for Angela Lansbury, the show's roots in the old end-of-the-pier conventions do become a lot more apparent.

Now, about the score. It is alleged by *Sweeney* doubters that it cannot be immediately hummed in the bath, to which I would reply that no great score ever can be. 'Maria' from *West Side Story* was not (contrary to myth) on everybody's lips the morning after the first night, but about a year later and I would have you know that 'Johanna' is just such a song. The constant achievement of Sondheim's score here is the way that it undercuts and counterpoints and contrasts with what is happening on stage (Sweeney's barber–chair murders are in fact accomplished to the strains of a lyrical number called 'Pretty Women' which is one of the most beautiful I have heard anywhere in the world).

The rest of the casting over here is admittedly a little more shaky (neither Austin Kent as the Judge nor Mandy More as Johanna have the assurance of their Broadway originals) but in Michael Staniforth there is a fine Tobias and Andrew C. Wadsworth has the right kind of inane juvenile-lead courage for Anthony.

I am prepared to admit that others are less enthusiastic, that this may not even be a majority view (though at the time of writing the critical count is far from complete); I am not prepared to believe that anyone who cares even remotely about the future of the stage musical could deny themelves the chance to judge *Sweeney* for themselves.

Freak Show

Three years after its original appearance at Hampstead, and more than a year after a triumphant Broadway opening, Bernard Pomerance's *The Elephant Man* has at last lumbered on to the National's Lyttelton stage in a production by its original director (Roland Rees) starring its original actor (David Schofield). But what we have here is not so much a play as a dramatized documentary of a kind normally associated with schools radio; the story of John Merrick is told in a series of sketchy little scenes from Victorian philanthropic life which add up to something less than might have been expected, given this extraordinary and terrifying subject.

Borrowing (whether consciously or unconsciously) a trick or two from Shaffer's *Equus*, Pomerance sets up a handsome and physically impeccable nude young actor and has him turn himself facially and vocally – not into a horse this time – but instead into the crippled, contorted and disfigured Merrick; he then has – not a psychiatrist this time – but instead a doctor suffering from pangs of Shafferian anguish about the rights of a medical man to impose his concept of normality on to a misfit. What makes *The Elephant Man* so much less successful than *Equus* is however Pomerance's refusal to engage in any real debate about Victorian ethics or charity; having set up various key figures (Peter McEnery as the anguished Doctor Treves, Peter Howell as the head of the hospital who sees in the Elephant Man a useful fundraiser, Arthur Blake as the Elephant Man's ever-hopeful fairground barker and Jennie Stoller as Mrs Kendal, who is virtually hired to give the Elephant Man female companionship because she as a trained actress can be trusted not to give any indication of fear or horror at his deformities) the play uses them as cartoon stereotypes to embody but not to explain or define certain Victorian attitudes.

We therefore get the facts, and very little else; we learn that Merrick was not in fact suffering from elephantiasis but did nevertheless have large brown cauliflower-like growths all over his body; we learn that money was raised via *The Times* to keep him in the London Hospital safe from prying fairground eyes, and that via the interest of celebrities such as Princess Alexandra (who makes a fleeting but pointless appearance) he was turned from a sideshow exhibit into a medical *cause célèbre* and a fashionable toy. For the first half of this short evening we seem to be approaching *The Miracle Worker* or *Children of a Lesser God*, plays about dedicated teachers taking on apparently lost causes whether medical or social; and by the time it becomes clear that Mr Pomerance does in fact have something different to say about people who appear to be curing others but are in fact only trying to cure themselves it is too late, for we are told nothing about the character or background of a man like Treves that would make us care about his own route to salvation.

In its own twisted way this is also of course the Frankenstein legend of the lovable monster, and in the second half we are also asked to consider (as we were in *Equus*) that the nearer a man is to normality the nearer he also is to death. In starting to write about *The Elephant Man* there were various routes Pomerance could have chosen, from straight history through social hypocrisy to the reversal of the patient–doctor relationship. His play peers down a number of those routes, but sets off on none of them. For all that, it does allow David Schofield to give one of the best performances currently to be seen anywhere in London, and there's a striking white-tiled hospital set by Tanya McCallin.

Meanwhile, to the National's Cottesloe stage have come three superb actors from the Johannesburg Market Theatre in Athol Fugard's own production of his *A Lesson from Aloes*, aloes being hardy cactus-like plants which unlike the people who grow them manage to survive the current South African climates. Mr Fugard's message here would seem to be that in order to be deeply unhappy and tormented in South Africa it is not necessary also to be black. Whites too are the victims of apartheid, and for the first act of this Ibsenesque family tragi-comedy we are concerned solely with an Afrikaner farmer and his mentally disturbed wife. He (Marius Weyers) is a bluff, pedantic fellow who, it transpires, may also have betrayed a black friend to the local police; she (Shelagh Holliday) is a refugee from a mental home and they are soon joined by the betrayed friend (Bill Curry). All have therefore recently been locked up in something, and that in essence is what Mr Fugard would have us know about South Africa; it is a lock-up for all, and in the end only the plants have any true freedom.

If you can imagine an Ayckbourn comedy transposed to a police state, that is Fugard territory; his characters are joky, lifelike ramblers trying to activate their own survival mechanisms while all around become increasingly hostile.

He too is a miniaturist, a writer who deals in characters and only then in themes; true, there are moments when the machinery of his dramatic writing seems to be grinding both loud and slow, but through it all shines such a fundamental love and optimism for humanity that the present situation of which he writes is made to seem all the more terrible. 'Politics and black skins,' as the wife here says, 'don't make the only victims in this country' and victims at their most hilarious and touching are the people about whom Fugard has always written best. In his own country he is still regarded as a licensed jester; here he should be regarded as that country's most reliable voice.

There's a Pal

'I have written some stories for the *New Yorker* about a nighclub singer called Joey,' wrote John O'Hara to his friend Lorenz Hart in 1940, 'and I think perhaps they might make a kind of a musical.' They did, and also a kind of musical history; *Pal Joey* was to become the last big Rodgers–Hart success, and it came only a matter of months before *Oklahoma!* with which Rodgers abandoned the dry-Martini acid lyrics of Larry Hart for the pumpkin-pie ditties of

Oscar Hammerstein. But *Pal Joey* is not only important because it marks the end of Rodgers–Hart; it's also important because it marks the beginning of the modern musical. For the first time on Broadway, here was a show in which the chorus line was intentionally tacky and the plot actually had something to do with the songs; here in fact was an integrated show.

All credit therefore to Robert Walker in his new Half Moon Theatre, some way down the Mile End Road, for giving London the first professional glimpse of *Joey* in more than a quarter of a century. Allowing that the Sinatra film was a travesty of the original, using its plot outlines as little more than a vehicle in which to transport the best of the Rodgers–Hart numbers from other shows, and given that the Lord Chamberlain even in 1954 was demanding cuts, it is indeed arguable that what we now have at the Half Moon is Britain's first ever original version of that classic show.

It has fallen into safe hands. Mr Walker, who with his choreographer Stuart Hopps last year gave us a superb small-scale *Guys and Dolls* at the old Half Moon premises, is such a master of the 1940s tacky that any day now I expect to find him directing pinball machines in Las Vegas. What he has understood about *Pal Joey* is that given a zonking great female star with a husky voice (and in this sense he has brilliantly discovered Sian Phillips), plus an unusually adequate hoofer (in this case Denis Lawson), the show itself can hardly fail.

True, its plot has the broken-backed structure that comes of adapting short stories (remember *Company*?) and like all great musicals *Pal Joey* is, when you analyse it, in fact about nothing very much. There's this failed nightclub host who meets a wealthy lady who is then blackmailed on account of her extramarital affair with him, and that's about it. But along the way we get 'I Could Write a Book' and 'Bewitched, Bothered and Bewildered' and a dozen other lesser-known triumphs: soaring Rodgers melodies pulled back to earth by the cynicism of Hart's lyrics.

True too, it would help the interests of accuracy if the showgirls in a supposedly 1930s Chicago nightclub were not reading an issue of *Variety* headlining Liberace and the coming of cable television, and there is no visible reason why a police chief of the time should be hooked on the Bogart–Cagney imitations of a decade later. But hedged in by the tight budget of the Half Moon (band of six, cast of twelve, setting about twenty feet by six) Mr Walker has found a genuinely local way of doing the big band shows of the past, and one which works very well. Robin Hooper turns in a manically sinister crooked agent, Jane Gurnett is a wonderfully frumpy Adele, and though Jean Hart's first-night zendering of 'Zip' was disappointing, there are signs that it too will one day mesh with the general bittersweet air of seedy confidence that this production revels in. Anyway, to hear Sian Phillips croak 'Vexed again, Perplexed again, Thank God I can be oversexed again' is in itself worth the journey to the Essex borders, and as one of the chorines tells Joey, to get to El Morocco he'd have to join the Foreign Legion first. Here the seediness is all, and it works triumphantly. The only remaining questions are how soon they transfer to the West End, and how well they will be able to preserve the crucial tackiness of the Mile End Road.

Fiasco Time

Now that at least some of the dust has settled around the O'Toole *Macbeth* (at the Old Vic, and arguably the greatest Shakespearian catastrophe since the burning of the Globe) we may perhaps be allowed to ask ourselves certain questions, not only about how the whole thing was allowed to happen in the first place but also about what it portends for the by no means assured future of the Vic itself.

The problem here is not just that a 1960s film star eager to clamber back into a theatrical lifeboat has been allowed to take the entire ship's crew down with him, though it is in this context perhaps worth noting that when Burton found himself similarly eager to get back to the American stage this summer he went back not in the long-threatened *King Lear* but instead in the musical *Camelot* as a way of getting himself back into condition. The real problem here is one of management.

Since Peter Hall pulled his National Theatre team out of the Vic in 1975, virtually nothing of any real value has happened there: occasional touring and children's companies have been allowed to come and go; Prospect made it a temporary home where they did an adequate Jacobi *Hamlet* and an appalling McCowen *Antony and Cleopatra*; and in casting around for a resident director at the beginning of this year the board came up with Timothy West, an interesting and valuable character actor with little experience of administration or regular theatrical production. In this context the Vic board decision (and I sometimes think our theatre will die not of VAT or falling tourism or the strengthened pound but quite simply of theatre boards) made about as much sense to me as giving Chichester to Keith Michell, though that too, may I remind you, was once done by a board.

Mr West is claiming, both publicly and privately, that the decision to give O'Toole total artistic control over this *Macbeth* (one which led not only to the appointment of Bryan Forbes as director – a man with no Shakespearian training of any kind – but also to the choosing of a cast many of whom would have been lucky to get work on a Wolfit tour of Rotherham in 1938) was reached before he took over the Vic and that he was therefore stuck with it. He could, however, not have taken the job, or better yet have made it a condition that the O'Toole deal be renegotiated. But West took the deal on, and indeed the Vic throughout the summer did run a curiously unattractive hard-sell advance ticket campaign whereby money was taken into the box-office, at one estimate around £600,000, for a totally untried and untested season. Given that the rest of the season is not only virtually starless but also curiously 1960s seaside rep in its choice of plays (*Godot, Merchant of Venice, The Importance*) it follows that the advance was taken in solely on the O'Toole magic. Indeed the massive pre-publicity announced that 'Peter O'Toole and Timothy West invite you to subscribe.'

What has emerged from the Waterloo Road these last few days has been the realization that the Vic cannot be saved by a 1960s film star who comes on stage, arch as the admiralty, to convey to us a state of deep trance-like inadequacy bathed in a glow of amber lighting of the kind MGM used to accord Esther Williams underwater. Nor can it be saved by an administration who believe that pre-publicity and pre-selling are any substitute for a coherent policy of casting and production. Even Harry Lauder, to whose memory Mr O'Toole made constant rehearsal allusion, could have run the Vic better than that.

There are directors around (indeed one of them, Frank Dunlop, is working rather less than 500 yards from the stage door) with the vision and the energy to save the Vic by imposing upon it some sort of coherent reason for continued existence. If none can be found with sufficient experience, then it might be as well to turn the Vic over to a permanent theatre museum where future generations could perhaps learn from the mistakes of the past. One of which, of course, is this production.

At the Royal Court, Caryl Churchill's *Cloud Nine* is an intriguing dose of surrealist humour in a reasonably serious play about sexual politics. By taking the same group of actors (in a Joint Stock production by Max Stafford-Clark and Les Waters) and having them play first in Victorian colonial Africa and then in a contemporary London park, *Cloud Nine* manages to be at the same time a transsexual farce and a savage indictment of role-playing in a society which has long since forgotten how and why the roles were cast in the first place. At the head of a strong and versatile team (though one of the few not required to work in drag) Graeme Garden continues to establish a non-'Goody' foothold in stage comedy, and seldom can a social tract have been quite so enjoyable on quite so many other levels.

Rhine Gold

Lillian Hellman called a volume of her memoirs *Pentimento* because of her fascination with the process that title denotes – the process whereby an old portrait can sometimes fade, leaving the outlines of a quite different portrait clearly visible beneath it.

In many ways, that same process can now be detected in the new National Theatre production by Mike Ockrent of her 1940 drama *Watch on the Rhine* which is getting (on the Lyttelton stage) its first major London revival in almost forty years.

On the surface, this is an American country-house melodrama inspired by Henry James but curiously situated somewhere midway from John Buchan to Enid Bagnold. A wealthily widowed dowager (Peggy Ashcroft, in a hugely welcome return to the stage after an absence of four years) living with her cantankerous housekeeper and her feeble son on a country estate in Maryland, in the months before Pearl Harbor but after the invasion of Czechoslovakia, takes into her very gracious home first a couple of rather shady Romanians and then her own daughter (Susan Engel) also on the run from war-torn Europe.

This daughter has been married for several years now to an

anti-Nazi freedom fighter (David Burke, in the performance of the evening) and it does not take us long to realize that he and the shady Romanian pro-Nazi husband (Sandor Eles) are soon to come to a parting of the ways. For the Romanian ('not a nationality,' sniffs the dowager, 'it's a profession') threatens the survival not just of the anti-Nazi but of all his friends still in Germany and clearly he has to be stopped in his treacherous tracks.

But on a deeper if still more faded level, through the outline of wartime heroics, can be discerned the framework of a quite different and very much stronger play about the morality of terrorism and about America's isolationist policies in 1940. On this level it's a play about arrogance, about wealth, about power and about the ending of the old pre-Roosevelt America in which being alone and aloof was still a possible posture for a nation formed specifically as an alternative to European self-destruction.

In a meticulously crafted, minutely observed and superbly played production, Hellman's stately mansion is opened up for our inspection like a 1940s' dolls' house: here are the three grandchildren, already old before their time because they have spent most of their short lives with father on the run from Hitler. Here is their mother, suddenly finding herself home again among the rolling lawns and the cribbage games but unable to recall the language of sundrenched rooms in which nobody is hiding. Here too, constantly crossing the barriers between country-house comedy and political thriller, is a play about Europe at war set entirely within twenty miles of Washington.

But the memories that linger are the performances: Burke (as the slowly and softly spoken father explaining to his children not only his next and probably last departure from them, but also the evil that men like him have been forced to do in the name of good), Eles as the archetypal Romanian failed hustler, Engel as the long-suffering wife and Ashcroft finally realizing that the war has now reached her very own doorstep. All are at the very top of their considerable form and the evening is, as a result, a splendid celebration of sheer old-fashioned but superbly fashioned theatricality.

Tripped Egos

A great deal of what is wrong, and some of what is right, with *They're Playing Our Song* (at the Shaftesbury) can be worked out by recalling the circumstances in which it was written three years ago. The composer Marvin Hamlisch and the playwright Neil Simon were at that time involved in an altogether different musical project, one that never in fact made it to the footlights. During that collaboration, Hamlisch began to tell Simon about an affair he was then having with the lyricist Carole Bayer Sager; Simon, seeing presumably in that 'odd couple' relationship a rerun of almost every New York comedy he had ever written, from *Barefoot in the Park* through twenty years to the present, began to outline a musical about a composer and a lyricist falling in and out of love between songs. Boy gets piano, boy gets girl, boy loses girl, boy keeps piano, boy gets girl back.

So far, so slick: an all-American musical, apparently devised by and for computers. It has already been playing to capacity for a couple of years on Broadway, and any day now they'll have Rock Hudson and Juliet Prowse doing it for Las Vegas. In the meantime, here it is in London with Tom Conti making his singing debut opposite Gemma Craven in a two-character and near-three-hour show. Backing them, a big brassy orchestra, a sextet of 'inner voices' and some glossily elegant cut-out skylines of Manhattan in a faithful reproduction of the original production.

Conti plays heavily on boyish charm, and manages throughout the evening to give an endearing and cunning impression of an actor who didn't really mean to be there at all. His is the performance of a man who has dropped into a ritual Broadway orchestral celebration and who feels that since he is there it would be churlish of him not to sing and dance a bit, which is precisely what he does. A bit.

Gemma Craven is altogether more at home, not surprisingly considering her distinguished musical track record, and the moments when this show does lift off are generally hers. But not even her manic vitality can disguise the fact that this is a very empty evening; it is as bright and as smooth and as glittery as the Pan Am skyscraper, but it looks like that skyscraper at night when the lights have been left on and the people have all gone home.

Neil Simon's especial brand of New York acid romanticism has never really worked in the West End; this time it may, because the songs are there to help it along. They're not great songs, and indeed you feel that you've been hearing them for years across hotel lifts and airport lounges; but that is precisely the familiarity of their appeal. The dialogue is Manhattan urban chic ('I was going to take a Valium but I couldn't get my teeth unclenched') and in terms of its origins this is probably the nearest that the Broadway musical has ever got to an autobiographical home movie. A theatre-going audience that can flock to this rather than *Sweeney Todd* (as happened on Broadway and may well be about to happen here) is not my kind of theatre-going audience; but if it's a mindlessly plastic, all-purpose, bland and no-thought show you're after, one as neatly and perfectly processed as an American Express card, then this is for you.

On the homegrown musical front, it needs to be added that *Colette* (at the Comedy) is not nearly as terrible as most of my colleagues would have you believe. That still makes it fairly terrible, but the real mistake here is to think of it as a musical at all. What John Dankworth has done, in response to his wife Cleo Laine's long-held desire to play Colette, is to put together a cycle of songs vaguely inspired by the life and times of the legendary French novelist. If heard on a record, or in a brief tele-concert, these songs would, I think, have considerable charm in an old 1950s Sandy Wilson convention.

True, the numbers in the first half do include a quota of clinkers, including one especially horrendous 'Ah Paree' song which if the evidence of my notes is to be believed contains the immortal couplet 'Mata Hari will get/All the dirt from Mistinguette', but they improve greatly after the interval, notably when we get to 'Love with Someone Younger' and Miss Laine and Mr Nelson (who plays all the other roles, two-character musicals now being something of a fashion) are able to give us an inkling of what this show might have been like if somebody had bothered to write a book for it.

Instead, what we have is effectively a concert evening, *Side by Side by Cleo and Colette*, jokily narrated by John Moffatt in *Irma la Douce* mood; Miss Laine is however no actress, and given dialogue like 'How's that hip of yours this morning?' she looks understandably a little lost. She is however a great dramatic singer, and when she is allowed to belt out the numbers all is briefly well. Then we get back to a sketchy kind of biography, told in Encyclopaedia

Britannica style, and one starts to think that perhaps the answer would have been to have Cleo sing Colette while somebody else acted out the story of her amazing life and times. Mr Nelson and Mr Moffatt cope valiantly on the sidelines, but cannot hide from us the fact that this is more a solo show with interruptions than a genuine three-hander. What we have, in the end, is a singer and some songs in search of a show; but for all that I'm still going out to buy the record.

Dublin Troubles

The surprising thing about *Juno and the Paycock* (now in a masterly revival by Trevor Nunn for the Royal Shakespeare Company at the Aldwych in celebration of the O'Casey centenary) is how little it turns out to be about its apparent theme. Set in 1922 in the two-room tenement home in Dublin of Juno Boyle and her 'Captain Jack', the strutting pub-peacock husband of the title, it was described by O'Casey himself as 'a play about the calamitous Civil War in Ireland, when brother went to war with brother over a few insignificant words in a Treaty with England'.

And so, in its final moment, this is indeed a play about the original Irish troubles. But only then. For two preceding acts we have in fact been treated to an altogether different play, a comedy of Irish manners centred around the 'Paycock' himself, marvellously comically played by Norman Rodway. In his refusal to go to work, in his sudden twinges of mythical leg-pains, in his phony blustering and makeshift memoirs, in his love-hate relationship with his treacherous neighbour Joxer (played in a fine double-act with Rodway by John Rogan) are the beginnings of every twentieth-century British television success from 'Coronation Steet' to 'George and Mildred'.

It was in the nature of O'Casey's brilliance to realize that neither the Abbey in Dublin nor audiences elsewhere would in 1924 accept a play of unremitting gloom about the then still current troubles. Better to give them a comedy, '*Macbeth* as viewed from the Porter's lodge', and then gradually turn it back on the customers so that the laughs would freeze on their lips. And still, half a century later, those laughs freeze.

It is only at the end of the second act that it happens: a sudden shadow of a gunman in the doorway, and Juno's already twitching son is led away to certain death. Now we learn why he has spent the first half of the play in a state of shock: not just to be the butt of his father's scorn, but because he knows he has betrayed a rebel and is to die. And that is just the beginning of the end. The legacy which Juno and the Paycock have been counting on to pay for their furniture turns out to be a mirage; their daughter's boyfriend then leaves her both pregnant and unmarriageable even to the one man (finely played by Frank Grimes) who does truly love her.

When therefore the Paycock gets back from the pub with Joxer in the play's chilling final scene, it is to a total unawareness that his son has been killed while his daughter and wife have left him in search of a home for the new and illegitimate child. He is now, and forever, with Joxer: their comedy has become a tragedy of death and destruction and they still don't know it.

In an immensely distinguished cast (Marie Kean turns up momentarily as the grieving neighbour) Judi Dench plays Juno with infinite courage; surrounded by the genuine Irish her accent occasionally wavers, and she still lacks the earth-mother quality that perhaps wrongly we have come to expect of a true Juno. But this is a performance that will mature and grow, and when it has we shall have at the Aldwych one of the finest O'Casey revivals I have ever seen.

Museum Piece

Way back in the late 1950s, at a time when Harold Pinter was still writing revues and Peter Cook just starting to do so, there was a curious fashion for blackout sketches in which a couple (usually played by Kenneth Williams and Fenella Fielding) would discuss the relative futility of their lives, the need for wall-to-wall carpeting and the possibility of there being either a God or a reliable bus service nearby. It comes however as something of a shock twenty years later to find a playwright I admire just this side of idolatry, a playwright who gave us in *Forty Years On* the finest postwar comedy of the British theatre and in *The Old Country* a spy drama which makes *Blade on the Feather* look like the pale rerun it in fact was, going back to those ancient revue jokes in search of a new script.

But that, alas, is what Alan Bennett has now done. His *Enjoy* (at the Vaudeville) appears to have been cobbled together from lines overheard on public transport, and is played by Colin Blakely and Joan Plowright in a kind of weary vaudeville double-act which suggests they may yet be right for *Red Peppers*. In a note attached to the Faber paperback edition of his play (which I read in the sadly vain hope that my ears had deceived me) Mr Bennett suggests that his scripts have in the past been 'altered and improved in rehearsal' and expects that the same thing will have happened again. It hasn't.

The idea here would seem to be the simple reverse of that in Peter Nichols' many comedies: nostalgia as a destructive force, memory lane closed for repair, and an elderly couple (living in the last back-to-back of a Leeds slum) about to be moved to a human museum where they can be admired as breathing relics of a bygone age. The social workers who invade their living-room as observers are, if I have understood Mr Bennett correctly, the playwrights and journalists and tele-interviewers and other busybodies who seem to believe that in our island past may lie some desultory clues to our bleak future. But all of that was said, and admirably said, in the closing moments of the headmaster's farewell speech in *Forty Years On*, the speech about tidying the old into tall flats and desolation at fifteen storeys becoming a view. Now, across two and a half endless hours, we get some good if random one-liners ('Our toilet was pre-grant, it came out of our own pocket') and the unnerving vision of a playwright desperately signalling that he thinks he might have a message for us if we could just hang on a bit while he does the jokes.

Along the way, a cast of thirteen (and when did you last see one of those in a West End comedy?) are thrown around the stage like props in the routine of some surrealist juggler; with the exception of Miss Plowright, doing a passable Beryl Reid, and Mr Blakely doing a good dour and frequently dead Dad, they could as well have been inflatable dummies. Mr Bennett's special talent is for creating or collecting resonant random comments, much after the fashion of an Inspector of Graffiti; lines like 'It takes more than a bit of vinyl to change humanity' and 'They give death grants now – I put Clifford towards some loose covers' ought to qualify him for some sort of permanent BBC employment as a human tape recorder of Britain at her most quirkily characteristic.

The trouble occurs when he starts looking for a play to house all of that. *Enjoy* is at its most ambitious and unlikeable when it tries to suggest some sort of sustainable framework for its comments; when it lurches into a brief corpse-disposal farce, or a simple monologue from the kind of interfering neighbour who can never understand why hers isn't a salaried profession, you remember Bennett's origins in revue and wish that he had gone back to them on this occasion. Not even the Pseuds' Corner pretension of the final backlit frozen-statue ending to Ron Eyre's production can convince me that what we have here is a coherent play; but nor, mercifully, can it take away the memory of one or two very funny isolated moments.

Whatever the dubious alliance of Sir Horace Cutler and Mrs Mary Whitehouse may have led you to believe, the scandal of *The Romans in Britain* (on the National Theatre's Olivier stage) has nothing at all to do with naked Romans and Celts going up each other like knives, nor yet to do with theatrical censorship. The scandal here concerns an artistic director engaged abroad when he could or at least should have been expecting trouble at home, and more importantly the artistic administration of a state-subsidized company which could allow this play to get beyond the Xerox machine, let alone into first rehearsal. Not because it is scandalous, or tasteless, or shocking, but because it is an underwritten and overproduced pageant which would look inadequate if performed as a school play. Ironically the publicity here, as for *Macbeth*, will doubtless encourage box-office queues; but where are those prepared to pay for a really good evening?

The question arises because at the Round House, on the only Monday night of its fortnight in London, Alan Ayckbourn's latest comedy, *Season's Greetings*, was playing to an audience of less than thirty per cent. True, there is currently an Ayckbourn glut in town, but the sad thing here is that not only is *Season's Greetings* a vintage anthology of all his best characters, it was also being played by the original Scarborough company considerably more wittily and touchingly than I have ever seen Ayckbourn played in London before.

Hollow Crown

In times of economic crisis, think big: the formula worked for Hollywood in the 1930s, hence all those Busby Berkeley Depression musicals, and it is working at the Royal Shakespeare Company right now. In what might well have been a year of cautious retrenchment they have so far given us a nine-hour rendition of *The Greeks* and a seven-hour *Nicholas Nickleby*. Now, to close the 1980 season on the main Stratford stage, they are giving us not just one but two Shakespearian King Richards: Alan Howard as Richard II and Richard III with roughly the same team of supporting players and the same director, Terry Hands. By opening them on consecutive nights, it may well be thought that in their current eventomania the RSC wish us to see some kind of a connection above and beyond the fact that both plays happen to be by Shakespeare and about kings called Richard. Doubtless next year we shall be getting *Twelfth Night* and *The Comedy of Errors* back to back in a major RSC season about Shakespearian twins. The trouble here is that *Richard II* and *Richard III* have no conceivable connection.

There have, so far as I can recall, been three major production theories about *Richard II* in living memory: the poet-King played by Gielgud, forever listening to the sound of his own melodious verse, the ravingly bisexual old queen-King played by Ian McKellen and the subtler Stratford mirror notion, whereby Richard and Bolingbroke were played (by Ian Richardson and Richard Pasco) as reflections of the same face.

Now we have a fourth: Richard as operatic hero, the actor-King who enjoys the throne the way some prima donnas enjoy the matinees. Thus we start in a rich golden setting with Richard in a campy yellow satin number visibly having himself a whale of a time on the throne, descending to interrupt the Mowbray–Bolingbroke duel for all the world like some mediaeval quizmaster running a royal generation game.

So far, so glittery; but already it's clear that we're going to have to pay a high price for the operatic convention. Gaunt, for instance: instead of the usual craggy dying prophet, new-inspired with a glimpse of England's collapse, we have a Tito Gobbi lookalike booming out the lines in rotund good health and then suddenly dropping off in the most unlikely death scene since Little Nell's. Gaunt is apparently playing at being old and ill in much the same way that Richard is playing at being King; the performance is all, and not only Richard and Gaunt but also York and Bolingbroke appear to be forever auditioning for some unseen royal gossip columnist.

The trouble with all this relentless theatricality is that it kills any real feeling for the verse or the drama; if they're all just actors, then it scarcely matters whether Richard or Bolingbroke retains the throne. Even the chain that ties Richard to his prison cell is long enough to have anchored the *Titanic*, and when Exton comes to do the murder he comes not stealthily but attended by nine, count them, nine assistants.

There are some fine performances here, not only from Howard and David Suchet as a rapidly ageing and wearying Bolingbroke, but also from Raymond Westwell as Gaunt, Tony Church as a giggly Duke of York and Bruce Purchase as a powerful and sinister Northumberland, already looking eager to get on to *Henry IV* wherein he has rather more to do. But in the end this *Richard* is flashy where it should be dazzling.

At the National, Bill Bryden is ending his current directorship of the Cottesloe stage with a curious production of *The Crucible* by Arthur Miller. This is one of the very few plays the National has done twice in its fifteen-year history, and in its rigidly stylized convention and its heightened use of language it is an odd choice for a company at the Cottesloe who have proved themselves in a diametrically different and considerably looser theatrical frame-work, that of *Lark Rise* and *The Passion*.

Seen now, a quarter-century on from the McCarthy hearings that gave the play its initial impetus (though were not, Miller is forever pointing out, its sole inspiration), *The Crucible* emerges as a desperately overlong melodrama owing considerable debts to the kind of Shavian debating that went into *The Devil's Disciple* and *Saint Joan*. Admittedly the first night at the Cottesloe was not much helped by a running time of three and a half hours (I have seen shorter *King Lears*) and a company most of whom seemed to be experiencing considerable difficulty with the density of Miller's prose. But even allowing that it may now have got sharper and quicker, it is hard to see what (except perhaps the massive success of *Death of a Salesman* at the Lyttelton) could have inspired Bryden to saddle up this old warhorse about Salem witch-hunting on a stage where it would have been so much more intriguing to have seen *After the Fall* or any of Miller's less classroom-clichéd scripts. Nor do I entirely understand why a play set in 1692 Massachusetts is being played in a thick Irish brogue; adequate rep performances come from Mark McManus as Proctor and Dinah Stabb as his Goodwife, but this production has nothing new to tell us about Miller and still less to do with the theatrical purpose and ethic of the Cottesloe.

Warren Piece

At the National Theatre, solemnly billed as a fiftieth birthday tribute to Harold Pinter which is nice of them considering that Shakespeare and Shaw, Rattigan and Coward, Osborne and Wesker have yet to enjoy anniversary honours there, a revival of *The Caretaker* has just opened on the Lyttelton stage directed by Kenneth Ives with Warren Mitchell, Jonathan Pryce and Kenneth Cranham. It is eminently respectable, if perhaps a little more joky and less menacing than usual. It has in fact all the qualities of one of those BBC1 classic 'Plays of the Month', Sunday-night revivals of acknowledged masterpieces which while never terribly good are never terribly bad either, and prove well worth watching if you happen to be home that night with a really bad old movie on ITV.

The reason this production of *The Caretaker* has all those qualities is that it *is* in fact a BBC1 'Play of the Month', to be transmitted next March but meanwhile lifted wholesale from television studio to National stage. Thus we are able to see, live but much after the fashion of an audience let in to watch a taping, Warren Mitchell's splendid, rubbery, spluttering Davies, Jonathan Pryce's unusually Steptoe-like Mick and Kenneth Cranham's finely obsessive Aston. But it would be nice to know how many more 'Plays of the Month' the National is proposing to hijack from television studios; an artistic directorship capable of *The Romans in Britain* is admittedly capable of anything, but assuming that Pinter's connection with the National qualifies him for this unique half-century tribute might it not have made more sense to mount a genuine National production of one of his less familiar works rather than one which has now had three major London revivals in the last decade?

My Dinner with Andre, which ran last week for five performances at the Royal Court's Theatre Upstairs and is now happily about to be filmed by its director Louis Malle, was an evening of rare and remarkable magic. The notion was simple and indeed unpromising: two men, playing themselves, meet in a New York restaurant for a reunion dinner after five years apart. One, Wallace Shawn, is a playwright and bit-part movie actor who looks and sounds like a refugee from a Woody Allen comedy. The other, Andre Gregory, is a director who once ran the Manhattan Project theatre where Shawn's first play was given an airing. But since then Gregory has dropped out, gone first to Poland to run a theatre group in a forest under the influence of Grotowski (the group, not the forest) and then to the Sahara and finally Scotland in search of deeper meanings and amazing spiritual revelations. Now, back off-Broadway, he is prepared to tell all and does so in a conversation with Shawn which lasts two uninterrupted hours. The set is two chairs, a table and a bottle of Perrier water; the conversation is the play, and to eavesdrop is what we are there for.

The two men form a marvellously odd couple; Shawn is thirty-six, squat, affable, living with a waitress, neurotically obsessed with a lack of cash and cheerfully prepared to admit at the start of the dinner that he 'only likes rational people who aren't going to surprise me' which would seem to rule out Andre since at forty-six Andre stands (or rather sits and talks) for an altogether other world, a world of Grotowski and Peter Brook and Ingmar Bergman films and christenings in Polish forests, a man who can admit that he and an entire group of actors once occupied themselves totally for several months by 'trying to create a hole to drop into'. He is in short the kind of man to whom the Arts Council used to give grants, a surrealist impresario who confusingly looks just like a classical Shakespearian tragedian while Shawn, arguing the orthodox alternative, looks like Peter Brook.

Inevitably, as the conversation wears on, you begin to take sides; is it really better to have travelled the Sahara with a renegade Japanese priest trying to work out a dramatization of *The Little Prince,* meanwhile abandoning not only home and loving family but also the actors you originally gathered together in Manhattan, or is it better to have stayed around New York cobbling together a living from day to day and retreating under an electric blanket from the more existential problems of western civilization? In the end, I came down firmly for Wally; he may still be reading the autobiography of Charlton Heston, his view of acting and indeed the world may be somewhat blinkered by the need to get through until tomorrow, but at least he isn't out there in the desert with a bag over his head pretending to be a hole in the ground. In the end, as he so rightly inquires of Andre, 'What does it mean just to sit there?' Andre remains unrepentant, Grotowski's Pied Piper, and I have a terrible feeling that any day now he'll be off to India with Peter Brook and the *Conference of the Birds*. But for as long as he stays around, and allows this conversation with Wally to be immortalized on celluloid, it does provide a splendid debate not only about conventional versus experimental art forms, but more importantly whether life is about getting to the bank before it closes or something altogether more ambitious, pretentious and in the end incomprehensible even to its participants.

Stage '80

Not the most wonderful of theatrical years, indeed one already famous for its on-stage disasters, though in fact neither the O'Toole *Macbeth* (at the Vic) nor the Brenton *Romans in Britain* (at the National) were as bad as the critics said. Both were a great deal worse. Elsewhere, specifically in the West End, managers have been looking so far backwards over their nostalgic shoulders as to be in imminent danger of breaking their necks: the year of Richard Rodgers' death brought *Oklahoma!* and *Pal Joey* back, but it also brought us Noël Coward (*Private Lives*), Mary Pickford and Lillian Gish (*The Biograph Girl*), Gilbert and Sullivan (*Hinge and Bracket*), Victorian melodrama (*The Streets of London*), Tom Lehrer (*Tom Foolery*), Terence Rattigan and Lillian Hellman at the National and Charles Dickens at the Aldwych.

Indeed so desperate was the Society of West End Theatre to find a Best New Play worthy of award this month that they gave their prize to *Nicholas Nickleby* which is neither new nor a play, though undoubtedly the best theatrical event of the year. Like Busby Berkeley's Hollywood in the Depression thirties, Trevor Nunn's Royal Shakespeare Company has this year been battling inflation and a slump with ever bigger and better productions – among them not only the eight-hour *Nickleby* extravaganza but a nine-hour John

Barton *Greeks* (an epic unfairly already forgotten in the rush to honour *Nickleby*) and a double helping of Alan Howard as Shakespearian *Kings Richard II* and *III* at Stratford.

The National has had by contrast a somewhat low-key year, unless you count the Cutler–Whitehouse yapping over the *Romans* which neatly sidetracked the issue into censorship when it should really have been about an appalling failure of management; that apart, its successes have been in getting Peggy Ashcroft back on to the boards after a four-year absence in an eminently respectable revival of Hellman's *Watch on the Rhine* and in getting Michael Gambon up to starring status in John Dexter's superlative revival of *Galileo,* while its failures include a curious thermonuclear saga called *Thee and Me* and the baroque miscasting of Alec McCowen as the old schoolmaster in Rattigan's *Browning Version.* There has also been a curious failure to recognize that Alan Ayckbourn's sprawling and very minor *Sisterly Feelings* comedies can only be justified in taking up a couple of nights a week of the Olivier space by the crudest box-office measurements, and here again there has been a terrible absence of anything very new.

What we have, all over the British theatre at the moment, is a crisis in management: once you have listed Trevor Nunn at the RSC, Alan Strachan at Greenwich, Giles Havergal at Glasgow and Michael Elliott at Manchester it is actually very hard to think of any other subsidized theatre in Britain that is being run as well as it could or should be, and non-subsidized theatres are by their very natures not being run at all, they are merely being leased out much after the fashion of rooms in a seaside boarding-house, over-expensively and often for short stays only.

A number of good theatrical managements have recently come to avoidable ends: Bill Bryden has left the Cottesloe where he gave the National its only really sustained run of success since the new building opened, Peter Gill has left the Riverside, and the Lyric Hammersmith has (until this month's arrival of Peter James from Sheffield) sorely lacked a visible and flamboyant administrator. In building terms we appear to have lost the Astoria for ever as a theatre but the Mayfair, after nine months in the dark, made a spectacular return to life at the end of the year with Bertice Reading in concert and now looks set to stay in business as a commercial theatre once again.

Perhaps the most important development of a financially difficult and (for shows) disastrous year has been the belated realization by commercial managements that instead of fighting each other for customers they would do better to band together against such common enemies as falling tourism, scandalous VAT charges, an increasingly sordid West End environment and an over-strong pound. Thus, and only ten years after it was first mooted, we at last have the cut-price ticket booth in Leicester Square and some indication that the commercial theatre is prepared to fight for a life it appeared to have already almost abandoned.

Elsewhere it has been a year of isolated but powerful delights: Sondheim's *Sweeney Todd* at Drury Lane was shamefully mistreated by most critics and therefore ignored by theatregoers but will eventually emerge (indeed is already emerging in award lists) as one of the most important and influential musicals of the century; Ralph Richardson, that greatest of all National treasures, is back in the West End (at the Comedy) in David Storey's fragile but poetic *Early Days*; Glenda Jackson (as *Rose*) and Frances de la Tour (as the crippled musician in *Duet for One*) and Tom Courtenay (in Ronald Harwood's Wolfit play *The Dresser*) all gave the kind of performances that will be remembered long after the year is over.

Three untimely deaths have taken from us the actress Rachel Roberts, the critic Kenneth Tynan and the playwright David Mercer; in those terms it has been an unusually sad year but the general air of doom and despondency in which it started proved to be (if only a little) premature. The most that could be said about the London theatre in 1980 is that it has survived largely intact, but that at present is no mean achievement.

1981

Altered Egos

Not since the mid-forties, when Mary Chase first produced her invisible rabbit out of the Broadway hat in *Harvey*, has there been the invention of a stage device quite so neat as that provided by Peter Nichols for his new *Passion Play*, now in an agile RSC production by Mike Ockrent at the Aldwych. The device is quite simply that of the alter ego: both main characters have by intermission appeared on stage in duplicate, so that while James and Eleanor are man and wife, visible to each other and neighbours, Jim and Nell are their consciences, inner souls and confidants, visible only to themselves and of course to us. Two characters, four actors.

So far so splendid, especially when you consider that the RSC has for Mr Nichols wheeled in a massively impressive guest-star quartet consisting of Billie Whitelaw, Eileen Atkins, Benjamin Whitrow and Anton Rodgers, the first two playing Eleanor and the second two playing James in their public and private incarnations.

The trouble however, and this seems to have gone unnoticed in an elsewhere generally ecstatic press, is that although he has found himself a superlative stage device Mr Nichols doesn't seem to have found himself anywhere much to put it. *Passion Play* is a depressingly soap-operatic account of a marriage on the rocks, desperately lacking the humour and the nostalgic insights of his earlier plays and oddly lacking, too, in any real developments of either plot or character.

James is a restorer of and dealer in paintings; Eleanor sings in the choir at the Albert Hall, thereby allowing James to start an illicit affair with the mistress of a deceased buddy while listening to radio broadcasts in order to ascertain the precise time of his wife's return home.

There's also a vindictive widow (Priscilla Morgan) who keeps

Eleanor informed of James' infidelities, plus the aforementioned mistress (Louise Jameson), the two splendid alter egos, and a number of extras whom the RSC, unlike any West End management, has been able to provide as party guests, restaurant diners, figures in one of Eleanor's nightmares and generally to fill out Patrick Robertson's huge and elegant setting, which would appear to be representing a town house in Blackheath roughly the dimensions of Windsor Castle.

As if exhausted by his invention of the *Doppelgänger* (which I long to see in a stronger play) Mr Nichols has fallen back on the hoariest of plot devices: the wife only discovers that the mistress is still having an affair with her husband when she mentions his visit to Switzerland and the mistress lets slip the word Zurich. The wife then says, 'But I never mentioned Zurich,' for all the world like an Inspector in the last reel of a British B picture of the 1940s.

Passion Play much resembles Pinter's recent *Betrayal* in that a stage device (there it was to begin at the end and work back to the beginning) is allowed to take the place of any real depth of feeling or personality; though Nichols writes passionate speeches about the death of marriage and the birth of lust, they fall interchangeably from lips it is very hard to care about. Thus we have a very clever but at heart curiously arid attempt to deal with the destructive powers of sex and marriage set against a lapsed Christian background (she sings the 'Matthew Passion', he restores religious paintings) which ends up in lines like 'You're overlooking the fact that I love this man,' lines that would not sound out of place in 'Crossroads' if only anybody there could remember them.

But Whitelaw–Atkins and Whitrow–Rodgers work so well together as aspects of the same two people that one ends up hoping they will abandon the increasingly turgid mechanics of a will-they-won't-they-stay-together plot and just settle for being a couple of marvellous double acts in search of a play.

She Woolf?

Before writing *Virginia* (Theatre Royal Haymarket) Edna O'Brien, we are told, threw herself to the Woolfs and spent several months 'immersed' in the writings of the blessed Virginia. The result of such immersion is much what you'd expect: a distinctly soggy play apparently written underwater and with a somewhat blurred vision of the subject. As an evening in the theatre, *Virginia* is saved by a remarkable and massive star turn from Maggie Smith who has recognized and rightly received acclaim for one of the great modern opportunities given to an actress. She never leaves the stage, seldom draws breath, constantly commanding and galvanizing attention in what is clearly not only a homecoming but also soon to be an award-winning performance after her five years in Stratford Ontario.

The trouble is, though, that we have here a solo show rather than a play: true, there are two other actors (Nicholas Pennell doubling as Virginia's father and husband, and Patricia Conolly doing a somewhat bossy Vita Sackville-West) but they are at best shadows, often left standing upstage with their backs to us, decorating a set by Phillip Silver who seems to have reached the eccentric conclusion that Virginia spent much of her life living in an otherwise deserted Japanese restaurant.

It is therefore as though we are at some form of literary lunch where Virginia Woolf has been asked for a couple of hours to address us on the subject of her life and Bloomsbury times; there is no real drama here, no confrontation, no development. Instead, a Sunday-supplement canter through the known facts of her life which takes for granted that we know most of them anyway. Thus, at the outset, the sound of rushing water is presumably meant to convey to us an instant image of Virginia sinking gently, pockets stone-filled, into the River Ouse. The trouble is of course, that theatregoers unacquainted with her tragic end might simply assume that she had left a tap running somewhere, and Miss O'Brien's particular brand of precious, hothouse intensity makes one long for that celebrated Alan Bennett parody, the one about him being distantly related to the Woolfs through some Alsatian cousins and therefore meeting the great lady herself, hot and sweaty from a hard day's reading in the London Library and proud holder of the *Evening Standard* award for the Tallest Woman Writer of 1927.

There is a terrible kind of reverence at work in Robin Phillips' static production, a coy and cloying adoration of Virginia which is only rescued by occasional moments of acid having more to do with Miss Smith's delivery than Miss O'Brien's remarkably dormant critical faculties. To hear Virginia deliver a line like, 'I had known there were buggers in Plato's Greece but it never occurred to me there could be buggers in our drawing-room at 46 Gordon Square' is to realize how much better this play would have been if written with a little more humour and a little less unquestioning adoration. There are also strong indications that Miss O'Brien has got the character of Vita wrong in several crucial respects; doubtless she would argue that she is not in the documentary business. My regret is that she's not really in the playwriting business either. The result is a fey glimpse of Virginia through a glass darkly.

At the Young Vic, Denise Coffey has a remarkably brisk and lively production of *Pygmalion* which uses Shaw's script for the Wendy Hiller–Leslie Howard film of 1938, thereby giving us several scenes not in the original play plus Shaw himself as a narrator to link them in the person of Donald Eccles.

This has the unexpected effect of shifting the focus of the play from Eliza and Higgins towards such usually more minor figures as Mrs Higgins and Colonel Pickering and it is those two perform-ances (by Judy Campbell and Tim Seely) which lend the evening most of its charm and distinction. For the rest, it's a brisk no-scenery romp through the plot with Lesley-Anne Down in her London stage début proving a thoroughly adequate if unexciting Eliza and David Henry doing an intriguingly cuddly bear-like Higgins.

At Greenwich until the beginning of March (and thereafter at the Vaudeville), Alan Strachan's production of *Present Laughter* con-firms him as our most able and trustworthy present-day director of Noël Coward. This is a hugely thoughtful if overlong revival of one of the most overtly farcical of all the Coward comedies; it has a third act which veers sharply into Ben Travers country, a central character at least fractionally autobiographical (and played with unusual restraint by Donald Sinden) and the masterly comic inven-tion of a loony playwright, taken over the top, and rightly, by Julian Fellowes.

Strachan has recognized, here as in his recent *Private Lives* revival, an underlying sadness about Coward's writing, and he has drawn from Donald Sinden precisely the right mixture of suavity and desperation as the leading man whose hair is going faster than his career. True, the voice still reverberates like a cathedral organ played by a demented alcoholic, but there are enough built-in booby traps ('Do stop acting,' other characters are forever telling him in one way or another) to allow the play to take off into a realm of manic character-studies linked by a plot which takes a long time to wind up and then runs away with breathtaking speed and confidence. In a strong cast Polly Adams, Dinah Sheridan and Gwen Watford hedge Sinden around with elegant savagery.

On Broadway

New York

America has done it again. The big news in New York this week is that of the talking tombstone, invention of a New Jersey undertaker who has discovered that by attaching a solar-powered tape recorder to his gravestones it is possible to have the dear departed address his or her mourners in a pre-recorded message of farewell and good cheer. Faced with such reality, what hope is there for showbusiness?

Quite a lot, as it happens. Broadway is booming this winter as never before: attendance is up twenty-five per cent on last year and they reckon that by the end of the season the total 1980–81 box-office take will be in the region of $200 million.

The English can still claim some of the credit for this, since the two hottest straight plays in town are Pam Gems' *Piaf* and Peter Shaffer's *Amadeus,* the former much as it was in London with Jane Lapotaire, but the latter tightened and rewritten for a proscenium stage, with Ian McKellen falling some way short of Scofield's massive National Theatre triumph.

For anyone returning as I am to New York after an eighteen-month absence, the major visible difference is, however, the way that New York seems at last to have become a part of America. The McDonalds and Burger Kings that were once only remarkable for their absence are now as omnipresent as in Boston or Cleveland, and the same process of Americanization is also visible on stage.

The big musical hits here now are almost all celebrations of the American past, though nostalgia doesn't come cheap. For *42nd Street,* tickets are up to $35 each, but this does at least mean that some are available each night. Whether the show justifies a £20 top depends on the extent of your Hollywood nostalgia.

Gower Champion, the director–choreographer whose sudden death was announced melodramatically from the stage as the

curtain fell on opening night, has here cobbled together a theatre
vision of the old Warner 1930s movie musical which ends up
looking more like a combined fashion show and tap-dancing
display than a stage musical. Tammy Grimes as the old-time star
appears to be phoning in her performance from somewhere under
several feet of water, and Jerry Orbach plays the producer in a state
of curious embarrassment, while Wanda Richert as the girl who
goes out there a chorus dancer and comes back a star looks about as
vulnerable and adorable as an armoured car. The rest is just a chance
to hear again all the best of Harry Warren's songs.

Barnum however, which opens in London this summer with
Michael Crawford in the role played here by Jim Dale, is a genuine
delight. The first ever circus musical, it tells the story of Barnum's
life through a series of sawdust sequences backed up by Cy
Coleman's brash and brilliant score. Acrobats tumble, jugglers and
clowns rampage through the theatre while Mr Dale on stage is
himself the greatest show on earth, to say nothing of being also a
one-man three-ring circus. Whether walking the high wire or doing
twenty-foot leaps on to the balcony, Mr Dale is a wonderful
Barnum and as all America loves a parade, that is more or less what
we have here in place of a plot. Michael Crawford has a hard act to
follow, but if the London production is even half as good it will still
be unmissable.

Satire, which used to be what closed here on Saturday night, is
now thriving off-Broadway in a savage and very funny parody of
modern American life called *Coming Attractions* and writen by Ted
Tally, who wrote the play about Scott of the Antarctic at last year's
Chichester Festival.

His story here is that of a failed hoodlum taken over by an alert
agent because of the serial rights, reckoning that the hoodlum has
the two things that have never failed in America, violence and really
bad taste. The agent then persuades his client to become the
Hallowe'en Killer. Predictably he then gets his own television
series, but the play rolls rapidly downhill as the death toll mounts
and the cops start writing their best-sellers. Mr Tally fires off at
random, hitting a good many New York targets but missing still
more. The play gains an awful relevance by having opened a week
or two before the Lennon murder, but inside its two shapeless hours
are about forty minutes of the funniest comic writing in town.

I have saved the best till last. Once in a very long while Broadway
takes over a British stage classic and improves it. Thirty years ago

there was the Mary Martin musical *Peter Pan,* still shamefully unseen in Britain, and now from Joe Papp's Public Theatre comes a superlative new production of *The Pirates of Penzance* which ought to be forcibly shown to every member of our own D'Oyly Carte Company. A cast headed by pop singer Linda Ronstadt (with George Rose as the very model of a modern Major-General) breathes life and fire and youth and blazingly good comedy into a show I had thought long dead, and the result is a miracle of resuscitation. Under a stony portrait of Queen Victoria, a wonderfully versatile company offer a celebration of Gilbert and Sullivan which has a young American audience on its feet to cheer, and rightly. The sooner we get these 'Pirates' over the Atlantic the better.

Meanwhile Elizabeth Taylor is about to open in a revival of *Little Foxes,* Lauren Bacall is doing a musical of the old Katharine Hepburn film *Woman of the Year* and there's now a sequel to *Bye Bye Birdie* called predictably *Bring Back Birdie.* Truly there's no business like old business.

Stills Life

'My name is Eadweard Muybridge, 1830–1904. In 1878 I invented the cinema.' And so begins, at Hampstead's New End Theatre, a remarkable and considerably critically underrated play by Nigel Gearing called *Snap.* Produced by Roland Rees for Foco Novo, the touring theatre company which originated *The Elephant Man,* this too is a kind of illustrated lecture about a life, though here we are dealing with a mental rather than physical affliction.

As one or two biographies have already established, it was the tragedy of Muybridge to photograph everything and see nothing. Born plain Edward Muggeridge of Kingston-upon-Thames (it is there, at the end of his life, that we find him delivering the account of himself which forms the basis for the series of blackout sketches that make up Mr Gearing's play) he moved to California, panned for gold, got hurled from a runaway stagecoach and ended up in San Francisco as the father of the motion picture. The first man to arrange photographs into sequences telling a story, he was also the first man to establish the precise movement of a racehorse, something he achieved by stationing a series of twelve cameras at regular intervals along a track and having them shoot as the horse was passing.

His other chief claim to fame was as the last man ever to be acquitted on a murder charge in the USA by a plea of *crime passionel,* something hitherto and thereafter regarded as rather more French than Californian. While photographing his wife and a ne'er-do-well actor called Harry Larkyns in a series of increasingly compromising poses, he had failed to notice that they had carried on after the photographic session came to its end. When this was brought to his attention, via the birth to Mrs Muybridge of a child bearing a remarkable resemblance to Larkyns, Eadweard promptly shot his male model and announced to a local cop that at the time he had been suffering brain damage due to the aforementioned fall from the stagecoach. Then he changed to the plea of *crime passionel,* became a distinguished fellow at the University of Pennsylvania, watched from the sidelines while Edison built on his work for the invention of the Kinescope, and eventually returned to a tranquil Kingston death.

Snap (not to be confused with a Maggie Smith comedy about venereal disease which opened under the same title several years back) is essentially a vaudeville in which four actors play all the characters in the Muybridge story; they are led through this by Oliver Ford Davies, who starts as the benevolent elderly hero and then sheds thirty and forty years to re-create the young photographer going out to the wild west. It is a remarkable, thoughtful and finally triumphant performance which reaches its climax in a resounding curtain speech to the burghers of Kingston about existence itself being, like a snap, the crack of light between two eternities of darkness and about the gift of photography to the world: 'We can arrest the moment, cross the Andes, do Niagara, all without leaving home; we can look at all pomposity and vanity through a three-inch lens.'

There are many moments of such lyricism in Mr Gearing's script and Mr Rees' suitably black-and-white production, and a tendency to go for the easy laugh (Larkyns 'bouncing as high as his cheques', Mrs Muybridge 'either overexposed or overdeveloped') should not blind us to this achievement in taking the format of the comic western burlesque and using it in a silent-movie convention to tell a simple and tragic story of a photographer unable to place himself in his own landscapes. Colette Hiller as the child-bride wife, Jonathan

Burn as Larkyns and Lucinda Curtis as the all-purpose Mrs Smith make up the company with remarkable verve, but *Snap* is Mr Ford Davies' evening and he establishes it as the most enjoyable time that has been had at the New End since *A Day in Hollywood, A Night in the Ukraine* started life there. Hasten along; if the show succeeds, it might just save the New End from shameful government-inflicted closure.

Kilroy Was Here

'Bloody typical,' commented John Osborne memorably, when informed that the English Stage Society which he helped create was this month celebrating its quarter-century at the Royal Court with a new all-Irish adaptation of *The Seagull* by Thomas Kilroy, though the precise nature of the angry old man's objection is not yet totally clear. Was it that the Court should be celebrating with a new play rather than a Chekhov revival? Or was it that *The Seagull* should be left in Russia rather than airlifted bodily to the West of Ireland?

The former objection is the easier to deal with, for since its very beginnings the English Stage Society has been in the revival business; what saved its first year at the box-office was not in fact *Look Back in Anger,* a slow starter commercially, but a money-making revival of *The Country Wife* which made Joan Plowright a star. Moreover within another two years Noël Coward was there directing his own translation of a Feydeau farce starring Vivien Leigh. The news was made at the Court by the new plays, but the money was usually made by the older ones.

The second objection takes a little longer to dispel, since it's the old one about messing about with the classics; though in this context how utterly faithful to its original Spanish is Osborne's adaptation of *A Bond Honoured*? Mr Kilroy's defence would seem to be that the demise of the Anglo-Irish estates, the existence there too of absentee landlords and the domination of the Land League all provide almost exact parallels between Ireland and Russia in the 1880s. Thus instead of Madame Arkadina we have Isobel Desmond, celebrated star of the London stage ('Just mention Ellen Terry to her and all hell breaks loose') returning to her Anglo-Irish country home with, instead of Trigorin, the well-known writer Mr Aston in tow. Her son Konstantin is still Constantine, but Nina has become Lily and the play she performs on the garden stage at the outset has become alarmingly like *Kathleen Ni Houlihan* or, as Isobel says, 'another of those Celtic things'.

The result of all these transpositions is a jokier but somehow smaller *Seagull*; I have never seen the play more strongly cast, but precisely because of that strength I longed to see them tackle the original. Anna Massey as Isobel–Arkadina gives the performance of her career, a wonderfully egocentric and neurotic turn, while the casting of Harriet Walter as Lily–Nina, she who was Ophelia to last year's Jonathan Pryce Hamlet on this stage, is no less impressive. True, it is a little odd to have as Aston–Trigorin an actor looking even younger than Constantine, odder when on that very stage are two other actors (T. P. McKenna as the Doctor and Stuart Burge as Peter) who would have been vastly more characteristic casting for the role. On the other hand we do have a tough, rebellious and mercifully unpoetic Constantine from Anton Lesser. Max Stafford-Clark's directing is crisp.

Out at the Redgrave Theatre, Farnham, the resident director David Horlock is currently offering the first-ever professional British revival of Noël Coward's epic *Cavalcade*. In the fifty years since it was first staged at Drury Lane, theatres elsewhere, among them both the National and the Aldwych, have been frightened off this project by the fact that it demands a cast of around 300 and more than a dozen changes of scene. But by brilliant use of an open stage, and an even more brilliant deal with Equity whereby only a dozen of the cast have to be professionals (the rest all drawn from local amateur groups) Farnham has achieved the impossible.

So now, for the first time in the theatre-going life of anyone much under sixty, we get the chance to look at the single most ambitious stage concept put together by a British playwright this century. When Coward wrote *Cavalcade* he was just thirty, and only a year away from *Private Lives*; his intention, having thus far made his name with small-cast comedies and big-cast revues, was to combine the best of both worlds while stretching the resources of stage management to their very limits. Thus we have a reasonably small play, about a household of masters and servants and how they survived and adapted to the changes in English life from 1899 to 1929, set within an infinitely larger pageant of historic events from the Relief of Mafeking through the *Titanic* to the end of the First War and beyond.

In reversing the two last scenes, so that we end not with the cynical 'Twentieth-century Blues' but with the jingoistic toast 'to England' and a mass singing of 'Land of Hope and Glory', Mr Horlock has perhaps left us with a false impression of *Cavalcade* as a work of mindless patriotism instead of a rather more complex hymn of love and hate to Britain; but that becomes a comparatively minor objection when set against his major achievement which is to have brought back to life a theatrical tapestry many of us had thought lost for ever. Somewhere in *Cavalcade* can be found almost everything that mattered about Coward as a playwright and as a man; the sense of the past, the fixation on duty and decent behaviour above all else, the brisk edginess of a forward-looking love scene set aboard a liner about to hit an iceberg, and a cascading sense of sheer theatre.

Carol Drinkwater as Jane Marryot, Granville Saxton as her husband and John Hughes as the drunken Bridges lead well for the professionals; but it is, in the end, the sight of the 300 others flocking on to that Farnham stage to watch the boats depart for the Boer and subsequent Wars that makes this *Cavalcade* such a marvellous procession.

Possum Power

Andrew Lloyd Webber's *Cats* (at the New London) is a vivid and marvellous gesture of transatlantic defiance; for years we have been told by Broadway that though we might have our Royal Shakespeare and our National, the one thing the London theatre lacked was an ability to do an all-dancing show. Now, and not before time, comes the answer; like Bob Fosse's *Dancin'* this is a choreographer's benefit, and not even a bomb scare could silence the cheering that rang through the auditorium on opening night.

True, this production leaves nothing to chance; customers taking their seats in at least half the stalls are, during the overture, transported in those seats on a circular conveyor belt around the set in pure Disneyland fashion so that the mound of dustbin rubbish which threatened to obscure all other views suddenly becomes the backdrop for the dance festival that is to follow. *Cats* has no plot, no book, no storyline; it is simply an arrangement of twenty of T. S. Eliot's *Old Possum* poems for dancers and orchestra, a revolutionary dance drama which, though occasionally both arch and twee, is vastly more often breathtaking in its confidence and ambition.

As cat-dancers poured through the auditorium, stroking the napes of unsuspecting necks and arching their backs for the next showstopper, it became clear that neither Lloyd Webber nor his director Trevor Nunn had attempted more than a celebration of Eliot's original verses; yet within those limits they have created a world total and unique, a world in which Gus the Theatre Cat can recall lost years at the Lyceum, Macavity can be not there and Mr Mistoffoles can bring back old Deuteronomy from behind a magic scarf. Number after number tears the place apart: Wayne Sleep doing the Jellicle Ball, Paul Nicholas as a rock-star Rum Tum Tugger, Elaine Paige doing the haunting, repetitive 'Memory' and Ken Wells as Skimbleshanks form the starriest all-singing all-dancing team in town, but in the end *Cats* is the utter and total triumph of one single talent: not Mr Lloyd Webber, who has already written many better scores; nor yet Trevor Nunn whose direction is to say the least unobtrusive; but for Gillian Lynne as choreographer. *Cats* is a show which not only brings the New London to full and proper life for the first time in its eight-year history but also, and again for the first time, proves that Britain can now muster thirty show dancers as talented, versatile and energetic as any team ever fielded on Broadway or in Hollywood. And all that while remaining entirely faithful to the weird mix of menace, melancholy and mayhem that exists in the original poems. *Cats* is a total and utter feline delight; it will doubtless lead more than nine other lives in more than nine other cities, but if the New London needs a new show much before 1985 I shall be more than a little surprised. Smash hits don't come more smash than this one.

Arthur Stanley Jefferson, born Lancashire, June 1895, was a music-hall comic who got his start understudying Chaplin; when times got still harder, he wound up on an Australian vaudeville circuit partnering a deadbeat Scots comedian and a still more talent-free lady known locally as the Kiwi because she was a fat bird from New Zealand. Eventually, back in America, Jefferson abandoned both those millstones around his talented if over-eager neck and went off to meet Oliver Hardy. By then he was of course calling himself Stan

Laurel, but it is solely with those early years that David Allen's play *Gone with Hardy* (briefly at the Tricycle and soon I hope to find a more central London home) is concerned.

It's a deft little piece which manages to be at one and the same time a stage biography and a vaudeville act; Sylvestre McCoy is the real Laurel, Jimmy Logan is the Scot and Toni Palmer the Kiwi as they act out Stan's beginnings in a series of silent-film comedy routines interspersed with the more real and unfunny truth of offstage life on a sequence of worsening tours of the Outback. This is another fine mess for Laurel to get himself out of, and a touchingly funny account of two failures and an eventual success.

Patrick Garland's first and highly promising Chichester season gets off to a somewhat desiccated start with a museum-piece revival of *The Cherry Orchard*; though strongly cast (Claire Bloom as Ranevskaya, Joss Ackland as Gayev, Sarah Badel as Varya) it offers no strong line or insights and seems content merely to declare the play open for our inspection. Emrys James and Angela Pleasance have good moments as Lopakhin and Charlotta, but the rest of the cast are respectfully arranged around Miss Bloom as if awaiting a stills photographer and the result is a sort of chamber concert without the music.

And talking of museum pieces, Peter Ustinov's new play *Overheard* (at the Theatre Royal Haymarket) is a curious holdover from the 1950s in which the British ambassador to some unnamed Ustinovian eastern state is beset by a native dissident whose demands appear to be asylum and the ambassador's wife in roughly that order. Ian Carmichael and Deborah Kerr play the ambassadorial couple as if out of some minor Coward comedy, Aharon Ipalé plays the dissident as if out of comic opera, and a heavy-handed fable of international whimsy dies slowly between breakfast and the after-dinner witticisms. It is as though some immensely learned Austrian professor had been asked to compose a drama for the old Home Service making light of East–West relations, and though it is very good to welcome Ian Carmichael back to the boards after far too long an absence, there is really nothing else of note here except the fact that Barry Dennen is wearing the worst-glued beard I have seen offered to paying customers since the death of Robert Atkins.

On the Map

We are in Donegal, the town of Baile Beag known to the English as Ballybeg; it is 1833, and a party of initially friendly redcoats has come over to chart the countryside and anglicize the local place-names. Ireland is to be conquered not by the sword but by the map; there is to be a process of 'erosion', whereby English will replace Gaelic first as a language and second as a way of life. So starts Brian Friel's new play *Translations* (at the Hampstead Theatre), arguably the most important drama to have come out of Ireland both theatrically and historically since the death of O'Casey, and one which deals not only with the roots of the present conflict but also with the cornerstones of the Irish character.

For we are not just anywhere in the village; we are in a hedge school, one of those secret corners which as early as the beginning of the nineteenth century had already begun to harbour those who objected to the banning by the English of Catholic education. Presiding over the occasional classes there, in a massively welcome return to the stage, is Ian Bannen as the drunken old pedant who is better in Latin or Greek or Gaelic than he is in English, and whose pupils are similarly uninclined to learn the language of the map-making redcoats. Already therefore we have a problem of interpretation and non-communication, though at first it seems no matter. A local girl who speaks no English falls in love with an English soldier who speaks no Gaelic; in an infinitely touching love scene they communicate only through the alternate place-names of the surrounding district, she speaking the originals while he intones the translations of the title.

But then, abruptly and inexplicably, the soldier disappears and as the play ends his captain is threatening to lay waste all the surrounding fields until he is found; within a matter of days, for the play takes place over less than a week, a group of harmless map-readers has become an invading army willing to devastate the fields that are their owners' only means of support. What began as a John Ford comedy of Irish misunderstanding has become a tragedy of epic proportions, one which is to last 150 years and bring us up to the present time. But the importance of Friel's play does not just lie in its awful topicality. What matters here is that he has taken the old

Abbey stereotypes, the drunken schoolmaster and his Joxer friend and the young lovers of folk comedy, and created for them a tapestry altogether new and chilling. The result is an ordnance survey of Irish humanity in which the present is shaped by the past and the map-maker becomes map-destroyer; Donald McWhinnie's production and the cast of ten led by Stephen Rea who join Bannen make this the most haunting and powerful new play of the year.

Out at the Riverside Studios in Hammersmith (and shortly to tour Brixton, Battersea and Croydon) Mustapha Matura's *One Rule* is a production by the Black Theatre Co-operative largely concerned with the moral problems inherent in becoming a reggae superstar. In the month of Bob Marley's sad death this might be thought to have a certain relevance, but as Mr Matura's concept of a superstar's life seems to consist largely of a black plastic sofa and a girlfriend of stunning inadequacy it is difficult to assess precisely what we are supposed to learn from or about it. An already shaky play (consisting for the first endless hour of a debate about whether black superstardom allows you to forget your roots and do the occasional Perry Como number or not) is finally destroyed in the closing twenty minutes when the star dies and is replaced by a black teenager bearing about as much resemblance to him as to Vera Lynn. This, says Mr Matura, will fool the world's press, though if it does then his play might just about stand the same chance.

Ring Master

When the curtain fell on the first night of *Barnum* (at the London Palladium) Michael Crawford was treated to an eight-minute standing ovation, the longest I have ever heard given to an actor in this country and one which so moved a leader-writer on the *Daily Mail* that the following morning readers of that paper were solemnly informed in an editorial that if more people in this great country of ours could be more like Mr Crawford, an end to our present little local economic and social difficulties could be arranged.

The idea of a nation led by song-and-dance men or women does admittedly have certain charms; America has settled for Ronald

Reagan when they could have had Ray Bolger, but over here a tap-dancing premier hoofing it down Whitehall to unveil statues to Walter Crisham and Jack Buchanan before executing a swift buck-and-wing on the tarmac at Heathrow *en route* to a conference choreographed by Gillian Lynne might well succeed where all else and Mrs Thatcher have failed.

What the *Mail* writer curiously missed, however, is a further analogy: like politics itself, *Barnum* is a massive only more success-ful confidence trick and at this point it becomes necessary to separate the very genuine achievement of Mr Crawford from the somewhat phonier but still dazzling achievement of the show.

After six months in a circus school in New York, he has con-quered the (fairly) high wire, mastered a certain amount of juggling and found the courage to slide down a rope anchored some fifty feet above stage and stalls; for an actor with a known affection for stunting (notably in the 'Some Mothers' TV series) this is still a remarkable conquest, and what makes Crawford considerably more fascinating in the role than was Jim Dale on Broadway is that he retains the very real possibility of failure. Every moment of the show therefore becomes a cliff-hanger; whether intentionally or not he gives the constant impression that his entire circus may be about to fall apart at the seams of the big top, and when it doesn't the mixture of relief and exultation that spreads first across his face, then across the stage and finally out into the auditorium becomes a wave of sheer theatricality the like of which you will find nowhere else in town or country.

Where Jim Dale's Broadway *Barnum* is a ringmaster in constant command, Crawford's is more like a circus-struck teenager who has suddenly been given the uniform and told to try it for size. The fact that both these interpretations suit the show equally well may suggest that the guide ropes supporting the structure of *Barnum* are a little loose, and indeed they are. Though there still are indications in the score (notably in the second-half number 'Black and White', one which will I suspect be largely incomprehensible to anyone without a working knowledge of Barnum's desire to be a city planner) that the musical was originally meant to be a more faithful reflection of the man's infinitely complex and often contradictory life, most of this has now been sacrificed to the stunting. Biographi-cal details are therefore now not so much sketchy as invisible, and we are left with what is effectively a three-hour finale incorporating some smashing big-band numbers, some brilliant solo stunts from

Crawford and the rock-solid belief that everybody loves a circus parade.

To prove Barnum's contention that there was a sucker born every minute, and that people will watch anything just so long as you give them somewhere to watch it, the penultimate first-half closer is sung largely in Swedish and the midget Tom Thumb turns out to be about five foot ten.

But at a time when all too many people are starting to think that Bertram Mills must have been Hayley's father, *Barnum* does at least manage a celebration of the spirit of circus; though it misses chance after chance to tell us who Phineas Taylor Barnum really was, and though it declines any *Cabaret*-like attempt to define a theatrical form through its performers or its audience, and though in its journey from Broadway it has become somehow more muddled and fluffy, this is still a great sawdust singalong made unforgettable by the energy, tenacity and bravura of its central performance, one admirably supported by Deborah Grant as Mrs Barnum and by Cy Coleman's oompah-pah score.

Leather Boys

I have seldom approached the National Theatre with less enthusiasm than for the opening of their new Olivier stage production of *The Shoemaker's Holiday*. In the first place it is directed by John Dexter, who like Peter Hall has been getting alarmingly operatic of late. Secondly, like Morris dancing and the Henley Regatta, *The Shoemaker's Holiday* has always seemed to me one of those ritual English celebrations which ought to be a lot more fun than they ever turn out to be, and thirdly it comes into that uneasy category of museum pieces which occasionally have to get revived simply because somebody somewhere once decided they were to remain a part of the national (and therefore National) repertoire.

So much for the prejudice. What you actually find when you get to the Olivier is an evening of considerable delight, a celebration of London perfectly timed for a St Paul's wedding and at long last proof that the National is beginning to think and work like a resident team instead of a collection of guest stars on the open stage.

Written in 1599, Dekker's comedy is in one sense the middle-class

Londoner's riposte to Shakespeare; its hero is the cobbler union-
leader who becomes Lord Mayor, its characters defiantly neither
princes nor paupers. Where Shakespeare exclusively concerned
himself with high life and low life, Dekker goes straight to the
middle and when the King does finally put in an appearance it is as a
supporting player at Simon Eyre's mayoral coronation.

A play much beloved of amateur dramatic societies, since it
allows large groups of people to stand around on stage drinking and

The Shoemaker's Holiday   Brenda Bruce *as Margery Eyre*, Alfred Lynch *as
Simon Eyre*, John Salthouse *as Firk*

hammering and roistering without much need for close acquaintance with the plot, *The Shoemaker's Holiday* is also a very careful
tapestry of London life at the turn of its century, and Julia Trevelyan
Oman's triple-arched set with its cluttered central shoemakers' den
is a marvellous reflection of that.

While over on the other side of Waterloo Bridge the RSC are
camping around with Michael Bogdanov's shamefully travestied
version of *Knight of the Burning Pestle*, Dexter has in contrast gone

for an utterly faithful rendering of the play which points up the essential simplicity of its structure. We therefore get Simon Eyre's rise to Guildhall matched by the two sub-plots about star-crossed lovers, but it is in individual moments that this production truly triumphs. When, for instance, Eyre's journeyman Rafe returns from the wars he throws open the top half of a stable door at the back of the set and there is general rejoicing at his safe homecoming. Until, that is, he throws open the lower half of the door and we see that the wars have left him without one leg. In lighter vein there are also marvellous jokes about the birth of unionism, both in the text and in Dexter's production where Hodge and Firk, Eyre's two henchmen, manage to spend an entire evening on the verge of downing often invisible tools.

Throughout there is a tremendous sense of a lost London; bells ring out, pisspots get emptied out of doors, ladies called Cicely Bumtrinket come in to be laughed at; Dekker's language is a thesaurus of localized geographic or scatological insults and all the basic jokes are here, from foreigners who have to be shouted at all the way through to a finale in which Eyre's wife comes on dressed as Elizabeth I while the King himself bears an alarming resemblance to Olivier's Henry V.

The danger, of course, is that the whole affair will degenerate into a period beer commercial, but Dexter avoids that through superb casting: though Alfred Lynch seems at first to lack the right showbiz *chutzpah* needed to get himself made Lord Mayor and Shrove Tuesday made a cobblers' holiday, he finally wins through on sheer quiet charm while Peter Lovstrom as Rafe, John Normington and John Salthouse as the two union brothers, and above all David Yelland as the King ensure a pageant of delight.

Short of calling his three central characters Freeman, Hardy and Willis, it is hard to see how Dekker could have written a play more intimately concerned with the origins of 'the gentle craft', but what Dexter and Oman have done is open it up so that it becomes a bawdy, lively parade in which you can almost smell the straw covering the city streets. The result is a production reeking of London, and if we get any hot summer nights they'd be well advised to move the whole thing out on to the Thames terraces and finish it with fireworks.

Viet Duet

In the wake of *Billy Bishop,* another two-man re-creation of a war: this time not Canadians in World War One but Americans in Vietnam, as seen by Amlin Gray who himself served as a medic there and is now a writer of *How I Got That Story* at the Hampstead Theatre. Essentially what we have here is 'Apocalypse Now and Then', a sketchy evocation of an appalling event achieved on stage by setting up an initially eager young war reporter (Robert Lindsay) against a vast collection of Vietnam locals, ranging from a dragon-queen President to an ultimately limbless American photographer still determined to get either shot or the award-winning shot, and all played by Ron Cook.

A vastly inventive production by Nancy Diuguid on a bare wooden stage allows Lindsay and Cook to play out a series of ever more awful war games until eventually Lindsay becomes Vietnamized to the point where he is trying either to marry or adopt himself into a permanent stay. Mr Gray is here mainly on about the farcical awfulness of war and the curious ability of certain Americans to feel more at home in Saigon than Minneapolis; true, Vietnam is never once mentioned by name (residents are described as 'Ambonese') and the play degenerates into a series of lightning sketches linked by the schmuck reporter who ends up supplying copy for a Robert Redford movie, albeit less than eagerly. But along the way there are some chillingly good jokes, and if it's a Viet Vaudeville you're after, then here it is.

For those of us who had not until now fully understood that the six sisters Mitford were in fact a sextet of Tiller Girls made good, the new Ned Sherrin–Caryl Brahms musical at Chichester may come as something of a surprise. It is in fact much like being hit over the head for several hours with bound back volumes of the *Tatler* for 1920–40: you emerge dazed, nostalgic, but not a lot the wiser.

The idea of *The Mitford Girls* seems in essence to have been a good one; short of doing 'Side by Side by the Sitwells', or 'Song by Song by Beverley Nichols', it's hard to think of a better way in to the pre-war world than through the gates leading to assorted Mitford lodgings. Thanks already to a television series and a huge number of biographies and autobiographies, everybody must have at least a vague idea of the members of this sorority: there was the dotty father and the placid mother, and then among the actual gels (and why the show is not called 'The Mitford Gels', thereby making an even more direct appeal to the theatregoers of West Sussex, I have yet to discover) there was the one who fell for Hitler, the one who invented Non-U, the one who went to America, the one who married a Duke, the one who married Mosley and the one who everybody forgets and is in fact called Pamela. The trouble is that if that's all you know about them before going into the theatre, that's also all you know about them by the time you come out.

Into a two-and-a-half-hour show the authors have decided to cram a complete and enchanting period-pastiche score by Peter Greenwell, plus eight additional songs by the likes of Coward, Kurt Weill and Vivian Ellis, plus six stage biographies and assorted high-society sidelights. That works out at roughly ten minutes per stage life, or at least it would if the first fifteen minutes of the show did not have to be spent in telling us precisely which Mitford is which.

So this cannot hope, and perhaps indeed was never intended, to be a stage biography. Instead it's a kind of cabaret through which assorted Mitfords flit interchangeably; the only two I ever knew were Nancy and Jessica, and it is not the fault of Patricia Hodge or Liz Robertson that for all the similarities they achieve in looks, voice or character they might as well have been playing Hedy Lamarr and Douglas Byng. But once you give real names to the inhabitants of Robin Fraser Paye's baroque thirties costumes, minds are apt to wander towards reality which is the point at which this whole white-piano sweeping-staircase edifice comes crashing to the ground. For while it is perfectly acceptable to have an anonymous torch singer in a lot of period satin crooning 'I'll fall in love with his funny face across the Ritz', it becomes somehow rather less tasteful when you realize that the funny face she's about to fall in love with is in fact that of the leader of the British Union of Fascists.

We are left, therefore, with a remarkable jumble of unsorted images. 'September Song' might for instance be ideal accompaniment for the lives of Walter and John Huston but seems to fit no particular Mitford, while the use of 'Thanks for the Memory' conveys the uneasy impression that one of them must also have married Bob Hope. In this helter-skelter scramble through half-opened family scrapbooks, the lasting impression is of six chorus girls in training for some 1930s Eurovision Song Contest; and whatever the Mitford girls were, they surely weren't that.

Patrick Garland's production (and the choreography of Anton Dolin and Lindsay Dolan) does however have a wonderfully period flair, and Oz Clarke struggles to convey impressions of Redesdale and various Mitford menfolk in the few seconds allowed for each.

Dangerous to Know

Really terrible historical dramas having rather disappeared since Dirk Bogarde last played Franz Liszt (on screen rather than piano), we should I suppose be grateful for the small mercies contained in Romulus Linney's new play at the Young Vic about Lord Byron. Short of persuading Peter Ustinov to disguise himself thinly as George III and cry, 'Stap me vittels, the feller's a damn poet,' it is hard to think of any Hollywood cliché left unturned by Mr Linney, who manages within the same half-hour to have Byron's daughter say, 'I am afflicted with a cancerous growth,' while her father helpfully notes that, 'A man named Berlioz is writing a great deal of music.' And there's better to come: 'You raped my mother,' Byron's daughter reminds him, lest presumably it had slipped his memory, 'unspeakably, while she was pregnant with me.' It's the 'unspeakably' that gets you in the end; that and having his daughter add seconds later, 'You travelled away from home into a scarlet sunrise to sink yourself in sherbert and sodomy.' They don't write plays like that any more, and it is indeed possible that they never did, not even for mid-afternoon schools radio back in the middle 1950s.

Undeterred by precedents, however, Mr Linney has cobbled together a biographical disaster of epic proportions not much helped by Frank Dunlop's production, which arranges the cast of eight on a series of plinths from where you expect them at any moment to burst out into one fast chorus of 'Missolonghi on My Mind'. Had indeed the whole misbegotten shambles been conceived as a musical, there might have been some sense in having David Essex play the mad, bad Lord. As it is, Mr Essex manages a shaggy haircut and a limp, thereby giving a curious impression of Long John Silver in search of his parrot, but not much idea of a great romantic poet. It could of course be argued that the play anyway is not about him at all; its title *Childe Byron* derives not so much from *Childe Harold,* of which Mr Linney seems to have made an only fleeting study, but from the notion that Byron's own child is now about to investigate her deceased father's life and flamboyant times. Thus in 1852 we find ourselves in Ada's study, where she is busily inventing the computer, when due to a nasty overdose of laudanum she hallucinates a meeting with Dad, whom she last saw when she was three months old. Sara Kestelman, in the only impressive performance of the evening, doubles daughter and mother, coughing occasionally into a blanket to indicate that curious wasting disease of which Norma Shearer and Garbo kept dying in period biographies of the 1930s.

True, nobody comes in saying, 'Morning, Byron, is that Shelley over by the fireplace and where's Keats?' but that one feels is only because within the confines of a rather limited company there simply aren't enough poetic young males to go round. Those that are there, apart from Essex, stand around playing assorted relatives and onlookers with a kind of frozen embarrassment, as if they know not only what they have to say next but also what they are going to have to say half an hour hence. Only Mr Essex manages to rise above the awfulness of the text, and he then plays Byron much the way Robert Taylor used to play Ivanhoe, with a mixture of infinite caution and the faint hope that the audience might know even less about the character.

As for Mr Linney, he seems to have taken some of Byron's better-known writings as per the *Oxford Dictionary of Quotations* and arranged them in no particular order, so that poems are broken up among several characters or else just left hanging incomplete on the air while the play drifts off to a further examination of whether or not Byron's daughter might have liked her father had she ever in fact managed to meet him. To suggest that this is an arch, coy, twee and terrible evening of truly stunning inadequacy does not begin to come to terms with the real problem of the play, which is Mr Linney's determination to give us within two hours all we need to know about Byron and then some. This particular collision of poetry and real life has always been a disaster area, as those who can still recall Sarah Miles and Richard Chamberlain camping around in *Lady Caroline Lamb* will doubtless testify; but to the minefield Mr Linney has brought his own personal explosives, notably a campus-lecture-circuit prose style and an extraordinary grab-all technique in which bits of Byron's poetry and prose are shovelled into the midst of Mr Linney's own tracts of dialogue, some of which are then repeated verbatim so that if we had been lucky enough to nod off the first time around there is still no chance of missing them on the repeat a scene or three later. 'Take your silly poems and swim to Greece,' is a line that I shall not easily forget, though the one that most aptly summarizes the whole mishmashed evening must be simply 'Byron, you need rest.'

English with Tears

From *French Without Tears* across thirty years, through *The Browning Version* to the last catastrophic film-musical rewrite of *Goodbye Mr Chips,* the late and great Terence Rattigan would return time and again to the classroom in search of some sort of well-made microcosm for the English character. Now Simon Gray, who has followed Rattigan into Africa and on to the cricket pitch in a latterday version of the same sort of search, also goes back to school. But where his first-ever West End play *Spoiled* was largely concerned with a pupil, his latest is concerned with the Rattiganesque bunch of social misfits who have landed up teaching English to a group of increasingly recalcitrant foreigners at the Cull-Loomis school of English at Cambridge in the early 1960s.

We never get to meet Cull, any more than we ever get to meet any of his students; Loomis however is an amiable old queen immortally underplayed by Robin Bailey, neatly sidestepping a minefield of absent-minded professor jokes to breathe new life into the only clichéd character of the entire evening. The other six are masterpieces of accurate and acidulous scholastic observation; there's the young and initially eager Anita (Jenny Quayle), forever lying about her philandering offstage husband; the failed novelist (Peter Birch) abandoned by his offstage family; the accident-prone supply teacher desperate to achieve permanent status (Glyn Grain); the woolly film-buff deputy (James Grout) with a neurotic offstage daughter and a chilling ability to turn ruthless; and the middle-aged Melanie (Prunella Scales) who may or may not have helped her ghastly offstage mother on a final journey down the staircase. Then and above all there's the ineffably vague St John who gives *Quartermaine's Terms* (at the Queen's) its title, its central focus and in the end its haunting and total triumph. As played by Edward Fox in a state of semi-detachment bordering on trance, St John Quartermaine is built into the furniture of the staff room but not, alas, able to be of much use in the classroom; otherwise engaged in a perpetual desire to be of help and an utter inability to manage it, he opens and closes a play he also holds together not so much by what he fails to do as by what other characters are forever about to fail to do to him.

On two occasions at least Gray himself nudgingly refers us to Chekhov, where the more accurate reference might well have been to N. C. Hunter; for we are back deep in the waters of the moon, where tight-lipped failure is acknowledged but never analysed and where anything of even faint dramatic value always happens offstage. For all that, *Quartermaine's Terms* is a masterly job of stagecraft; seven character sketches, each complete in itself, each interlocked with all of the others, come together to make up the best modern play in town if you allow that *Translations*, though of course about the Irish present, is in fact securely locked in the Irish past. In one sense *Quartermaine's Terms* is the coming together of *Butley* and *Otherwise Engaged,* both also by Gray and directed by Pinter; in another it is simply and splendidly an excuse for seven smashing performances.

For the final offering of Patrick Garland's first season there, Chichester has gone distinctly downmarket and is presenting a joyous tribute to the Crazy Gang cobbled together by Garland himself, Brian Glanville and Roy Hudd who plays Bud Flanagan. For those of us who grew up with the Gang at the Victoria Palace in the 1950s, ageing through our teens while they got younger and younger through their seventies, this is in the nature of a religious revival experience, not least because Chichester has managed to gather some of the Gang's old understudies (Peter Glaze and Monsewer Eddie Gray's brother Billy) to reincarnate their old masters rampaging through stage and stalls. True, the book of *Underneath the Arches* is a broken-backed and spineless shambles, uncertain whether to be a life of Bud and Ches or a history of the Gang or a survey of pre-war variety techniques. A large number of the original Bud-and-Ches songs (not one of which is credited to a composer or lyricist in the programme) are left out to make way for a bizarre and irrelevant Florrie Forde compilation, and, of those that are in, it makes no conceivable sense to have 'F. D. R. Jones' sung

several years before Roosevelt achieved the Presidency, while setting 'Grey-Haired Lady' in the First rather than the Second War also
makes utter gibberish of its lyrics. All that and more can however be
forgiven for the totally magical moment when from backstage they
bring out Chesney Allen himself, now eighty-six, for a first-half
closer. On the stage where Olivier gave his Othello and Plowright
her Saint Joan he got the loudest and longest standing ovation I have
heard, and rightly; the old gentleman who had given up Gang
warfare in 1945 because of failing health had outlived all the others
to have the last laugh and hear the last applause.

Unfair Hearing

After a less than wonderful start with *Eastward Ho!* the new
Mermaid looks to have a winner (and I would guess a lengthily
profitable West End transfer) with its second production, Mark
Medoff's Broadway award-winning *Children of a Lesser God.*
Perched somewhere halfway from *The Miracle Worker* to *Whose Life
Is It Anyway?* this is a sketchy but very powerful account of the case
for what can only be called Deaf Liberation, and it leads to an
eventual awareness that the state of being deaf, like the state of being
black, is not made better by any attempts to modify it. In a cast of
seven, three of the characters (and actors) are totally deaf; two of
them make the attempt to talk, to lip-read, to accommodate themselves to a world in which the unthinking majority can hear. One
does not, and the play is essentially about her refusal to conform, to
pretend, to learn to do badly what she can never do well.

This is in that sense a play about a rebellion; just as the hero of
Whose Life? refuses to prolong a hopeless hospital existence, so
Sarah Norman (marvellously played here by Elizabeth Quinn) wins
in the end the right to be true to her own future – to live deaf, and
even to find pride in what makes her different. *Children* follows a
number of well-tried routes on its way to an original ending; twenty
years ago, you feel, this heroine would have been black in a white
area, or a teenager among adults, or simply from the wrong side of
the tracks, and true to *Miracle Worker* there's the understanding
teacher (Trevor Eve in an equally impressive performance) who
comes to understand her, while true to *Equus* there are peripheral

visitations from uncomprehending parents and well-meaning officials trying to come to terms with an existence they can never share.

But where Medoff scores is in the variations he plays on these familiar patterns and in the way that his play analyses communication between two worlds, not just that of the deaf and of the hearing, but also that of the actors and the audience. *Children* is a sign-language *Translations*; it sets up the barriers, shows how they might but probably won't be hurdled, and ends with a commendable lack of sentimentality. It's a play about love and about control and about defiance; above all it's a play about the fact of deafness, about it being a state not the opposite of hearing but instead full of its own sounds and rules and codes of behaviour where, as in L. P. Hartley's past, they do things differently, not always because they have to but sometimes because they want to. It's an evening on no account to be missed, and Gordon Davidson's production is so fresh and so strong that you could be forgiven for thinking he hadn't already done it on at least three other stages in America including his own in Los Angeles.

The British have never understood about Neil Simon, any more than Americans have ever really understood about Alan Ayckbourn. The two most successful living comic dramatists have consequently found the Atlantic crossing consistently hazardous and often disappointing; plays by Simon that have survived three years on Broadway have been known to collapse in as many months in London, and where London has in the past fifteen years virtually never been without at least one and often three Ayckbourns, more than half his work remains unplayed on Broadway.

Simon's London hits have usually not been his plays at all but rather the negligible books he has written for such plastic-coated, ready-mix, dehydrated musicals as *Little Me* and (currently) *They're Playing Our Song* which makes it all the more important that we should at last have the chance over here to see one of the few plays on which his claims to be something more than a gag-man actually rest. *Chapter Two,* now receiving its British premiere at the Lyric Hammersmith, was a Broadway hit of some five seasons back and then became a glossily vacuous Hollywood movie with James Caan; what separates it from much of Simon's earlier work is that it is at times a painfully autobiographical account of a writer trying to come to grips with the death of a beloved first wife and the possibility of starting out again with a second.

When we first meet George Schneider (played by Garry Waldhorn, who bears a certain accurate resemblance to Simon at his most depressed) he is newly returned from the European vacation he has taken with his brother Leo to get over the funeral. It has not been a success: 'London was bankrupt, Italy on strike, France hated me and Spain was still mourning Franco,' he notes in a kind of Michelin guide to woe which is a fair indication of the shape of the dialogue to come. But Simon's unequalled dexterity as a comic writer ought not to blind us to his very remarkable achievement in here writing nothing less than a comedy about death and despair and a very funny one.

Most of his stage hits have been some form of autobiography: *Barefoot in the Park* was about life with his first wife; *Odd Couple* about life with his brother. Now, in *Chapter Two,* we still have the brother (played by George Layton) and we also have the character unashamedly modelled on the second and present Mrs Simon, actress Marsha Mason (intelligently and sharply played by Maureen Lipman).

The director Peter James, in his first assignment at the theatre he now manages, has paid Simon the compliment of a serious production in which the company of four are sharply confined to what lies in and beneath the text. True they have the usual English difficulty with the New York Jewish humour, but they also have the courage to play for drama and let the gags take care of themselves. In the end, Simon offers his audience the customary Broadway cop-out of a happy ending, precisely the one Medoff avoids; but then again, that's showbusiness.

Goodbye Dolly

There are going to be precious few members of the National Theatre audience not aware in advance of the outcome of Tom Stoppard's latest comedy *On the Razzle* (Lyttelton); it's the one about the two grocery clerks having a day out in the big city, and it was first written by John Oxenford in 1835 London as a one-acter called *A Day Well Spent.* A few years later Johann Nestroy turned it into a full-length Viennese comedy, but it first came to modern notice in 1938 when Thornton Wilder rewrote it for America as *The Merchant of Yonkers*; fifteen years later, for Wilder was not a man to waste much, he added a new central character and got another Broadway hit comedy called *The Matchmaker*. That in turn became *Hello Dolly!*, and what we have now at the National is a return to the Nestroy in an admittedly somewhat faithless translation by Tom Stoppard.

It is then in a mood of '*déjà revue*' that the play needs to be approached and has indeed been staged; as if aware that the original vehicle was getting a little overcrowded and rusty, the director Peter Wood has had some razzle-dazzle production ideas, not the least of which is the casting of Felicity Kendal as one of the male clerks. There is no textual reason for this, nor indeed is there much of a reason why our most distinguished comic dramatist should have been spending his recent time cobbling some new jokes into a dog-eared plot; but in a remarkable triumph of energy and eccentric invention the old engine is cranked up again and made to run one more time.

From the moment of Dinsdale Landen's first appearance as the master grocer, three-time winner of the Johann Strauss medal for duck-shooting but unable to separate his niece from his knees, at least phonetically, it is clear that we are already some way over the top. Mr Landen pitches his performance as a vaudeville turn somewhere halfway from Groucho to Chico Marx, and the rest of the company are left to follow his suit, a baroque affair which jingles his approach long before he actually camps into view. Abandoning, mercifully, the original local Viennese allusions Stoppard has come up with a wordplay of his usual daunting, dazzling, Scrabbled and scrambled brilliance. Some of the jokes, notably the one about Alpha and Omigod, might look better in a crossword but by the time, two hours later, that we've reached 'He'll alter you before the dessert, no, no, I mean he'll desert you before the altar' most lines of resistance have long since been worn down.

In that sense Stoppard's turn is about as outrageous as Landen's: 'I woke up this morning feeling like a new man so I went out and got one.' 'Personal servant, is he?' 'Yes, a bit' is dialogue that doesn't leave a lot of room for comment, and *On the Razzle* has the precisely correct air of a bank holiday, one on which a hitherto fairly studious writer has suddenly been allowed his turn as a stand-up comic. 'One false move,' says Landen early in proceedings which are eventually to involve a ladder, a sex-mad coachman and a maid who appears to have wandered in from Feydeau to clean up the rest of the jokes, 'and we could have a farce on our hands,' and that is of course exactly what we get. There's not much sense of Vienna, or the grocery trade, or escape from suburban routine, and without those elements it is true that the running jokes stop running somewhere around the middle of the third and last act. At that point I did start missing the songs a bit, and thinking about how brave it is of Mr Wood to try the running-waiter gags that Gower Champion made such magic in *Hello Dolly!* without having a choreographer, a score or any dancers, let alone Carol Channing on that lengendary staircase. But if you want to see how it's possible to balance twenty-five people on nothing more than a dictionary and the realization that with enough puddings on the table there's even a joke in just desserts, then this dazzling evening is the one to go for. National Christmas treats are coming around a little early this year.

The Royal Exchange in Manchester, which show for show has a recent track record as impressive as that of the National or the RSC, now has another winner in Adrian Noble's masterly production of *Doctor Faustus*. It takes one or two remarkable liberties, such as giving us the last classic 'Faustus is gone' speech as a programme note instead, but in all the essentials this is a spare and tense triumph not only for Noble but also for his two principal players. Ben Kingsley offers a nomadic, existential scholar prepared to sell his soul to the devil but not then prepared to get in return nothing more than a Cook's tour of Europe and a couple of conjuring tricks. His final appeal to Mephistopheles at the jaws of hell is thus a petulant shriek of rage rather than agony, while James Maxwell as the devil's runner manages a marvellously Ancient Mariner mix of glint and steel. Within the confines of Bob Crowley's set a magic circle is established, one which reflects the larger magic circle which is that theatre itself, and there are some breathtaking special effects, not least the descent of Mephistopheles on a crucifix from the Gods, the better to taunt Faustus with his lost divinity. There is a clarity and a confidence here, as well as the arrival of Kingsley at major straight-stage stardom. London ought to get the opportunity of a look at it.

Strong Sea

Having already established a powerful line in Coward, first with the Maria Aitken *Private Lives* and now with the Donald Sinden *Present Laughter,* it is good to see Alan Strachan turning his Greenwich Theatre's attention to Rattigan. For, like the late Sir Noël, the late Sir Terence has been abjectly ignored by the RSC and generally messed up by the National, leaving his plays wide open to redis-covery by adventurous pub, regional and repertory theatres but largely unseen in central London.

Indeed *The Deep Blue Sea,* which has just opened at Greenwich, is getting its first ever London revival in the thirty years since it was first seen here with Peggy Ashcroft, and in a blazingly powerful and confident production it emerges as perhaps the strongest of all mid-century British dramas. Not that it has ever been recognized as such; when it first opened, although Rattigan was at the height of his fame and fortune and still four years away from the destruction that came to him with the arrival of Osborne at the Royal Court, most critics proceeded to get both his intentions and his achieve-ments here radically wrong.

Briefly, the story is of Hester Collyer, played now by Dorothy Tutin in one of the focal performances of her career; separated from an eminent judge, she is living with a fatally weak-willed test pilot (Clive Francis in the role which originally made a star of Kenneth More) and as the play opens is retrieved by well-meaning neigh-bours from a suicide which seems to be her only possible solution. On the first night in 1952 Ivor Brown took the view that all she needed was a good marriage guidance counsellor, which is roughly akin to suggesting that all Hedda Gabler needs is a halfway decent interior decorator. Indeed, in so far as we have an English *Hedda Gabler, The Deep Blue Sea* is it.

Tynan, though still a supporter when the play first opened, managed to deliver himself of that one great line about Rattigan being the theatre's Formosa, occupied by the old guard but geo-graphically inclined toward the progressives, but then he too got the play deeply and totally wrong by suggesting that having opened with Hester's failed suicide it ought to have ended with her success-ful one. It took Rattigan several years to point out regretfully but tactfully that the whole point of the play is Hester's survival, in itself an infinitely greater tragedy than her death.

The Greenwich programme notes gives us no indication of the play's original reception, which is why I dwell on it here; nor, and this is the greater pity, do they give us any indication of the play's true origins. It is in essence a triangular piece, cornered by Hester, her older and richer husband, the judge, and her younger but sexier lover, the pilot; that triangle was originally a real one, albeit homosexual. There was no Hester but there was Rattigan himself, caught briefly between an older and richer male lover, the MP and diarist Chips Channon, and a younger passion for an actor called Ken Morgan who had been in the film version of Rattigan's first great hit, *French Without Tears*. In the end it was Morgan, not Rattigan, who opted for suicide and successfully took his own life. Had there been no theatrical censorship in Britain in 1952 it is possible, though by no means certain, that *Deep Blue Sea,* instead of seeming the well-made throwback to Galsworthy and Pinero that it now does, would in fact have emerged as our first great homosexual tragedy.

As it is, what we have here is a play in which minor characters, such as a joky landlady and a priggish young married couple living in the flat above Hester's, are beginning to creak a bit, and in which an awful lot of cigarettes seem to get lit and clenched between stiff upper and lower lips. But apart from that, it is all still in remarkably good working order; not only the character of Hester but also those of the Judge (immaculately played by Peter Cellier) and the sinister struck-off doctor (Tony Jay also in cracking form) are superlatively drawn and fulfilled. The only problem is that of Freddie Page, the alcoholic pilot. At the time of his first creation, on both stage and screen, by Kenneth More, men like that were still to be found in all the best pubs; the war not yet a decade over had left a generation of congenitally unemployable cheery misfits who were trading on a kind of seedy RAF charm and not a lot else. Now, forty years on from the battles for Britain, those men have entirely vanished and it is no fault of Clive Francis that the type has become almost unplayable by or to a generation who never knew them.

And talking of lost generations, lost Empires, lost Englishmen, to the Mayfair Theatre has come a remarkable if curious one-man show based on Jerome K. Jerome's ineffable Thames bestseller *Three Men in a Boat*. Rather than take the easy way out, by either playing Jerome himself or hiring another two actors, Jeremy Nicholas has opted to give us just one of the men who were on the boat, now back on dry land and preparing a dinner party for the other two. While he and we await their non-arrival he reads for us the highlights of the journey from Kingston to Oxford, leaving out Hampton Court Maze and their crisis within but including most of the other adventures in a likeable performance pitched about half-way from Richard Briers to John Cleese. A kind of daft innocence coupled with random charm gets us through what is in fact a production idea borrowed from *George and Margaret* to retrieve what would otherwise be pure radio.

Beastly Good

There are times, and they are coming around with ever increasing frequency, when I despair of my critical colleagues in the daily press or what is left of it and them; for several years now the complaint has been, and justifiably, that the West End is full of elderly American musicals and mindless English comedies and not a lot else. So when at long last we get a new play (admittedly novel-based) which is both a comedy and a tragedy, a lyrical, lilting joy containing in the performance of Simon Callow far and away the funniest comic turn in town, what happens? Vague disconsolate murmurs that it is 'neither one thing nor the other' and that perhaps it might have been better to have left the whole thing on the printed page.

The play is of course *The Beastly Beatitudes of Balthazar B*, adapted by J. P. Donleavy from his own novel and to be found at the Duke of York's, to which make all possible speed since the box-office is likely to need your help. What you will find there is a rambling, randy and wholly enchanting account of two 1946 Trinity College Dublin undergraduates being rapidly expelled (for keeping ladies of uncertain virtue in a cabin trunk) and propelled on a journey through life, London and Harrods which veers from high farce to an ending of – unless you've read the book – utterly unexpected sadness.

The title character is admittedly something of a problem; as the play opens we know nothing of him beyond that he's wealthy, Paris-born and has, while apparently still almost in infancy, managed to get his nanny with child. Patrick Ryecart plays him angelic and vacuous, but by the end of the evening we know little more; about his friend Beefy however we know almost too much. The magnificent masturbator, skidding along on infamy towards holy orders but forever interrupted by the need to get his hands on his all too lively grandmother's fortune, Beefy is one of the great comic creations of our time and from the moment of his first stage appearance, a butch, latterday Oscar Wilde in search of his audience, Callow plays him to the hilt and then way beyond. Beefy and Balthazar, childhood colleagues in prep-school smut, survive their expulsion from Trinity in much the way they survived their old headmaster, the dread bicycle-seat sniffer. They move to London, where Balthazar makes an unhappy marriage (having mysteriously lost his only true love in Dublin) while Beefy ends up in command of a lift until there is the inevitable crash. But whether charging into unlit bedrooms, clad only in an assortment of bicycle chains, defiling widows, orphans and motor mechanics, or merely muttering 'Blessed are they that lay down their garments,' Beefy is a source of constant amazement and delight. Can his name really be getting smaller year by year in Debrett? Can his family motto really be 'I'll thank you not to fuck about with me'? Has he really arranged for the Fortnum's picnic hamper to be served to him during a Soho strip show? Does he really live otherwise on a daily tin of dogfood, 'honest nourishment at an honest price'? The answer is indeed yes, and at his final departure from Balthazar's life ('I go now to Maida Vale, from where only the hardiest ever return') the loss is ours too.

The supporting cast seems to be made up largely of cut-price Lady Bracknells (Lally Bowers, Sylvia Coleridge), but when did you last see a company of fifteen on a commercial London stage not doing a musical or emanating from a subsidized house? Ron Daniels, the director, keeps them all in a kind of order and the result is an unmissable adult treat.

Stephen Lowe, hitherto best-known for plays of localized English life, has been courageous in attempting a parable about Tibet immediately before and after the Chinese invasion during the 1950s, and braver still in shaping it in such a way as to invite comparisons with Brecht's *Caucasian Chalk Circle* or *Good Woman of Setzuan*. The fact that *Tibetan Inroads* (at the Royal Court) doesn't altogether work on that level is apt to mask its success on a number of others. What Mr Lowe is, I think, on about here is the way that a people, any people, will use religion and politics to further their own ends

The Beastly Beatitudes of Balthazar B Patrick Ryecart *as Balthazar*, Simon Callow *as Beefy*

while believing they are still acting for the greater good.

Thus as the play begins we find our hero (Kenneth Cranham in a fine, gritty performance) in first imminent and then realized danger of castration for having slept with the wife of a wealthy local landowner; the castration is demanded by his own brother, a powerful neighbourhood monk (memories of Gielgud and 'I come from a nearby Llamasery' in the musical of *Lost Horizon* should at this point be banished). Anyway our hero then summons up devils and demands revenge, which sure enough arrives in the shape of the Chinese People's Liberation Army.

So much for the first half; act two of *Tibetan Inroads* is largely concerned with working out whether it was better to have a lot of monks going around castrating local adulterers than a lot of Chinese forcing the villagers to build roads and listen to the thoughts of Chairman Mao. No very firm conclusions are reached, though there is time for the irreverent thought that the Dalai Lama was right to get the hell out of there altogether, even if he did choose

India instead. Along the way, however, there are some strong performances, notably from Sharon Duce and Paul Brooke, though I somehow doubt that the production has been sponsored by the Tibetan Tourist Board.

Broadway Nicked

New York

In so far as it is possible to take a waxwork display by storm, the RSC's *Nicholas Nickleby* has stormed Broadway; some previews were sparsely attended but the official opening brought the expected raves (shows here are reported either as second comings or as natural disasters, and last accordingly five years or one night) and tickets at a hundred dollars apiece are now hard to come by. Nevertheless, with a union-dictated closing date of 3 January and a total budget of $4.5 million, the expectations are of *Nickleby* losing at least $100,000 even if every last ticket is sold.

That in itself gives some indication of the present economic climate along the Great White Way – shows playing to upwards of $300,000 a week, among them *My Fair Lady*, are doing little better than breaking even while of last season's seventy new productions less than half a dozen will ever show a New York profit.

Accordingly, Broadway has become the land of the living dead, final proof that there is indeed life long after artistic demise. Here you will still find Rex Harrison grinding out his Professor Higgins eight shows a week, Claudette Colbert proving that if you look closely she is still alive and working albeit in a thriller (*A Talent for Murder*) of alarming inadequacy, and Richard Harris warming over his ten-year-old screen portrayal of the once and apparently forever future King Arthur in *Camelot*.

Of the thirty-four shows currently on Broadway, less than a dozen have been written since 1975 and only about half those are straight plays; the rest is a massive musical mausoleum where Lena Horne, Mickey Rooney, Ann Miller and Lauren Bacall make nightly personal appearances for out-of-town movie addicts who at thirty-five dollars a ticket find some sort of oblique reassurance in their stage presence. If all those old 1940s Hollywood stars are still alive and kicking through eight shows a week, then surely their audiences must have survived too?

The Lauren Bacall show, *Woman of the Year,* is in fact lifted from
an old Tracy–Hepburn screen comedy to which has been added a
score by Kander and Ebb which manages to echo the *Applause* that
was Miss Bacall's last stage hit so closely you wonder why they
have bothered adding new lyrics. Miss Bacall, who is rapidly turning into Marlene Dietrich, stands around a lot in spotlights as if
waiting to sign autographs while Harry Guardino, as the cartoonist
who falls in love with her, makes you wonder where on earth she
manages to find co-stars who offer such little competition. In the
absence of a book, the producers have borrowed the Gene Kelly
cartoon-dancing routine and managed to get it wrong, while in the
absence of a finale, Miss Bacall has borrowed the wet-hair routine
from *South Pacific* and got that wrong too. The result is a shameful
shambles (winner incidentally of this year's Tony Award) from
which only Roderick Cook, as a campy secretary, emerges with
something akin to dignity.

It is against this background of appalling rewrites that the flags
need to be hung out yet again for Stephen Sondheim. True, his new
musical *Merrily We Roll Along* is also based on an old thirties
comedy (by Kaufman and Hart) and from the first preview I witnessed it was clear that a lot needs to be done before this Hal Prince
production officially opens on 3 November. But there is more
invention, courage and intelligence in a single moment of this show
than in the rest of Broadway's twenty current musicals put
together. The original play created a device (later borrowed by
Pinter for *Betrayal*) whereby it started at the end, with a group of
depressed and corrupt forty-year-olds, and followed them back
scene by scene across twenty years to their youthful optimism and
ideals, so that the final image is of them setting out on a road we
know they can never follow.

Sondheim and his dramatist George Furth have updated this end
from the thirties to the fifties, and instead of having the show played
by middle-aged actors getting younger Prince has cast it with
twenty late teenagers, most making Broadway débuts and all
having to age up to forty and then down again. That the show
works at all is thus something of a miracle, and that it will soon
work a great deal better I do not doubt.

Like Sondheim's *Follies* it is about the present in the past, and like
his *Company* it has a fragmented structure more akin to a sequence
of short stories than a book. It is a musical about lost dreams and
discovered nightmares, and it contains (in 'Old Friends' and 'Our

Time') two of the most haunting and lyrical numbers that even he has ever written. Whether it will appeal to a Broadway audience capable of giving Lauren Bacall a standing ovation without being struck by lightning remains to be seen; this is a difficult, dangerous and spasmodically brilliant show. It is also, at the time of this writing, in some trouble.

Amadeus (John Wood now starring) and *Children of a Lesser God* apart, the only good straight play on Broadway is Lanford Wilson's wonderfully Chekhovian *Fifth of July*; set in Lebanon, Missouri, this is one of those multi-generation family sagas at which in this country Enid Bagnold and N. C. Hunter once excelled. An anecdotal piece (as was Wilson's *Talley's Folly*) concerning the walking wounded of the American sixties, it's about drugs and drink and homosexuality and Vietnam and the rock business but in the end it's mainly about the selling of a family home and may very well be American's own *Cherry Orchard*.

National Disaster

The time has come once again, I fear, to ask ourselves who is managing the National Theatre and when he proposes to start. The easy answer is of course that it is Peter Hall and that as he is currently rehearsing an epic Christmas production of *The Oresteia* – just the thing for family audiences – he cannot be expected to be everywhere at once. That perhaps is why the one coherent and genuinely successful stage in the building, the Cottesloe, has been allowed to abandon all the permanent-company ideals of Bill Bryden and take instead a random selection of ill-assorted work from Wesker to Dario Fo while simultaneously the Lyttelton is becoming a West End rerun house full of transfers from Hampstead, undemanding Stoppard diversions and a forthcoming Pinero ideal for the Theatre Royal Haymarket.

But if two stages have lost any sense of being a National Theatre, that still leaves us the open Olivier under the personal direction of Peter not only Hall but also Gill; surely what is happening there might have some sense of purpose or occasion, offer some faint clue as to why that vast edifice sits on the South Bank swallowing our tax-paid millions? Not in fact. What is happening there at the moment is *The Hypochondriac,* a Michael Bogdanov production some way after Molière which would have looked inadequate if staged a decade ago at the Young Vic for one Saturday-morning schools audience who didn't mind watching amateurs on their way to drama school. Mr Bogdanov has achieved the not inconsiderable feat of taking a team of talented professionals (among them Daniel Massey, Michael Bryant, Anna Carteret and Polly James) and making them into a collection of campy, posturing muggers apparently under the impression that nobody in the audience will remain seated or awake unless the stage is turned into a tacky carnival filled with people who appear to have just come fifteenth in a Ken Dodd lookalike contest.

The alibi for this shambling wreck would appear to be *commedia dell'arte*; the notion that as Molière allowed a certain amount of dancing and miming between scenes then anything goes. It has however apparently escaped the notice of both Mr Bogdanov and his lacklustre choreographer that for *commedia dell'arte* routines to work they need to be put together with the infinite precision of *Cats.* To fill the Olivier stage with a lot of uneasy extras desperately trying not to look embarrassed as they perform sequences which have all the charm and entertainment value of an earthquake, and then to have that mood spill over into the actual plot so that Massey in the title role looks as if he has just failed a 1950 audition for Brian Rix, does such desperate disservice to an intriguing play that you are left, like the audience at 'Springtime for Hitler', open-mouthed in amazement that the affair was allowed to get to a first rehearsal, let alone a first night.

This is Molière's last play and has a great deal to say about the nature of doctors, disease and the power of imagination; the fact that it is better known over here in the schoolrooms than on the stage is no excuse to treat it as unplayable. Better in that belief not to have done it at all than to have come up with this halting apology, one which uses a translation by Alan Drury of such mind-bending inanity that it is finally forced to resort to old which–doctor–witch-doctor chestnuts in the hope of bludgeoning its audience into an involuntary giggle. The cast is about evenly divided between those who look as though they would like to be doing something else for a living and those who look as if they are awaiting the first read-through of a Wolf Mankowitz musical. The result is a desperate, raving, ranting, ramshackle evening put together in an arch, coy, 'classics can be fun' frame of mind which insults the intelligence of all its participants and witnesses.

Miller's Tale

One of the larger mysteries of the postwar London theatre has been its failure to come to terms with the greatness of Arthur Miller; the National has in fifteen years managed just one revival of *Death of a Salesman* and two of *The Crucible*, the RSC has not managed even that, and commercially we still await London premieres of *After the Fall* (1967) and everything Miller has written thereafter.

But now, to Wyndham's in a stunningly powerful production by Michael Blakemore, comes the first London revival in more than thirty years of the play that made Miller's name and established the guidelines of his work: *All My Sons* is about guilt and family and survival in small-town America and in its central figure, Joe Keller, the guy that knowingly sold the cracked cylinder heads that sent twenty-one pilots and his own airman son to a flaming death, we have already the beginnings of Willy Loman. Joe, too (played here by Colin Blakely in a performance of such controlled brilliance that even the armpits seem to sweat on cue), is out there working the territory on a smile and a shoeshine, and like *Death of a Salesman* this play too is *Our Town* rewritten in acid and poison and blood.

Doubtless Miller had a more lofty model than Thornton Wilder; the fallen tree that stands centre stage as a symbol of Joe's fallen son, the conscious use of family patterns established by O'Neill many years earlier, the lengthy prose soliloquies all suggest a pattern of classical Greek tragedy compressed within the fences of the archetypal mid-Western backyard. Even the neatly arranged sets of neighbours, one couple living each side of Joe, are no more than onlookers, a chorus of ordinary people brought up against one extraordinary happening in the past that all for different reasons would like now to forget.

In that sense *All My Sons* is a play of deep cynicism about postwar America's ability to kill in the name of commerce, and about its belief in the overriding and all-forgiving importance of family loyalty. But Miller is on about something else here too; like Ibsen in both *The Wild Duck* (which this play much resembles) and *Enemy of the People* he is on about a community within which one individual is holding up too many mirrors for the others, mirrors which eventually have to get smashed if that community is to survive. On that level, what separates *All My Sons* from *The Crucible* is that at curtain fall Joe has the grace, or perhaps just enough panic, to take his own life before others start doing that for him.

Yet the supreme achievement of Blakemore here has been to take an *ad hoc* company, few of whom have ever worked in the American theatre or with each other before, and mould them within a month's rehearsal period into a deeply convincing community; you may hear the occasional creaking of Miller's three-act, three-hour plotting, you may wonder whether the notion that all postwar affluence is blood-stained loot might not be a little simplistic, but you will not easily forget the look in Rosemary Harris' eyes as she finally comes to terms with the tragedy she has helped to write, nor the moment when Colin Blakely as her Joe finally and all too late accepts the parental responsibility of the title. This is *the* American postwar tragedy, and we shall not see it better played in the foreseeable future.

Out at Greenwich, Julian Mitchell's *Another Country* is a new play intelligently and intriguingly derived from some recent newspaper headlines. A year or so ago, during the Blunt spy scandal, journalists the world over leapt to the easy and understandable conclusion that Cambridge in the late twenties and thirties was the breeding ground for upper-class homosexual treachery. Mr Mitchell takes a somewhat different view; he reckons that characters are formed, and even ideals selected, some time before arrival at undergraduate status and that therefore we should root around further back, into the British public schools that sent those men to Cambridge. Thus we have here a play about the schooldays of Guy Burgess; true, the school in the play is not specifically Eton, and the character is called Guy Bennett, but beyond that Mitchell has not made much attempt to disguise his subject matter. Like two other recent and similarly titled plays, Alan Bennett's *The Old Country* and Trevor Griffiths' *Country,* this is a drama about the way that modern England comes ready-wrapped in old school ties. In allowing only one of his cast of ten (David Williams as a camp pacifist lecturer) to be over seventeen on stage, and in setting the entire piece within the school, Mitchell has taken some considerable theatrical risks but Stuart Burge's fluent production meets that challenge very well, and the result is an

enthralling school play which establishes that every single require-
ment for the trade of traitor (ambition, disillusion, cunning and a
talent for hypocrisy) is amply matched by the requirements of a
good British public school. Shades of the prison house are beginning to close fast around these golden lads of the thirties, among
whom Rupert Everett (as the Burgess character) and Joshua le
Touzel (as the one modelled on John Cornford) are especially
impressive.

Royal Flush

Once in a while, and luckily not too often, a play comes along
which is so stunningly, mind-bendingly terrible that it transcends
all the normal laws of criticism and one such is now to be found at
the Palace Theatre. It's called *Her Royal Highness?* and it's written by
the director, Ray Cooney, along with Royce Ryton who is to the
English theatre roughly what Crawfie once was to English journalism, that's to say he writes truly awful things about royalty. I don't
mean awfully unkind or unfair, just awfully bad; his heart is clearly
somewhere near the right place but his typewriter is alas not, and
the result is the kind of play which might get even Willie Hamilton a
good name among Royalists.

Billed in what seems to me direct contravention of the Trades
Description Act as 'a comedy', *Her Royal Highness?* is set across the
first six months of this year, months leading up to the Royal
Wedding, and its central notion is that during those lengthy
preparations Lady Di gets cold feet and runs home to mother to
have a bit of a think about the whole affair, while an Australian
lookalike model (played of course by the same actress) is flown in to
impersonate the future Princess of Wales at various public events.

This allows Ryton and Cooney to borrow virtually an entire act
of *Pygmalion* and restage it as Palace officials try to teach the model
to walk and speak like a Fair Lady, but the rest of the play appears to
have been not so much lifted from Shaw as cobbled together from
old gossip-column headlines. Set on a bare stage occupied only by a
flight of stairs apparently left over from some prehistoric Miss
World competition, the play gives you the impression that you've
been locked up amid the royal waxworks at Madame Tussaud's for

two and a half hours, only without so many laughs.

In a sizeable cast of more than twenty players, all of whom commendably manage to get through the entire evening without tearing up their Equity cards, actresses manage to play the Queen and the Queen Mother and Mrs Thatcher all looking more like Danny La Rue in drag, and the audience is given free flags to wave, though I rather wish they'd also given out earplugs and those sleep masks you get on aeroplanes. Lines like 'You're taking on an awful reponsibility, Diana – look at Lord Snowdon – he never got used to it' suggest that Ryton and Cooney should be royally incarcerated in the Tower for a lengthy course in dramatic construction, but the really alarming thing about *Her Royal Highness?* is that it is, I suspect, going to make a great deal of money. A hefty advertising campaign coupled with a brilliant choice of the Palace Theatre (the next best thing would, I suppose, have been to stage 'Springtime for Hitler' at Berchtesgaden) looks to me like a winner, while all the finale lacks is Anna Neagle and the massed bands of the Grenadier Guards.

The fact that we have here a script of such breathtaking inadequacy that when nothing much is happening on stage (as often it isn't) the cast feel obliged to turn to their audience with little homilies on the future of the Monarchy suggests a strong case for the return of the Lord Chamberlain and his powers of stage censorship; it is not that the play is offensive to royalty, but that it is offensive to paying customers who expect more for their £6 stalls than dialogue apparently copied off the inside of a cracked Coronation souvenir mug. The whole affair has all the awful fascination of watching somebody constructing Windsor Castle out of old marshmallows, and I only hope Cooney and Ryton have the decency to send the royalties to royalty. You will note that I have not mentioned any of the cast by name; one day they will thank me for that.

To the Aldwych from last year's Stratford season has come the Alan Howard *Richard III* in a somewhat subdued version of Terry Hands' original production, though clearly still intended as a companion piece to the current Howard–Hands *Richard II* also in the RSC repertoire for London. The plays stand as twin pillars at either end of the history cycle, and *Richard III* ends in the same way as *Richard II* begins, with a new king bathed in a kind of holy light. Beyond that however they have not a lot in common, and it is indeed arguable that both director and star have actually been hampered in their approach to *Richard III* by having to work on it in tandem with *Richard II*.

But this is a production full of wonderfully theatrical images set against a slatted jet-black background, none finer than the last where Richard is actually pinioned to the battlefield of Bosworth by the ghosts of all those whom he has destroyed, so that Richmond may then run him through with a lance; the parts here (notably Howard's as the King, Derek Godfrey as a splendidly wry Buckingham and Sinead Cusack as a tragically sexy Lady Anne) add up to rather more than the whole but as a kind of anti-Coronation, a pageant of blood and corruption, it works well enough.

Masked Greeks

Within the past fortnight two of the National Theatre's three leading directors (Peter Gill being presumably otherwise engaged) have written to me indicating somewhat regally that my enthusiasm for their recent work has not quite come up to their own very high standards. The same could of course be true of their work and my standards, but I had hoped to be able to be more enthusiastic about Sir Peter Hall's new *Oresteia* (on the Olivier stage), not least because it is in a version by our greatest modern theatrical poet, Tony Harrison, has been fully five years in the making, and does meet the minimum requirements that the National ought from time to time to be offering something on a scale and in a style not readily available elsewhere.

Sadly that is the most to be said for what is currently happening at the Olivier; coming as it does almost two years after the broader and infinitely more accessible *Greeks* cycle at the Aldwych, this is more in the nature of a classroom exercise. For all three plays that make up the *Oresteia* (*Agamemnon, Choephori* and *Eumenides*) Hall has opted to have a cast-chorus playing in heavy immobile masks behind which they are then effectively buried alive. Not for the first time on the Olivier stage, a deadly operatic ritual has overtaken live drama; a programme note of unusual inanity informs us that these masks are not in fact being worn to re-create the anyway unknown conditions of original production, but then adds that they do nevertheless have an effect comparable 'to the protective masks worn by welders'. The fact that nobody pays nine pounds a ticket to sit for upwards of five hours watching welders at work seems not to have occurred to anyone on the South Bank, and as a result what might have been an infinitely powerful visual and aural experience is reduced to the static dimensions of a radio play produced by the inmates of some mid-Western American university drama depart-ment intent on returning the classics to their roots.

It is an academic experiment of considerable tedium, largely because for better or for worse we have now come to expect more of actors than movements of the voice and arms: we need eyebrows and eyes and cheeks and chins and mouths not frozen into immobility, and without that kind of life and detail we are left with a carefully choreographed museum display of what Greek drama might have looked like to the Greeks, one which not even the brilliance of Harrison's language and a stunning Harrison Birtwhistle score can bring to anything more than very occasional flashes of life. Excellent actors whose range, subtlety and differen-tiation are the hallmarks of their trade are here strapped into solid puppet headframes through which they are then supposed to relate to a modern audience the remarkable story of Agamemnon's sacrifice and Clytemnestra's revenge and the final verdict on Orestes, and I suppose we were lucky they didn't also have to have one arm strapped behind their backs. The production ends, incidentally, with the most shamelessly engineered standing ovation I have ever seen in a theatre; as one distinguished veteran critic said to me afterwards, 'When I want a religious experience, I'll go to church.'

Those of you 'Crossroads' addicts still worried about the eventual fate of Noele Gordon will be relieved to learn that she's still alive and well and slogging through eight shows a week at the Haymarket Leicester in an adequate rep revival of *Gypsy,* one of the greatest of all Broadway musicals since it combines in a single score the lush showbiz music of Jule Styne and the acid, anti-showbiz lyrics of Stephen Sondheim. Miss Gordon has a certain difficulty capturing the essence of an all-American vaudeville mother, the same kind of difficulty Anna Neagle might find in playing Eleanor Roosevelt, but as a show it remains pretty invulnerable and in Roger Redfarn's briskly efficient production Fiona Fullerton is an enchanting (if also over-English) Gypsy Rose Lee.

Similar problems of the transatlantic crossing are better handled at the Ambassadors, where James Roose-Evans has devised and directed a faithful stage adaptation of the bestselling *84 Charing Cross Road* by Helene Hanff. Miss Hanff is a little middle-aged American lady whose main claim to fame is that for twenty years she wrote, like Alistair Cooke, a series of letters from America; this writer was, when the letters start, an impoverished New York TV scriptwriter who could never quite raise the fare to London, and indeed had Laker then existed we might to this day not have heard of her. Instead, she began to express her yearning to be in London along with her orders for books to make that city feel somehow closer, and the ultimate tragedy is that when she does finally make it across the Atlantic most of her penfriends and the shop itself are all but gone. Radiant performances by Rosemary Leach as Miss Hanff and David Swift as her favourite salesman make this a Christmas treat; somehow you feel the Ambassadors' box-office should accept book tokens.

And finally, two productions at the Lyric Hammersmith; on the main stage, a dullish revival of *The Soldier's Fortune* made bearable by a marvellously camp turn from Hugh Paddick as the pandering Sir Jolly Jumble, and in the Studio *Trafford Tanzi,* Claire Luckham's brilliant account of a life and a marriage seen over ten rounds in the wrestling arena. Some falls, some submissions and a final no-holds-barred knockout contest between Tanzi and her chauvinist pig husband; unmissable.

Stage '81

A year not of massive economic despair but of persistent gloom and a curious lack of excitement or enthusiasm; after the Arts Council cuts of last year perhaps the greatest theatrical achievement was sheer survival, and in that context it's good to note that the major casualties have been fewer than forecast. True, we have lost the Old Vic as a permanent classical house, and further out towards the fringe the Round House, Riverside and the Mermaid have all lost a lot of ground in straitened circumstances. In the West End, too, many houses have been too dark for too long but what seems currently to be most lacking is any real sense of a coherent policy for the eighties.

Certain theatres still seem to have a definable idea of what they are doing and where they are going: David Aukin at Hampstead and the management of the Bush are, for example, both still managing on minimal budgets to run playhouses where there is a distinct style. Equally, the RSC is still rolling superlatively along tracks laid down twenty years ago by Peter Hall, while ironically it is the failure to build just another set of such tracks that is currently besetting the National under Hall. And not only the National; what, now, is the purpose or policy of the Royal Court? Or of the Lyric Hammersmith? Or of the Young Vic? All these and more have been forced economically to succumb to a random hit-and-run or flop-and-fail policy.

Outside London, larger theatres from Chichester north to Nottingham and Leicester seem to have found some sort of salvation in a lot of big old musicals often complete with big old stars, while the good news from inner London is the turning of the Fortune into a home for the best of the Fringe; meanwhile precious few other central London managements want to risk their investors' money on any but the very safest of bets; like publishers, impresarios have been running for cover at the first breath of cold air. When they emerge from their caves and find that the weather has changed, there may well be nobody out there to enjoy it with them.

For all the noble noises sounded by its organizers, the West End is still a wasteland of crumbling theatres, surly box-office managers, overpriced bars and impossible parking. It took Broadway more than a decade to realize that its only hope of salvation was a deal with the City of New York on matters environmental and social as well as economic and theatrical; it is apparently going to take London theatre managers even longer to do a sensible deal with their proprietors (who should bear at least half the show risk), the GLC and the Metropolitan Police.

So much for what has been wrong with 1981 in the theatre; what has been right with it includes the first major Irish play since O'Casey (Brian Friel's *Translations*) and a couple of smashing comedies, Nell Dunn's female Turkish Bath chatterama (*Steaming*) and Jack Rosenthal's backstage *Smash* which for reasons still unclear never got further in than Richmond.

From awards already announced it is clear that Mark Medoff's deaf-liberation *Children of a Lesser God* is set to scoop the pool though (like *The Miracle Worker*) more for its cause than its actual writing. In sheer performance terms I cannot think of a better production this year than Michael Blakemore's revival of *All My Sons,* though it is run a very close second by Harold Pinter's production of Simon Gray's English-With-Tears school play *Quartermaine's Terms.* What is especially remarkable on both these stages (the Albery and the Queen's) is that the level of company playing achieved with a group of actors who met only in rehearsal a month before opening is actually much higher than anything achieved this year by either of our major permanent companies.

On the musical front *Cats* is a clear winner, and indeed the first homegrown musical we can send to Broadway with a feeling of pride rather than deep embarrassment; Michael Crawford is proving himself the best three-ring circus in town in *Barnum,* but London curiously rejected one of the best Broadway scores in years, perhaps because *The Best Little Whorehouse in Texas* was a less than ideal title for the Drury Lane billboards.

Two of the best individual performances of the year undoubtedly came from Daniel Massey in the National's *Man and Superman* and Dorothy Tutin in the Greenwich *Deep Blue Sea,* though had Edna O'Brien's *Virginia* been less of a literary-lunch monologue and more of a play then Maggie Smith would have been in that league too. John Wells as Denis Thatcher turned in an excellent topical cabaret of the old 'TW3' tradition, though I reckon the best comedy performance in town is that of Simon Callow as the unbelievably randy Beefy in Donleavy's superb *Beastly Beatitudes of Balthazar B.*

Disappointments of the year included Ustinov's lacklustre embassy comedy *Overheard* and the failure of *The Accrington Pals* to make it beyond the Warehouse. Appalling mistakes of the year included Richard Huggett's belief that he could play Evelyn Waugh, and Emile Littler's that he could fill the Palace with Colin Welland's old school play. I am still undecided whether *The Sound of Music* or *Childe Byron* or *Her Royal Highness?* is actually the most mind-bendingly awful evening I've had in a theatre all year, though I firmly believe that all three may well be contenders not only for Worst of the Year but also for Worst of the Decade.

On the brighter side, 1981 has also been the year of Manchester's *Duchess of Malfi,* Brighton's *Brothers Karamazov,* C. P. Taylor's haunting Nazi musical *Good* and, at the Court, a lyrical Irish *Seagull* as well as (at the National) John Dexter's superb *Shoemaker's*

Holiday. All in all, a fair old mix.

Stage '82

January: Ray Cooney denies that, following the success of *Her Royal Highness?* at the Palace, his next production will be a musical about the early life of Prince Philip tentatively entitled *Bess, You Is My Woman Now*. Noele Gordon does however indicate that, if terms could be agreed, she might be willing to appear at Wembley in the life of Anna Neagle on ice. Anna Neagle says she would prefer to appear as Noele Gordon, and if possible under water. The National Theatre is considering whether or not it might be more sensible to let the audience wear the masks in *The Oresteia*, thereby freeing the actors for facial expression.

February: Thousands of angry ticket holders demonstrate outside the Victoria Palace when it is discovered that *The Little Foxes,* in which Elizabeth Taylor makes her London stage début, is not in fact a searing behind-the-scenes account of her marriages to Mike Todd and Eddie Fisher but instead a boring old Lillian Hellman revival. Meanwhile Petula Clark, still recovering from the shock of a totally unfounded shoplifting inquiry, refuses to sing 'These Are a Few of My Favourite Things' at *Sound of Music* matinees.

March: John Osborne's mother starts a long and profitable tour in a one-woman show in which she reviews her son's autobiography and describes the heartbreak she suffered when he refused to accept the Terence Rattigan Award for promising young dramatists with very nice eyes. On Broadway, Richard Nixon denies that he is taking over from Mickey Rooney in *Sugar Babies* but indicates that he might be willing to tour as King Lear if somebody could explain the bits about madness and over-zealous daughters.

April: The Old Vic, having now auctioned off all fixtures and fittings, is thinking of hiring out Peter O'Toole for private parties. Anna Neagle has decided not to appear in a life of the Queen Mother on roller skates, but the Queen Mother has indicated that she might be willing to film the life of Jessie Matthews if the money was right and she could wear all her own tiaras.

May: A survey of declining West End box-office business indicates that the public at large really only wants to see actors when they are appearing at memorial services or taking part in awards ceremonies. Accordingly, at least one London theatre now promises to seat its audiences in pews, while another will offer them tables at which to eat and vote during the show.

June: The appeal fund for the defence of Michael Bogdanov, director of *The Romans in Britain,* has now reached half a million pounds and the National Theatre has threatened that unless this is doubled by Christmas they will revive the production nightly on all three stages. Ned Sherrin is reported to be working on a sequel to *The Mitford Girls* entitled *The Mitford Boys* and starring David Kernan as the late Sir Oswald Mosley with Wilfrid Hyde White as the Duke of Devonshire.

July: To encourage theatregoers to make their way through the City of London to their new Barbican premises, the Royal Shakespeare Company is offering rent-controlled overnight accommodation in the skyscraper blocks and a 'lucky ticket' draw in which the winner gets to be Lord Mayor for a week. The Mermaid Theatre is now being run by Lord Bernard Miles' parrot and there is a good chance of *Treasure Island* being revived again for Christmas only with a slight change of emphasis. The Society of West End Theatre announces a drastic new training scheme for box-office attendants which will include the art of picking up telephones and actually encouraging customers to book tickets. Moreover bar staff will be urged to work during intervals and programme sellers may even be asked to carry change and know the precise order of letters of the alphabet when seating audiences.

August: Barbara Woodhouse and the Queen Mother jointly deny that they are to appear together on stage in a revival of *Corgis and Bess*. Meanwhile American tourists who wish to impress the folks back home without having to suffer long boring evenings indoors are now able to purchase a London Theatregoer's Kit which includes six torn ticket-stubs, several theatre programmes already pre-thumbed and a ready-reckoner cocktail party quotation chart including ten variations on 'It was really great' and 'That Alan Howard sure can say Shakespeare.'

September: Executors of the Jessie Matthews Estate reveal that they have turned down an application from Danny La Rue but are still considering the suitability of the Queen Mother and Barry Humphries for a starring role in her stage musical biography. The first Julian Slade music festival opens in Budleigh Salterton.

October: Following the success of *Cats* on Broadway, it is bought for Hollywood and there are rumours that T. S. Eliot will now become the first major poet ever to win a posthumous Oscar; meanwhile Tim Rice and Andrew Lloyd Webber are considering a musical of *The Waste Land* starring Elaine Paige as Mrs J. Alfred Prufrock. Michael Foot agrees to make a nationwide personal appearance tour in the stage version of *Worzel Gummidge* so long as Peter Tatchell agrees to play his Aunt Sally.

November: Now that Gilbert and Sullivan are safely out of D'Oyly Carte clutches, there is to be an all-male production of *The Pirates of Penzance* in aid of *Gay News* at a sauna-and-solarium complex not far from the Charing Cross Road. Joan Plowright declines to play Vivien Leigh in the stage version of Lord Olivier's new autobiography. Evelyn Laye agrees to play Jessie Matthews in the new musical of her life, but only for the early years; Flora Robson has been asked to play her in later scenes.

December: The BBC, having launched itself into stage productions with 'Captain Beaky's Musical Christmas', denies that it is now planning to do the 'Nine o'Clock News' live at the Palladium in front of an invited audience. Buckingham Palace officials ask Downing Street if it is still constitutional for the monarch to impose life exile from Great Britain on all those involved in planning Royal Variety Shows.

1982

Taylor Made

This still being the awards time of year, when critics are in an unusually giving vein, and actors and dramatists required in return to give some of their finest renditions of surprise, humility and gratitude on podiums rather than stages, most of my Fleet Street colleagues seem to have decided that either Brian Friel's *Translations* (at the National from Hampstead) or Peter Nichols' *Passion Play* (briefly at the Aldwych) was the best new play of 1981. In both those selections they are of course deeply mistaken.

Far and away the best new play of last year was one which turned up in the RSC repertoire at the Warehouse for a very few performances in the autumn and has now just reopened there for what will I trust be a much longer stay, though tragically this return to the RSC repertoire comes just a month after the sudden and early death of its writer C. P. Taylor. Having now had a second chance to see his *Good* confirms my belief not only that it was the major achievement of his remarkable playwriting career, but also that it will live long after some current award-winners have been forgotten.

A chamber concert in death and destruction, pitched somewhere halfway from *Cabaret* to *Pennies from Heaven*, *Good* tells the story of a semi-detached German professor called Halder, played in a performance of exquisite otherworldliness by Alan Howard. In the four months since I first saw Howard blinking myopically through this role I have been trying to think why it seemed so strongly reminiscent, and of precisely what, since the performance is unlike anything else I have ever seen Howard do for the RSC; seeing the play again this week it finally dawned on me that what he is doing here is precisely what Mr Howard's uncle Leslie used to do in such English films of the early forties as *Pimpernel Smith*, the creation of a character so totally self-absorbed that new rules have to be invented for his integration into the surrounding society.

In *Good*, that society is the immediately pre-war Germany; Halder is a well-meaning academic who happens to have written somewhat casually a novel suggesting that in certain special circumstances euthanasia might not, on balance and all things considered, be such a terribly bad idea. Hitler gets to hear of the book, and across six years from 1933 Frankfurt to 1939 Auschwitz, we follow Halder's decreasingly dreamlike involvement with the Nazis. On stage throughout the evening is a company of ten actors and five musicians, though only Halder and we can ever hear the band: they exist in his head, a permanently portable palm court quintet who play everything from 'A Night in Monte Carlo' to 'You Are My Heart's Delight' in ever increasingly ghastly jovial counterpoint to the book-burning and the Jew-baiting and the euthanasia that take up more and more the centre of the stage. And then, at the last, when Halder starts to run Auschwitz for Eichmann, not especially because he wants to but just because it seems the thing to do at the time, the band finally becomes a reality and it is of course a band of Jewish prisoners.

Taylor himself called *Good* a comedy with music, and in the blackest possible way that is perhaps what it is; but it's also a play about the power of popular music, about the infinite possibilities of self-delusion, and about the daft notion of virtue in the abstract. Halder is not essentially evil, and he's not just obeying orders, at least not in the beginning; nor is he especially ambitious, or corrupt, or stupid, or afraid. Like Don Quixote (and predictably he ends up at the Auschwitz railway station reading just that) he would wish the world to pull its socks up and prove benevolent, and if his contemporaries do at the moment seem a little over-inclined to set fire to books and Jews, well then, perhaps sooner or later they might give up and go home and all will be vaguely right again under a German heaven.

In one sense, *Good* has a lot in common with both *Arturo Ui* and *The Good Soldier Schweik*; where Brecht showed us Nazi history as a comic strip, Taylor shows it to us in the form of a concert by some Bavarian Mountain Ensemble; true, they are still playing 'September Song' a decade or so before it was written, which is curious given the minutely detailed historical documentation offered us by the programme, but that apart this Howard Davies production seems to me as near faultless as any of the eighties thus far. It boasts an immensely strong cast, with Domini Blythe and Penelope Beaumont among the women in Halder's life and Joe Melia in the performance of his career as the wry Jewish friend who insists on injecting reality into Halder's otherwise-engaged existence. Not since the Trevor Nunn/Ian McKellen *Macbeth* almost five years ago has the RSC come together on a small-scale production of such intensity and triumph, and their achievement has been to turn what might have veered towards nightmare farce ('I'm in love with you and the children but I'm not a hundred per cent sure about Hitler,' says Halder to his wife in one of his few moments of lucid doubt) into a play about moral compromise and political uncertainty. Halder's sole aim is survival without harm to others; when that aim is seen to be impossibly idealistic, he has no other. All that's left him is the band, and the band plays on; Howard's final shocked realization that it has come to life in the midst of death is a stage image as powerful as any you will find in any contemporary theatre.

Blue Max

'He was a popular hero more than a comic. He was cheeky because he was a genius . . . he was flashiness perfected and present in all things visible and invisible – the common, cheap and mean parodied and seized on as a style of life . . . Hardly a week passes when I don't miss his pointing star among us.' Thus John Osborne, in his recent autobiography, on Max Miller, and though Osborne has always been the first to deny that his Archie Rice in *The Entertainer* was the failed mirror-image of Miller, there's not a lot of doubt that Max's influence on the legitimate theatre was probably greater than that of any other music-hall comedian of the day. Olivier and Tynan were among the first to mourn his death in 1963, both remarking that in a time of increasing mechanization Max was one of the last to live really dangerously on stage. As he himself used to say, 'There'll never be another. When I'm dead and gone, lady, this game's over.'

Max has been dead and gone for the best part of twenty years, and the music-hall game is indeed long over, but now, to the stage of the Fortune Theatre, comes *Here's a Funny Thing*, a semi-solo show written by R. W. Shakespeare (no, lady, not that Bill Shakespeare) in which John Bardon, aided only by a somewhat recalcitrant pianist, attempts to bring Max back to the boards. Physically the resemblance is not that great, but then again if Bardon is not in real life much like Max Miller, nor was Max Miller.

He was born Thomas Henry Sargent in the slums of Brighton during November 1895, only acquiring his new name after his wife saw a Max Factor poster on the back of a bus; and though the gaudy splendour of the white trilby and the flowered suit was to become his stagemark, the real Max was much more like the rather down-at-heel old trouper we meet in the first act here, clutching his sandwiches and cursing Val Parnell. Mr Parnell, it will be recalled, was the Palladium manager who, having allowed Jack Benny to do fifteen minutes during the 1950 Royal Variety Show, then tried to haul Miller off after a mere five. Treating this as an affront to his patriotism rather than his professionalism, Miller stayed on to do the full fifteen; backstage afterwards, a livid Parnell told him he would never work the Palladium again. 'Mr Parnell,' said Miller, 'you are ten years and a hundred thousand pounds too late.' He'd made his fortune, and was happy to retire on it to Brighton, except of course that public demand brought him back to the Palladium for a triumphal return two years later.

Contrary to popular belief (including Osborne's) Miller was not Jewish, and his humour was rooted instead in a kind of hard-edged neutrality; at a time of predominantly Northern comics he was a Southerner, and at a time of fundamentally cosy entertainment he was ruthless, waspish, invulnerable and very funny. In the course of an eccentric career he once filmed with Gielgud (in *The Good Companions*) and topped the bill at every Palace of Varieties in the land. He was a seaside postcard brought to life, a stick of Brighton rock made flesh, and to see him whole you had to see him live. Mr Bardon manages, in the second half, an adequate impression and, in the first half, a sketchy stage biography; I'm however inclined to wish he'd developed the first half further, for it is there that we begin to see the contrasts between Thomas Henry Sargent and Max Miller at their most interesting.

When *The Sound of Music* first opened at the Apollo Victoria last August, I was careful to arrange my summer holiday so as to avoid exposure to it; a thin, not to say skeletal, week for new productions coupled with the inescapable fact that the tills are still alive with the sound of singing nuns and Petula Clark has, however, forced me belatedly towards that bizarre entertainment and I have to report that it is not nearly as bad as I had feared. On the contrary, it is a great deal worse.

In the first place the show is the most schmaltzily objectionable of all Rodgers and Hammerstein's musical collaborations; in almost every other, the seedy cornball sentimentality of Rodgers' music was counteracted to some extent by the icier urban intelligence of Hammerstein who was to become Sondheim's great tutor and friend. But by the time (1959) of *Sound of Music* Hammerstein was already dying of cancer and the show painfully reflects his weakness; instead of the chilly brilliance of a lyric like 'You Have to Be Carefully Taught' (*South Pacific*, 1949) we get references to 'larks who are learning to pray', presumably in some combined aviary and seminary.

It is fractionally to the credit of Petula Clark that she manages to get through the show without breaking into fits of uncontrollable giggles, something I have to admit I failed to do; Michael Jayston, playing the Baron von Trapp, has the grace to look deeply embarrassed even when not required to sing, but only Honor Blackman as the Countess truly gets away with the evening, largely because she sensibly behaves like royalty opening some peculiarly underprivileged church fête. It is, I fear, a collector's evening, not least because it has been staged in a cinema where the stage apparently only allows for two kinds of choreography: the kind where you line the cast up in a straight footlights row from left to right according to height, and the other kind where you let them move very slowly either off or on to the stage. It would be nice to think that this production, which manages to be simultaneously tacky and extravagant, rather like the Tower of London reconstructed in marshmallow, would put an end to the current London theatrical vogue for reviving very old musicals very badly, but if you believe that you will doubtless have already enrolled your lark in a religious training establishment.

Tour of Hampstead

In a week when the London theatre at last awoke from its unusually and unnervingly prolonged post-Christmas slumber, we have seen no less than five female performances of immense and unusual strength, three of them given in a play at Hampstead which also marks the arrival of a female dramatist of considerable promise.

Catherine Hayes' *Skirmishes*, first seen last year in the studio theatre of the Liverpool Playhouse, is the account of a dying mother (Anna Wing) and her two bedside-bickering daughters (Frances de la Tour and Gwen Taylor in what is arguably the ugliest sister act since *Cinderella*). Played over a brisk eighty minutes without an interval, this is a bleak, cynical and yet often also vitriolically funny family album in which death itself eventually becomes of minor importance when compared to the greed, envy, insecurity and jealousy that it unleashes.

What is most impressive about Miss Hayes as a writer is that her play manages like a grainy old family snapshot to tell you more about the shadows than about the light, though at first it seems almost too simple. We have the one daughter Jean (Frances de la Tour) who at the risk of making a shaky marriage still shakier has stayed home nursing an incontinent, deaf and bedsore old mother, while the other (Rita, played by Gwen Taylor) has escaped several years earlier, only now to return bossily confident for the last rites. But it very soon transpires that there is not a lot to choose between them; Jean has stayed at least partly so as to get her hands on the inheritance, while Rita only departed because she was forced out by a mother who disapproved of her marriage to a man already once divorced. And Mother is, in the few lucid moments when she does get to speak, no better: having driven Rita out and watched while Jean desperately fought both her illness and her loneliness ('At least when Father died the Timber Trades Federation kept phoning'), she now rounds on Jean and demands that Rita should be her sole heiress.

In a prolonged sketch about the messy process of dying, Miss Hayes would seem to be telling us that it does not lend its partici-pants any kind of nobility; people who have been horrible in life will go on being horrible as they croak their last, and those gathered around the bedside will not improve either in the circumstances. At a time when physical and/or mental affliction lies at the heart of most Broadway and a good many London stage hits, here I would guess is another winner.

Edward Bond's *Summer* (on the National's Cottesloe stage) is also about a dying woman, though in this case her actual death is of minor dramatic importance; what matters here is her life and the debatable conclusion which Bond himself draws from it. We are in an unnamed European country, almost certainly Yugoslavia, at the height of the tourist season; a wealthy London fashion dealer (Anna Massey) has returned to her native soil, in this as almost every other postwar summer, to spend a vacation reliving some uneasy wartime memories. Her family were the undisputed royalty of the village when the Germans invaded in 1940; because of their power, she was able to get a faithful maidservant (Yvonne Bryceland in the fifth of this week's stellar turns) away from a firing squad. When, however, the partisans ousted the Germans, this same maid gave evidence which allowed them to put the rich lady's father in a work camp where he died. They also took over the family home for conversion to a block of holiday flats and it is there that the two women have since been meeting annually – only now it is the maid who is sentenced to a death of cancer.

Again, therefore, a play of guilt and revenge and dying. Mr Bond clearly wants us also to see here a play for the European postwar conscience, though his message that in the end justice matters vastly more than kindness seems to me highly arguable. Yet in directing his own play as essentially a conversation piece for the two women (there are a couple of minor young lovers and a wonderfully obtuse German tourist played by David Ryall to fill out the frame) the author has drawn from both Miss Massey and Miss Bryceland two of the best performances of even their remarkable careers.

Fraud Squad

If I were the writer G. F. Newman I would not, I think, be parking on many yellow lines or hanging around dark alleys in the vicinity of New Scotland Yard for the next twenty years or so. For what Mr Newman has given us, in his first stage play, *Operation Bad Apple* at the Royal Court, is a remarkably detailed and lifelike account of a massive and abortive investigation into Metropolitan Police corruption. The title is, I suspect, intended to recall Operation Countryman, and the resemblance to that real-life internal police inquiry (one which, it will be recalled, lasted two years at a cost of two million tax-paid pounds and has thus far led to all of four prosecutions) is enhanced by having here as there an external and rustic force brought in to examine the big-city dealings of the Met.

Mr Newman is in one sense a documentary man rather than a dramatist; you feel he could well have written the current BBC 'Police' series, had a writer been required. He is not especially concerned with fleshing out his characters, with giving them wives or children or homes or motives other than naked greed. He works in short, sharp, televisual scenes mainly set in offices or cells as one-to-one confrontations, and his dialogue has the constant and alarmingly plausible ring of a police transcript taken off a concealed microphone.

From the Assistant Commissioner's marvellously loaded opening speech to the investigative force, in which while telling them to leave no stone unturned he manages also to imply that every stone they do turn will then be used to beat them insensible, it is clear that we are in a world of utter and total cynicism: 'Looking for corruption in the Met,' says one character early on, 'is like drilling for water in Ireland.'

At this point we have of course to ask ourselves precisely how much we should believe; among the play's principal accusations are that the recent rioting in Britain's streets was police-induced so as to create a demand for stronger (and therefore less accountable) policing, and that corruption in the CID is now running at about ninety per cent of the force and starting at the top. If this had been an article or a television documentary instead of a play, Mr Newman would doubtless already be in the company of several libel lawyers; as it is we have to accept his privilege here, withhold a verdict ourselves and merely note that in Max Stafford-Clark's excellently spare production it is a chilly little play which, if even a quarter true, ought to be giving the Home Secretary some very sleepless nights.

Meanwhile at the Theatre Royal, Drury Lane the programme sellers are now carrying aerosol cans of deodorant, donations to the Royal Australian Prostate Fund are welcomed and a notice warns 'Ethnic Minorities Not Encouraged' all of which means that Barry Humphries is now in solo residence starring in, as the flashing neon sign so tastefully puts it, *An Evening of Intercourse with Edna*. In a belated attempt to keep the dread Dame in her place (presumably before she strangles her creator, like the ventriloquist's dummy in *Dead of Night*) Mr Humphries also now offers us his impersonations of the cultural attaché Sir Les Patterson, the 'new wave' Australian film-maker Phil Philby and the dear departed Sandy from one of Melbourne's lesser suburbs. All these are monologues in the Ruth Draper–Joyce Grenfell tradition and might have worked

An Evening's Intercourse
Barry Humphries

wonderfully in a smaller theatre, but in the vast open spaces of the Lane it is only Dame Edna who can truly fill the stage and her audience insults have reached new heights of wonder as she drags stagehands out centre stage to examine a lady in the stalls 'with a face like a poultice hanging over a hospital balcony'.

Later, following the commercial for self-destructing sanitary towels and the suggestion that East Berlin must be just like the Adelaide Festival only all year round ('mime one night, puppets the next and on Saturdays miming bloody puppets'), Edna herself descends from an outsize chocolate box to explain why she has moved up to the Lane from 'Molester' Square. Humphries as Edna now plays the audience the way that Robert Newton used to play Long John Silver, with a mixture of stunning bravado and utter fearlessness. The mother, megastar and millionairess has found in Drury Lane not only a massage parlour of the human spirit but also a social services centre where this upmarket Mother Theresa can bestow a compulsory barbecue on those unfortunates in the front row who have already had to forfeit their shoes to the Dame ('This? This isn't a shoe – it's a cry for help'). Like a pantomime dame on speed, Mr Humphries ends this manic evening by firing gladioli through cannons into the dress circle; as an entertainment it is fractionally shorter than *The Ring* and a lot funnier.

Greater Loesser

The National looks set for a long Runyon. Fully ten years after Olivier's ill health caused him to abandon his plan to play Nathan Detroit, the stage that bears his name at last has its *Guys and Dolls* and with it, I would guess, the first mass populist box-office smasheroo sell-out in the often troubled history of Hall's South Bank administration. In that sense the wait of a decade has been worthwhile, and true to Damon Runyon's gambling instinct the success has been achieved at odds of about eight to five against.

Guys and Dolls may be one of the true classics of the Broadway musical but it is a curiously intransigent show to stage; its songs are its plot, its characters are its action, and in the end it lives or dies by its choreography and its cast's understanding of the original Frank Loesser/Abe Burrows three-cent opera convention.

In this case the casting has been brave to foolhardy: the four principals, Bob Hoskins (as Nathan) is more Hammersmith than New York Broadway, Julia McKenzie (as Adelaide) is patently too great and good a singer ever to have been confined to the crummy Hot Box nightclub, Ian Charleson (as Sky) is years too young and innocent, and Julie Covington (as Sister Sarah) oddly lacks the requisite Major Barbara fervour. The fact that all four manage to rise above these character drawbacks is due partly to the afore-mentioned choreography (and if there is a single triumph in this evening it is that of David Toguri), and partly to the vast amount of help they receive from a contrastingly perfectly cast supporting team.

I never expect to see a better Nicely-Nicely Johnson than David Healy, nor a more sinister Big Jule than James Carter; Bill Paterson as Harry the Horse, Barrie Rutter as Benny and Harry Towb as Brannigan are equally superb down to their patently aching feet, and what was always a company show (the title song and the second-half showstopper are both sung by minor characters) becomes in Richard Eyre's brisk production a victory of mass stagecraft over individual turns.

From its filmic opening titles, which sensibly haul the memory back into the Warner Brothers' black-and-white 1940s from the false Goldwyn Technicolor image of Brando and Sinatra, right through to John Normington doing 'More I Cannot Wish You' quite beautifully, this is a production in which the whole is always greater than its parts. It is a tapestry of small-time losers and big-band numbers, and though Eyre's overall concept may lack the acid edge of the recent Half Moon revival, it manages to fill the Olivier stage with the brassy sound and tacky soul of Runyon's Broadway.

There is, however, one point about this success which my critical colleagues seem curiously willing to overlook, and at the risk of incurring yet again the wrath of Sir Peter Hall I would like to point it out. A smash hit at the National Theatre is not precisely the same thing as a National smash hit; this revival has been achieved by a director and a choreographer totally new to the National with a cast among whose four principals only one has ever before played a leading role on a main National stage. In that sense *Guys and Dolls* is a triumph for the National in just the way that the recent *My Fair Lady* revival was a triumph for the Adelphi Theatre; it is not a show which emerges (as say, did the RSC's *Nickleby* or *Swan Down*

Gloves) from the bowels of the company, nor is it one which says anything about the nature or existence of a National policy on musicals.

But to go from the glorious memory of Runyon's Broadway past to the forty-years-on reality of Broadway today is a deeply depressing experience. Currently there are twenty-six shows playing along the Great White Way; thirteen of those are musicals which opened more than a year ago, two are straight plays in from London (*Amadeus* and *The Dresser*), one is a five-year-old thriller (*Deathtrap*) and three are shaky star vehicles for Lauren Bacall, Katharine Hepburn and Lena Horne. That leaves a total of just seven shows which could remotely be described as new American theatrical events.

Broadway has become a desert of the intellect, and any believer in the possibility of it still featuring great legitimate performances should be taken forcibly to the Winter Garden Theatre where two notable actors, James Earl Jones and Christopher Plummer, are to be seen in a travesty of *Othello* which all too perfectly summarizes the problems of New York's commercial theatre.

This appalling Peter Coe production bears the same relationship to real Shakespeare that an airline meal bears to real food; it is a plastic, instantly packaged and dehydrated attempt to serve up a classic to an audience who have neither the time nor the interest to take it in, and Mr Jones and Mr Plummer are now walking through it in what would appear to be a mechanized trance during which lines emerge from their mouths without apparently having ever passed through their brains. Whole speeches are transposed, presumably in the interests of getting the more famous lines out up front before the customers fall into a deep sleep, and when an especially significant development of the plot is reached, stage lights are switched on and off as a kind of early warning system for audience attention. As Iago, Mr Plummer seems to be warming over a once-famous Richard III, and as Othello, Mr Jones has the grace to look deeply embarrassed; the rest of a distinctly scratch company stand around a lot wondering what to do with their arms and legs.

Elizabeth Regina

In a Victoria Palace programme note much recommended for quiet reading during those all too frequent moments when the plot of *The Little Foxes* proves less than entirely gripping, the producer Zef Bufman (an ex-First Lieutenant in the Israeli Army commandos, and therefore ideally trained for the portage of Elizabeth Taylor to London) reveals that Lillian Hellman's creakingly ancient melodrama was only selected for Miss Taylor's stage début after both *Hay Fever* and *Who's Afraid of Virginia Woolf?* had been carefully considered. Noël Coward and Edward Albee have had a remarkably lucky escape.

The Hellman Deep South saga, one dedicated to the notion that the family which decays together stays together, will perhaps be familiar from an original Broadway performance (in 1939) by Tallulah Bankhead and a film two years later which starred Bette Davis. Both those ladies had a redoubtable quality of performance evil which lifted this turn-of-the-century 'Dallas' into a soap-opera of distinction; few will forget Miss Davis watching Herbert Marshall (as her invalid husband) dying at her feet after she has graciously declined to pass him the medicine bottle.

Miss Taylor however, after years of formative training in some MGM charm school, is unable to scale those melodramatic heights, and indeed the big scene of the husband's death now happens offstage; we are left therefore with a lady who in certain studio-like conditions (notably the final confrontation with her daughter) can manage to be powerful, but who for the rest of a long evening is hopelessly unable to relate to a stage full of other characters. Admittedly she has not been much helped by a set which looks as though it is on the last legs of a long bus-and-truck tour and a supporting cast who look much the same; seldom can so many B villains from minor television movies have been assembled on the same stage at the same time, and it is intriguing that the one actress who distinguished this revival when it first opened on Broadway last year (Maureen Stapleton as Birdie) has now disappeared from the cast-list.

The result is a curiously tacky, crumbling and dilapidated evening, much like watching *Gone with the Wind* in an Atlanta cinema

shortly after the burning. Miss Taylor gives a very small performance inside a very large costume, unlike the rest of the company
who give very large performances inside a restricted playing area
caused largely by the fact that whenever their star enters they retreat
upstage as if in the presence of minor Balkan royalty. All in all, an
evening for stargazing rather than stardom.

But if the worst of Broadway is now in London, conditions along
the Great White Way are not much better; the hottest ticket there,
selling at forty dollars over the counter and a hundred under it, is
Dreamgirls, a curious Michael Bennett extravaganza which looks as
though it started with a lighting plot into which somebody then
decided to insert live singers. Based loosely and unofficially on the
career of the Supremes, this is a show lacking both a book and a
score but choreographed to within an inch of its life by Mr Bennett
who has here carried the ethic of his *Chorus Line* to its ultimate
dehumanized extension. *Dreamgirls* is a rock concert performed in
theatre; its plot is minimal (one Dreamgirl leaves the group only to
triumph solo and return at the last to the fold) and the standing
ovation which it nightly receives is the sound not of genuine enjoyment but of an audience desperately trying to reassure itself that
money has not been wasted. Were the score any better, one might
have cause to regret the screams in which it is drowned from the
very beginning of the first number; but now, as so often on
Broadway, the best and noisiest performances are invariably given
by people sitting in the stalls.

Katharine Hepburn has, as usual, got it about right; Broadway
for her has become not the ultimate American theatrical achievement but just one more stopover (and in fact the last) on a long
coast-to-coast tour. *The West Side Waltz*, in which she is currently
making a personal appearance at the Barrymore, is the work of
Ernest Thompson who also wrote her current screen hit *On Golden
Pond* and has cornered a useful line in Westchester Chekhov,
thereby enabling age-old movie stars to instruct their fans in how to
reach a graceful senility.

Miss Hepburn sensibly plays it centre stage and very fast, as if
opening some singularly underprivileged old people's home rather
than closing a comedy of doubtful merit.

There is, however, better news off-Broadway, since Playwrights
Horizons on West 42nd Street are currently staging the best new
American play I have seen in many a long season; A. R. Gurney's
The Dining Room is another instalment in his continuing saga of the

decline of WASP America, but this one conceived and directed in a single room across sixty years, so that a stunningly versatile cast of six play (without changes of costume or make-up or setting) three generations in gradual states of professional and private decay. At times the play resembles nothing so much as Eliot's *Family Reunion* rewritten by Alan Ayckbourn; at others its debt to Thornton Wilder's *Long Christmas Dinner* is still more in evidence. Yet Gurney has repaid all those debts with interest and come up with a human history of recent America which is as funny as it is touching and as clever as it is true. The sooner it is seen in London the better for us all.

Fascist Angels

Two immensely wealthy women closeted over a meal in a luxurious apartment, one getting paralytically drunk while the other assaults the only male unwise enough to venture into the sanctum: Noël Coward, of course, in *Fallen Angels* (1925), his first commercially triumphant comedy. Now, at the Lyric, we have an intriguing if unacknowledged variant: the two women in Robert David MacDonald's *Summit Conference* happen to be Eva Braun and Clara Petacci, mistresses of Hitler and Mussolini, but at first here it looks as though Mr MacDonald intends to use them for nothing more than a light comedy, set in admittedly unpropitious circumstances.

It is 1941 in Berlin; the two Axis dictators are in conference, leaving their womenfolk to an uneasy meeting over tea in Eva's gracious apartment, one she has decorated with hand-sewn swastika cushions and a drinks cabinet roughly the size of the Reichstag. As the women are played by Glenda Jackson (a curiously subdued Eva) and Georgina Hale (a way-over-the-top Clara) we would appear to be in for a marathon bitching session, one which indeed gets off to a splendidly icy start with Eva remarking that whereas Caesar came, saw and conquered, Mussolini only comes when he sees that somebody else has conquered. Clara in revenge notes that one German is a philosopher, two are a public meeting and three are a war, leaving Eva to respond that one Italian is a tenor, two are an opera and three a retreating army; she also notes that the only way a clever German Jew would speak to a stupid German Jew would be over the telephone from New York, but there the jokes seem to run out, halted not so much by their own appalling taste as by the sudden realization that Mr MacDonald is in fact on about something very much more serious.

He wants us to see, in the mythical meeting of these two ladies, some sort of a commentary on the war, on Fascism, on anti-Semitism and on feminism and the trouble is that his chosen comic framework simply can't stand it. Rather than settle for character studies of two still comparatively unknown ladies, or even a consideration of 'The Mistress in History' always delivered like bread to the back door, he has decided to use them as stereotype puppets for one of those 'what if' dialogues once beloved of BBC radio writers who would bring together Napoleon and George III for a dialogue about European history.

As a result, Georgina Hale is allowed by the director-designer Philip Prowse to play Clara in full pantomime vein as the kind of bottom-wiggling Italian mistress you might expect to see in a bad pizza commercial, while Glenda Jackson gets little more opportunity to make of Eva anything more interesting than a mouth-piece for the playwright's own somewhat eclectic view of recent sexual, racial and political warfare. Her assault on the unfortunate young soldier sent to serve the tea (Gary Oldman) is I think meant to symbolize both the Nazi assault on the Jewish population and, in a role reversal, male assault on women over the years. That is, however, asking a lot of an actress given little more to do on stage than remove a waiter's trousers, and the play suffers a similar credibility gap between what can be done in its two short acts and what they are supposed to suggest to us.

The pity of this is that when, all too briefly, Mr MacDonald works within the confines of what he has got (three people trapped in a room with a tea trolley and a world war outside the door) he is both very funny and very effective. The social bickering of Eva and Clara as they try to sort out supremacy, the dream of Eva to go to Hollywood after the war and play herself in the movies, and above all the superlative bitchery of Clara who, told by Eva that by 1945 every German home will have its own television set, merely inquires precisely how many German homes Eva expects there to be by then, all add up to an immensely promising double-act which is then blown to pieces by its own delusions of grandeur. Much, I suppose, like that of Hitler and Mussolini in the first place.

Hedda First

By the bad luck of the West End draw, a new and worthy but immensely dull Susannah York *Hedda Gabler* has ended up at precisely the same theatre, the cavernous Cambridge, which was a decade ago electrified by Maggie Smith in Ingmar Bergman's classic production of this same play. Try as one may, it is impossible to banish the echoes of that other *Hedda*; though there have been many since, some much worse than the present one and a few rather better, it is still the Bergman version which illuminated the manuscript and not only in that melodramatic moment when Hedda is actually burning it.

What we have here is a brisk, cool, hugely adequate but curiously undramatic canter through the text, put together by Donald McWhinnie in a regional rep tradition of about the middle 1950s. Miss York offers us neither Hedda the ice queen nor Hedda the demon lover luring Lovborg to his doom; instead she glides through the drama as if on roller skates, central to the events around her yet so totally not of their making that her final suicide is indeed no more than the social inconvenience complained of by Judge Brack in the curtain line.

This therefore becomes Brack's evening: in Tom Baker's wonderfully sinister, manic turn it is he who holds centre stage, he (far more than Tom Bell's distinctly unpoetic Lovborg) whom we expect to see wearing the vine leaves in his hair, he who finally galvanizes this creaking production into some sort of life. Irene Handl also does a remarkable scene or two as the old aunt, memorably conceiving her as a sort of Norwegian Miss Marple on the prowl, but elsewhere the casting is fatally bland – this must be the first Hedda of recent times in which Tesman and Lovborg have been virtually interchangeable.

Meanwhile out in West Sussex, Patrick Garland's Chichester is rapidly establishing itself as the showbiz answer to Glyndebourne; two of last year's four shows were old musicals and this year we are already getting a return to *Valmouth*, Sandy Wilson's long-lost classic of the late 1950s in its first stage revival. Classic in score, that is: no musical written in England in the thirty years that separate Coward's *Bitter-Sweet* from Lionel Bart's *Oliver!* has a more impressive sequence of numbers from the title song through 'Magic Fingers' and 'Big Best Shoes' all the way to the 'Cathedral of Clemenza' and 'I Will Miss You'. The trouble, now as during an original and all-too-brief London run twenty years ago, is of course the book; though the composer has brought in Cardinal Pirelli from an altogether different novel to boost the second half, plots were never Ronald Firbank's strongest suit and nor indeed have they been Sandy Wilson's, as any synopsis of *The Boy Friend* might indicate.

What we get therefore are some marvellous characters and some superlative songs in search of a central focus; the dialogue, especially when spoken by Fenella Fielding who is now so far over the top as to be almost out of sight, sounds like Evelyn Waugh rewritten by Oscar Wilde, and you can't ask much more than that when dealing with high-camp Catholicism run riot. But in treating the whole affair as a minor and eccentric spa operetta which had best be left to sort itself out, John Dexter has curiously and unusually failed to give the show the shape and discipline it crucially needs if it is not to subside into a baroque shambles. The scenes, for instance, involving Mrs Hurstpierpoint and Mrs Thoroughfare need to be played as swiftly and precisely as the tea-party sequence in *Pygmalion*; if, as on the first night, they are played through a fog of uncertainty, and if Sir Robert Helpmann as the Cardinal is so badly miked that he looks like a ventriloquist who has thrown his voice and failed to get it back, then clearly there's a lot more rehearsing to be done. But when it is done, in there somewhere remains a magical entertainment; *Valmouth* has many problems in terms of a new lease of London life, not least the fact that it is a big musical (cast of twenty, orchestra of six stuck up a palm tree) in need of a small theatre. But Firbank himself was a master of the unlikely ('Order me,' he once commanded my late godfather Sewell Stokes while they were supposed to be having tea in a Lyons' Corner House, 'herons' eggs whipped with wine into an amber foam') and it would be lovely if this unlikeliest of musicals, complete with Bertice Reading dressed like a driver-operated bus and Doris Hare as the 120-year-old Granny Tooke, could at last reach a mass audience; where else in the world but in *Valmouth* do people still amuse themselves by smacking the hermaphrodite?

Papal Bull

Ever since the days of its occupancy by Moral Re-Armament there has been something distinctly uneasy about the goings-on at the Westminster Theatre, and the current offering there (though definitely non-MRA) does little to restore public confidence in the curious policies of that playhouse. Having no particular desire to be struck by either lightning or any of my three extremely Catholic children, I would like to make it clear right away that in principle I can see no earthly reason why an ex-playwright should not become Pope. Indeed in my admittedly inexpert theological view, that would seem an admirable and reassuring qualification for the Vatican.

But when he had become Pope, and had decided splendidly to visit Britain in a difficult time, it was surely unforgivably opportunist for a commercial management to dig out an old play of his and stage it in the hope, presumably, of some spun-off publicity. Short of requesting His Holiness to wave at faithful theatregoers from atop the cut-price ticket booth in Leicester Square, this management has not been exactly reticent in its timing. No matter that the playwright's royalties will doubtless be going to a deserving cause; all other aspects of this production are nothing if not deeply commercial, and seem to me in roughly the same appallingly tasteless league as the selling for profit of Papal T-shirts.

The moral test here is really a very simple one; had Karol Wojtyla not become Pope John Paul II, for reasons which had nothing whatsoever to do with his work as a dramatist, is it remotely conceivable that a commercial management and a team of star actors would now be within a hundred miles of *The Jeweller's Shop*, a play he wrote in 1960 in the form of a series of monologues on the nature of love? Is it likely that Robin Phillips, to mark his return from Stratford, Ontario, would have chosen to direct a script which not only by its very form denies all possible dramatic activity on stage, but is also couched in the kind of appallingly fey and whimsical language (for which the translator Boleslaw Taborski must assume responsibility) of those biblical verse dramas that the BBC used to inflict on us during Holy Week in the very earliest days of religious broadcasting?

The notion of a man who hangs around a jeweller's (Paul Daneman) operating as father confessor and religious-romantic adviser to three interlinking pairs of parents and children who seek some sort of symbolism in their wedding rings may also be inclined to establish undesirable links between high church and high finance, though in this context the only really strong speech in the play is concerned with the denial of such material values. A strong cast (Hannah Gordon, Gwen Watford, John Carson, Lalla Ward) seem to be forever in search of the radio microphone to which this play might well be better directed; as a ring cycle it remains defiantly untheatrical.

To the Theatre Royal, Drury Lane from Central Park by way of Broadway have come Wilford Leach's swashbuckling *Pirates of Penzance*, not (contrary to widespread belief) an updating or a mockery or even a parody of the original, but instead a celebration of Gilbert and Sullivan designed for an age which has replaced the operetta with the musical. It is as though the Peter Brook *Midsummer Night's Dream* had come not out of the Royal Shakespeare Company but out of a British theatre which had frozen all Shakespearian production around 1930. Because neither the director, nor the choreographer, nor many of the original cast or their first audiences had ever seen a D'Oyly Carte production, they simply treated the *Pirates* as a theatrical discovery and gave it all they'd got. The result was a flamboyant big-band show which looked as though somebody had decided to do the '1812' with actors instead of an orchestra.

Now, in the chandeliered setting of Drury Lane, a production which originally traded on sheer bravura has begun to look faintly nervous, as if neither its Pirate King (Tim Curry) nor its lovely Mabel (Pamela Stephenson) are quite sure of the exact length of tongue to be left in cheek. As a result the London production goes a bit further over the top and is a bit more inclined to bludgeon us with its vitality and noise; no buckle is ever left unswashed, no corner of the stage left without five somersaulting pirates and a maiden rampant. Nevertheless the sheer energy and joy of this production are finally unbeatable, and even if it has become a muggers' paradise at least two of the performances (George Cole as the very model of a modern Major-General and Annie Ross as the pirate maid with 'the remains of a fine woman about her') manage to improve on the originals.

Those of you with fond memories of Garbo on the deck of that ship, hair blowing in the MGM wind as she bade farewell to her beloved Sweden, should banish them before arriving at the Tricycle where the title character in Pam Gems' *Queen Christina* resembles instead the head prefect at some particularly seedy transvestite academy. The notion here would seem to be a feminist exploration of the agony of being a Swedish queen when most people would have preferred a king; but in cobbling together a chronicle of her celebrated abdication Miss Gems has fallen into almost every one of the socio-historical traps she avoided when dealing with *Piaf*. At least Garbo had a writer who realized that lines like 'Shall I call for the leeches, Ma'am?' and 'Can Poland give me a son?' were apt to cause rolling about the aisles in the wrong places.

The Barbican Chronicles

I have seen the Barbican and it works; difficult to find your way to, harder still to find your way about inside, it nevertheless contains at the heart of its concrete maze a gem of a theatre eleven hundred seats large yet retaining a feeling of intimacy and acoustic privacy which the builders of the Olivier must now be gnashing their teeth over. It is indeed to rejoice in the architecture of the playhouse, and of John Napier's stunningly carpentered set, that I'd recommend an early visit to Trevor Nunn's inaugural production of *Henry IV* Parts One and Two and suggest that you see the two plays (as is possible on certain summer Saturdays) across one single seven-hour day.

Part One, judged alone, is a massive disappointment. Nunn seems content to use it as a primer, bringing to the text none of the flair or intellectual discipline that one remembers from the Terry Hands and Peter Hall excursions into this same Stratford territory over the past two decades. Instead the play is left there, sprawled out across the wide stage while the cast amiably ramble around both apparently in search of a map. As a pageant to show off the new RSC premises it is just about all right; as a rediscovery or enlightenment of the text it seems remarkably lacking in both style and coherence. Only Timothy Dalton's starry Hotspur begins to approach the sense of personal danger that can bring these battle-field chronicles to life; the rest of a distinctly undercast and under-strength company seem to have settled for a plod through the text in traditional Shakespeare-for-schools fashion.

But then, and this is why I suggest the full day, as Part Two begins to pull itself into shape (and it is admittedly a vastly better play) the old virtues of the company tradition begin to reassert themselves; Joss Ackland's muted Falstaff, Gerard Murphy's long-haired Hal and Patrick Stewart's unobtrusive Henry IV start to make sense as characterizations, and by the time we reach Ancient Pistol (Mike Gwilym in marvellously manic form) leading the company in a rooftop chase across the set, what has been up to then a worthily dull and defiantly unspectacular history lesson is suddenly galvanized into the kind of life and excitement that typifies the RSC at their epic *Nickleby* best. What began as an example of adequate stage-management becomes, as the newly crowned Henry V finally rejects his Falstaff, a triumphal arrival in the heart of both real and stage City.

Paper Chase

The first thing to be said in favour of *Windy City*, a new musical of *The Front Page* at the Victoria Palace, is its score: a smashing, lilting, big-brass, sentimental, singalong succession of fifteen numbers by an English composer new to me (Tony Macaulay) and a lyricist (Dick Vosburgh) now so steeped in American showbiz folklore that he will doubtless end up as a special nostalgia consultant to the White House. The second thing to be said about it is that though the first half does not altogether hang together, for reasons to which I will return in a paragraph or three, the second half lifts off into such a series of musical and dramatic triumphs that you leave the theatre on a considerable high, only later to have to come to terms with the somewhat grudging reaction of a number of other professional observers.

No one doubts that *The Front Page* (written in 1928 by Ben Hecht and Charles MacArthur as a result of their own Chicago newspaper experiences, thrice filmed and much revived on stage most recently by the National Theatre in 1972) is a classic of deadline lunacy, but to suggest, as some have, that it is therefore untouchable and does not need songs makes about as much sense as wondering why anybody ever bothered adding songs to *Romeo and Juliet* or *Pygmalion*. The problem is not the songs themselves but what has to be sacrificed in order to get them in, and the first thing to go has been the intricate first-act structure of the play, one in which a whole group of reporters were individually established and introduced to us.

But what Mr Vosburgh (also responsible for the book) has realized is that *The Front Page* is as perfect a representation of its tumultuous times as any Cagney–Bogart movie, and though it may have been the avowed intent of its original authors to point up the callous indifference with which pre-war Chicago viewed accidental or intentional death, what they in fact ended up with was a sentimentally devout tribute to journalists who (unlike the police or the politicians of the story) are ultimately forgiven everything in the name of their eccentric calling. The play treats reporters with all the reverence accorded by *The Sound of Music* to nuns: they may be, indeed here are, incompetent, alcoholic, bloodthirsty numskulls but by Jesus they're newspapermen and that explains it. Walter Kerr once called *The Front Page* 'a machine for surprising and delighting the audience regularly, logically, insanely and accountably' and what the Vosburgh–Macaulay team with their director Peter Wood have had to do is strip down that fifty-year-old machine and reassemble it in working order.

At first you wonder if they're going to make it: a lot of splendid original material (such as Sheriff Hartman's habit of putting two hundred of his relatives on the city payroll to defend Chicago against the Red Army 'which is leaving Moscow any minute now') has disappeared to be replaced by a lightning canter through the plot, one which inevitably only has time to focus on about half a dozen of the principals. But this stripping–down to basics, this rapid tour of the beginnings of a complex tale involving a mad killer, a Hollywood heiress and a reporter called Hildy Johnson so hooked on print that his fingers seem to come with typewriters already attached, does at least allow us to realize that, uniquely, *Windy City* is to be an actors' musical. No choreographer is credited, no set-piece dance routines are allowed to interrupt newsroom activity as manic as anything ever dreamed up by Mr Vosburgh's beloved Marx Brothers, whose period this of course also was. Indeed the show appears to have been nailed together by and for men who have never danced much in their lives and see no reason to start now. Dennis Waterman (as Hildy) and Anton Rodgers as his treacherous, irascible editor are not exactly Fred Astaire and Jack Buchanan, but they have an oddly clumsy, rambling charm which turns their 'I Can Just Imagine It' into a genuine showstopper.

And given that most of the supporting cast needed for this show are already gainfully employed in *Guys and Dolls* at the National, Peter Wood's triumph has been to pull together in London an Anglo-American team who plausibly have been spending their lives peering through the cigar ash and the poker hands in search of a derelict scoop. On the other side of their grubby desks the 'real people' are well represented by Robert Longden doing a wonderfully manic turn as the killer, Amanda Redman as the Hollywood girl with the encyclopaedic knowledge of Dolores del Rio (Mr Vosburgh is not a man to waste much), and Diane Langton as the tart with the heart of pure marshmallow.

But in the end what happens here, as in all good musicals, is that the songs paper over the cracks in the original fabric; just when the show seems to be in danger of losing its footing, uncertain whether to parody what was anyway a satire and unsure just how much of the original still makes sense, along comes another rousing number and we're back to the typewriters. Only Waterman's closing solo seems messily staged, as though the singer and director had suddenly lost faith in it as a conventional number and therefore imported a likeable but irrelevant drunk to help it along. Elsewhere, even on the first night, there was a confidence here which you still find all too rarely in new English musicals, and though I hope that the Victoria Palace can hold this *Front Page* for many months to come, it's also good to know that we now have, after *Evita* and *Cats*, a third new musical to send to Broadway.

Princes of Denmark

By a freak accident of timing, the London fringe theatre is currently offering one of the best and one of the worst productions of *Hamlet* I've ever seen. The one to avoid is at the Young Vic where Edward Fox, a likeable and intelligent actor, has chosen to give his Prince in surroundings which suggest that the staff of some very minor British prep school in about 1950 have suddenly been asked to mount the play for parents' day without quite enough rehearsal or a director. The Ghost has the traditional affliction of the larynx, the Gertrude looks understandably appalled not so much at her husband's murder as at the quality of the acting going on around her, and the audience at the interval, which was when I have to admit I made no excuse and left, were wearing the stunned expressions last witnessed on the faces of those who have just sat through a party political broadcast for the Social Democrats.

If Mr Fox can ever find himself a director and a cast he might yet prove an interesting Prince; in the meantime, head for the Warehouse which is where Jonathan Miller is staging the play for his third and last time, last because he has announced that this will be his farewell to the non-operatic theatre. If so, it is a remarkable swansong; his control of the play has strengthened considerably since he first directed it at Cambridge and Greenwich more than a decade ago, so that we now have a hugely intelligent, surgically incisive and enthralling evening played on the bare boards of the Warehouse as a chamber thriller much after the fashion there of the great Trevor Nunn *Macbeth*.

The casting here is all: not only Anton Lesser's nervy, jumpy young thoroughbred Dane but Philip Locke's wonderfully theatrical Player King and a strong Rosencrantz–Guildenstern double from Ken Stott and David Firth which suggests they could go from this into the Stoppard.

Dr Miller also gives us a predictably graphic and clinical mad scene, with Kathryn Pogson a memorably neurotic Ophelia from the start, and an unusually young and subtle Claudius from John Shrapnel. True, the last two acts drop a lot in tension, and it may be pushing the luck a bit to have Fortinbras giggle on his final sight of the massed corpses, but these are minor cavils at an evening of huge assurance, excitement and dynamism.

Meanwhile the Chichester Festival management, having already cast Joan Plowright as Britain's best-loved nurse (*Cavell*) and then left her stranded in the middle of that vast open stage without a play, now complete the double by casting John Mills as Britain's best-loved schoolmaster and leaving him without a musical. An appallingly inadequate Leslie Bricusse score from a ten-year-old O'Toole movie fiasco (also nominally *Goodbye Mr Chips*) has been hauled out of oblivion and attached to a new book (by Roland Starke) of equally amazing inadequacy, and the whole mishmash has then been given a production (by Patrick Garland and Christopher Selbie) which manages to turn Hilton's once-great short story into a gang show that even Ralph Reader might have had his doubts about.

Looking like a walrus who has somehow lost his carpenter, Sir John drifts through this tackily choreographed shambles with a marvellously good grace, even managing in the second half to haul the show up from being unbelievably terrible to being at moments only endearingly inadequate. That a director of Garland's subtlety, who once had to deal with some very similar issues of historical and patriotic English traditionalism in that other school show *Forty Years On*, could have allowed this *Chips* to degenerate into a desperate attempt to recreate *Underneath the Arches* with midgets is as mysterious as the current collapse of Chichester overall. Unless you wish to discover Nigel Stock as a comic baritone, a discovery somehow akin to finding that Mrs Thatcher can play the spoons, forget it.

Wilde Night

That the National Theatre should only now, some twenty years into its existence, be coming to terms with *The Importance of Being Earnest* (Lyttelton) is I suppose some sort of back-handed tribute to the late Edith Evans, who made Lady Bracknell so securely her own for almost half a century that few other leading actresses seemed willing to take up the challenge, at least in central London, though I do recall Irene Handl tackling the role at Greenwich in a heavy German accent so as to avoid all possible comparison.

Sir Peter Hall has had an even better idea, which is to entice Judi Dench away from the RSC (presumably with the promise of the forthcoming Pinter trilogy) and then cast her as an amazingly though accurately youthful Lady B; because Dame Edith played the role over so long a period of time, we are inclined to forget that with a daughter of only twenty there is no reason why her ladyship has to be much more than forty and this revelation gets the new production off to a cracking start.

Hall has discovered something else of importance about *The Importance*, which is that if it is played with immense solemnity by people for whom muffins are a way of life and cucumber sandwiches no laughing matter, then it becomes an even funnier play.

The Importance of Being Earnest   Martin Jarvis *as John Worthing*, Judi Dench *as Lady Bracknell*, Nigel Havers *as Algernon Moncrieff*

Thus we have an Algernon (Nigel Havers) of manic intensity, a Worthing (Martin Jarvis) of scholarly pomposity and an utterly magnificent Prism–Chasuble pairing by Anna Massey and Paul Rogers, working together as the bemused professional help in a world where the amateurs still rule.

One might have wished that the National had done their academic duty and given us the full four-act version, or that Hall had begun to think about what I believe is the infinitely darker side of what is now regarded only as a drawing-room comedy; a play written just as the shades of the prison-house were beginning to close around Wilde, a play about false identity and furtive weekends and the art of not being found out, has always seemed to me to have a great deal more to do with Victorian attitudes to homosexuality and social corruption than is generally admitted. That, perhaps, is why Bernard Shaw found it 'a hateful play', why H. G. Wells thought it only 'fairly funny' and why Wilde himself, going back-stage to George Alexander's dressing-room on that fateful first night when Queensberry had failed to deliver the bouquet of vegetables, congratulated the actor–manager on a glossy triumph. 'Well?' asked Alexander. 'Charming,' replied Oscar, 'and do you know from time to time it reminded me of a play I once wrote myself called *The Importance of Being Earnest.*'

By abandoning the fourth act then as now, producers from Alexander across eighty years to Hall have taken *The Importance* far too lightly; Hall has begun to correct that balance, with the first postwar production that even attempts to look behind the jokes. On a steeply raked, shinily tiled setting by John Bury this *Importance* is done like a very upmarket *Charley's Aunt,* extremely fast and with considerable elegance. Characters are given an off-stage existence, too; Judi Dench is encouraged to make of the unseen Lord Bracknell an all too realistic and less than ideal husband, one whose crashing boredom explains her evident infatuation with Algy. Similarly, Zoe Wanamaker's Gwendolen has a sharp anger that suggests the beginning of a New Woman, one unlikely to get far into the twentieth century without becoming a suffragette.

What Hall has done is therefore to realign the play and rethink its relationships; he has hauled it out of the pretty-pretty, stylized picture frame into which Gielgud and Beaton had locked it for most of this century, and it is perhaps ungrateful to wish he had hauled it even further toward the darker reality which underlies this most famous of all comedies of appalling manners.

Treble Chance

The National Theatre is currently offering a complete and utter guide to one of its own directors, Harold Pinter, which should on no account be missed despite the fact that the usual appallingly incompetent NT scheduling means that it is only available for four doubtless already sold-out performances in the whole of November. The guide comes in the form of three short plays on the Cottesloe stage, directed by Peter Hall himself and played under the overall title *Other Places.* The first of these plays, *Family Voices,* has already been around a bit both on BBC radio and as a National platform performance last year; the other two are however totally new and taken together, cross-cast across one single evening, they add up to a remarkable insight into Pinter past and present.

Family Voices is the one about the letters, written but probably never posted, of a mother and son and recently deceased husband/ father; these are spoken aloud, radio-style, by Anna Massey and Nigel Havers with Paul Rogers as the third voice from the grave and there is no attempt here at any real dramatization. It remains a radio play, but one of intense fascination because it recaps all the familiar Pinteresque themes of his past plays, from *The Room* through *The Caretaker* to *The Homecoming*: menace is here, and non-communication, and sinister sexuality, and the rearrangement of truth depending on who is to speak next. Half-heard whispers from the past are mingled with screams of reality from the present to form a vocal tapestry that might in a less reverential atmosphere seem almost a parody of Pinter circa 1965.

But then, for the second play, we go even further back, back in fact to the Harold Pinter who first made his name writing revue sketches for Kenneth Williams in shows like *Pieces of Eight*. Here, in a new play called *Victoria Station,* is a sudden return to that eerie jokiness: its only two characters are a minicab controller (Paul Rogers again) and his luckless driver, wonderfully played by Martin Jarvis. The cab and its driver are, we're told, deeply lost; there may or may not be a body on the back seat, and if there is it may or may not still be alive. That, oddly enough, doesn't much matter; what does, is the sense that the world may suddenly have come to an end leaving one cab driver and his organizer desperately trying to make some sort of sense out of what they have got left. Brilliantly staged by Hall so that we only ever see Jarvis through the windscreen of a real on-stage car, while Rogers set in an office high above him goes gradually to pieces in perfect counterpoint to his driver's increasing calm, this is a double-act of considerable skill which comes as a sharp reminder that Pinter can still do the jokes.

But both these plays are really only curtain-raisers for the last, *A Kind of Alaska,* which instead of harking back to past triumphs suggests that Pinter is in fact now moving forward into some altogether new direction. In the first place, and extremely unusually for him, the play is derived from a book, and a book of medical fact. Oliver Sacks' *Awakenings* was a 1974 account of the arousal from years of catatonic lethargy of a large number of sleeping-sickness patients, brought back to life by the wonder-drug L-dopa. Pinter shifts the location to England and considers the awakening of just one patient, played by Judi Dench in what has to be the performance of even her remarkable career.

She plays Deborah, who at the age of sixteen fell into sudden and total coma; some twenty-nine years later, she awakes to find her doctor (Paul Rogers now going for the treble) and her sister (Anna Massey) watching over her, beginning the attempt to explain how she has come to lose three decades of her life in sleep.

But what makes *A Kind of Alaska* so haunting is the technique Pinter has devised for telling the story from Deborah's own eyeline; 'You've aged, substantially,' she tells her sister and it is an accusation, as if she had put on weight in all the wrong places. This is a play about the unfreezing of the body while the mind remains desperately unable to thaw out quite so fast, and Judi Dench's ability to conjure up the soul and voice of a teenager in the body of a woman nearly fifty should win her just about every one of this winter's acting awards.

Real Magic

When they come to write the textbooks on Tom Stoppard, if they haven't already started, his new *The Real Thing* (at the Strand) is the play that's going to give them the most trouble since it fits almost no preconceived notion of the kind of playwright he is thought to be. It is not, for instance, a brilliantly Scrabbled wordplay like *Rosencrantz* or *Jumpers*; nor is it as socially or politically committed as *Night and Day* or *Every Good Boy*, nor even as quickfire-comic as a sketch like *The Real Inspector Hound*.

Instead it's a romantic comedy of a tragic nature, corresponding perhaps most closely to less successful attempts in this same field recently made by our other two leading British dramatists, Harold Pinter (in *Betrayal*) and Peter Nichols (in *Passion Play*). Like them, it's a story of rearranged marriages and furniture in the affluent London architect-and-actor belt; in its first Cowardly moments we get what appears to be a stylish comedy of bad manners, full of cuckoo-clock jokes about Old Basle and Swiss Frank, but no sooner are we getting used to those *Private Lives* than we realize that they're not what the play is about at all. We are in fact watching a play-within-a-play and its central characters are about to fade away, since their only real function is to introduce us to the two people the play is really about, who just happen to be their offstage marital partners in real life and who are therefore *The Real Thing* if you're still with me.

But *The Real Thing* is also love, and divorce, and jealousy, and innocence, and anguish and in writing about all of that within the context of a marital drama about an actress and a playwright Mr Stoppard has come up with the warmest and the most touching play he has ever written. In a purely artistic sense, this is also an auto-biographical play since it is about a dramatist trying to write a play about indescribable love; it is a stunning variant on the eternal square (since both central characters, wonderfully well played by Roger Rees and Felicity Kendal, have other marital and professional partners whom we are allowed to meet and often to like as much as laughs; while rehearsing his forthcoming appearance on 'Desert Island Discs', the playwright recalls an earlier brush with the musical classics: 'I was taken to Covent Garden to hear Callas in a foreign musical without dancing; people were giving kidneys to get tickets.'

Buried somewhere deep in *The Real Thing* are also some marvellous insights into the nature of the theatre in which its central characters work: 'If you get the right words in the right order,' says the dramatist, at a time when he is signally failing to do so, 'you can nudge the world.' *The Real Thing* is not, perhaps, going to nudge the world: but it is going to nudge a lot of people into a realization of what theatre and love and betrayal are all about, and for that we should be more than grateful. It is a play which lends some much-needed dignity and life and purpose to a West End that is currently desperately in need of all of that, and Peter Wood's production is a miracle of discreet stagecraft: not only in his central casting of Kendal and Rees, but also in performances from Jeremy Clyde and Michael Thomas and above all Polly Adams he has drawn together the best teamwork in town.

Loewe Rating

If the moribund West End theatre is remarkable for anything this Christmas, it will be for the number of dehydrated old movie stars returning from Hollywood exile to go spectacularly over the top in rusting vehicles that probably saw service in the Dardanelles. At this rate we'll have Stewart Granger in *The Prisoner of Zenda* at the National by Easter and Greer Garson in the musical of *Mrs Miniver* by mid-summer. Meanwhile however there is Peter O'Toole in *Man and Superman* and Richard Harris on the last leg of his long transatlantic bus-and-truck tour of *Camelot,* making a final stopover at the Apollo Victoria where an English company has been respectfully grouped around him by Michael Rudman.

Camelot has always been something of a curiosity; the best score and the worst book that Lerner and Loewe ever wrote, it has been resolutely loathed by critics and loved by audiences (not least the Kennedy family who made its title song the anthem for an entire Presidency) for twenty years, and it comes up now looking like the last of the great pantomimes on a set by Desmond Heeley that appears to have been not so much built as iced.

What we have here is, in Noël Coward's celebrated review, *Parsifal* without the jokes, and Rudman has rightly organized it as a series of marathon panto-walkdowns in which the company are encouraged not to bump into the furniture or their leading man especially when he is waving Excalibur about with reckless abandon. It is indeed arguable that Excalibur gives the least wooden performance in the show, and it's a pity that Mr Harris seems (possibly as a result of a nervous first night which at one point had him crawling on all fours beneath the curtain to escape the audience at the interval) to have forgotten some of the superlative phrasing of the lyrics that he managed in the great 1967 Josh Logan film version. It's also unfortunate that Lancelot (Robert Meadmore) has been encouraged to wear a frizzy wig strongly reminiscent of Hermione Gingold, and that Guinevere (Fiona Fullerton) looks more like Mr Harris' daughter than his wife. Still there's a superlative comic turn from Robin Bailey as Pellinore and, as the gentleman behind me said on the way out, it does make such a nice change from going to the theatre.

The much-advertised recall of another screen star, Peter O'Toole, to stage legitimacy has all but obliterated the most interesting aspect of his performance in *Man and Superman* at the Theatre Royal Haymarket. What Mr O'Toole makes here is a bizarre return to the barnstorming, eye-rolling stellar flamboyance that may well have been a feature of touring actor–management in his Irish youth. Micheàl MacLiammòir and Donald Wolfit would have been the first to recognize what is going on at the Haymarket. In a desperately slow and deadly dull production by Patrick Dromgoole, surrounded by a cast who range from the ponderously adequate to the barely employable (the two exceptions here being the dour Michael Byrne as Shaw's 'New Man' and the splendid veteran Joyce Carey as the mother), Mr O'Toole goes flamboyantly into an entire deep-freeze full of ham taking most of the play with him. Those who saw the supremely intelligent National Theatre revival of this sexist debate last year will have trouble recognizing in this Edwardian shambles the same basic text, but despite evident trouble with his vocal chords its star does turn in a remarkably mesmeric if dotty central performance which suggests that the sooner O'Toole starts touring as Higgins in the ice-rink version of *My Fair Lady* the better for us all.

1982: Played Out?

A year which saw the arrival of the Royal Shakespeare Company at the Barbican, major new plays from both Pinter and Stoppard and the storming of Broadway with *Plenty* and *Cats* and *Good* can hardly be described as a disastrous one for the British theatre in general. Yet 1982 also saw a moment in early October when no less than twelve (or just over one in three) main and central London playhouses were dark, with four of those actually for sale; it saw the permanent loss of Riverside Studios which had operated continuous World Theatre seasons of a kind long since abandoned by the RSC, and it saw the demise of the Talk of the Town and the Astoria as cabaret theatres. It saw an American (James Nederlander) buy the Aldwych and a Canadian (Ed Mirvish) buy the Old Vic. It saw theatre budgets being slashed all over the country as Arts Council grants failed to keep pace with inflation, and it saw an increasingly desperate determination in the commercial West End to rely on old stars and even older musicals to keep theatres open. It was perhaps symbolic that the one really successful theatrical campaign fought this year had nothing to do with the present or future of the British theatre but was solely concerned with its past in the continuing attempt to save the British Theatre Museum.

But annual theatrical reports are too often inclined to descend rapidly into non-specific accounts of doom and gloom, and it might make sense to start with a few facts. By my reckoning, in London alone, no less than 286 shows opened this year; some of those were in the repertoires of the two big culture palaces run by the National and the RSC, some were in the pubs and clubs, a few were even in the West End. Some are now moving into their second year, some barely made it to the end of their first week, and a few only ever meant to stay a day or two on some prolonged tour north to or south from the Edinburgh Festival.

All the same, no city which can open nearly 300 productions in twelve months can claim to be in terminal theatrical trouble, whatever the depredations of a Government which seems to regard actors, in so far as it regards them at all, as a useful sub-division of troop entertainment. It is true that we now have an Arts Minister (Paul Channon) to whom at the age of five a play was dedicated by Terence Rattigan; it would be even better if he did not sometimes give the impression that it was also the last play he ever saw.

The essential problems have not in fact changed much since this time last year: a West End suffering increasingly from inner-city decay, so that its traditional local audiences find it hard to get to, harder still to park in, expensive to attend and unattractive to visit while the tourists who once took their place in the golden early seventies are also now coming to much the same conclusion – theatre-going, like charity, should begin either at home (in this case with cut-down television versions of such archetypal stage classics as *Nickleby*) or else in a local playhouse where the costs and the inconvenience can be at least cut by half. Meanwhile a once-thriving pub circuit is now also severely strapped for cash both over the counter and backstage, while increasingly any money spent too visibly at the National or the Barbican (the river-boat disaster that was Ayckbourn's *Way Upstream,* for instance, or the brave attempt at an angry pantomime in the Barbican *Poppy*) begins to look dangerously like profligacy.

Like Mrs Thatcher and her once-famous kitchen larder, the

British theatre is now desperately about storing and preserving and cutting back: in a world where *The Mousetrap* can run thirty years on a shoestring, who needs epic adventures in great stagecraft? The answer is of course that we do: in a time of recession, as Busby Berkeley discovered in the Hollywood 1930s, there's nothing quite like an extravaganza but try telling that to the banking theatre managers of Shaftesbury Avenue. The success of *Guys and Dolls* is of course living proof that Berkeley was right, but then again *Guys and Dolls* is playing maybe two nights a week at most on a heavily subsidized stage at the National.

So much for the doom and gloom I was trying to avoid; on the credit side this has been the year of Pinter's superb triple bill *Other Places*, the year of Stoppard's untypical and therefore hugely underrated *Real Thing*, the year of Jonathan Miller's stunning theatrical farewells with the Anton Lesser *Hamlet* and the English National Opera *Rigoletto*, this last far and away the best musical in town. For new work it has also been the year (at the Royal Court) of Terry Johnson's intriguing Marilyn Monroe play *Insignificance*, and for performances it has been the year of Joss Ackland's Falstaff, Judi Dench's amazingly youthful Lady Bracknell, Michael Gambon's Stratford King Lear and Anna Massey and Yvonne Bryceland in Edward Bond's (also much underrated) *Summer*.

It was also the year when Barry Humphries in his Dame Edna drag managed to turn Drury Lane into a massage parlour of the human spirit, bestowing like some manic Mother Theresa a compulsory barbecue upon the audience who had already forfeited their shoes and much of their dignity in an evening which made even Elizabeth Taylor in *The Little Foxes* seem almost credible by comparison.

Enough there to keep the drama–critical mind alive for a year, and sometimes not just alive but also blown.

1983: Forthcoming Detractions

January: Dame Anna Neagle announces at the end of the pantomime season her availability for the role of Mrs Thatcher in the forthcoming musical version of *Anyone for Denis?* Greer Garson agrees to play *Mrs Miniver* on ice at the Apollo Victoria as soon as the current Richard Harris *Camelot* grinds to a halt. Sir Peter Hall again declines to publish his salary for 1983 but agrees that it is probably no greater than the National's staging costs for the new Alan Ayckbourn comedy set symbolically aboard the *Lusitania* in early 1917.

February: Fifteen more empty central London theatres come on the property market and plans are announced for the conversion of the Theatre Royal Haymarket into Haymarkets One, Two and Three; these will be small-stage auditoria with very thin walls, so that it should be possible to attend Shakespeare's *Henry VI* in its entirety within about three hours.

March: Following the success of Peter O'Toole in *Man and Superman* on stage, it is announced that Hollywood has purchased all screen rights; it is hoped that Dudley Moore and Charlton Heston will play the title roles. Meanwhile there is to be a special Hollywood Greats season on stage at the Barbican; Cary Grant's *King Lear* will be followed, probably a night or two later, by Julie Andrews as *Hedda Gabler*.

April: Box-office surveys of the West End now indicate that the average theatregoer along Shaftesbury Avenue is a fifty-year-old Japanese industrialist with about half-an-hour to spare between engagements. All playwrights are being asked to study the average length of time that elapses in dress circles between the buzzing of electronic watches, and to confine their major speeches to those intervals.

May: Bar prices for a single interval gin crash the £10 barrier at last. Parking is forbidden within a fifteen-mile radius of central London except between the hours of 5 and 8 a.m. Offenders are liable to have their cars removed and both legs at the kneecaps.

June: Dame Anna Neagle announces her summer-season availability for the role of Ronald Reagan in the forthcoming Broadway musical *Hello, Ronnie!* This has already had a considerable success in Peking where it was widely understood to be a tribute to the music of Lonnie Donegan. Meanwhile in London, cab drivers threaten to stick the name of the murderer in *The Mousetrap* to the glass partitions of all taxis unless they get an immediate five-pound surcharge on all journeys involving playgoers on their way home from the St Martin's who wish to discuss the significance of its plot.

July: Theatre owners announce that for every London playhouse sold before the end of the month, the purchaser will qualify for two free seats to any matinee of *Cats*.

August: Lord Miles announces that unless the City of London agrees to a large and immediate cash increase in grants to the Mermaid, he will have no alternative but to revive *Treasure Island* and play Long John Silver there throughout the autumn with Bonnie Langford as his parrot. And following triumphant 1982 London seasons by such solo entertainers as Barry Humphries and Spike Milligan, the economically embattled National Theatre details a special winter season of 'The Goodies', one of whom will be appearing on each of its stages nightly until Christmas.

September: Declining to grant the theatre the VAT relief it enjoys in almost all other European countries, Mrs Thatcher's Government points out that simply because a once-great industry happens to be dying, that is no reason not to carry on strangling it. How else could the many theatre-going coal and steel workers of South Wales be expected to understand the logic of the Government's position?

October: Mrs Thatcher announces her likely availability from next Spring for the role of Dame Anna Neagle in a forthcoming Andrew Lloyd Webber musical tentatively entitled *Hats*. The Archbishop of Canterbury will play Norman St John-Stevas and it is hoped that His Holiness the Pope will make a special guest-starring appearance as Kitty Muggeridge.

November: Following the triumphant example of British Airways, the National Theatre now also announces plans to sell itself off in sections to private industry. The South London Ten-Pin Bowling Association has already made a sizeable bid for the Olivier lobby, and it is believed that the sandwich bars are to be moved to Gatwick as part of a dynamic new programme for cash savings on subsidized cheesecakes.

December: The Society of West End Theatre announces its awards for 1983. The Terence Rattigan Award for thinly-disguised dramas about handsome young poofs goes jointly to Julian Mitchell for *Another Another Country* and to the late J. M. Barrie for *Peter Pan*. The award for the most number of awards presented to the British theatre goes once again to the *Evening Standard*, and this year's special prize for the only original star of *The Mousetrap* to have made an epic three-hour movie about a world-famous Indian religious leader of diminutive stature goes by a narrow vote to Sir Richard Attenborough.

1983

Designs for Living?

Caryl Churchill's *Top Girls*, back briefly at the Royal Court from a Broadway triumph, has been hailed by at least one of my critical colleagues as 'the best play ever written in Britain by a woman': up against *Richard of Bordeaux*, even up against *Dusa, Fish, Stas and Vi*, that seems to me a risky claim, not least because it begs one of the play's most central issues which is the precise definition of female achievement in a male world. Even if we accept it, we have still to face the fact that *Top Girls* is essentially not one but three excellent short plays.

The first is a table-top discussion between some legendary historical figures, not least Pope Joan and the Victorian explorer Isabella Bird, about the precise nature of feminine survival and at what cost through the ages. The second is a tough little documentary set in a modern employment agency featuring some case-histories of ambitious management secretaries. And the third is a tight, taut and marvellous domestic drama about two sisters, one of whom abandons her baby to the other in a bid for professional and personal freedom. True, these plays are linked by one character: Marlene (Gwen Taylor), the giver of the dinner party, is also the manager of the employment agency and the sister who has abandoned her baby. True, too, the other six women all double up so that the debate about feminism and freedom continues across centuries and countries throughout the two-hour evening. But in the end, we have still got three short plays even if they do all contribute to one central theme.

Top Girls is not a stridently feminist work of propaganda: instead it's an immensely carefully weighted argument, starting in Shavian debate and gradually narrowing down to domestic particulars, about the cost of emancipation and equality. What makes it so

La Prima Donna Employment Agency

Amo Amas Amas

The Mirror of Venus = Feminine.

Hewison

Top Girls   Carole Hayman *as Dull Gret*, Gwen Taylor *as Marlene*, Deborah Findlay *as Isabella Bird*, Selina Cadell *as Pope Joan*

powerful is a curious kind of passionate detachment that Caryl Churchill has achieved through her start in history, and what makes it such a splendidly powerful evening is the group playing of a wonderfully strong cast in Max Stafford-Clark's hugely powerful production.

At the Bush, Doug Lucie's *Hard Feelings* is billed as 'a viciously funny play set in Brixton in 1981' and that seems no violation of the theatrical trades' descriptions act, though it doesn't tell you the whole story. What Mr Lucie has done here, exactly half a century on from Noël Coward, is to come up with a modern *Design for Living* in which six characters are used to hold a mirror up to the nation and the times which have bred them.

But we are not into documentary reality: the riots of that Brixton summer happen way off-stage and affect only one of the characters.

He, Tone (Stephen Tiller), is anyway a butch journalist outsider, using the group's milk bottles for anti-police missiles; though ironically it is also he who gives the others their only real glimpse of a moral code.

Then there's Viv (Frances Barber) whose parents have given her the house and with it a final, chilling, proprietorial authority over all of its inhabitants; there's also Annie (Diana Katis from the marvellous Oxford undergraduate film *Privileged*) who's a laid-back model dabbling in pornographic movies; Rusty (Ian Reddington), a new-romantic singer whose tragedy is a successful father and an inherent talent for disaster; Jane (Jennifer Landor), a Jewish solicitor expecting to be forgiven for it; and Baz (Chris Jury), a Sheffield wimp hoping to end up as something big on the managerial side of frisbees.

These characters are Mr Lucie's play: they lunch at Routiers, shop at Camden Lock, wonder whether to rename their house Dunthinkin and gaze in wonder at Tone, the newcomer, a born-again pagan with a deep, understandable fear of Sir Geoffrey Howe. He (Tone) is the only one of the group not to have been through Oxford, and there too Mr Lucie is I think trying to tell us something of the incestuous dangers of a university education. His play is an acidulated, acerbic and often very funny look at power and property and the self-destructive mechanism therein. Like Evelyn Waugh in *A Handful of Dust*, he's trying to show us how laws of the jungle can still apply in a jungle of the cities, and he's on about the clan mentality. By the time all *Hard Feelings* have been expressed, some of the members have been ignominiously expelled from the group but Queen Viv remains at least outwardly unharmed, and presumably soon to start on the long march to Downing Street.

It's a play about greed and selfishness and insecurity and racial intolerance, made all the more powerful by its refusal to allow a Brixton brick in through the window. Mr Lucie's only weapon is (like Caryl Churchill's) that of language, and he too uses it with the economy, confidence and wit of a dramatist of twice his age and experience. He also deserves some sort of special award for allowing *Casablanca* to play on a video screen in full view of his audience for most of the second act; how many other dramatists would let in that sort of competition, and how many of those would win through to the point where I wasn't even looking at the set when Bergman and Henried sang the 'Marseillaise'? Mr Lucie is a writer to watch for in the future, and *Hard Feelings* is a play to see now.

Vivat Rex

In the ten years or so since Olivier gave up the National and most other great stars gave up the West End, we have grown accustomed – for better and often for worse – to an essentially academic theatre where the writers and directors reign unchallenged. Faced with a Bernard Shaw revival such as that of *Heartbreak House* now at the Theatre Royal Haymarket, my critical colleagues therefore look instinctively to see what the director rather than the actors have brought to it and as a result of that one-sided quest John Dexter's new production has been unfairly attacked for lacking the ensemble coherence of a recent National revival by John Schlesinger.

But this is to deny not only the flamboyant and marvellously quirky theatricality of what Dexter has produced, a theatricality which Shaw would have been among the first to recognize and grudgingly approve; it is also to deny the remarkable achievement of the new production in bringing Rex Harrison back into his own. Twenty-five years on from *My Fair Lady*, years which he has spent working in a fair amount of old rubbish, Harrison is at last home in his rightful Shavian territory and if this definitive Captain Shotover doesn't get him the knighthood then nothing will. Sure he is a little fluffy on some of the longer speeches, and there are indeed moments when he appears to be neither coming nor going but merely hovering like some benign Prospero over a British isle that is still full of noises and somehow no longer very magical. Yet all of that is a perfect role description of Shotover himself, and when Harrison gets himself into the great speech about England ('The Captain is in his bunk, drinking bottled ditchwater; and the crew is gambling in the forecastle. She will strike and sink and split. Do you think the laws of God will be suspended in favour of England because you were born in it?') it is to be reminded with a sudden shock of what an extraordinary talent we have allowed to disappear over the Atlantic in these last forty years.

The play, admittedly, remains more of a problem: Shaw seems to have thought he was writing an English *Cherry Orchard* (the subtitle is 'a fantasia in the Russian manner on English themes') and come up instead with an Edwardian *Hay Fever* in which the true star apart from Shotover is the house itself, a house where hearts and nations can be broken with equal ease while the inhabitants debate the virtues of selling your soul to the devil in Zanzibar. Around Harrison in this rambling structure, apparently run up by an unholy alliance of Ben Travers and Turgenev, Dexter has assembled one of the starriest casts even the Haymarket has recently enjoyed: Diana Rigg looking like Lady Ottoline Morell is Hesione, Rosemary Harris is an aristocratic Ariadne, Paxton Whitehead (as Hector) is back to these shores after twenty years in Canada and still sounding uncannily like Jonathan Miller, Simon Ward is a twit-of-the-year Randall Utterword and the indomitable Doris Hare is the aptly named Nurse Guinness. You might, if you were very lucky, see a more intelligent production of this play sometime in the next half-century; I doubt you will ever see a more quintessentially, unmissably theatrical one.

Monroe Doctrine

'I am Camera' announces the singing narrator early in the catastrophic musical that is *Marilyn!* (at the Adelphi) to which the only possible reply is the immortal Broadway reviewer's 'Me no Leica'. What is wrong with this deeply uneasy stage life and especially death of the late and great Miss Monroe is just about everything, so we had better start with the lyrics by Jacques Wilson which are, I fear, only too aptly summarized by the unforgettable 'Maybe he'd like to know me better, Wait till he sees me in a sweater.' Mr Wilson is also responsible for the book, such as it is, which consists largely of having Miss Monroe's many husbands whisked rapidly on and off stage while she stands watching them with a look of understandable bemusement. One of them does pause long enough at the footlights to announce 'I am Arthur Miller: I know everything'; the pity of it is that the real-life Mr Miller apparently didn't know enough lawyers to keep this travesty of himself and indeed of Miss Monroe off the stage of the Adelphi.

It is the kind of show which would, only a few years back, have opened and very possibly also closed in Philadelphia: quite why it has been brought to London pre-Broadway by its American management remains unclear, except that they do seem to have been hugely influenced by the success of *Evita* from which they have borrowed not only the choreographer (Larry Fuller) and star (Stephanie Lawrence) but also the whole notion of a David Essex lookalike narrator to anchor an extremely sketchy piece. *Marilyn!* is admittedly not helped by its score (Mort Garson) which manages to sound throughout much like the kind of Muzak you forget even while you are hearing it in hotel lifts. The trouble is that it also takes up a very great deal of time for the cast to plod through nearly thirty undistinguished songs, so that there's precious little left for any but the most threadbare plot and characterization. In the end what we need is either some sort of coherent attitude to Miss Monroe's sad life and Hollywood times, or else to learn something about her that could not be gathered by flicking through the pages of some tattered old movie magazine. Here we get neither: we are, however, treated to a final and breathtaking five-minute sequence of old film clips demonstrating only too clearly the utter failure of *Marilyn!* to come to any real understanding of Marilyn.

Showbiz sagas are never the easiest of theatrical forms, and it was therefore brave of the director Michael Rudman to set his first script as dramatist at a couple of committee meetings for the selection of an award-winning new play. This is an incestuous world Mr Rudman knows well enough, and what he has come up with in *Short List* (at the Hampstead Theatre) is a script strongly reminiscent of middle-period John Osborne, one of those plays like *Time Present* or *Hotel in Amsterdam* where a group of larger-than-life theatrical types are gathered to discuss some offstage giant while not a lot else happens.

In this case the giant is Harry Wyecroft, a late lamented and apparently legendary theatre director at least faintly modelled on George Devine, in whose honour there is, of course, a real-life theatrical award given .annually. But Rudman is not essentially concerned here with an attack, however tempting, on those Royal Courtiers who still seem to live in Devine's long shadow; rather has he taken a group of leftover and all-too-recognizable dramatists and directors from the fifties and sixties and watched them at work and play, much after the fashion in which Michael Frayn took a group of leftover actors and watched them in *Noises Off*.

The problem is, however, that Rudman is not, or at least not yet, a writer in anything like Frayn's league; his play is therefore inclined to come to the occasional grinding halt in mid-act. What it does provide, though, is a chance for a group of the best actors in town to have themselves a ball. Ian McKellen as the panel's natural leader, Bernard (Yosser) Hill as the loony Marxist, Glyn Owen as the monosyllabic Northern reality writer and Philip Voss in a savagely wonderful parody of an Arts Council committee stalwart, have all found themselves characters they can run and run with, and the result is a splendidly bitchy attack on the British theatre at its most clannish.

Mr Rudman has, in truth, gone for one or two extremely ancient jokes (the Woody Allen character forever phoning his own answering service and 'what's the play about – about three hours' routine) but he has also managed some waspishly good moments of committee madness and he has been more than a little lucky in gathering a director (Mike Ockrent) and a cast who could doubtless play the *Spotlight* casting directory on stage if asked. What we now need from Mr Rudman are dramatized accounts of his backstage dramas with Richard Harris and Sir Peter Hall.

Alan Ayckbourn's bizarre conviction that apart from being the finest comic dramatist of the postwar British theatre he is also the Stephen Sondheim of Scarborough has led him and us into another deeply disappointing musical called *Making Tracks* at Greenwich. There is, I suspect, still a very funny play to be derived from Mr Ayckbourn's own years of experience as a BBC radio studio manager in the early 1960s; here, however, all we get is a distinctly duff account of six people and three visitors in a rundown pop-recording studio trying to cobble together a hit single, and the desperate pace at which the author has directed his own piece suggests that he too has seen the cracks in its flimsy structure. The music is by Paul Todd who also puts in a pleasant appearance as a drummer in the midst of a strong playing team.

Chips with Everything

When I began going to the theatre thirty years ago, the West End was full of plays like Michael Wilcox's *Lent* now at the Lyric Hammersmith Studio. Gentle, literate, elegiac pieces to do with childhood or old age, the work of people like N. C. Hunter and Wynyard Brown, which frequently turned up at the Haymarket with cast-lists studded by dames and knights of the British theatre.

They (the plays, rather than the dames or knights) got swept away by the Court revolution of 1956 just as surely as old revues got swept away by *Beyond the Fringe*, and since then, though it has occasionally found a resting place in the middle of a Radio Four afternoon, the well-made play has been about as evident around London as the well-made ocean liner. All the more reason, therefore, to welcome Mr Wilcox's remarkably unfashionable and extraordinarily enthralling piece. Apparently cobbled together by an unholy alliance of Enid Bagnold and Terence Rattigan, it concerns one man's memories of his last year at a boys' prep school in 1956. He, our narrator (Jonathan Kent), is admittedly a rather special pupil in that his grandmother owns the school; his parents have been killed in an air crash, which means that the school is his life all through the holidays as well as all through the term, and it is from that unusual perspective, the schoolboy as eventual owner of all he surveys, that we are allowed to glimpse the off-duty staff.

There are in fact only four other characters in the play: Patience Collier in wonderful form as the eccentric old grandmother, Jean Anderson and Dennis Edwards as the sour couple who have been brought in to run the school until the boy himself can take charge, and Wensley Pithey as the resident Mr Chips in an old-schoolmaster performance which ought, unless this is to prove a quite exceptional year, to win him just about every supporting-actor award that is going. I do not believe you could currently find a better-acted play than *Lent* in the whole of London; whether or not you could find a better play will depend largely on your fascination with the English private school system and its effects on the later life of its participants.

It would not be hard, in fact, to make a case for *Lent* being a plea for total and compulsory closure of all private schools in this country tomorrow morning: it explores memories of a place quite alarmingly cut off from outer realities, into which only 'The Goon Show' is occasionally allowed to intrude via the radio, where the adult inhabitants are either mad, greedy, treacherous or have a faintly dubious sexual interest in their youthful charges. But that, I suspect, is not what Mr Wilcox is on about here at all: these are merely incidental insights into the people who made up what could very well have been parts of his own youth. At the centre of this play is, instead, an extremely powerful and almost Chekhovian lament for a lost world: a world, for all its failings and eccentricities, which contained something of value even if it was only isolation and spare time.

Seeing *Lent* is like having somebody flip through an old album of their school photos for you; some are of extreme dullness, some are a bit blurred around the edges, but now and then are sudden moments of quite remarkable clarity when you see what that school must have been like for that pupil. For Mr Pithey alone, giving the most touching and nostalgic account of an old Englishman I have seen since the late Nigel Bruce gave up playing Dr Watson to Basil Rathbone's Sherlock Holmes, *Lent* should be seen; it should also be seen by anyone who believes that the war, indeed the 1950s, did anything to change what both *The Browning Version* and *Goodbye Mr Chips* were all about.

To Wyndham's from a much-acclaimed fringe run at the Old Red Lion has come Phil Young's improvised *Crystal Clear*, a play about blindness which happily manages to avoid the pitfalls of becoming 'Children of an Even Lesser God'. Thus far, plays about blindness have either been thrillers (*Wait Until Dark*) or sentimental romances (*Butterflies Are Free*) unless of course you count *King Lear*. But what Mr Young and his admirable company of three (Anthony Allen, Philomena McDonagh and Diana Barrett) have come up with is a play about the importance of seeing into yourself even if you can't see anything much around you. What raises it to the level of such other plays about physical affliction as *Duet for One* is that this is neither a patronizing nor a crusading piece of theatre: it is simply the story of three people, one sighted, one blind and one going blind during the play, trying to come to terms with themselves and their relationships regardless of their lack of vision.

In one sense, *Crystal Clear* is about the power politics of blindness, the way that some blind schools advise their pupils not to marry other blind people for fear of total inaccessibility to the sighted world. In another, it's a play about commitment to yourself as much as to other people, and in a third it's an icily waspish play about public attitudes to blindness: at a hospital, one of the characters tells the receptionist he has suddenly lost his sight; 'But have you,' she asks him, 'an appointment?' He may not have an appointment but what he does now get, the officials tell him proudly, is a pound off the cost of his television licence. Devised and performed in the style of a Mike Leigh workshop improvisation of extreme care, *Crystal Clear* is a simple no-interval succession of five scenes each involving two characters at least one of whom is having trouble with internal or external vision. What we have here is a play about clarity of the spirit as well as of the eye, and as such it works very well indeed.

West End Story

Fabulous invalids have a habit of getting better very suddenly. A month or so ago, you may recall, you could hardly open a paper or magazine (or indeed listen to radio or television) without learning about how London's commercial theatre was in the final stages of cardiac arrest. Richard Harris hauled off in his *Camelot* prime, twelve theatres dark, government shock horror refusal yet again to lift the VAT on theatre tickets, Shaftesbury Avenue closed to through playgoing traffic, all of that and more. Only one thing was overlooked: the fact that it was early February.

Morley's Third Law of Theatre has always held that no sane actor will rehearse over Christmas. From this it follows that almost no new shows can open between about 1 January and 15 February, while large numbers of shows can and do close in that period due to the ending of the school holidays. Accordingly, it is nearly always possible for arts journalists round about 10 February to earn themselves a few bob writing pieces about the imminent collapse of the London theatre; these have the distinct advantage of being self-explosive, so that a month later a few more bob can usually be earned denying the whole thing. Because early in March a huge number of shows that have been cobbled together since the Christmas holidays start making their way into town, with the result that you now can't hire yourself an empty London theatre for love nor money. While we're at it (and this being a week singularly devoid of major first nights) you might like one or two other playgoing facts: 9,000,000 people went to London theatres last year, a figure that is five per cent up on 1981. There are now more theatres open in London than there were at this time in either 1980 or 1981. In the last decade, seven London theatres have either been built, reopened or converted back from cinemas. Thirty thousand people a night go to a West End theatre, and two-thirds of the 8,000,000 people who came to visit London last year gave the live theatre as one of their main reasons for coming. There are, as any European traveller will tell you, more theatres open in London any night of the week than in most continental capitals combined, and indeed rather more than you will usually find even in New York.

Why all of this matters, and why it needs to be noted that the present government took £7½ million in tax out of the London theatre last year without so much as a 'thank you', is because there has grown up in recent years a dangerous belief that the British theatre can actually get by without the West End. We have, it is true, a thriving pub–theatre circuit, an extremely healthy regional theatre network and a booming couple of subsidized companies at the National and the Barbican. But that is like saying that since we have a House of Lords and a Students' Union, who needs a House of Commons? The West End is the one place where theatre can truly be tested against market forces. Everywhere else, it operates on some kind of hidden economy, whether the subsidy comes from Arts or local Council or simply from a publican who is doing well on his beer profits and can therefore afford a few actors in the back room. Only in the West End is there a genuine test of public appeal: shows that people are willing to pay money for stay on. Shows that they are not willing to pay money for come to a sudden halt. It is as immediate, and sometimes as alarming, as the Stock Exchange, but at least it's a barometer of popular theatrical taste in 1983.

And what it means, of course, is a certain amount of rubbish. Nobody looking down a West End theatre guide for this week could claim that every one, or even half, of the forty or so shows advertised represent major intellectual breakthroughs in the art of drama. But it seems to me that a West End which can support Cheryl Campbell's doubtless soon to be award–winning *Miss Julie* (at the Duke of York's) or a play like *Crystal Clear* is not altogether to be dismissed as nothing more than a resting-place for old comedies and even older musical comedies.

And the West End is now even beginning to learn how to look after its own triumphs: where once a comedy like Michael Frayn's brilliant backstage *Noises Off* (at the Savoy) would have been left to disintegrate slowly with a succession of less and less distinguished visiting stars above the title, it has instead been totally recast and redirected for its second year so that audiences approaching it now are seeing a show which has effectively been in existence for less than three months.

The all-new company of ten are perhaps no better than the

originals who started out at the Lyric Hammersmith eighteen
months ago, but they are extremely different: Ben Whitrow as the
long-suffering director, for instance, has replaced Paul Eddington's
suppressed rage in the role with an eerie kind of calm, while Robert
Flemyng now plays the old actor on the fringes of certifiable lunacy
where Michael Aldridge merely played him drunk and deaf. But all
of these variations merely go to prove the extraordinary efficiency
of Frayn's stage machine. It is not that his play about sub-standard
actors falling to pieces in seaside theatres is especially original:
indeed Philip King wrote a farce thirty years ago called *On Monday
Next* about just the same subject. Rather is it that here (as in his
novel *Towards the End of Morning* and such earlier plays as *Clouds,
Alphabetical Order* and *Donkeys' Years*) Frayn has taken a particularly
enclosed order of people and allowed them to disintegrate from
within before our eyes. The sight is alarmingly funny because it
depends on so much more than just the classic routines of farce
coming apart at the seams: it depends on characters immensely
carefully constructed over three long acts then being solemnly
dynamited one at a time. Mr Frayn's own fictional programme
notes for his cast are alone worth the price of admission.

Index

Individual productions of, for example, the Royal Shakespeare Company or the National Theatre should be looked up under their respective play-titles.

Abbey 37, 210, 242, 269
Abigail's Party 88–9
Above Us the Waves 122
Absent Friends 82
Accidental Death of an Anarchist 199
Accounts of a Journey through Madness 166
Accrington Pals, The 302
Ackland, Joss 17, 97, 139, 267, 330, 343
Ackland, Rodney 217–18
Adams, Jonathan 225–6
Adams, Polly 146, 259, 339
Addams, Charles 130, 146
Adelphi 16–17, 163, 319, 353–4
Adrian, Max 11, 189
Aeschylus 211
After the Fall 248, 294
Agamemnon 298
Agate, James 87, 140
Ages of Man 11, 158
Ain't Misbehavin' 172–3
Aitken, Maria 17, 62, 62, 82, 215–16, 285
Albee, Edward 122, 176, 321
Albery 302
Aldridge, Michael 19, 360
Aldwych 22, 29, 39, 43, 45–6, 69–71, 81,
    89–90, 112, 120, 130, 158, 164–5,
    197–8, 211–13, 227–9, 242–3, 250, 255,
    264, 297–8, 298, 309, 341
Alexander, George 335–6
Alfie 147
Allen, Anthony 152, 357
Allen, Ches 279–80
Allen, Dave 28, 157
Allen, David 267
Allen, Woody 28, 249, 355
All My Sons 294–5, 302
Almost Free 59–60
Alphabetical Order 13–14, 360
Amadeus 200–1, 259, 292, 320

Ambassadors 11, 176–7, 225, 300
Anatol 48–9, 77, 187
And a Nightingale Sang 190–1
Anderson, Jean 179, 356
Anderson, Lindsay 43
Andrews, Harry 106
Andrews, Julie 344
Angel, Barry 151
Anhalt, Edward 34–5
Anhalt, Tony 124
Anna and the King of Siam 186
Annie 132–3, 151, 155, 157, 185, 230
Annie Get Your Gun 86
Annis, Francesca 57, 58
Another Country 295–6
Anouilh, Jean 34–5, 140
Antony and Cleopatra 148–50, 158, 236
Anyone Can Whistle 61
Anyone for Denis? 343
Apocalypse Now 184
Apollo 17, 55, 75–7, 109, 312–13, 340, 343
Applause 185, 291
'Archers, The' 127
Ardrey, Robert 45
'Are You Being Served?' 220
Are You Now or Have You Ever Been . . .?
    95–6
Arliss, George 216
Armfield, Neil 220
Arts 52
Arts Council 14–15, 117, 118, 159,
    199–200, 249, 300, 341, 359
Arturo Ui 89, 310
Ashcroft, Peggy 238–9, 251, 285
Asher, Jane 47, 124, 217–18
Aspects of Max Wall 3–4, 11
Astaire, Fred 64, 332
Astoria 251, 341
As You Like It 174, 194

Atkins, Eileen 8–9, 88, 140–1, 255–6
Atkins, Robert 21, 223, 267
Atkinson, Barbara 152
Atkinson, Rowan 143
Attenborough, Richard 345
At the Drop of a Hat 143
Attwell, Mabel Lucie 146
Aubrey, John 11–12
Audley, Maxine 106, 165
Augins, Charles 105
Aukin, David 301
Austin, Robert 170
Avon, Roger 190–1
Awakenings 337
Ayckbourn, Alan 19–20, 82–3, 117, 118,
    128–9, 154, 159, 170–1, 226–7, 234, 245,
    251, 281, 323, 342, 344, 355
Aylmer, Felix 183

Bacall, Lauren 261, 290–1, 292, 320
Bacharach, Burt 5
Badel, Sarah 267
Bagnold, Enid 141, 176, 238, 292, 356
Bailey, Robin 179, 278, 340
Baker, Frank 138
Baker, George 140
Baker, Tom 325
Bankhead, Tallulah 321
Bannen, Ian 95, 268–9
Baptiste, Thomas 96
Barber, Frances 351
Barbican 119, 304, 329–30, 341, 342, 344,
    359
BARC 189
Bardon, John 312
Barefoot in the Park 240, 282
Barker, Harley Granville 29, 96–8
Barker, Howard 32–4, 208–9, 220
Bar Mitzvah Boy 151–2, 155, 157
Barnes, Clive 12
Barnum 260, 269–71, 302
Barnum, Phineas Taylor 270–1
Barnum and Bailey 210
Barrett, Diana 357
Barrie, J.M. 19, 203, 345
Barrymore 322
Bart, Lionel 118, 126, 227, 229–30, 325
Barton, John 58–9, 67, 211–12, 250–1
Bates, Alan 49–50, 203
Battle of Life, The 4
Baum, Vicki 188
Baxter, Keith 93
Baxter, Stanley 81, 118
Bay, John 166
Baylis, Lilian 88
Beacham, Stephanie 141, 168
Bear, The 166
Beastly Beatitudes of Balthazar B, The
    287–8, 302

Beaton, Cecil 336
Beaumont, Penelope 311
Beavis, Ivan 58
Becket 34
Beckett, Samuel 18
Beckinsale, Richard 48
Bed Before Yesterday, The 40, 43
Bedroom Farce 82–3, 159, 168, 170–1
Beecham, Thomas 209
Beerbohm, Max 112
Before the Party 217–18
Bell, Tom 181, 325
Belt and Braces 199–200
Ben-Hur 140, 175
Benmussa, Simone 141
Bennett, Alan 101–3, 191, 218, 222, 243–5,
    257, 295
Bennett, Jill 50–1, 75–7, 94, 195
Bennett, Michael 65, 322
Benny, Jack 312
Benson, Frank 21
Bent 181
Benthall, Michael 135
Bentley, Eric 95–6
Bergman, Ingmar 16, 249, 325
Bergman, Ingrid 351
Berkeley, Busby 178, 192, 246, 250, 343
Berkoff, Steven 107
Berlin, Irving 86
Berman, Ed 59–60, 189–90
Bernhardt, Sarah 108
Best Little Whorehouse in Texas, The 302
Betjeman, John 101
Betrayal 155–7, 159, 182, 256, 291, 338
'Bewitched, Bothered and Bewildered' 235
Beyond a Joke 143–4
Beyond the Fringe 13, 143, 189, 356
Beyond the Rainbow 157, 163
Bicât, Nick 213
'Big Best Shoes' 326
Billingham Forum 95
Billy 151
Billy Bishop 274
Bingo 36
Biograph Girl, The 250
Birch, Peter 278
Birmingham Rep 8
Birthday Party, The 18
Birtwhistle, Harrison 299
Bitter-Sweet 214, 325
Black, Don 151
'Black and White' 270
Black Comedy 47
Blackman, Honor 313
Black Theatre Co-operative 269
Blade on the Feather 243–4
Blaikley, Alan 54–5
Blair, Joyce 151
Blake, Arthur 190, 233

Blake, Jonathan 138
Blakely, Colin 8–9, 108, 112, 244, 294–5
Blakemore, Michael 43, 76, 81, 152, 294–5, 302
Bland, Peter 110
Blessed, Brian 91
Blezard, William 5
Blithe Spirit 61–3, 155
Bloom, Claire 267
Blunt, Anthony 295
Blythe, Domini 311
Bodies 122–3, 176–7, 182
Bogarde, Dirk 276
Bogart, Humphrey 178, 235, 331
Bogdanov, Michael 272, 293, 304
Bolam, James 47
Bolger, Ray 64, 270
Bolt, Robert 90–1, 118
Bolton, Guy 56
Bond, Christopher 230–1
Bond, Edward 19, 36–7, 315, 343
Bond, Gary 52
Bond Honoured, A 263
Boulting Brothers 23
Bowke, Peter 15
Bowers, Lally 288
Bowker, Judi 119–20
Bowles, Peter 59
Bown, John 31
Boy Friend, The 326
Boys from Syracuse, The 118
Boys in the Band, The 181
Braden, Kim 164
Bragg, Melvin 54–5
Brahms, Caryl 228, 274
Brand 133–4
Brandes Theatre 134
Brando, Marlon 319
Brassneck 100
Brecht, Bertolt 89, 91, 178, 288, 310
Brenton, Howard 19, 100–1, 220, 250
Bring Back Birdie 261
Bricusse, Leslie 126–7, 157, 333
Bridges, Robert 79
Brief Lives 11–12, 201
Briers, Richard 19, 128, 287
British Theatre Museum 342
Bron, Eleanor 80, *80*
Brook, Faith 103
Brook, Peter 44–5, 119, 147–8, 148–50, 158, 249–50, 328
Brooke, Paul 7, 290
Brooks, Mel 163
Brooks, Ray 191
Brothers Karamazov, The 302
Brown, Ivor 285
Brown, John Russell 135
Brown, Pamela 30, 140
Brown, Tina 91–2, 99

Brown, Wynyard 355
Browne, Coral 63
Browning Version, The 114, 251, 278, 357
Bruce, Brenda *272*
Bruce, Lenny 29
Bruce, Nigel 357
Bryant, Michael 39, 91, 134, 187–8, 194, 226, 293
Bryceland, Yvonne 197, 315, 343
Bryden, Bill 37–8, 98, 127, 144, 154, 184, 247, 250, 292
Brynner, Yul 186–7, 216
Bubbling Brown Sugar 104–5, 119
Buchan, John 101, 238
Buchanan, Jack 332
Bufman, Zef 321
Buggy, Niall 79
Bull, Diane 128
Bull, Peter 140
Burge, Stuart 167–8, 264, 295
Burgess, Guy 295–6
Burke, Alfred 80
Burke, David 122, 176–7, 239
Burn, Jonathan 262–3
Burrows, Abe 318
Burton, Richard 140, 202, 236
Bury, John 38, 85, 119, 135, 336
Bush 91–2, 95–6, 213–14
Bush 301, 350–1
Butley 50, 145, 225, 279
Butterflies Are Free 357
Buxton, Judy *212, 213*
Bye Bye Birdie 185, 261
Bygraves, Max 28
Byrne, Eddie 37
Byrne, Michael 341
Byron, Lord 276–8

Caan, James 281
Cabaret 77, 181, 271, 309
Cadell, Selina *350*
Cagney, James 178, 235, 331
Cahoot's Macbeth 189–90
Caird, John 228
Callow, Simon 167, 194, 201, 287–8, *289*, 302
Calvert, Phyllis 217
Cambridge 163, 177–8, 325
Camelot 19, 35, 113, 164, 202, 236, 290, 340, 344, 358
Camino Real 94
Campbell, Cheryl 359
Campbell, Judy 31, 258
Campbell, Mrs Patrick 87, 132
Candida 112, 146
'Candy Man' 126
Cannan, Denis 45
'Captain Beaky's Musical Christmas' 305
Caretaker, The 224, 248

Carey, Joyce 341
Cargill, Patrick 124
Cariou, Len 231
Carmichael, Ian 19, 267
Carpenters, The 144
Carr, Jane 100
Carroll, Belinda 63
Carson, John 328
Carter, James 319
Carter, Jimmy 204
Carteret, Anna 187, 197, 226, 293
Casablanca 107, 351
Casarès, Maria 26
Cashin, Fergus 112
Casino *see* Prince Edward
Casson, Lewis 183
'Cathedral of Clemenza' 326
Cats 265–6, 293, 302, 305, 332, 341, 345
Caucasian Chalk Circle, The 288
Cause Célèbre 152
Cavalcade 179, 264–5
Cavander, Kenneth 211
Cavell 333
Cazenove, Christopher 20, 170
Cellier, Peter 286
Cellini, Benvenuto 10
Chakiris, George 147
Chalk Garden 141
Chamberlain, Richard 277
Champion, Gower 259–60, 284
Changeling, The 158, 167
Changing Room 167
Channing, Carol 142, 284
Channon, Chips 286
Channon, Paul 342
Chaplin, Charlie 266
Chapman, John 109–10, 112
Chapter Two 281–2
Charge of the Light Brigade, The 22
Charles Dickens 4
Charleson, Ian 319
Charley's Aunt 165, 336
Charly 185
Charnin, Martin 151
Chase, Mary 15–16, 255
Chater, Gordon 157
Chekhov, Anton 79–81, 91, 119–21, 166,
    193, 222, 263–4, 279, 292, 322, 356
Chelton, Nick 150
Chern, Penny 208
Cherry Orchard, The 29, 119–21, 158, 267,
    292, 352
Chetwyn, Robert 181
Chicago 94, 177–8
Chichester 53, 66, 120, 142–3, 194–6, 267,
    274–6, 279–80, 301, 325–6, 333–4
Chicken Soup with Barley 131–2, 138
Childe Byron 276–8, 302
Children of a Lesser God 233, 280–1, 292,

302
Children of the Sun 197–8
Chkhikvadze, Ramoz 210
Choepori 298
Chorus Line, A 64–5, 105, 200, 322
Christie, Agatha 31–2, 124
Church, Tony 67, 213, 247
Churchill, Caryl 238, 349–50, 351
Clare, John 36–7
Clark, Brian 123–4
Clark, Petula 303, 313
Clarke, Oz 276
Clarke, Warren 78
Class Enemy 129–30
Cleese, John 287
Close of Play 182–3, 219, 222
Close the Coalhouse Door 190
Cloud Nine 238
Clouds 154, 159, 360
Club, The 219
Clyde, Jeremy 339
Cobb, Lee J. 30
Coburn, D.L 193–4
Code of the Woosters, The 19
Coe, Peter 185, 320
Coffey, Denise 258
Colbert, Claudette 290
Cole 60, 126, 173, 191, 215
Cole, George 210, 328
Coleman, Cy 260, 271
Coleridge, Sylvia 288
Colette 241–2
Collegiate 189
Collier, Ian 215
Collier, Patience 356
Collins, Barry 45
Comedians 28–9
Comédie Française 52
Comedy 152, 169, 241–2, 252
Comedy of Errors, The 118, 246
Coming Attractions 260
Como, Perry 269
Company 16, 61, 230, 235, 291
Compton, Edward 69
Compton-Burnett, Ivy 17
Conduct Unbecoming 122
Conference of the Birds 250
Confusions 82
Connolly, Cyril 195
Connor, Martin 226
Conolly, Patricia 257
Conrad, Joseph 184
Conti, Tom 124, 217–18, 240
Contractor, The 167
Cook, Peter 243
Cook, Roderick 291
Cook, Ron 274
Cooney, Ray 117, 118, 159, 296–7, 303
Cooper, Giles 152, 183

Cooper, Gladys 179
Cooper, Rowena 63
Cooper, Tommy 199
Coppola, Francis Ford 184
Coriolanus 106–7, 158
Cornford, John 296
Cornish, Anthony 132, 137
Cornwell, Charlotte 13
Cornwell, Judy 52
'Coronation Street' 242
Cosman, Leonie 151
Cottesloe 21, 53, 98, 107, 123, 127, 154–5,
    158, 184, 222, 233–4, 247–8, 251, 292,
    315, 336–8
Cotton, Oliver 29, 133
Country 295
Country Wife, The 263
Courtenay, Margaret 76
Courtenay, Tom 36–7, 154, 223–4, 252
Courtneidge, Cicely 117
Covent Garden 168
Covington, Julie 131, 319
Coward, Noël 19, 23, 46, 60, 61–3, 75, 76,
    81, 86, 113, 125, 128, 142–3, 155, 164,
    173, 178, 179, 188, 190–1, 195, 203,
    214–15, 218, 248, 250, 258, 263, 264–5,
    267, 275, 285, 321, 323, 325, 338, 340,
    350
Cowardy Custard 60, 173, 191, 215
Cranham, Kenneth 98, 168, 248, 289
Craven, Gemma 192, *192*, 240
Crawford, Joan 98
Crawford, Michael 185–6, 260, 269–71,
    302
Crazy Gang 81, 279–80, 333–4
Cribbins, Bernard 169
Crime and Punishment 218
Crisp, Quentin 60, 157
Criterion 68, 71, 225–6
Cronyn, Hume 193
Crosby, Bing 56
Cross, Ben 178
'Crossroads' 48, 256, 299
Croucher, Roger 19
Crowden, Graham 8, 106, 228
Crowley, Bob 284
Crowther, Bosley 113
Crucible 177
Crucible, The 247–8, 294–5
Crucifer of Blood, The 171–2
Cruickshank, Andrew 226
Crystal Clear 357–8, 359
Crystal Palace 125
Culver, Roland 39
Cummings, Constance 32–3, *33*, 217
Cure for Freedom, A 60
Curry, Bill 234
Curry, John 117
Curry, Tim 328

Curtis, Lucinda 263
Curtis, Tony 36
Cusack, Sinead 197–8, 298
Cutler, Horace 245, 251
Cymbeline 173–5, *174*
Cyrano de Bergerac 20–1

Dahl, Roald 4
Daily Mail 48, 269
Dale, Jim 260, 270
'Dallas' 321
Dalton, Timothy 329
Dancin' 159, 265
Dane, Clemence 217
Daneman, Paul 328
Daniels, Billy 105
Daniels, Ron 90, 288
Dankworth, John 241
Dante, Nicholas 65
Darrow, Clarence 11
Dastor, Sam 7
David, Joanna 81, 176
Davidson, Gordon 281
Davidson, Ian 55, 166
Davies, Howard 310
Davies, Oliver Ford 213, 262–3
Daviot, Gordon 217
Davis, Bette 165, 321
*Day in Hollywood, A Night in the Ukraine,
    A* 165–6, 263
Day in the Death of Joe Egg, A 81, 124, 186
Day Well Spent, A 282
Dead of Night 317
Dean, Isabel 37
Deane, Hamilton 147
Dear Octopus 180
Dearth, Lynn 213
Death of a Salesman 30–1, 144, 247, 294
'Death of a Teddy Bear' 152
Deathtrap 152, 320
Deep Blue Sea, The 114, 285–6, 302
de Filippo, Eduardo 108–9, 132
de Keyser, David 213–14
Dekker, Thomas 271–3
de la Tour, Frances 213–14, 252, 314
Delfont Organization 54
Delmar, Elaine 105
deMille, Cecil B. 66, 210, 229
Dench, Jeffery 165
Dench, Judi 58–9, 67, 104, *174*, 175, 243,
    334, *335*, 336, 338, 343
Deneuve, Catherine 220
Denison, Michael 140
Dennen, Barry 267
Derby Day 100
de Retz, Gilles 60
'Desert Island Discs' 103, 339
Design for Living 46, 156, 350
de Souza, Edward 59, 224

Destiny 89–90
Devil's Disciple, The 247
Devine, George 54, 167, 354
Devlin, J.G 37, 39
Dewhurst, Keith 155
Dews, Peter 195
Dexter, John 27, 194, 251, 271–3, 303, 326, 352–3
Dial M for Murder 124
Dickens, Charles 4, 10–11, 227–8, 250
Dietrich, Marlene 5–6, 291
Dining Room, The 322–3
Dirty Linen 59–60
Dispatches 184
Diuguid, Nancy 274
Dobie, Alan 168
Doctor Faustus 284
Doctor's Dilemma, The 146
Doctor Zhivago 90
Dogg's Hamlet 189
Dolin, Anton and Lindsay 276
Donegan, Lonnie 344
Donkeys' Years 360
Donleavy, J.P. 287, 302
Donner, Clive 6
'Don't Cry for Me, Argentina' 138
Dotrice, Roy 11–12, 147
Double Dealer 158
Douglas-Home, William 32, 63, 119, 180
Dove, John 87
Down, Angela 13, 176–7
Down, Lesley-Anne 258
Doyle, Conan 171
D'Oyly Carte 10, 261, 305, 328
Dracula 146–7
Drake, Alfred 20, 186
Draper, Ruth 11, 317
Dreamgirls 322
Dresser, The 222–4, 252, 320
Drinkwater, Carol 265
Dromgoole, Patrick 341
Drury, Alan 293
Drury Lane 64–5, 229–32, 252, 264, 302, 317–18, 328, 343
Dublin Theatre Festival 78
Duce, Sharon 290
Duchess of Malfi, The 302
Dudley, William 187
Duet for One 213–14, 252, 357
Duke in Darkness, The 216
Duke of York's 94–5, 154, 287–8, 359
Duncan, Sandy 203
Dunlop, Frank 237, 276
Dunlop, J.B. 78
Dunn, Nell 301
Durden, Richard 31, 58, 68
Dusa, Fish, Stas and Vi 91, 349
Duvitski, Janine 88
Dyer, Chris 56

Dyson, Anne 52

Ealing Studios 77
Early Days 222, 252
Eastward Ho! 280
Eaton, Wallas 218
Ebb, Fred 178, 291
Eccles, Donald 258
Economist 89
Eddington, Paul 128, 360
Eddison, Robert 27, 39, 66, 88, 140
Eddy, Mary Baker 203
Eddy, Nelson 166
Edgar, David 89–90, 166–7, 227
Edison, Thomas Alva 262
Educating Rita 224–5, 226
Edwards, Dennis 356
84 Charing Cross Road 300
Elen, Gus 68
Elephant Man, The 232–3, 261
Eles, Sandor 239
Elgar, Avril 176
Elgar, Edward 101
Eliot, T.S. 18, 34–5, 141, 175–6, 266, 305, 323
Elizabeth, the Queen Mother 117–19
Elliott, Denholm 39
Elliott, Michael 80, 169, 175–6, 251
Elliott, Paul 169
Ellis, Antonia 178
Ellis, Vivian 275
Elocution of Benjamin Franklin, The 157, 219
Elphick, Michael 168
Elvis 157
Encounter 91
Enemy of the People 134, 295
Engel, Susan 238–9
English Stage Society 263
Enjoy 244–5
Entertainer, The 145, 224, 311
Entertaining Mr Sloane 19, 209
Epsom Downs 100–1
Equus 100, 123, 177, 201, 232–3, 280
Esquire 184
Essex, David 138, 276–7, 354
Eumenides 298
Euripides 26, 211
Evans, Edith 13, 113, 334
Eve, Trevor 280
Evening of Intercourse with Edna, An 317–18
Evening Standard 49, 345
Evening with GBS, An 11
Everett, Rupert 296
Every Good Boy Deserves Favour 136–7, 338
Evita 138–9, 151, 155, 157, 191, 203, 332, 354–5
Ewing, Barbara 52
Expresso Bongo 191
Eyre, Richard 22, 29, 319

Eyre, Ronald 164, 245

Fahy, Katherine 52
Fairbanks, Douglas, Jr 63
Fallen Angels 323
Fall of Eagles, The 67
Fall of the House of Usher 107
Family and a Fortune, A 17
Family Reunion, The 175–6, 323
Family Voices 336–7
Farago, Peter 167
Farleigh, Lynn 183
Farrow, Mia 29, 203
Fawdon, Michele 220
'Fawlty Towers' 208
'F.D.R. Jones' 279–80
Feast, Michael 18, 51
Fellini, Federico 57
Fellowes, Julian 170, 258
Fellows, Don 178
Ferrer, José 20–1
Ferris, Barbara 14, 179
Festival Hall 136
Feydeau, Georges 23, 83, 142–3, 164, 168,
     195, 198, 263, 284
Field, Shirley Anne 6
Field, Sid 15
Fielding, Fenella 142–3, 243, 326
Fields, Gracie 118, 119
Fifth of July 292
Fill the Stage with Happy Hours 22
Films and Filming 98
Filumena 108–9, 132
Findlay, Deborah *350*
Finlay, Frank 43–4, 50–1
Finney, Albert 38–9, 53, 66, 80, *80*,
     119–20, 134–5, 158
Firbank, Ronald 326
Firth, David 333
Firth, Tazeena 82
Fisher, Eddie 303
Fiske, Alison 179
Flanagan, Bud 279
Flashpoint 213
Fleetwood, Susan 37, 39, 51, 66, 119–20
Flemyng, Robert 360
Flood, Gerald 222
Flowers for Algernon 185–6
Flying Down to Rio 94
Fo, Dario 199, 292
Foco Novo 261–3
Follies 61, 291
Fonda, Henry 11
Fonda, Jane 6
Fontanne, Lynn 193
Fool, The 36–7
Foot, Michael 305
Forbes, Bryan 237
For Colored Girls Who Have Considered

Suicide When the Rainbow is Enuf 200
Ford, John 268
Ford-Davies, Oliver 15, 106
Forde, Florrie 279
Forget-Me-Not-Lane 81, 190
For Services Rendered 179–80, 183
Forster, E.M. 225
'Forsyte Saga, The' 17, 97
Forsyth, Bruce 125–7, 185
Fortune 225, 301, 311–12
Fortune, James 163
Forty Love 169
42nd Street 259
Forty Years On 103, 243–4, 334
Fosse, Bob 265
Foster, Barry 121
Foster, Julia 141
Fox, Edward 175–6, 279, 332–3
Fox, William 176
Francis, Clive 122, 143, 285–6
Fraser, Bill 20, 37
Fraser, Ronald 19
Frayn, Michael 13–14, 119–20, 153–4, 159,
     209–10, 354, 359–60
Freeman, John 169
French Without Tears 113, 278, 286
Friel, Brian 268, 301, 309
Friend, Martin 132
Front Page, The 195, 330–2
Fry, Christopher 21, 75, 139–41, 183
Fugard, Athol 233–4
Fuller, Larry 138, 354
Fullerton, Fiona 299, 340
Fulton, Rikki 210
Funny Girl 151, 203
Funny Peculiar 48
*Funny Thing Happened on the Way to the
     Forum, A* 126
Furth, George 291

Gaetani, Raimonda 109
Galbraith, Angela 51
Gale, Richard 181
Galileo 251
Galsworthy, John 113, 286
Gambon, Michael 49–50, 156, *156*, 183,
     226, 251, 343
Garbo, Greta 76, 277, 329
Garden, Graeme 238
Garland, Patrick 11–12, 143, 267, 276, 279,
     325, 333–4
Garrick 3–4, 11, 133, 152
Garrick, David 22
Garson, Greer 217, 340, 343
Garson, Mort 354
Gaskill, William 98
Gay News 305
Gearing, Nigel 261–2
Gee, Donald 121

Gelzer, Helen 105
Gems, Pam 259, 329
'Generation Game, The' 108
Gennaro, Peter 151
George, Tricia 226
George and Margaret 287
'George and Mildred' 242
Gibbs, Matyelok 128
Gielgud, John 11, 18, 30, 84–5, 140, 158, 183, 246, 289, 312, 336
Gilbert and Sullivan 250, 261, 305, 328
Gile, Bill 55–6
Gill, Peter 120, 158, 251, 292, 298
Gillespie, Robert 79
Gin Game, The 193–4
Gingold, Hermione 17, 340
Giovanni, Paul 171–2
Giraudoux, Jean 211
Gish, Lillian 250
Glanville, Brian 279
Glass Menagerie, The 92
Glaze, Peter 279
Globe 122, 128–9, 170–1, 191–3
Glover, Julian 106
Glyndebourne 135
Gobbi, Tito 246
'God Bless the Child' 105
Godfrey, Derek 48–9, 147, 298
Godfrey, Patrick 70
Goldie, Hugh 124
Gone with Hardy 267
Gone with the Wind 321
'Gonna Build a Mountain' 126
Good 302, 309–11, 341
Goodbye Mr Chips 278, 333–4, 357
Goodchild, Tim 34
Good Companions, The 312
Good Earth, The 165
'Goodies, The' 238, 345
Good Soldier Schweik, The 310
Good Woman of Setzuan, The 288
Goolden, Richard 59–60
'Goon Show, The' 356
Gordon, Noele 299, 303
Gordon, Hannah 328
Gordon, Peter 7
Gorey, Edward 146
Gorky, Maxim 29, 197–8
Gostelow, Gordon 217
Götterdämmerung 135
Gough, Michael 27, 51, 66, 82, 123, 154, 217
Grade, Lew 119
Gradually Last Summer 93
Graham, Billy 118, 134
Graham-Jones, Sebastian 127, 154
Grain, Glyn 107, 278
Grainger, Gawn 154
Grand Hotel 76

Granger, Stewart 340
Grant, Cary 344
Grant, Deborah 271
Gray, Amlin 274
Gray, Billy 279
Gray, Charles 195
Gray, Eddie 279
Gray, Simon 49–50, 122, 123, 152, 155, 158, 182–3, 219, 222, 278–9, 302
Greeks, The 211–13, 229, 246, 251, 298
Green, Benny 86
Greene, Graham 39
Greenwell, Peter 275
Greenwich 12–13, 210, 215–16, 251, 258, 285–6, 295–6, 302, 333, 334, 355
Greenwood, Rosamund 195
Greenwood Theatre 31
Gregory, Andre 249–50
Grenfell, Joyce 11, 189, 317
Grey, Joel 94
'Grey-Haired Lady' 280
Griffiths, Trevor 28–9, 295
Grimes, Frank 243
Grimes, Tammy 142, 260
Grotowski, Jerzy 249–50
Groucho Letters, The 107–8
Grout, James 278
Guadagni, Nicky 8
Guardino, Harry 291
Guinness, Alec 17, 101–3, *102*, 113, 228
Guitry, Sasha 142
Gurnett, Jane 236
Gurney, A.R. 322–3
Guthrie, Tyrone 54, 66, 85
Guys and Dolls 96, 235, 318–20, 332, 343
Gwilym, Mike 182, *212*, 213, 330
Gypsy 61, 151, 203, 299

Hack, Keith 95
Haigh, Kenneth 143
Hair 65
Hale, Georgina 323–4
Half-Life 183
Half Moon 199, 235–6, 319
Hall, Peter 8, 22, 24, 28, 38, 53, 66, 83, 84–5, 114, 117, 119, 134–5, 157, 158, 200–1, 227, 236, 271, 292, 298, 301, 319, 329, 334–6, 336–7, 344, 355
Hall, Willis 108
Hamlet 38–9, 53, 66, 107, 123, 134, 149, 189, 212, 220, 236, 264, 332–3, 343
Hamlett, Dilys 35
Hamlisch, Marvin 65, 240
Hammerstein, Oscar 86, 117, 185–7, 235, 313
Hammond, Kay 215
Hampshire, Susan 172
Hampstead 13–14, 88–9, 122–3, 143–4, 154, 182, 224, 232, 268–9, 274, 292,

301, 309, 314–15, 354–5
Hampton, Christopher 33, 46–7, 77–8, 123
Hancock, Christopher 168
Hancock, Sheila 133, *230*, 231
Handful of Dust, A 351
Handl, Irene 13, 325, 334
Hands, Terry 14–15, 46, 106, 198, 246, 297, 329
Hanff, Helen 300
Happy Days 53
Happy Family 152, 183
Happy Yellow 91–2
Harbert, James 35
'Harbour Lights' 78
Hard Feelings 350–1
Harding, Gilbert 76, 195
Harding, John 188
Hardwicke, Cedric 179
Hardy, Oliver 266–7
Hare, David 24–6, 33, 130–1, 158, 182, 220
Hare, Doris 326, 353
Harris, Richard 290, 340, 344, 355, 358
Harris, Rosemary 295, 353
Harrison, John 8
Harrison, Rex 49, 186, 290, 352
Harrison, Tony 26–8, 58, 298–9
Harrow, Lisa 70, *70*
Hart, Jean 236
Hart, Lorenz 234–5, 291
Hart, Moss 195–6
Hartley, L.P. 281
Harum, Eivind 64
Harvey 15–16, 255
Harvey, Martin 223
Harwood, Ronald 169, 222–4, 252
Havergal, Giles 251
Havers, Nigel 335, *335*, 337
Hawthorne, Nigel 81
Hayes, Catherine 314
Hayes, Patricia 108
Hay Fever 61, 321, 352
Hayman, Carole *350*
Haymarket, Leicester 299
Hayworth, Rita 76
Hazlitt, William 69
Healy, David 191–2, *192*, 319
Heartbreak House 7–9, 50, 352–3
Heart of Darkness 184
Hecht, Ben 330
Hedda Gabler 32, 285, 325, 344
Heeley, Desmond 340
Helen 211
Hellman, Lillian 238–9, 250, 251, 303, 321
Hello Dolly! 178, 185, 283–4
'Hello Dolly!' 79
Hellzapoppin 148
Helpmann, Robert 326
Hemmings, David 19–20

Henried, Paul 351
Henry IV 14, 46, 247, 329–30
Henry V 14–15, 45–6, 106
Henry VI 87, 106, 130, 344
Henry, David 258
Henson, Basil 146
Henson, Nicky 55, 119–20, 134
Hepburn, Katharine 165, 261, 291, 320, 322
Herbert, Jocelyn 222
Here's a Funny Thing 311–12
Her Majesty's 19–20, 34–6, 125–7, 151–2, 171, 172–3, 221
Heroes 207–8
Herr, Michael 184
Her Royal Highness? 296–7, 302, 303
Hersey, David 197
Heston, Charlton 140, 250, 344
Hewitt, Christopher 203
Heywood, Pat 100
Hicks, Barbara 97
Hickson, Joan 82–3
Higgins, Colin 45
Hill, Bernard 355
Hill, Jimmy 135
Hiller, Colette 262
Hiller, Wendy 258
Hilton, James 333
Hinge and Bracket 250
Hodge, Patricia 92, 275
Hodiak, Keith 165
Hoffman, Dustin 143
Hogg, Ian 179
Holbrook, Hal 11
Holden, Jan 110
Holder, Ray 163
Holinshed, Raphael 26
Holliday, Shelagh 234
Holloway, Stanley 100
Home 18, 222
Homecoming, The 133, 337
Homer 211
Honolulu Community Theatre 30
Hood, Marag 182
Hooper, Robin 236
Hopps, Stuart 235
Horden, Michael 32–3, *33*, 169
Horlock, David 264–5
Horne, Lena 290, 320
Hornung, Ernest W. 39
Horovitch, David 13
Horwitz, Murray 172
Hoskins, Bob 319
Hotel in Amsterdam The 51, 98, 354
Hotel Paradiso 188
Hothouse, The 224
'Hound Dog' 221
Housewife! Superstar! 55
Howard, Alan 15, 46, 69–70, *70*, 106–7,

149–50, 158, 197–8, 246–7, 251, 297–8, 304, 309, 311
Howard, Branson 164
Howard, Ken 54–5
Howard, Leslie 258, 309
Howell, Peter 233
Howes, Bobby 219
How I Got That Story 274
How I Won the War 22
How the Other Half Loves 82
Hudd, Roy 279
Hudson, Rock 117, 240
Huggett, Richard 302
Hughes, John 265
Humperdinck, Engelbert 112
Humphries, Barry 55, 68, 157, 304, 317–18, *317*, 343, 345
Hunt, Martita 143
Hunter, N.C 182, 279, 292, 355
Huntley, Raymond 76
Huston, John 275
Huston, Walter 275
Hypochondriac, The 293–4

I am a Camera 112
Ibsen, Henrik 9, 146, 234, 294–5
ICA *see* Institute of Contemporary Arts
'I Can Just Imagine It' 332
'I Could Write a Book' 235
'If I Ruled the World' 126
'I Got It from Agnes' 226
Ik, The 44–5
Importance of Being Earnest, The 12–13, 70, 214, 237, 334–6, *335*
Importance of Being Oscar, The 11
I'm Talking About Jerusalem 137–8
Inadmissible Evidence 144–5, 158
Inman, John 220
Innocent, Harold 179
Insignificance 343
Institute of Contemporary Arts 24
International Centre for Theatre Research 45
Ipalé, Aharon 267
Iphigenia in Aulis 211
Ipi Tombi 54, 117
Irma La Douce 191, 241
Irons, Jeremy 70, 121, *121*
Irving, Henry 134
Isherwood, Christopher 78, 112, 181
'Is That All There Is?' 221
'It Ain't Half Hot Mum' 58, 81
Ivanov 188
Ives, Kenneth 248
'I Will Miss You' 326

Jackman, Hope 178
'Jackson' 221
Jackson, Glenda 84, 94, 119, 149–50, 158,

252, 323–4
Jacobi, Derek 88, 140, 220, 236
'Jailhouse Rock' 221
James, Emrys 15, 46, 267
James, Henry 238
James, Peter 177, 251, 282
James, Polly 165, 293
Jameson, Louise 256
Jameson, Pauline 176
Jarry, Alfred 147–8
Jarvis, Martin 335, *335*, 337
Jay, Tony 286
Jayston, Michael 215, 313
Jeeves 19–20, 34
Jefford, Barbara 20, 66
Jeffrey, Peter 23, 180
Jenkinson, Philip 165
Jerome, Jerome K. 286
Jesus Christ Superstar 139
Jewel, Jimmy 28
Jeweller's Shop, The 327–8
Jewsbury, Edward 209
Jingo 22–3
'Johanna' 231
Johannesburg Market Theatre 233–4
John Gabriel Borkman 9, 53
Johnson, Celia 23
John, Paul, George, Ringo . . . and Bert 25, 225
Johns, Stratford 132–3
Johnson, Richard 35, 62
Johnson, Terry 343
Joint Stock company 100, 238
Joking Apart 170–1
Jones, David 29, 173–5
Jones, Freddie 223–4
Jones, Gemma 133, 190
Jones, Griffith 57, 104, 175
Jones, James Earl 157, 320
Jonson, Ben 84–5
Joplin, Janis 25, 202–3
Joseph, Keith 119
Joseph and the Technicolor Dreamcoat 139
Journey's End 81, 122, 184, 208
Judgement 45
Jumpers 338
Juno and the Paycock 242–3
Jury, Chris 351
Just Between Ourselves 170
Justice, Barry 195

Kafka, Franz 148, 224
Kahaut, Pavel 189
Kancheli, Gia 210
Kander, John 178, 291
'Kansas City' 221
Kathleen Ni Houlihan 264
Katis, Diana 351
Katsulas, Andreas 45

Kaufman, George S. 195–6, 291
Kay, Charles 88, 133
Kean, Marie 57, 243
Keel, Howard 35
Keith, Penelope 118, 128
Kelly, Gene 64, 185, 291
Kelly, Matthew 48
Kemp, Jeremy 197
Kemp, Roger 168
Kempinski, Tom 213
Kempson, Rachel 17, 102, *102*
Kendal, Felicity 154, 201, 283, 339
Kendall, Kay 17, 62, 215
Kennedy, Jimmy 78
Kennedy, John F. 92–3, 202, 340
Kennedy's Children 6–7
Kent, Austin 232
Kent, Jonathan 95, 356
Kern, Jerome 54, 56
Kernan, David 17, 61, 304
Kerr, Deborah 76, 187, 267
Kerr, Walter 331
Kestelman, Sara 194, 277
Keyes, Daniel 185
Kilroy, Thomas 263
Kind of Alaska, A 337–8
King, Dave 25
King, Hetty 5
King, Philip 360
King & Clowns 157
King and I, The 132, 185–7
King Lear 8, 56, 67–8, 69, 111, 117, 149, 174, 202, 223–4, 236, 247, 344, 357
King's Head 6–7, 60, 78, 157
Kingsley, Ben 85, 119, *174*, *175*, 228, 284
Kingston, Mark 31, 225
Kipling, Rudyard 90
Kirkwood, James 65
Kissinger, Henry 226
Kiss Me Kate 86
Kissoon, Jeffrey 217
Kitchen, Michael 133
Kitovitz, Katherine 167
Kleban, Edward 65
Knight of the Burning Pestle 272
Knuckle 24
Kohler, Estell 93
Koltai, Ralph 134, 197
Kulukundis, Eddie 117
Kustow, Michael 53, 107
Kyle, Barry 56–7, 67

'Ladies in Waiting' 86
Lady Caroline Lamb 277
'Lady's Got Potential, The' 138
Lady's Not for Burning, The 30, 140–1
Laine, Cleo 241–2
Laing, R.D. 167
Laker, Freddie 104

Lamarr, Hedy 113
Lambert, Annie 212
Lancaster, Burt 76
Landen, Dinsdale 14, 43–4, 122, 146, 176–7, 283
'Land of Hope and Glory' 265
Landor, Jennifer 351
Langella, Frank 147
Langford, Bonnie 345
Langton, David 63, 153
Langton, Diane 192, *192*, 332
Lansbury, Angela 39, 231
Lapotaire, Jane 259
Lark Rise 127, 154–5, 158, 247
Lark Rise to Candleford 127
Larkyns, Harry 262
La Rue, Danny 117, 297, 304
Lasdun, Denys 22, 66
Lau, Patrick 195
Lauder, Harry 237
Laurel, Stan 266–7
Laurenson, James 165
Law, Phyllida 180
Lawrence, D.H. 29
Lawrence, Gertrude 186, 195, 214–15
Lawrence, Stephanie 354
Lawrence, T.E. 215
Lawson, Denis 235
Laye, Evelyn 305
Layton, George 282
Lazarus, Frank 166
Leach, Rosemary 300
Leach, Wilford 328
Lean, David 90, 228
Lee, Bernard 23
Lee, Eugene 231
Lee, Peggy 221
Lee, Shelly 107
Leech, Richard 124
Leeds Playhouse 8
Lefevre, Robin 182
Lehrer, Tom 225–6, 250
Leiber, Jerry 221
Leigh, Mike 88–9, 357
Leigh, Vivien 142, 263, 305
Leigh-Hunt, Barbara 67
Leighton, Margaret 17, 75
Leland, David 93
Lennon, John 260
Lent 355–7
Leon, Annie 183
Lerner, Alan Jay 225, 340
Lesser, Anton 264, 333, 343
Lesson from Aloes, A 233–4
Letter, The 179, 218
le Touzel, Joshua 296
Leventon, Annabel 79
Levin, Bernard 113, 118
Levin, Ira 152

Liberace 235
Liberty Hall 210
Life Class 28
'Lili Marlene' 5
Lill, Dennis 172
'Lillie' 172
Lillie, Beatrice 11
Lindsay, Robert 274
Linney, Romulus 276–8
Lipman, Maureen 282
Little Dorrit 4
Little Foxes, The 261, 303, 321–2, 343
Little Me 281
Little Night Music, A 16–17
Little Prince, The 249
Littler, Emile 302
Littler, Susan 82
Liverpool Playhouse 314
Lloyd Webber, Andrew 19, 138, 265–6, 305, 345
Locke, Philip 38, 66, 333
Loesser, Frank 318
Loewe, Frederick 225, 340
Logan, Jenny 178
Logan, Jimmy 267
Logan, Joshua 19, 340
'Lola' 5
Lombardi, Michael 163
London Assurance 69, 164
London Cuckolds, The 168
'London is London' 126
Long Christmas Dinner 323
Longden, Robert 332
Look After Lulu 142–3
'Look at Life' 54
Look Back in Anger 50, 75–6, 145, 263
Loren, Sophia 108
Lost Horizons 289
Love, Patti 167
Love Letters on Blue Paper 123
Love of a Good Man, The 208–9
'Love with Someone Younger' 241
Lovstrom, Peter 273
Lowe, Stephen 288
Lucie, Doug 207–8, 350–1
Luckham, Claire 300
'Lucky Lips' 221
Lunghi, Cherie 58
Lunt, Alfred 193
Luther 145
Lyceum 134
Lynch, Alfred *272*, 273
Lynn, Jonathan 192
Lynn, Vera 81, 126
Lynne, Gillian 226, 266
Lyric 11, 40, 43, 108–9, 251, 281–2, 300, 301, 323–4, 355–6, 360
Lyttelton 21, 52, 61–3, 82–3, 90–1, 118, 130–1, 145–6, 155–7, 179–80, 182–3,

232–3, 238–9, 247, 248, 282–4, 292, 334–6

McArdle, Andrea 132
MacArthur, Charles 330
Macaulay, Tony 330, 331
Macbeth 89, 104, 112, 113, 117, 134–5, 148, 149, 158, 189–90, 236–7, 242, 245, 250, 311, 333
McCallin, Tanya 233
McCarthy, Joseph 76, 247
McCowen, Alec 88, 149, 157–8, 236, 251
McCoy, Sylvestre 267
McDiarmid, Ian 59, 90, 136, 208–9
McDonagh, Philomena 357
MacDonald, Robert David 323–4
McDowell, Malcolm 19, 143
McEnery, Peter 227, 233
McEwan, Geraldine 142–3
McGinity, Terry J. 107
Maciver, Donald 79
Mackay, Fulton 98
McKellen, Ian 57, 58, 104, 106, 134, 136, 181, 246, 259, 311, 355
McKenna, T.P. 152, 264
McKenna, Virginia 187
McKenzie, Julia 61, 128, 319
McKern, Leo 79–80, *80*, 120
MacLaine, Shirley 94, 142, 148
MacLiammòir, Micheàl 11, 125, 341
McManus, Mark 248
McPherson, Aimee Semple 215
Macrae, Gordon 35
McWhinnie, Donald 269, 325
Machin, Peter 153
Madras House, The 96–8
Maen, Norman 35
'Magic Fingers' 326
Magnificence 100
Making Tracks 355
Malle, Louis 249
Maltby, Richard Jr 172–3
Mame 178
Man and Superman 302, 340–1, 344
Man for All Seasons, A 90
Manhattan Project 249
Mankowitz, Wolf 293
Man Who Came to Dinner, The 63, 194–6
March, Elspeth 97
Marcus, Frank 48
Mardi Gras 54–5
'Maria' 231
Marie Antoinette 216
Marilyn! 353–4
Marley, Bob 269
Marlow, Christopher 66
Marowitz, Charles 48
Marriott, Anthony 109–10
Marrying of Ann Leete, The 29

Marshall, E.G. 98
Marsden, Betty 20
Marshall, Herbert 321
Martin, Mary 261
Martin, Millicent 61
Martin, Rosemary 222
Marx, Chico 148, 166, 283
Marx, Groucho 82, 107–8, 166, 283
Marx, Harpo 166, 195
Mary Barnes 166–7
M.A.S.H. 184
Mason, Marsha 282
Massey, Anna 8, 23, 183, 264, 315, 335, 337–8, 343
Massey, Daniel 19, 134, 156, *156*, 293, 302
Master Builder, The 134
'Mastermind' 219
Mastroianni, Marcello 108
Matchmaker, The 283
Matthews, Jessie 117, 202, 303, 304, 305
Matura, Mustapha 269
Maugham, Somerset 27, 59, 76, 87, 102, 113, 159, 178–80, 182, 183, 217–18
Maxwell, James 284
Mayer, Louis B 34, 165
Mayes, Dermot 227–8
Mayfair 224, 251, 286–7
Meadmore, Robert 340
Medoff, Mark 280–1, 301–2
Melia, Joe 311
'Memory' 266
Mercer, David 182, 252
Merchnt of Venice, The 237
Merchant of Yonkers, The 283
Mermaid 60–1, 85–6, 117, 123–4, 136–7, 191, 215, 280–1, 300, 304, 345
Merman, Ethel 151
Merrick, John 232–3
Merrily We Roll Along 291–2
Metropolitan Opera 194
Michell, Keith 20–1, 172, 237
Midler, Bette 148, 202–3
Midsummer Night's Dream, A 44, 118, 149, 328
Mikaël, Ludmila 15
Miles, Bernard 117, 304, 345
Miles, Sarah 277
Millay, Edna St Vincent 209
Miller, Ann 202, 290
Miller, Arthur 30–1, 247–8, 294–5, 353
Miller, Jonathan 12–13, 143, 333, 343, 353
Miller, Mary 154
Miller, Max 311–12
Milligan, Spike 345
Millionairess, The 159
Mills, John 75–7, 228, 333–4
Minelli, Liza 94, 148
Miracle Worker, The 233, 280, 302
Mirren, Helen 25

Mirvish, Ed 341
Misanthrope, Le 26–7
Miss Julie 359
'Miss Otis Regrets' 86
'Mister Cellophane' 178
Mitchell, Julian 17, 295, 345
Mitchell, Warren 68, 248
Mitford Girls, The 274–6, 304
Moffatt, John 241–2
Moiseiwitsch, Tanya 26–7
Molière 20, 26, 69, 293
Molina, Alfred 199
Molly 152, 158
Monroe, Marilyn 343, 353–4
Montgomery, Robert 214
Monty Python 18
Moore, Dudley 344
Moore, George 141
Moore, Stephen 47, 59–60, 82–3, 91, 131, 226
Morahan, Christopher 91, 133–4, 145–6, 196–7
More, Julian 191
More, Kenneth 285–6
More, Mandy 232
'More I Cannot Wish You' 319
Morgan, Ken 286
Morgan, Priscilla 255
Morley, Robert 11, 218, 219
Morrell, Ottoline 9
Morris, William 137
Moscow Art 120
Mosley, Oswald 68, 131
Mousetrap, The 4, 11, 112, 117, 119, 343, 344, 345
Mrs Miniver 340, 343
Much Ado About Nothing 58–9
Muggeridge, Kitty 345
Mullen, Barbara 31–2
Muller, Robert 48, 113
Muni, Paul 30
Muppets, the 119
Murder at the Vicarage 31–2
Murder in the Cathedral 34, 141
Murphy, Gerard 330
Muybridge, Eadweard 261–3
My Dinner with Andre 249–50
My Fair Lady 64, 138, 185, 186, 290, 319, 341, 352

Napier, John 56, 58, 211, 227–8, 329
National Film Theatre 98
National Opera 343
National Theatre 7–9, 18–19, 21–2, 23–4, 26–8, 28–9, 37–8, 38–9, 43–4, 50–2, 52–3, 61–3, 66–7, 75, 77–8, 82–3, 84–5, 90–1, 96–8, 107, 108, 112, 114, 117, 118, 119–21, 123, 130–1, 133–4, 134–5, 145–6, 155–7, 158, 168, 178–80, 182–3,

203, 297, 299, 303, 343, 344, 345
Nederlander, James 341
Nelligan, Kate 8, 78, 130–1, 158
Nelson, Kenneth 86, 241–2
Nestroy, Johann 282–3
Newark, Derek 82, 107, 224
New End 141, 165, 207–8, 261–3
New-Found-Land 59–60
Newley, Anthony 126–7
New London 265
Newman, G.F. 316
New Statesman 153
Newton, Robert 135, 318
New Yorker 234
New York Times 12, 113
Nicholas, Jeremy 286–7
Nicholas, Paul 266
Nicholas Nickleby 227–9, 246, 250–1, 290, 319, 330, 342
Nicholas Tomalin Reporting 24
Nichols, Beverley 178
Nichols, Dandy 43–4
Nichols, Mike 193
Nichols, Peter 81, 124, 186, 190–1, 244, 255–6, 309, 339
Night and Day 153, 155, 159, 338
Night at the Opera, A 166
Night in Casablanca, A 107
'Night of a Thousand Stars' 138
Nimrod 219–20
Niven, David 76
Nixon, Richard 126, 303
Noble, Adrian 284
Noble, Larry 108
Noises Off 354, 359–60
No Man's Land 18–19
Norden, Denis 165
Norman, Monty 191
Norman Conquests, The 82, 128, 170, 226
Normington, John 37, 197, 201, 273, 319
Norton, Deborah 6, 168
No Sex Please – We're British 109
Nossek, Ralph 28
'Nostalgia' 193
'Nothing Can Stop Me Now' 126
Not Now Darling 112
Nottingham Playhouse Company 28–9
Novello, Ivor 147
'Nowadays' 178
Nunn, Trevor 56–7, 58, 67, 104, 118, 134, 228, 242, 250, 251, 266, 311, 329, 333

O'Brien, Edna 256–8, 302
O'Brien, Timothy 82
Observer 113
O'Callaghan, Richard 59
O'Casey, Sean 78, 242–3, 268, 301
Occupe–toi d'Amélie 142
Ockrent, Mike 225, 238, 255, 355

Odd Couple, The 181, 282
Odets, Clifford 222
Of Thee I Sing 56
Oh Calcutta! 200
Oh Mr Porter 85–6
Oida, Katsuhiro 45
O'Keeffe, John 69–71
Oklahoma! 185, 186, 193, 209, 234, 250
Old Country, The 103, 218, 222, 243, 295
'Old Dope Peddler, The' 226
Oldfield, Richard 6
Old Flames 52
'Old Friends' 291–2
Oldman, Gary 324
Old Movies 98
Old Possum 266
Old Red Lion 357
Old Vic 8–9, 26–8, 28–9, 37–8, 38–9, 43–4, 50–2, 53, 57, 61, 67, 87–8, 104, 118, 135, 140–1, 149, 159, 219, 236–7, 250, 300, 303, 341
Oliver! 132, 138, 157, 230, 325
Oliver, Stephen 227
Olivier 21, 53, 66–7, 77–8, 84–5, 96–8, 120–1, 133–4, 134–5, 158, 187–8, 194, 196–7, 200–1, 226–7, 245, 251, 271–3, 292–4, 298–9, 318–20, 329
Olivier, Laurence 15, 53, 80, 104, 106–7, 113, 124, 140, 196–7, 215, 273, 280, 305, 318, 352
O'Malley, Mary 99–100, 151
Oman, Julia Trevelyan 272–3
Once a Catholic 99–100, 129, 158
Once in a Lifetime 196, 229
'One' 65
O'Neil, Paddie 165
O'Neill, Eugene 294
One Rule 269
On Golden Pond 322
Only in America 221–2
On Monday Next 360
On the Razzle 282–4
On the Twentieth Century 221
'Onward to Jerusalem' 163
Open Space 48–9
Operation Bad Apple 316–17
Orbach, Jerry 260
Ordeal of Gilbert Pinfold, The 169
Oresteia, The 292, 298–9, 303
Orlando Furioso 127
Orton, Joe 19, 133, 208, 224
Osborne, John 30, 50–2, 75, 98, 142, 144–5, 158, 224, 248, 263, 285, 303, 311–12, 354
Othello 69, 97, 149, 174, 320
Other Places 336–8, 343
Otherwise Engaged 49–50, 279
O'Toole, Peter 236–7, 250, 303, 333, 340–1, 344

Otto, Barry 220
'Our Time' 291–2
Our Town 55, 294
Outward Bound 9
Overheard 267, 302
Owen, Glyn 355
Owen, Kate 92
Oxenford, John 282
Oxford Playhouse Company 30–1, 208–9

Pacific Overtures 61
Pack, Roger Lloyd 133
Paddick, Hugh 85, 300
Pagett, Nicola 17
Paige, Elaine 139, 266, 305
Palace 296–7, 302, 303
Pal Joey 234–6, 250
Palladium 94, 112, 118, 148, 185–7,
    269–71, 305, 312
Palmer, Toni 267
Papp, Joe 261
Pappas, Robin 92
Parker, Don 6
Parker, Dorothy 166
Parker, Stewart 78–9
Parnell, Val 312
Parr, Chris 34
Parry, Natasha 197
Parsifal 113, 164, 340
Pasco, Richard 29, 246
Passion, The 154, 247
Passion of Dracula 147
Passion Play 255, 309, 338
Paterson, Bill 319
Patience 10
Patrick, Nigel 63, 100
Patrick, Robert 6
Paye, Robin Fraser 275
Peach, Blair 199
Peacock, John 216
Peacock, Trevor 15
Peck, Bob *174*, 175
Pedley, Anthony 209
Peer Gynt 78, 134
Peers, Donald 99
Pennell, Nicholas 257
Pennies from Heaven 309
Pennington, Michael 57, 90
Pertimento 238
Pericles 175
Perkins, Anthony 203
Peter Grimes 231
Peter Pan 132, 203, 261, 345
Petherbridge, Edward 172, 229
Phaedra Britannica 26–8, 58
Phèdre 26
Phelps, Samuel 69
Philadelphia Story 204
Philanderer, The 145–6, 158

Philanthropist, The 47
Phillips, John 102–3, *102*
Phillips, Leslie 203
Phillips, Robin 257, 327
Phillips, Sian 235–6
Phillpotts, Ambrosine 76
Phoenix 63–4, 153, 159, 215
Piaf 259, 329
Piaf, Edith 221
Piccadilly 55–6
Pickford, Mary 250
Pickup, Ronald 97
Pieces of Eight 143, 337
Pimpernel Smith 309
Pinelli, Guiseppi 198–9
Pinero, Arthur 95, 113, 286, 292
Pinewood Studios 100
Pinter, Harold 18–19, 62, 122, 133, 155–7,
    159, 182–3, 224, 243, 249, 256, 279,
    291, 302, 334, 336–8, 341, 343
Pirandello, Luigi 18, 190, 222
Pirates of Penzance, The 261, 305, 328
Pithey, Wensley 356–7
Playboy of the Western World, The 37–8
Playhouse 179
'Play of the Month' 248
Playwrights Horizons 322–3
Pleasance, Angela 267
Pleasance, Donald 216–17
Pleasure of His Company, The 63–4
Plenty 130–1, 158, 182, 341
Plowright, Joan 40, 108–9, 244, 263, 280,
    305, 333
Plummer, Christopher 320
Plunder 43–4, 53, 146, 158
Poe, Edgar Allen 107
Pogson, Kathryn 333
'Police' 316
Pollock, Ellen 78
Pomerance, Bernard 232–3
Porter, Cole 60, 85–6, 139, 173, 195
Poppy 342
Portman, Eric 75
Posta, Adrienne 138
Power, Tyrone 216
Pravda 118, 136
Prayers for My Daughter 158
Prentice, Reg 118
Present Laughter 63, 203, 258–9, 285
Presley, Elvis 99, 221
'Pretty Women' 232
Previn, André 136–7
Priestley, J.B. 75
Prime of Miss Jean Brodie, The 99–100
Prince, Hal 16–17, 138, 203, 229, 231, 291
Prince Edward 138–9
Prince of Wales 15–16, 54–5
Prisoner of Zenda, The 340
Private Lives 122, 150, 152, 155–6, 214–16,

184, 187–8, 194, 196–7, 200–1, 222,
226–7, 232–4, 236, 238–9, 245, 247–8,
250, 251, 252, 259, 264, 271–3, 282–4,
285, 292–4, 298–9, 301, 302, 303, 304,
309, 315, 318–20, 330, 332, 334–6,
336–8, 341, 342, 343, 344, 345, 352, 359
Neagle, Anna 20, 34, 113, 117, 119, 187,
250, 258, 264, 285, 338
Privates on Parade 81
Privileged 351
Producers, The 163
Prospect Theatre Company 87–8, 118,
140–1, 159, 236
Protheroe, Brian 168
Prowse, Juliet 240
Prowse, Philip 324
Pryce, Jonathon 29, 150, 248, 264
Psycho 203
Public Theatre 261
Pumpkin Eater, The 157
Punch 43, 180
Purchase, Bruce 247
Pygmalion 186, 225, 258, 296, 326, 331

Quartermaine's Terms 278–9, 302
Quayle, Anthony 16, 66, 124, 142
Quayle, Jenny 215, 279
Quayle, John 180
Queen Christina 329
Queen's 103, 147, 185–6, 190–1, 217–18,
222–4, 278–9, 302
Quentin, John 172
Quick, Diana 66
Quilley, Denis 38, 66, 81, 152, *230*, 231
Quinn, Elizabeth 280
Quinn, Patricia 33, *33*

Racine, Jean 26
Raikes, Raymond 168
Randall, Leslie 169
Rathbone, Basil 357
Rattenbury, Alma 152
Rattigan, Terence 62, 75–7, 113–114, 118,
130, 152, 207, 248, 250, 251, 278,
285–6, 303, 342, 345, 356
Ravenscroft, Edward 168
Ray, Robin 225–6
Ray, Trevor 98
'Razzle Dazzle' 177–8
Rea, Stephen 37, 78, 269
Reader, Ralph 334
Reading, Bertice 221, 251, 326
Reagan, Ronald 269–70, 344
Real Inspector Hound, The 189, 338
Real Thing, The 338–9, 343
Rear Column, The 121–2, *121*, 158
Red Devil Battery Sign, The 92–4
Reddington, Ian 351
Redfarn, Roger 299

Redgrave 264–5
Redgrave, Michael 113, 183, 219
Redgrave, Vanessa 119, 173
Redman, Amanda 332
Redman, Joyce 187–8
Redmond, Liam 37
Red Peppers 244
'Red Sails in the Sunset' 78
Rees, Roger *174*, *175*, 227, 339
Rees, Roland 232, 261–2
Reflections 216–17
Reid, Beryl 19, 244
Return of A. J. Raffles, The 39
Reynolds, Debbie 221
Rice, Tim 20, 138–9, 305
Richard II 246–7, 251, 297–8
Richard III 95, 196–7, 210, 246–7, 251,
297–8
Richard, Cliff 118
Richard of Bordeaux 216, 349
Richards, Gavin 199
Richardson, Ian 246
Richardson, Ralph 18, 23, 119–20, 179,
222, 252
Richert, Wanda 260
Rich Man, Poor Man 94
Richmond 301
Rigby, Terence 18, 91
Rigg, Diana 27, 153, 353
Rigoletto 343
Ringwood, Bob 34, 92
Rippon, Angela 119
Rivera, Chita 94
Riverside 158, 251, 269, 300, 341
Rix, Brian 109, 118, 143, 200
*Roar of the Greasepaint and the Smell of the
Crowd, The* 127
Roberts, Rachel 252
Robertson, Cliff 185
Robertson, Liz 275
Robertson, Patrick 256
Robeson, Paul 157
Robson, Flora 179, 305
Rodgers, Anton 30, 96, 191–3, *192*, 255–6,
331–2
Rodgers, Richard 56, 117, 185–7, 234–5,
250, 313
Rodska, Christian 191
Rodway, Norman 70, *70*, 197, 242
Rogan, John 99–100, 242
Rogers, David 185
Rogers, Paul 8–9, 29, 39, 78, 85, 97, 335,
337–8
Romans in Britain, The 245, 248, 250, 251,
304
Romantic Comedy 203
Romeo and Juliet 56–7, 58, 150, 174, 331
Romilly, Elizabeth 179
Ronde, La 49

Ronstadt, Linda 261
Rookery Nook 142
Room, The 337
Rooney, Mickey 202, 290, 303
Roose-Evans, James 300
Roots 137–8
Rope 124
Rosa, Dennis 147
Rose 252
Rose, George 261
Rose, The 202–3
Rosemary's Baby 203
Rosencrantz and Guildenstern Are Dead 338
Rosenthal, Jack 151, 157, 301
Ross, Annie 328
Rostand, Edmond 20
Round House 44–5, 92–4, 100–1, 169,
   175–6, 210, 245, 300
Rousseau, Jean-Jacques 29
Routledge, Patricia 190
Roveta, Sandy 65
Royal Court 19, 24–6, 32–4, 36–7, 46–7,
   54, 99–100, 113, 129–30, 142, 144–5,
   158, 166–7, 169–70, 181, 208–9, 238,
   263–4, 285, 288–90, 301, 302–3,
   316–17, 343, 349–50, 354, 356
Royal Exchange 80, 169, 175–6, 284, 302
Royal Hunt of the Sun 201
Royal Shakespeare Company 12, 14–15,
   22–3, 29, 39, 45–6, 56–7, 58–9, 69–71,
   81, 90, 104, 106–7, 112, 117, 118–19,
   134, 138, 148–50, 158, 164–5, 168,
   173–5, 196, 197–8, 211–13, 224–5,
   227–9, 242–3, 246–7, 250–1, 255–6,
   272, 285, 290, 294, 297–8, 301, 304,
   309–11, 319, 328, 329–30, 341, 342
Royalty 105, 200
RSC *see* Royal Shakespeare Company
Rudman, Michael 13, 143–4, 179–80, 340,
   354–5
Runyon, Damon 318–20
Russell, Willy 224–5
Rustaveli Theatre Company 210
Rutherford, Margaret 32, 62, 128, 215
Rutter, Barrie 319
Ryall, David 315
Ryan, Helen 97
Ryecart, Patrick 287–8, *289*
Ryton, Royce 296–7

Sacks, Oliver 337
Sackville-West, Vita 209, 257–8
Sacred Flame, The 159, 179, 218
Sager, Carole Bayer 240
Salad Days 78
Salthouse, John 88, *272*, *273*
Samarth, Alaknanda 27
Saint Joan 87–8, 141, 247
Same Time Next Year 203

Sanderson, John 13
Sands, Leslie 179
Saratoga 164–5
Satton, Lon 55, 105
Saturday Review 111
Saturday, Sunday, Monday 108, 132
Saunders, James 122–3, 176–7
Savages 47
Savident, John 140
Savoy 31–2, 124–5, 359
Sayers, Dorothy L. 124
Saxton, Granville 265
Scales, Prunella 49, 278
Schafer, Lawrence 185
Schell, Maximilian 77–8
Schlesinger, John 8, 81, 352
Schnitzler, Arthur 48–9, 187–8
Schofield, David 232–3
Scofield, Paul 7–8, *7*, 84–5, 97, 112, 140,
   149, 201, 259
Scoop 13
Scully, John 6
Seagull, The 263–4, 302–3
Season's Greetings 245
Seely, Jim 258
Selbie, Christopher 333
Selby, Nicholas 37, 78
Selznick, David O. 227
'Send in the Clowns' 17
Seneca 26
Separate Tables 75–7, 207
'September Song' 275, 310
1789 127
Sewell, Stephen 219–20
Shaffer, Peter 47, 177, 200–1, 232, 259
Shaffer, Tony 124–5
Shaftesbury 146–7, 240–1
Shakespeare, R.W. 312
Shakespeare, William 7–8, 11, 12, 14–15,
   26, 36, 38–9, 56–7, 66, 67–8, 87, 106–7,
   118, 134–5, 148–50, 173–5, 190, 196–7,
   236–7, 246–7, 248, 272, 320, 330
'Shall We Dance?' 132
Shange, Ntozake 200
Sharpe, Bernard 105
Shaw 92, 131–2, 137–8
Shaw, George Bernard 7–9, 11, 52–3,
   87–8, 97, 111, 137, 145–6, 158, 175,
   225, 247, 248, 258, 296, 335, 349, 352
Shaw, Glen Byam 39
Shaw, Robert 167
Shaw, Sebastian 124
Shawn, Wallace 249
Shearer, Norma 216, 277
Shelley, Barbara 57
Shepherd, Jack 184
Sheppard, Morgan 55
Sheridan, Dinah 63, 259
Sherlock Holmes 39, 159, 164

Sherman, Martin 181
Sherriff, R.C. 23
Sherrin, Ned 60, 221, 228, 274, 304
'She's the Girlfriend of the Whirling
    Dervish but She's Giving Him the
    Runaround' 165
Shevelove, Burt 126
Shoemaker's Holiday, The 271–3, *272*, 303
Short List 354–5
Show Boat 54
Shrapnel, John 95, 198, 212–13, *212*, 333
Shulman, Milton 118
Shut Your Eyes and Think of England
    109–10, 112
Side by Side by Sondheim 60–1, 86, 126, 173,
    191, 230
Sign of Four, The 171
Signoret, Simone 113
Silver, Philip 257
Sim, Alistair 33
Simmons, Jean 17
Simon, Neil 169, 170, 202, 203, 240–1,
    281–2
Sinatra, Frank 235, 319
Sinden, Donald 58–9, 67, 110, 112, 258–9,
    285
Singular Life of Albert Nobbs, The 141
Sisterly Feelings 226–7, 251
Skinner, Cornelia Otis 63
Skirmishes 314–15
Slade, Bernard 203–4
Slade, Julian 304
Slag 24
Sleep, Wayne 266
Sleuth 124–5, 152
Small Craft Warnings 6
Smash 301
Smike! 228
Smiles of a Summer Night 16
Smilie, James 35
Smith, Dodie 120, 176, 180
Smith, Maggie 94–5, 215, 257, 262, 302,
    325
Smith, Roger 214
Smith, Stevie 84
'Soldiers of the Queen' 128
Some Like It Hot 181
Snap 261–3
Soldier's Fortune, The 300
'Some Mothers Do 'Ave 'Em' 186, 270
Sondheim, Stephen 16–17, 60–1, 86, 173,
    204, 229–32, 252, 291–2, 299, 313, 355
Songbook 191–3, *191*
Song of Bernadette 99
Sophocles 211
Sound of Morley, The 11
Sound of Music, The 186, 302, 303, 312–13,
    331
South Pacific 291, 313

Speight, Johnny 68
Spoiled 278
Spokesong 78–9
Spriggs, Elizabeth 62, *62*, 78, 85, 123
'Springtime for Hitler' 163, 293, 297
Stabb, Dinah 248
Stafford-Clark, Max 100, 238, 264, 317,
    350
Stallybrass, Anne 122
Stamp, Terence 147
Standing, John 23, 146, 183
Staniforth, Michael 232
Stanislavsky, Konstantin 120
Stanton, Barry 168
Stapleton, Maureen 321
Star is Born, A 202–3
Starke, Roland 333
Starr, Pat 6
State of Revolution 90–1, 118
Steadman, Alison 88, 170
Steafel, Sheila 166
Steaming 301
Steele, Tommy 112
Stephens, P. G 37
Stephens, Robert 119–20, 134, 158, 215
Stephenson, Pamela 328
Stern, G.B. 214
Stern, Tim 88
Stevens, Ronnie 7
Stevie 84
Stewart, James 16
Stewart, Patrick 150, 330
St John-Stevas, Norman 345
St Martin's 344
Stock, Nigel 143, 334
Stoker, Bram 147
Stokes, Sewell 326
Stoller, Jennie 233
Stoller, Mike 221
Stone, Paddy 54
Stoppard, Tom 59, 122, 136–7, 153, 155,
    159, 187, 189–90, 282–4, 292, 333,
    338–9, 341, 343
Storey, David 18, 28, 167, 222, 252
Stott, Judith 63
Stott, Ken 333
Stott, Mike 48
Strachan, Alan 17, 215, 251, 258, 285
Strand 71, 338–9
Strand Magazine 171
Stratford 38, 45, 56–7, 58–9, 67–8, 106–7,
    130, 148–50, 173–5, 246, 251, 297, 343
Streets of London, The 250
Streisand, Barbra 105, 148
Strindberg, August 19, 109
Stripwell 32–4, *33*
Strouse, Charles 185
Stubbs, Una 86
Student Prince, The 67

Studio 300
Sturua, Robert 210
Styne, Jule 151, 165, 203, 299
Success Motivation Institute of Japan 163–4
Suchet, David 247
Sugar Babies 202, 303
Sugden, Mollie 220
Summer 315, 343
Sunday Telegraph 48
Sunday Times 23
Supremes, the 322
Suzman, Janet 94–5, 212–13, *212*
Swan Down Gloves 319–20
Swan Lake 49
Swann, Robert 13
Sweeney Todd 204, 229–32, 241, 252
Sweet Charity 94
Swift, Clive 145
Swift, David 300
Synge, J.M. 37–8

Tabarski, Boleslaw 327
'Take It from Here' 218
'Take the "A" Train' 105
Talent for Murder, A 290
'Tale of an Oyster, The' 86
Tale of Two Cities, A 4
Tales from the Vienna Woods 77–8, 188
Talk of the Town 55, 341
Talley's Folly 292
Tally, Ted 260
Tamburlaine 53, 66, 134
Tandy, Jessica 193
Tatchell, Peter 305
Tatler 112, 274
Taylerson, Marilyn 67
Taylor, C.P 190, 302, 309–10
Taylor, Elizabeth 261, 303, 321–2, 343
Taylor, Gwen 314, 349, *350*
Taylor, Robert 277
Taylor, Samuel 63
Teeth 'n' Smiles 24–6
Tempest, The 7–8, *7*, 149
Tennyson, Alfred Lord 174
Ten Times Table 128–9, 159, 170
Terry, Nigel 36
'Thanks for the Memory' 275
Thatcher, Margaret 119, 270, 334, 342–3, 345
Thaw, John 153
Theatre Royal 4, 63, 119, 142, 171–2, 183, 216–17, 256–8, 267, 292, 341, 344, 352, 355–6
Theatre Upstairs 129, 249–50
Thee and Me 251
Then and Now 182
'These Are a Few of My Favourite Things' 303

'These Foolish Things' 215
They're Playing Our Song 240–1, 281
This Happy Breed 190
Thomas, Dylan 140
Thomas, Michael 339
Thomas, Nina 168
Thomas and the King 34–6
Thompson, Eric 19
Thompson, Ernest 322
Thompson, Flora 127
Thomson, William 111
Thorndike, Sybil 87–8, 113
Thornton, Frank 110
Thoughts of Chairman Alf, The 68
Three Men in a Boat 286–7
Threepenny Opera 231
Three Sisters, The 180
Thring, Frank 219
Tibetan Inroads 288–90
Tiller, Stephen 351
Time Present 51, 354
Times, The 23, 101, 122, 140, 153, 180, 233
Timon of Athens 174
Todd, Mike 303
Todd, Paul 355
Togivi, David 319
Tomalin, Nick 23–4, 153, 184
Tom Foolery 225–6, 250
Took, Barry 49
Top Girls 349–50, *350*
Towards the End of Morning 154, 360
Towb, Harry 151, 319
Toye, Wendy 86
Tracy, Spencer 291
Trafford Tanzi 300
Traitors 219–20
Translations 268–9, 279, 281, 301, 309
Travelling Music Show, The 125–7, 157
Travers, Ben 40, 43–4, 53, 70, 82, 110, 128–9, 142, 146, 158, 168, 210, 258, 353
Treasure Island 117, 304, 345
Treats 46–7
Tree, Beerbohm 171
Treves, Frederick 146
Tricycle 267, 329
Troubadour 163–4
Turgenev, Ivan 353
Turnbull, Colin 45
Turner, Bridget 37
Turner, John 20, 88
Turner, Lana 139
Tutin, Dorothy 119–20, 135, 149, 187–8, 216–17, 285, 302
Twain, Mark 11
Twelfth Night 174, 246
Twelve Angry Men 122
'Twentieth-century Blues' 265
'TW3' 61, 302
Tynan, Kenneth 5, 113, 140, 176, 195, 252,

285, 311

Ubu 147–8
Ubu Enchaîné 147
Ubu Roi 147
Umbrellas of Cherbourg 220–1
Uncle Vanya 16–17, 79–81, *80*, 120–1, 198
Uncommercial Traveller, The 4
Underneath the Arches 279–80, 334
Undiscovered Country 187–8
'Upstairs, Downstairs' 63
Ure, Mary 167
Us 44
Ustinov, Peter 267, 276, 302

Valmouth 325–6
Very Good, Eddie 55–6
Variety 235
Vaudeville 78–9, 84, 157, 244–5, 258
Vaughan Williams, Ralph 101
Veterans 22
Victoria Palace 132–3, 279, 303, 321–2, 330–2
Victoria Station 337
Villiers, Caroline 35
Virginia 256–8, 302
Vivat! Vivat Regina! 90
Vogue 150
Volpone 84–5, 112
Voltaire 87
von Horvath, Odon 77–8
Vosburgh, Dick 165–6, 330–1
Voss, Philip 355

Wadsworth, Andrew C. 192, *192*, 232
Wagner, Richard 38, 50
Waiting for Godot 237
Wait Until Dark 357
Waldhorn, Garry 282
Walker, Elspeth 143
Walker, Robert 235
Walker, Zena 76, 183
Wall, Max 3–4, 11
Waller, David 57
Waller, Fats 172–3
Waller, Lewis 97
Walter, Harriet 264
Walters, Julie 48, 225
Wanamaker, Zoe 70, 336
Ward, Eliza 213
Ward, Lalla 328
Ward, Simon 39, 121, *121*, 353
Warehouse 104, 112, 224–5, *226*, 302, 309–11, 333
Warner, David 38
Warren, Harry 260
Wars of the Roses, The 211
Washbourne, Mona 16, 84
Watch It Come Down 50–2, 53

Watch on the Rhine 238–9, 251
Waterhouse, Keith 108
Waterman, Dennis 164–5, 331–2
Waters, Les 238
Waters of the Moon 159, 182
Watford, Gwen 122, 176–7, 259, 328
Watts, Jennifer 92
Watts, John 164
Waugh, Evelyn 13, 101, 169, 326, 351
Way Upstream 342
Weapons of Happiness 100
Wedekind, Benjamin 83
Weill, Kurt 275
Welland, Colin 302
Welles, Orson 199
Wells, H.G. 335
Wells, John 302
Wells, Ken 266
Wesker, Arnold 123, 131–2, 137–8, 248, 292
West, Lockwood 223
West, Timothy 88, 133, 236–7
Westminster 327–8
West Side Story 16, 57, 61, 64, 94, 229, 231
West Side Waltz, The 322
Westwell, Raymond 247
Weyers, Marius 234
Whatham, Claude 92
'What Kind of Fool Am I?' 126
Wheeler, Hugh 231
'When You're Good to Mama' 178
'Where Have All the Flowers Gone?' 5
Whicker, Alan 169
White, Wilfrid Hyde 63–4, 304
White Cargo 113
Whitehead, E.A. 52
Whitehead, Paxton 353
Whitehouse, Mary 245, 251
Whitelaw, Billie 14, 152, 213, 255–6
Whiteley, Thelma 88
Whitemore, Hugh 84
Whiting, John 75, 140, 209
Whiting, Margaret 37
Whitlam, Gough 55
Whitrow, Benjamin 13, 59, 255–6, 360
'Who Can I Turn To?' 126
Who's Afraid of Virginia Woolf? 88, 176, 321
Whose Life Is It Anyway? 123–4, 159, 218, 280
Wickham, Jeffry 176
Wilcox, Michael 355–6
Wild Duck, The 294
Wilde, Cornel 36, 216
Wilde, Oscar 10–11, 12–13, 49, 70, 109, 140, 41, 288, 326, 335–6
Wilder, Thornton 283, 294, 323
Wild Oats 69–71, 164, 168
Williams, Bransby 223
Williams, Clifford 54, 70

Williams, Emlyn 4, 10–11, 75, 119, 227
Williams, Esther 19, 237
Williams, John 35
Williams, Kenneth 81, 143, 224, 243, 337
Williams, Michael 23, 67
Williams, Nigel 129–30
Williams, Tennessee 6, 92–4
Williamson, David 219
Williamson, Nicol 106, 144–5, 158
Willmore, Alfred *see* MacLiammóir, Micheál
Wilson, Effingham 52
Wilson, Jacques 353
Wilson, Lanford 292
Wilson, Peter 143
Wilson, Sandy 241, 325–6
Wilton, Penelope 146, 156, *156*, 226
Wimbush, Mary 197
Windsor, Frank 136
Windy City 330–2
Wing, Anna 314
Winslow Boy, The 114
Winter Garden 320
Witness for the Prosecution 124
Wodehouse, P.G. 19–20, 56
Wojtyla, Karol 327
Wolfit, Donald 66, 67, 85, 134, 210, 222–3, 237, 252, 341
Woman of the Year 261, 291
Wood, Charles 22–3
Wood, David 20
Wood, John 136, 152, 187–8, 196–7, 292

Wood, Peter 187, 283–4, 331–2, 339
Wood, Victoria 225
Woodhouse, Barbara 304
Woods, Aubrey 55
Woodthorpe, Peter 190
Woodvine, John 57, 58–9, 104, 136, 229
Woodward, Tim 33, *33*
Woolf, Virginia 256–8
Woollcott, Alexander 194–6
World Turned Upside Down, The 154–5
Wright, Norman 30
Wylton, Tim 106
Wyndham, Charles 69
Wyndham's 7–8, 294–5, 357–8
Wynne, Ken 110, 196

Yakir, David 221
Yarwood, Mike 120
Yates, Marjorie 145
Yelland, David 27, 273
York, Michael 202
York, Susannah 141, 325
'You Have to Be Carefully Taught' 313
Young, Barbara 132
Young, Phil 357
Young Vic 147–8, 258, 276–8, 293, 301, 332–3
'You're the Cream in My Coffee' 64

Zeffirelli, Franco 57, 108–9
'Zip' 236
Zukor, Adolph 165

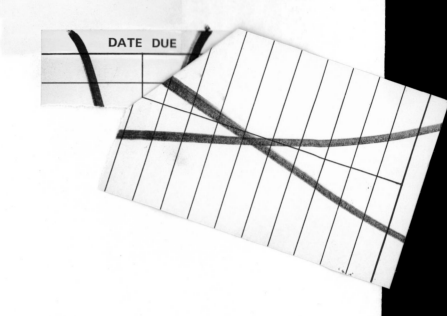

DATE DUE